"Nalanda Roy's book, *From Epic Tales to Digital Trails: Understanding New Mediascapes in Activism*, is a meticulously crafted exploration of the complexities of the mediascape. It is an indispensable read that offers valuable insights and is worth every penny. Delve into this book and learn from one of the best."

– **Adebowale Akande, Professor and Editor, IR GLOBE Crosscultural Inc, Vancouver, BC**

"The book From *Epic Tales to Digital Trails: Understanding New Mediascapes in Activism* provides a very useful overview of the use of how the current digital world provides an important platform for activism by using social media from Facebook to X to Instagram and beyond but can also be used to harm activists and democracy as well. It provides an important perspective on how the management of technology can be used to either help or harm democratic values and highlights the need for ethical and inclusive guidelines in their use."

– **Victor Asal, Phd, Director of the Center for Policy Research, Professor of Political Science, Rockefeller College, University at Albany, SUNY**

"The edited volume *From Epic Tales to Digital Trails: Understanding New Mediascapes in Activism* is an important book that highlights the challenging applications of technology through the lens of access and accountability. By looking at how ICT, particularly social media technologies, can organize activists and broaden their reach by sharing new, alternative narratives across the media frontier, this volume explores critical areas of social movement mobilization and activism. The willingness to engage in the careful analysis of the benefits and pitfalls of ICT in this turbulent time makes it more compelling."

– **Joseph W. Roberts, Ph.D., Chair and Professor of Politics and International Relations, Roger Williams University, Department of Politics and International Relations.**

"It is a truism that technology can be used for both good and evil, while the human and institutional factors behind a technology are decisive in shaping its uses. How specifically a given technology is used; for instance, to foster democracy or to foster authoritarianism, is the real question, which requires a well-informed and detailed investigation. Professor Nalanda Roy's edited volume entitled *From Epic Tales to Digital Trails: Understanding New Mediascapes in Activism* by Routledge is precisely such a needed and timely investigation of questions that development of new digital technologies pose. Specifically, the volume, through various case studies of digital technology uses in fostering translational activism, shaping of online narratives, and creating of digital communities provides the readers with mostly positive examples of new technology applications, and with specific ideas of how new technologies can be used for good. Highly recommended."

– **Jacek Lubecki, Professor of Political Science and International Studies, Georgia Southern University**

FROM EPIC TALES TO DIGITAL TRAILS

This book offers a critical perspective on the digital landscape and examines how societies can ensure that technology serves the public good without exacerbating existing inequalities. It advocates for a proactive approach to addressing the challenges presented by digital media, emphasizing the need for ethical guidelines and inclusive decision-making processes. Rather than merely outlining problems, the volume offers potential solutions and frameworks for navigating the future and advocates new forms of political engagement and innovative approaches to governance that leverage technology while safeguarding democratic values and human rights. Through a multidisciplinary lens, the chapters dissect critical issues, from the contours of digital landscapes to social media's impact on communication patterns and the transformative power of digital mobilization. Journeying into diverse facets of human engagement with digital media, the book also explores how actors navigate the geographies of digital spaces and the resources at their disposal. The volume will be essential reading for scholars and researchers of media and communications studies, sociology and politics.

Nalanda Roy holds the position of Professor within the Department of Political Science and International Studies at Georgia Southern University, USA. At GSU, she holds the titles of Certified Diversity Executive and Inclusive Excellence Faculty Fellow. In 2024, Dr. Roy was recognized with the prestigious Professor A. Noam Chomsky Shining Star Research Award. An accomplished author, Dr. Roy, has penned several books, numerous peer-reviewed journal articles, and many book chapters. She has served as the section program chair for the International Studies Association's (ISA) South Asia in World Politics. She holds a senior editor position on the *Oxford Research Encyclopedia of International Studies*.

FROM EPIC TALES TO DIGITAL TRAILS

Understanding New Mediascapes in Activism

Edited by Nalanda Roy

Routledge
Taylor & Francis Group
LONDON AND NEW YORK

Designed cover image: Getty Images

First published 2025
by Routledge
4 Park Square, Milton Park, Abingdon, Oxon OX14 4RN

and by Routledge
605 Third Avenue, New York, NY 10158

Routledge is an imprint of the Taylor & Francis Group, an Informa business

British Library Cataloguing-in-Publication Data
A catalogue record for this book is available from the British Library

Library of Congress Cataloging-in-Publication Data
A catalog record has been requested for this book

ISBN: 978-1-041-03886-3 (hbk)
ISBN: 978-1-041-04575-5 (pbk)
ISBN: 978-1-003-62891-0 (ebk)

DOI: 10.4324/9781003628910

Typeset in Sabon
by Taylor & Francis Books

CONTENTS

ILLUSTRATIONS

Figures

CONTRIBUTORS

Nalanda Roy holds the position of Professor within the Department of Political Science and International Studies at Georgia Southern University, USA. At GSU, she holds the titles of Certified Diversity Executive and Inclusive Excellence Faculty Fellow. In 2024, Dr. Roy was recognized with the prestigious Professor A. Noam Chomsky Shining Star Research Award. An accomplished author, Dr. Roy, has penned several books, numerous peer-reviewed journal articles, and many book chapters. She has served as the section program chair for the International Studies Association's (ISA) South Asia in World Politics. She holds a senior editor position on the *Oxford Research Encyclopedia of International Studies*.

Georgina Chami is a Lecturer at the Institute of International Relations, University of the West Indies and was a recipient of the Central America/Caribbean Fulbright Visiting Scholars Program in 2010. Her research interests include Peace and Security, Diplomacy, Civil Resistance, Migration, Artificial Intelligence and Higher Education. Her co-edited *Managing New Security Threats in the Caribbean* was published by Palgrave Macmillan in 2022. She currently serves as the Member of Faculty of Social Sciences Committee on Distance Learning and Outreach, Faculty Advisor, Harvard National Model United Nations (HNMUN) and UWI STA Model UN Club.

Sriparna Basu is the Dean and Professor of Communication at the FORE School of Management, New Delhi, India. She holds an MA from Jadavpur University, Kolkata and obtained her master's and PhD in Cultural Studies from the University of Illinois at Urbana-Champaign, USA. She has more than 23 years of teaching experience, which also includes consulting experience across various industry sectors. Her current research is in the intersection of digital cultures, interactive technologies, user-behavior, responsible AI, and digital inclusivity. She has worked in policy projects relating to digital policy impact evaluation in rural India.

Sujatha Alla holds a PhD in Engineering Management and Systems Engineering from Old Dominion University, USA. Her research comes from systems engineering perspective and she aims to develop sociotechnical readiness tools for healthcare service robots. She did her BSc in Computer Sciences and MSc in Pure Physics at Andhra University, India. Later she pursued a second master's in engineering management from Old Dominion University, Virginia, USA. Currently she is working on healthcare process optimization and nanosurgical robot path planning optimization. Her research interests include emerging technologies in healthcare: healthcare robotics, human-machine interaction, machine-learning, decision-making in complex environments, cybersecurity, and data science.

Vijay Kumar Chattu is a global health physician specializing in medicine, public health, management, and social sciences. Dr. Chattu is currently based at Temerty Faculty of Medicine at the University of Toronto and is an Adjunct Professor at the University of Alberta, Canada. Dr Chattu did his Bachelor of Medicine Bachelor of Surgery (MBBS) and MD in Community Medicine in India, his MPH in Health Policy and Management in Belgium, his MPhil in Global Health Governance in South Africa, and his PhD in International Relations at the University of the West Indies.

Shivani Sharma is Assistant Professor in the Communication Area at the Indian Institute of Management (IIM), Sambalpur. Her research interests include Strategic Communication, Semiotics, Negotiation, and Media Studies. She is a recipient of Shastri Indo-Canadian Fellowship and Charles Davis Award from the Rocky Mountain Modern Language Association, University of Texas, USA. She has published articles in peer-reviewed journals and presented her research at international conferences.

Ned Rinalducci is the Chair of the Department of Social Sciences at Miami Dade College, North Campus, Florida, USA. Dr. Rinalducci spent 25 years teaching at Armstrong State University and Georgia Southern University in Savannah, Georgia, USA, where he taught courses including Global Sociology, the Sociology of Media, the Sociology of Terrorism, the Sociology of Tourism, the Sociology of Nationalism, the Sociology of the Family, and Deviance and Social Control. Dr. Rinalducci holds a PhD in Sociology from Georgia State University, an MS in Social Psychology from Mississippi State University, and a BS in Sociology and Psychology from Florida State University, USA.

ACKNOWLEDGMENTS

I offer my deepest gratitude to the Almighty, whose grace and guidance have been with me at every turn. This work stands as a testament to Your wisdom, strength, and love, which continue to inspire me in all that I do. I also want to express my sincere thanks to my husband and daughter for their unwavering love and support. My heartfelt appreciation goes to my undergraduate honors student, Chris Ortiz-Gonzalez, for his invaluable assistance in editing the bibliography and helping me with the index. Chris is currently pursuing a Bachelor of Arts in Political Science with a minor in Asian Politics in the Department of Political Science and International Studies at Georgia Southern University, USA. Additionally, I extend my profound thanks to Dr. Ned Rinalducci, Chair of the Department of Social Sciences at Miami Dade College, for his ongoing interest in my work and for graciously agreeing to write the foreword for this book.

PREFACE

In the past two decades, the world has witnessed a profound transformation in the ways we communicate, organize, and advocate for change. The rapid expansion of Information Communication Technology (ICT) and the proliferation of social media platforms have not only redefined our everyday interactions but have also created new spaces for collective action and discourse. From informal friendship groups and chat rooms to professional discussion boards and newsgroups, these digital spaces have become breeding grounds for self-forming, self-organizing movements that transcend traditional geographical and political boundaries.

The edited volume *From Epic Tales to Digital Trails: Understanding New Mediascapes in Activism* arrives at a critical moment. In the post-COVID era, our reliance on digital communication has deepened, making the exploration of online humanitarian movements and their socio-political stakes more important than ever. Dr. Nalanda Roy's timely edited volume captures this transformative moment, offering a comprehensive examination of how technology and social media have empowered self-organizing movements and facilitated the emergence of alternative discourses advocating for diverse agendas.

Dr. Roy has curated an impressive group of contributions that extend and challenge existing theoretical frameworks. Her work brings together voices that explore the ethical dimensions of digital activism, the challenges of maintaining the vitality of digital commons, and the intricate dynamics of content production and dissemination. This volume is a testament to her vision of fostering a deeper understanding of the intersection between technology and humanitarian advocacy.

The central themes of this book—collaborative engagement, ethical obligations, and the socio-political implications of digital connectivity—are deeply relevant to ongoing conversations among policymakers, activists, and scholars. Each essay invites readers to consider the emerging fault lines in the digital landscape and to reflect on the responsibilities we bear as participants in these evolving spaces.

As we look to the future, the transformative power of digital technology promises to continue reshaping the landscapes of communication, activism, and collective action in ways that are both profound and unpredictable. The next generation of digital tools, including advances in artificial intelligence (AI), expanded access to high-speed internet, and even more sophisticated social media platforms, will further challenge and redefine the boundaries of connectivity and influence. While these developments bring the potential for deeper engagement and more accessible participation, they also introduce new ethical dilemmas and responsibilities, particularly as digital divides persist across communities worldwide.

From Epic Tales to Digital Trails: Understanding New Mediascapes in Activism is, therefore, both a reflection on our current moment and a roadmap for navigating the complexities that lie ahead. Dr. Roy's curated contributions offer a comprehensive foundation for anyone interested in understanding—and shaping—the future of digital engagement, emphasizing that while digital technology evolves rapidly, it is up to us to determine how it will best serve the needs of our interconnected world.

As a past collaborator and enthusiastic follower of Dr. Roy's work, I am excited by the depth of analysis and the breadth of perspectives that this volume encompasses. It not only challenges us to think critically about our roles in shaping and being shaped by the digital world but also encourages us to consider the ethical and practical dimensions of our digital lives.

Ned Rinalducci, Ph.D.
Chair, Department of Social Sciences
Miami Dade College, North Campus
Miami, Florida, USA

1

INTRODUCTION

Understanding the Digital Divide in a Connected Age

Nalanda Roy and Sriparna Basu

Unequal Access: The Challenges of the Digital Divide in Modern Society

In his thought-provoking book *Future Politics*, Jamie Susskind astutely observes that "power will lie with those who control the technology, not necessarily those who own it" (Susskind, 2018, p. 154). Susskind further contends that tech firms wield significant influence, not only during the initial design phase but also in determining the formal and technical properties, as well as the range of possible uses for their technologies. In an era marked by rapid technological advancements, the intersection of digital landscapes and human agency has become increasingly significant. The book *Future Politics: Living Together in a World Transformed by Tech* explores how emerging technologies will shape the future of politics, society, and individual lives. In this book, Susskind talks about the technological transformation of politics and argues that technology is not just a tool but a transformative force that will fundamentally reshape political systems. He discusses how advancements in artificial intelligence, blockchain, and other technologies will affect governance, political participation, public administration, law enforcement, policymaking, and democratic processes.

Susskind explores how governments might use technology to improve efficiency, transparency, and public engagement. He also addresses the potential risks, such as the erosion of privacy, surveillance, and the concentration of power in the hands of a few tech-savvy elites. The book examines the impact of technology on democratic institutions and processes and highlights how social media can amplify misinformation, deepen political polarization, and influence election outcomes. The book stresses the need for new regulatory frameworks and innovations to protect democratic integrity in the digital age. However, it also raises concerns about bias, accountability, and the potential for AI to be

DOI: 10.4324/9781003628910-1

used in ways that undermine democratic principles and delves into the ethical implications of technological advancements.

Today, the digital divide poses a considerable challenge, revealing the gaps in access to technology and the internet. Although digital connectivity has revolutionized economies and improved communication, many communities—especially those in rural and low-income areas—still encounter significant obstacles to access. This disparity intensifies existing inequalities, restricting educational opportunities, economic growth, and social participation for those left behind. As essential services increasingly transition online, individuals lacking reliable internet or technological resources find themselves marginalized, unable to engage fully in the fast-changing digital world. Tackling these issues demands collaborative efforts from governments, organizations, and communities to ensure that everyone has equitable access to technology.

The edited volume *From Epic Tales to Digital Trails: Understanding New Mediascapes in Activism* offers a critical perspective on the digital landscape, and questions how societies can ensure that technology serves the public good and does not exacerbate existing inequalities. The central thesis is that technology can either enhance or undermine democratic values, depending on how it is managed. The book also advocates for a proactive approach to address these challenges, emphasizing the need for ethical guidelines and inclusive decision-making processes. Rather than merely outlining problems, this volume offers potential solutions and frameworks for navigating the future, and advocates for new forms of political engagement and innovative approaches to governance that leverage technology while safeguarding democratic values and human rights.

From Epic Tales to Digital Trails journeys into diverse facets of this intersection, exploring how actors navigate the geographies of digital spaces and the resources at their disposal. Through a multidisciplinary lens, the chapters dissect critical issues, from the contours of digital landscapes to social media's impact on communication patterns to the transformative power of digital mobilization. As Sundar Pichai, CEO of Google said, "The key to thriving in the digital age is embracing collaboration beyond borders and cultures."

Social media has emerged as a potent tool for civil society movements, facilitating unprecedented levels of connectivity, mobilization, and activism. Platforms such as Twitter/X, Facebook, Instagram, and TikTok offer new avenues for organizing, advocacy, and discourse, impacting everything from local community issues to global humanitarian crises. Shirky, an expert on social media and digital communication, has written extensively about the role of digital technologies in facilitating collective action and social change. His work highlighted how digital platforms enable new forms of organization and activism (Shirky, 2008). However, while social media has empowered civil society movements in many ways, it also presents a range of challenges and limitations. This critical analysis explores both the positive contributions and the problematic aspects of social media in the context of civil society movements. Social media platforms have revolutionized the way civil society movements mobilize supporters and spread awareness. Hashtags such as #BlackLivesMatter, #MeToo, and #FridaysForFuture have demonstrated how digital campaigns can swiftly gain traction and galvanize public opinion (Roy, 2022, p. 135). The viral nature of social media enables movements to reach a global audience, making it easier to rally support and raise awareness about critical issues.

Types of social media movements	*What did it achieve?*
#BlackLivesMatter	Originating in the United States, this movement gained international traction on social media, advocating against systemic racism and police violence. It sparked global protests and discussions about racial justice.
#MeToo	This movement began to spread quickly around the world to raise awareness about sexual harassment and assault. It encouraged survivors to share their stories and prompted significant conversations about consent and workplace culture.
#FridaysForFuture	Initiated by Greta Thunberg, this youth-led movement mobilized students around the world to demand action on climate change. Social media played a crucial role in organizing strikes and sharing climate science.
#BringBackOurGirls	Following the kidnapping of Nigerian schoolgirls by Boko Haram, this hashtag became a rallying cry, drawing attention to issues of violence against women and girls and the need for action against extremist groups.
#SaveTheAmazon	This movement highlighted deforestation and environmental issues in the Amazon rainforest. Activists used social media platforms to raise awareness and pressure governments and corporations to act.
#LoveIsLove	Advocating for LGBTQ+ rights, this hashtag gained momentum during the fight for marriage equality and beyond. It has been used globally to promote acceptance and challenge discrimination.
#ClimateStrike	Closely linked to FridaysForFuture, this movement encouraged people to take part in climate strikes. Social media is essential for organizing events and sharing information on climate issues.
#EnoughIsEnough	This movement addresses gun violence in the United States and has sparked discussions and protests about gun control policies, mobilizing young activists through social media platforms.

FIGURE 1.1 Some notable global social media movements that have made significant impacts. These movements demonstrated the power of social media in mobilizing people, raising awareness, and fostering global solidarity around social justice issues

Social media democratizes the public sphere by allowing individuals from diverse backgrounds to share their perspectives and experiences. This democratization is particularly significant for marginalized and underrepresented groups who might otherwise lack access to traditional media platforms. By giving voice to those who are often unheard, social media fosters a more inclusive and pluralistic discourse. We need to understand that the ability to communicate in real time is one of the most significant advantages of social media for civil society movements. Organizers can disseminate information quickly, coordinate activities, and respond to emerging developments with agility. This real-time capability is crucial for organizing protests, rallies, and other forms of collective action. Social media platforms facilitate fundraising and resource mobilization through crowdfunding and online campaigns. This capability is particularly important for grassroots movements that may not have access to traditional funding sources. Platforms such as GoFundMe and Kickstarter, etc., along with social media sharing, enable movements to raise funds and gather material support from a broad audience.

While social media can amplify voices, it also has its own challenges and limitations, such as the potential to create echo chambers in which users are exposed primarily to information that aligns with their pre-existing beliefs. This reinforcement of ideological boundaries can contribute to political and social polarization, making it more difficult to achieve consensus and foster constructive dialogue across different groups. Besides, the rapid spread of information on social media comes with the risk of misinformation and disinformation. Misinformation can erode the credibility of movements, create panic, and even incite violence. For example, as the global protests calling for justice for the brutal rape and murder of a female doctor at R G Kar Hospital in Kolkata, India—known as "Justice for Abhaya"—have gained momentum, distinguishing reliable sources from false narratives has become increasingly challenging. This issue has raised significant concerns for civil society movements that depend on social media for advocacy (Wucker, 2020). In San Francisco, protesters have formed a human chain, chanted slogans and held placards that read "We demand justice" (Mukherjee and Roy, 2024). Despite these global expressions of outrage, social media is facing surveillance from governments and other entities, leading to the repression of dissenting voices and the criminalization of activism (Rheingold, 2002). Tufekci, for example has provided in-depth analyses of how social media and other digital tools impact political movements and activism. Her research on the Arab Spring and other movements has contributed to the understanding of digital activism (Tufekci, 2017).

It has become extremely important to understand strategies for navigating the overwhelming digital environment and focus on how individuals can reclaim control over their digital lives. Additionally, the collection of personal data and the monitoring of online activities pose risks to the privacy and safety of activists, which may deter participation and compromise security. It is important to understand that the benefits of social media are not equally distributed. The digital divide, characterized by disparities in access to technology and the internet, means that not everyone could participate in or benefit from social media-driven movements. This divide can exacerbate existing inequalities and limit the reach of movements to those who are already digitally connected.

Beyond Boundaries: The Digital Transformation of Society

During the past two decades, access to Information Communication Technology (ICT) and social media platforms have led to many new digital spaces for communicating—ranging from friendship groups, to chat rooms, to professional discussion boards, newsgroups, etc. The past couple of decades have also witnessed the growth and creation of many self-forming and self-organizing movements online, with their focus on shared humanitarian concerns and vulnerabilities leading to social listening across borders, and subsequent shared and emerging discourses. The edited volume *From Epic Tales to Digital Trails: Understanding New Mediascapes in Activism* will identify how applications and access to technology and social media platforms enable the creation of self-forming, self-organizing movements capable of sharing alternative discourses in advocating for diverse agendas. The volume will explore the 'digital landscapes,' a term that refers to the "complex and overlapping contours of online information flows" (Webster et.al, 2020), and explain how actors navigate the geographies of this landscape and whether and how they have the resources to do so.

In an era marked by rapid technological advancements, the intersection of digital landscapes and human agency has become increasingly significant. As technology transforms the fabric of society, influencing every facet of daily life, the way we interact with and exert control over these digital landscapes has profound implications for our future. Technology has evolved at an unprecedented pace, reshaping how we communicate, work, and govern. The rise of digital platforms, from social media to blockchain, has not only altered the way information is disseminated but also redefined power structures and social norms. The omnipresence of digital technologies has led to a profound shift in human behavior and societal expectations.

Digital transformation encompasses various domains, including artificial intelligence (AI), big data, and the Internet of Things (IoT). These technologies offer remarkable opportunities for innovation and efficiency, but they also introduce complex challenges related to privacy, security, and ethics. As technology becomes more integrated into our lives, the need for a nuanced understanding of its impact on human agency becomes increasingly crucial.

The digital landscape is a comprehensive and evolving environment shaped by the interaction of various digital platforms, technologies, and information flows. Understanding this landscape involves recognizing its complexity, interconnectedness, and dynamism, as well as its impact on individuals and society. As technology continues to advance, navigating the digital landscape requires both awareness of its current state and adaptability to its ongoing changes. It's important to mention the concept of digital activism, which emerged as researchers and practitioners began to recognize the transformative impact of digital technologies on traditional forms of activism. The rise of the internet, social media, and mobile technologies provided new opportunities for organizing, mobilizing, and engaging in political and social causes.

While the exact origin of the term 'digital activism' may not be attributed to a single individual, the collective contributions of these scholars and practitioners have played a crucial role in defining and advancing the field. The term itself reflects the broader trend of integrating digital tools into activism and advocacy efforts, shaping how contemporary social movements operate in the digital age. The collection of essays aims to probe the socio-political stakes of online humanitarian groups by extending the current theorizations of social constructivism (Vygotsky, 1986; Luckin & Du Boulay, 1999) and how they apply to self-developing online movements. The volume asks questions such as: how do digital tools empower global civil society, what strategic realities emerge from this 'digital mobilization', and how are digital technologies transforming various aspects of work and organizational dynamics? It thereby provides insights into the evolving digital landscape. It aims to look at the ethical concerns and obligations that lie at the heart of developing digital commons—the challenge of value depletion or destruction that often takes away the vitality of the commons. For humanitarian self-organizing processes, it will be important to trace and establish the aspects of constructivism (collaborative engagement and negotiated goals, facilitation, etc.), as well as how online humanitarian communities (which are in many ways designed communities) establish and drive relationality and reciprocity goals. The volume will bring together the discursive, ethical, and informational aspects of the digital landscape, to update academicians and policymakers on how content is produced, disseminated, and consumed as well as the emerging fault lines in this process.

Chapter one, "Understanding the Digital Divide in a Connected Age", sets the stage by asking the fundamental question: what are these virtual terrains and how do we traverse them as actors, whether as individuals, organizations, or communities? It engages with the intricacies of the dynamics of digital environments vis-à-vis our engagement with it.

An important shaper of the digital terrain is social media. Social media platforms have now rewritten communication dynamics and power. Chapter two, "Social Media as a Conduit for Civil Society Movements" talks about social media, which has emerged as a significant influence on the global landscape, creating several new ways/methods of communication and interaction through the internet: relay chats, Facebook, Instagram, email, Twitter/X, video chat, information sharing, blogging, and discussion groups. Very importantly, it has enabled communication globally and to anyone who has interests and activities across political, social, economic, and geographical boundaries. In recent times, there has been considerable debate worldwide about the distinctive impact and influence that social media has on public opinion and expression. This chapter attempts to recognize and examine how social media alter communication patterns and engage and influence the public in frank, critical discussions on different social and political issues which can ultimately lead to mass civil society movements which eventually provoke societal change. Undoubtedly, the literature suggests that social media is emerging as a definite influencer on civil society actions and engagements on matters of vital importance within the global political landscape. Consequently, there must be scrutiny and the creation of policies that support democratic principles and encourage civic engagement.

Chapter three, "Platformizing the Epic: A Semiotic Reading of the New Mediascapes and the Narrative Threads of the Mahābhārata: A Case Study", examines how hashtags and fragmented linguistic expressions reshape ancient narratives. In artistic expression, the transformative power of digital storytelling is giving new meaning to historical texts. The Mahābhārata, once confined to epic texts, now thrives in the mediascapes of Twitter/X, bridging tradition and innovation. The new media retellings of the Mahābhārata have 'turned' the epic toward an experimental mode, creating metaphoric threads of narrative. This chapter focuses on C. Sreedharan's two Twitter/X tales of the epic entitled *The Epic Retold* (2014) and *The Autobiography of a Villain* (2019), narrated from the perspectives of Bhima and Duryodhana, respectively. Through the hashtag network of tweets, the epic has undergone a diegetic shift with the new mediascapes foregrounding the popular renditions of the Mahābhārata.

This chapter draws on digital metaphors as vital cues to the process of retelling. It deals with the following research questions: how does the fragmented and restrictive access of linguistic expression on Twitter/X capture the depth of narration without necessarily discontinuing the epic traditions? Particularly, how does the extension of characters from 140 to 280 inflect the semiotic narration in tweets? In what manner does the temporality of the new media age impact the pastness of the epic? It seeks to analyze the following semiotic layers: (a) a critical examination of tweets as semiotic units within literary narration, including the metaphorical use of hashtags; (b) the portrayal of the hero, Bhima, and the antihero, Duryodhana, as the narrators of the Twitter/X Mahābhārata; and (c) the tweeting of the chronicles from the eighteen days of war. Additionally, it investigates how the reception of these epic twictions has shaped the evolving dynamics of narrative metaphors on new media platforms.

Chapter four, "The Growing Influence of ICTs on Online Communities in Post-Covid Era: Opportunities and Challenges", explores the need for technology adaption and evolution in a post-Covid era in employee groups, self-organizing groups, and self-forming groups. The necessity of the ICTs promoted capital investment and technological innovation. This chapter is divided into five sections. The first section is focused on the evolution and the era of ICTs. The second section is focused on the types of online groups and the degree of technologies they are expected to use. The third section focuses on the influence of ICTs on computer literacy, internet availability, and the global digital reset. The fourth section focuses on the Unified Theory of Acceptance and Use of Technology

(UTAUT) theory and users' perceptions and attitudes toward technology use. The fifth section focuses on challenges related to ICTs and the change of behavior intention affected by social isolation and insufficient financial support. The conclusion includes implications for managing and mitigating the negative impacts of ICTs. This chapter discusses various conditions that led to virtual teams, personality types, motivation models, leadership traits, behavioral aspects, and the interweave between these aspects.

The chapter further explores that in the post-Covid era, globally, 16 % of companies have gone fully remote, and 66 % of U.S. employees still work remotely in 2024. The COVID-19 pandemic has led to the emergence of organization-led, self-forming, and self-organizing online communities as people have turned to digital platforms to connect with others and share information during a crisis. Technology cooperation and the rapid development of Information and Communication Technology (ICTs) has led to the emergence of the 'connected world' characterized by how smart technologies impact everyday life. The application of smart technologies redefines the way people live, interact, and conduct business. Since the big lifestyle reset following the COVID-19 pandemic, every aspect of human life still relies heavily on ICTs. However, there are also challenges associated with organization-led, self-forming, and self-organizing online communities. The aspects related to self-motivation (Taylor & Alla, 2018), performance expectancy, effort expectancy, social influence, conflict management (Taylor & Alla 2018), and other behavioral and health factors must be explored comprehensively. When it comes to self-forming and self-organizing groups, they can be vulnerable to misinformation and polarization, and the lack of formal organization can make coordinating actions or addressing issues within the group difficult.

The concluding chapter five, "Fostering Synergy: The Next Chapter of Digital Engagement", synthesize the book's themes. Technology and social media empower self-forming, self-organizing movements, and alternative discourses emerge, advocating for diverse agendas. The transformative potential of digital spaces is undeniable; it is no doubt a force reshaping our world. However, accelerated digital transformation also brings considerations of data privacy and security, and above all the responsible actions of individuals and organizations. As technology advances rapidly and new innovations continually emerge in digital spaces, the challenges of misinformation spread, while echo chambers and threats to privacy and security must be balanced with the need to connect and mobilize opinion. Overall, "Fostering Synergy: The Next Chapter of Digital Engagement" provides a comprehensive analysis of how networks and digital technologies shape social structures and global interactions, providing context for understanding self-organizing communities.

Conclusion: The Future of Digital Synergy Across Borders

As globalization accelerates and technology continues to evolve, the concept of digital synergy across borders is becoming increasingly significant. This edited volume explains the potential developments, challenges, and opportunities associated with cross-border digital collaboration in various sectors, including business, education, healthcare, and governance. The proliferation of the internet and mobile technologies has made it easier for individuals and organizations to connect regardless of geographical location. Social media platforms, online collaboration tools, and remote working solutions have democratized access to global networks.

The findings suggest that fostering digital synergy can lead to enhanced innovation, improved and streamlined services, and strengthened global collaborations. As digital initiatives expand, there will be a growing emphasis on sustainable practices. Cross-border collaborations will increasingly prioritize environmental impact, leading to the development of green technologies and practices. However, cross-border collaboration often encounters challenges due to cultural differences. Hence, it is crucial to understanding and respect diverse perspectives for effective communication and teamwork. By adopting these strategies, stakeholders can maximize the benefits of digital synergy and contribute to a more interconnected and innovative global landscape.

To fully harness the potential of digital synergy and self-organizing communities, scholars and experts should consider several strategies. For example, promoting digital literacy and enhancing digital skills across communities can empower more individuals to participate and contribute meaningfully. Besides, it is extremely important to create an inclusive platform to ensure equitable access to technology and resources, which will help bridge the digital divide and foster diverse participation. Alongside this, implementing strategies to combat misinformation and promote fact-checking can strengthen trust within communities. Organizations can provide resources and support to help self-organizing communities maintain their activities and engagement over time.

Digital synergy and self-organizing communities represent a transformative force in today's interconnected world. By harnessing technology, individuals across borders can collaborate, innovate, and advocate for change. However, addressing the challenges that accompany this digital landscape is crucial for sustaining these communities and ensuring that they contribute positively to global society. As we move forward, fostering inclusivity, enhancing digital literacy, and promoting responsible communication will be key to realizing the full potential of digital synergy. As Amartya Sen said, "Globalization, when combined with technology, has the potential to create a shared future built on mutual understanding and collaboration."

References

Johnson, B. L. (2003). Ethical obligations in a tragedy of the commons. *Environmental Values*, 12(3), pp. 271–287.

Luckin, R., & Du Boulay, B. (1999). The importance of the learner's perspective in the design of educational software. In *Proceedings of the 9th International Conference on Artificial Intelligence in Education*, pp. 35–42. IOS Press.

Mukherjee, S., & Roy, A. (2024). Worldwide protests held over Indian trainee medic's rape and murder. Reuters.com. https://www.reuters.com/world/india/worldwide-protests-held-over-indian-trainee-medics-rape-death-2024-09-08/.

Rheingold, H. (2002). *Smart mobs: The next social revolution*. Perseus Publishing.

Roy, Nalanda, ed. (2022) *Nonviolent Resistances in the Contemporary World: Case Studies from India, Poland, and Turkey*. Routledge.

Shirky, C. (2008). *Here comes everybody: The power of organizing without organizations*. Penguin Press.

Susskind, J. (2018). *Future politics: Living together in a world transformed by tech*. Oxford University Press.

Taylor, A. K., & Alla, S. (2018). Influence of reward systems on motivation-pros and cons based on current literature. *Proceedings of the International Annual Conference of the American Society for Engineering Management*, pp. 1–8. American Society for Engineering Management (ASEM).

Tufekci, Z. (2017). *Twitter and tear gas: The power and fragility of networked protest*. Yale University Press.

Vygotsky, L. S. (1986). *Thought and language* (A. Kozulin, Ed. & Trans.). MIT Press. (Original work published 1934)

Webster, A., Svalastog, A. L., & Allgaier, J. (2020). Mapping new digital landscapes. *Information, Communication and Society*, 23(8), pp. 1100–1105.

Wucker, M. (2020). *The digital transformation of labor: The role of social media in the 21st century*. Routledge.

2

SOCIAL MEDIA AS A CONDUIT FOR CIVIL SOCIETY MOVEMENTS

Georgina Chami

Introduction

The 21st century has witnessed unprecedented technological advancements that have fundamentally transformed societal interactions and global connectivity. Among these advancements, social media platforms stand out as a pivotal force reshaping how we communicate, interact, and engage with worldwide issues. In the field of social science, scholars frequently describe social media as the 'third place', a concept originally introduced by sociologist Ray Oldenburg (Oldenburg, 1999). 'Third place' suggests that our lives revolve around three primary spaces: home, work, and a third space where community is formed, ideas are exchanged, and leisure time is enjoyed. Traditionally, this third place was linked to physical venues such as pubs, clubs, parks, or churches. However, with the rise of social media, this concept has evolved into a virtual space.

Increasing connections to social media is a significant aspect of modern civic activism. Major events in regions such as the Arab world, Ukraine, and Turkey have unfolded alongside vigorous internet-sharing activities by those involved (Anderson, 2011; Tufekci & Wilson, 2012). Social media platforms have played a crucial role in the shift from face-to-face communication to the virtual space. This shift has allowed people from various backgrounds and similar interests to communicate in real-time, share information, and engage in collective actions on an unparalleled scale. As a result, social media has become a potent tool that surpasses geographical boundaries, bridging gaps between individuals, communities, and even nations, while also increasing their visibility. It enables the swift dissemination of information, initiatives, and movements far beyond their initial geographic origins.

Social networks can address two primary challenges faced by civic activism: identifying supporters within a large and dispersed group united by a common

DOI: 10.4324/9781003628910-2

issue and aiding these supporters in progressing toward the cause's objectives (Olson, 1971). Social media can boost grassroots involvement with social and political matters on local, national, and global scales. Academic research indicates that online social networks support grassroots civic activism in three main ways: spreading information, exerting social influence, and creating critical mass dynamics. Social media platforms have turned into crucial arenas for activism due to the extensive mediatization of all aspects of human life (Castells, 2015; Bennett & Segerberg, 2012.

Social media has been lauded for empowering citizens and fostering democracy (Unwin, 2012; Jha & Kodila-Tedika, 2020). The widespread adoption of social media and the expansion of virtual spaces have also led scholars from various disciplines to recognize negative consequences, especially concerning their effects on social interactions, communication, and political engagement/institutions (Vosoughi et al., 2018). These include privacy concerns, political polarization, cultural biases, and misinformation, to name a few. However, in recent years, social media has become a potent instrument for civic activism, revolutionizing how people participate in political and social matters. It offers numerous opportunities to expand civic involvement, promote public discourse, and improve citizens' access to information. These opportunities become especially important as we witness an increasing trend of governments limiting political activities in physical spaces.

Individuals employ social media and various online platforms as avenues for political engagement. These platforms play a crucial role in fostering public accountability and broadening access to unbiased information regarding social, economic, and political matters relevant to their communities or nations. Additionally, citizens utilize tactics such as naming and shaming campaigns and #Hashtag Activism to raise awareness and garner attention for specific events and issues (Goswami, 2018). These actions serve to spotlight the inadequate performance of public authorities, compelling them to address concerns raised by citizens. This dynamic foster greater public accountability and contributes to the promotion of democratic governance.

The accessibility and broad adoption of social media platforms have democratized access to information, empowering the public and marginalized communities to share their narratives, spotlight their struggles, and express their voices directly, without intermediaries. Platforms such as Twitter/X, WhatsApp, Instagram, Facebook, and TikTok have transformed how individuals access and distribute global news and information, facilitating the swift dissemination of content across the globe. Exposure to diverse global events, societal issues, and personal narratives through social media has expanded people's perspectives and illuminated previously overlooked or inaccessible issues. Moreover, social media's significance in human rights advocacy lies in its capacity to cultivate empathy, increase awareness, and spur collective action, a trend increasingly recognized by scholars studying human rights activism. With increased social media use, it becomes critical to assess its effects on the global political landscape and create policies that uphold democratic principles and encourage civic engagement.

Historical Context

Before the advent of social media, civic activism relied primarily on traditional methods of communication and organization, such as face-to-face meetings, phone calls, and printed materials. The pre-social-media era represents a distinct period in human history characterized by diverse modes of communication, community interaction, and societal dynamics. While social media has undeniably transformed the landscape of communication and society, understanding the foundations laid by previous eras is essential for contextualizing contemporary challenges and opportunities. Reflecting on this era prompts us to critically evaluate the impact of technological advancements on human relationships, cultural exchange, and the fabric of society, guiding us toward a more informed and nuanced understanding of our digital age.

The advent of social media has revolutionized the way we communicate, interact, and perceive the world around us. However, it is essential to reflect on the era preceding this digital transformation, a time characterized by different modes of communication and societal dynamics. The pre-social-media era, spanning from prehistory to the late 20th century, played a crucial role in shaping human connections, cultural exchange, and the dissemination of information. This section delves into the key characteristics and impacts of this era, highlighting its significance in understanding the evolution of communication and society.

Communication Before Social Media

Before the advent of social media, communication was fundamentally different in its mechanisms, speed, and reach. The methods of communication were more direct and personal, and often required physical presence or tangible mediums. Types of communication before social media included face-to-face interactions, written correspondence, and, in modern times, telephone conversations and mass media.

Face-to-Face Communication

One of the most significant forms of communication before social media was face-to-face interaction (Edwards, 2015). This mode of communication allows for immediate feedback, non-verbal cues, and human interaction that is often lost in digital interactions. Face-to-face communication facilitates deeper relationships and trust, as individuals can read body language, facial expressions, and tone of voice (Schlosser, 2020). These nuances play a crucial role in building and maintaining social bonds.

Written Correspondence

Written correspondence, such as letters and postcards, was another primary method of communication. This form required time and effort, both in writing and in waiting for a response, which often led to more thoughtful and deliberate exchanges. The anticipation of receiving a letter added emotional weight to the communication process. Additionally, handwritten letters were personal artifacts, often cherished and preserved as keepsakes, which added to their sentimental value.

Telephone Conversations

The invention of the telephone marked a significant shift in communication, allowing for real-time conversations over long distances (Wells, 2018). Telephones bridged the gap between face-to-face interaction and written correspondence by providing immediate voice communication. This technology enabled people to maintain personal connections despite physical separation. However, it still required a degree of planning and coordination, as calls were typically scheduled and, for a time, limited by cost and availability.

Mass Media

Before social media, mass media played a pivotal role in information dissemination. Newspapers, radio, and television were the primary sources of news and entertainment. These mediums had the power to reach large audiences simultaneously, shaping public opinion and culture (Liao, 2023). Unlike the interactive nature of social media, mass media was a one-way communication channel, with limited opportunities for audience feedback. This often meant that information was consumed passively, with little chance for immediate discussion or rebuttal.

The methods of communication before social media had profound social implications. Relationships were often more localized, with communities tightly knit due to the necessity of physical proximity for interaction. Trust and reputation were built through consistent and direct contact, and social networks were smaller but more intimate. Information spread more slowly, allowing for more in-depth processing and discussion. The absence of instant communication meant that people were less likely to experience the information overload that is common today.

Communication before social media was characterized by personal, deliberate, and often slower interactions. Each method, whether face-to-face, written, or telephonic, required a level of effort and presence that fostered deep, meaningful connections. Mass media, while influential, did not offer the same level of interactivity that social media provides today. The shift to digital communication has transformed how we connect and share information, but understanding past methods highlights the value of personal and thoughtful interaction in a way that is increasingly rare in the age of social media.

Unlike previous eras, where civic participation often required physical presence at meetings or protests, social media enables instantaneous communication and broad dissemination of information. This accessibility has democratized engagement, allowing individuals from diverse backgrounds to contribute to public discourse and participate in civic affairs from virtually anywhere (Shirky, 2008).

Contemporary Period

The contemporary period is marked by unprecedented connectivity and digital transformation, largely driven by the emergence of social media platforms. These digital tools have revolutionized how individuals interact, organize, and participate in societal issues, significantly altering the dynamics of activism and advocacy (Adhiarso, Utari & Hastjarjo, 2018). These technologies have both positive and negative implications for social dynamics. On one hand, technology has made it easier for individuals to maintain relationships over long distances and to form communities based on shared interests rather than geographic location. Online platforms facilitate quick information-sharing, collective action, the mobilization of social movements, and space for marginalized voices to articulate their views (Chen, Ho & Chen, 2021).

On the other hand, digital communication can lead to superficial interactions and a sense of isolation. The widespread use of social media has been associated with heightened feelings of loneliness and anxiety (Verduyn et al., 2017), as people compare themselves to carefully curated portrayals of others' lives. Furthermore, it is more challenging to develop meaningful relationships through online interaction compared to with face-to-face communication. The interplay between traditional and digital forms of community interaction has profound implications for contemporary society. Social dynamics are now influenced by a combination of personal, local, and global factors. Communities are no longer bound by physical proximity, but rather by networks of interest and affinity.

This shift to digitalization has both enriched and complicated social life. The ability to connect with like-minded individuals across the globe has expanded opportunities for learning, collaboration, and cultural exchange. However, it has also contributed to the fragmentation of public discourse and the creation of echo chambers, where people are mostly exposed to information and opinions that confirm their preexisting beliefs (Dubois et al., 2020). The challenge for contemporary society is to balance the benefits of digital communication with the need for genuine, in-person interactions. Building strong communities requires fostering environments where individuals can engage meaningfully, both online and offline. This involves creating spaces for dialogue, promoting inclusivity, and encouraging active participation in community life.

Social dynamics and community interaction are fundamental to the fabric of society, shaping how individuals relate to each other and the world around them. The evolution of these interactions, particularly in the context of technological advancements, highlights the changing nature of the community and the importance of adapting to new modes of communication. The influence of social media on the modern global political landscape is intricate and multi-faceted, prompting significant questions about the relationship between technological advancements and democratic governance. Thus, policies must be designed to promote democratic values and encourage civic participation, while also understanding how social media can shape political discourse, mobilization, and governance worldwide.

Social Media

This section of the chapter will examine the concept of social media, its influence on the present-day international political landscape and civic engagement. Social media, as we know it today, is a product of technological advancements that have revolutionized the way people communicate and interact. The history of social media is marked by significant milestones that reflect the evolution of digital communication from simple forums to complex networks that influence global politics, culture, and society. The roots of social media can be traced back to the late 1970s and early 1980s with the advent of Bulletin Board Systems (BBS) (Dhingra & Mudgal, 2019). These platforms allowed users to exchange messages, share files, and participate in discussions through a centralized server. Similarly, Usenet, created in 1980, enabled users to post news and messages in newsgroups, forming one of the earliest online communities.

The late 1990s saw the emergence of the first recognizable social networks. Six Degrees, launched in 1997, is often credited as the first social networking site, allowing users to create profiles and connect with friends. Despite its innovative approach, Six Degrees was short-lived, shutting down in 2000. Several service providers, such as Asian Avenue, Black Planet, and MiGente, emerged between 1997 and 2001, offering a mix of features like profile creation, friend requests, and the ability to identify friends on personal profiles (Boyd & Ellison, 2007). Friendster, launched in 2002, improved on this concept by giving users control over whom they wanted to connect with rather than offering a computer-managed environment (Winder, 2007). It quickly gained popularity but eventually declined due to technical issues and competition.

MySpace, launched in 2003, marked a significant leap in social networking by offering customizable profiles, music-sharing, and a strong community focus. It became the most visited social networking site by 2006. However, its dominance was challenged by the rise of Facebook, founded in 2004 by Mark Zuckerberg and his college roommates. Initially restricted to Harvard students, Facebook expanded rapidly to other universities and eventually to the public. Its clean interface, real-name policy, and innovative features such as the News Feed propelled it to become the leading social network globally.

The mid-2000s saw the diversification of social media platforms, each serving different purposes. A variety of tools to connect people, including social networking sites (Facebook and Twitter), photo-sharing sites (Instagram and Flickr), and video-sharing sites (YouTube and Vimeo) (Ellison & Boyd, 2013;

Burgess & Green, 2018). Social media has drastically transformed the communication patterns of citizens in their daily lives. It is undeniable that social media has made social life more dynamic. Moreover, social media influences greater political discourse, the mobilization of social movements, and political communication and participation. As a public entity, social media has become popular for connecting citizens' aspirations through virtual communication processes. Social media enables two-way communication, allowing organizations to tailor content and interact with communities and society.

Social media has been transformative in communication and remains a pivotal factor (Edwards, 2011). As a modern communication platform, social media is defined in various ways. One definition provided by Carr and Hayes (2015) gives a comprehensive definition of social media, describing it as platforms that empower users to create, share, and exchange information and ideas within virtual communities and networks. According to their analysis, social media facilitates interactions and connections among individuals and organizations, making it possible for users to engage in personalized communication. These platforms support a variety of activities, including content creation, information-dissemination, and community-building. By enabling real-time, two-way communication, social media enhances the ability of users to engage with and influence their communities and society at large. Carr and Hayes highlight the transformative impact of social media on the way people interact, form relationships, and participate in civic and social activities. From Carr and Hayes's perspective, social media emphasizes two-way communication between the sender and the receiver, enabling the exchange of messages simultaneously.

According to Beer (2008), social media can be conceptualized as a group of online tools that facilitate expression and interaction. The term 'social media' refers to the different internet-based networks that allow users to interact with others verbally and visually (Carr & Hayes, 2015). This definition emphasizes the ability of persons to share, cooperate and dialogue, highlighting two-way interaction and message delivery through content creation and sharing on social platforms. Shirky (2008) argues that social media enhances the capacity to share, collaborate, and engage in collective action beyond the confines of conventional institutions and organizations Shirky underscores the potential of social media to facilitate collective action, suggesting that it enables citizens, particularly digital citizens, to engage in collaborative activities such as fundraising, online petitions, and civic engagement initiatives.

The expansive array of functions and influences of social media has elevated it from being merely a communication tool to what is often referred to as 'new media.' New media encompasses the convergence of digital communication technologies that are computerized and networked. It encompasses anything capable of transmitting information (intermediaries) from information sources to data recipients. New media is characterized by two primary elements: digitization and convergence. The internet serves as a prime example of convergence as it integrates various other media functions such as audio, video, and text (McQuail, 2010). New media denotes shifts in media production, distribution, and utilization. It tends to be freer from centralized control, in contrast to the conventional media landscape. The emergence of social media platforms such as Facebook, Twitter/X, Instagram, and others has revolutionized the way civic activism operates and mobilizes.

Facebook

Facebook plays a significant role in fostering civic activism by providing a platform for information-dissemination, community-organizing, and mobilization. It allows activists to share news, updates, and calls to action quickly and broadly, reaching a diverse and extensive audience. Facebook groups and pages enable users to connect, facilitating the formation of communities around specific causes and issues. This connectivity enhances collective action, allowing activists to coordinate events, rallies, and campaigns effectively. Additionally, Facebook's tools, such as live streaming and event creation, support real-time engagement and organization, making it easier for activists to maintain momentum and visibility for their causes. Overall, Facebook serves as a powerful tool for civic engagement, amplifying voices and driving social and political change. This capability also enables social and political scientists to analyze political discourse effectively (Stieglitz & Dang-Xuan, 2013.

Instagram

Similar to other social media platforms, Instagram facilitates social connectivity by allowing users to follow each other, with those being referred to as 'followers' (Hu et al., 2014). Instagram plays a vital role in promoting civic engagement by leveraging its visual and interactive features to raise awareness and mobilize communities. The platform's focus on images and videos allows activists and organizations to create compelling and easily shareable content that can capture attention and convey messages effectively. Instagram Stories, Reels, and IGTV provide dynamic ways to share real-time updates, behind-the-scenes looks, and educational content, keeping followers informed and engaged.

Hashtags on Instagram facilitate the discovery of movements and causes, enabling users to connect with wider communities and join conversations around specific issues. Influencers and public figures on Instagram can amplify civic messages, reaching large audiences and inspiring action. Additionally, the platform's interactive features, such as polls, questions, and live sessions, encourage user participation and dialogue, fostering a sense of community and collective purpose. Overall, Instagram enhances civic engagement by making activism visually appealing, easily accessible, and highly interactive, thereby encouraging more people to get involved in social and political causes.

WhatsApp

WhatsApp significantly contributes to civic engagement by offering a secure and efficient platform for communication and organization. Its end-to-end encryption provides a sense of privacy and security, encouraging open discussions and the sharing of sensitive information related to social and political issues.

WhatsApp groups allow users to connect with others who share similar interests and goals, facilitating the rapid spread of information and coordination of activities such as protests, community meetings, and awareness campaigns. The app's multimedia capabilities enable the sharing of photos, videos, documents, and voice messages, enriching communication and making it more dynamic and engaging. It has become a popular application used for messaging, especially among young people (Jisha & Jebakumar, 2014; Kiran & Srivastava, 2018). Additionally, WhatsApp broadcast lists and status updates help disseminate important messages to a broad audience quickly. Overall, WhatsApp serves as a valuable tool for civic engagement, enhancing connectivity, information-sharing, and collective action in a secure environment.

Twitter/X

This platform facilitates connections with a broad range of people, including strangers, and has become a popular social media tool. Twitter/X has emerged as a vital platform for civic activism, enabling individuals and groups to mobilize and advocate for social and political change on a global scale. Its real-time nature allows activists to rapidly disseminate information, organize protests, and coordinate collective actions. Hashtags such as #BlackLivesMatter and #MeToo have been transformed from social media trends into powerful movements that challenge systemic injustices and amplify marginalized voices. Twitter/X facilitates direct engagement with policymakers and authorities, influencing public opinion and policy agendas by highlighting issues that traditional media might overlook. Despite challenges such as misinformation and echo chambers, Twitter/X remains a dynamic tool for civic activism, fostering grassroots movements and promoting transparency in civic discourse. Its functional features have made it particularly popular among journalists, media organizations, politicians, scholars, and civil activists for sharing news and ideas (Stieglitz & Dang-Xuan , 2013; Mohammadi et al., 2018). Citizens can easily access information, engage in discussions, and mobilize support for causes they care about. Twitter/X and Instagram facilitate real-time updates and enable individuals to connect with like-minded peers globally, fostering a sense of community and solidarity (Boulianne, 2009).

Civic Engagement

Civic engagement or participation is a broad term. There appears to be no agreement among scholars on its usage and interpretation (Gibson, 2000;

Mohammadi et al., 2011). Academics define civic participation or engagement based on the context and necessity. It encompasses a wide range of activities from voting and volunteering to participating in community organizations and public demonstrations. Civic engagement is vital for fostering a vibrant, participatory democracy where citizens are actively involved in shaping their communities and influencing policies. Civic engagement is essential for a vibrant democracy as it ensures that citizens have a voice in governance and community development.

The term 'civic engagement' gained prominence through Robert D. Putnam's book *Making Democracy Work* (Putnam, 1993). In his work, Putnam underscores the significance of 'social capital' as a crucial component of a democratic society. It is the cornerstone of a vibrant and participatory democracy, where individuals actively contribute to the betterment of their communities and society. It encompasses a spectrum of activities and behaviors through which people express their commitment to civic values and responsibilities. Voting in elections is perhaps the most fundamental form of civic engagement, where citizens exercise their right to choose representatives and shape the direction of governance. Beyond voting, civic engagement includes volunteering time and skills for community service projects, such as helping at local food banks, participating in neighborhood clean-ups, or mentoring youth.

Additionally, civic engagement involves actively participating in public discourse and advocacy efforts. This can range from attending town hall meetings and voicing concerns to policymakers to organizing or joining grassroots movements that advocate for social justice, environmental sustainability, or other causes. Social media and digital platforms have also become powerful tools for civic engagement, enabling individuals to raise awareness, mobilize support, and influence public opinion on a global scale. Ultimately, civic engagement fosters a sense of shared responsibility and solidarity among citizens, promoting a more inclusive and responsive society where everyone's voice can contribute to positive change.

Definition of Civic Engagement

Civic engagement is broadly defined as the participation of individuals in activities aimed at influencing public policy and decision-making processes, as well as contributing to the betterment of their communities (Adler & Goggin, 2005). Ekman and Amnå (2012) characterized civic engagement as a form of collective action. Mohammadi et al. (2011) stated that participation promotes good governance. Consequently, civic engagement and public participation support each other and influence governance. Civic engagement is also defined as "any activity where people come together in their role as citizens" Diller (2001, 22). It involves both political actions, such as voting and campaigning, and non-political actions, such as volunteering and community service.

Civic engagement is an interdisciplinary field that includes political science, citizenship, psychology, anthropology, and other disciplines. Conceptually, civic engagement is a fundamental concept in community civics, emphasizing citizen involvement in various aspects of life (Darmawan et al., 2016). This involvement encompasses activities such as political participation, social networking, association membership, and even newspaper-reading (O'Connor, 2006; Putnam, 1993). Traditionally, these activities have been conducted in the physical world, directly involving citizens. However, the advent of the Fourth Industrial Revolution has made the internet the backbone of citizen activities, and many of these engagements have shifted to the digital realm, particularly on social media. Consequently, the role of digital citizens in social media involvement is becoming increasingly crucial.

Mossberger, Tolbert, and McNeal define digital citizens as "those who use the Internet regularly and effectively" (Mossberger et al., 2008, 1). According to their perspective, anyone who frequently uses the internet in their daily life can be considered a digital citizen. Mossberger et al.'s definition includes individuals who engage in online activities for various purposes, such as obtaining political information to fulfill their civic duties or using technology for economic purposes. Therefore, the number of digital citizens corresponds to the number of people who access the internet daily.

Thomas Ehrlich offers a more specific definition of civic engagement, stating: "Civic engagement has been defined as the process of believing that one can and should make a difference in enhancing his or her community" (Ehrlich, 2000, vi). In this definition, Ehrlich emphasizes the central idea that individuals have the capacity and responsibility to contribute to improving their community. He further elaborates that achieving meaningful change in community well-being requires a combination of knowledge, skills, and values, encompassing both political and non-political processes (Ehrlich, 2000; Hylton, 2018). Ehrlich's definition provides a clear and inclusive perspective, acknowledging that civic engagement activities extend beyond political involvement, although political activities may form part of partisan civic engagement.

Adler and Goggin have made significant contributions to the understanding of civic engagement, particularly in their exploration of how digital media and communication technologies influence participatory democracy. They argue that platforms such as Twitter/X and other social media networks play a crucial role in enhancing civic engagement by lowering the barriers to entry for public participation and expanding the reach of civic discourse beyond traditional boundaries. Their work emphasizes that digital platforms offer new avenues for citizens to engage with political and social issues, facilitating real-time communication, the mobilization of collective action, and the amplification of diverse voices. They highlight how these technologies empower individuals and communities to organize around shared concerns, challenge established power structures, and advocate for policy changes (Adler & Goggin, 2005).

Moreover, they discuss the potential of digital media to foster deliberative democracy, where informed and inclusive discussions lead to better decision-making processes. By studying the dynamics of online communities, they illustrate how digital spaces can both democratize access to information and create new challenges such as echo chambers and misinformation. In essence, Adler and Goggin's research underscores the transformative impact of digital media on civic engagement, emphasizing its potential to strengthen democratic practices while also highlighting the importance of addressing its limitations and ensuring equitable access to digital resources for all citizens. Their insights contribute to ongoing discussions about the role of technology in shaping the future of civic participation and democratic governance.

In recent decades, there has been significant advancement in information technology, particularly in digital communication. The convergence of network structures and increased accessibility, along with advancements in hardware and software, have empowered individuals to transform and revolutionize the dynamics of communication in public life. These changes in communication methods ultimately impact individual experiences in the social realm, particularly in their involvement or participation in civic life. This includes changes in how people engage in civic activities and how these engagements are measured (Gordon et al., 2013).

The emergence of new media, particularly social media, necessitates a re-evaluation of citizen involvement, particularly among young citizens. For young individuals, civic engagement takes on a non-traditional form, moving away from conventional methods. The Millennial generation exhibits a preference for utilizing technology, which significantly impacts their modes of participation (Lee & Circella, 2019). Millennials are those born between 1981 and 1996. This generation interprets political involvement beyond traditional party structures, extending into broader social realms. Activities such as initiating online petitions, critiquing governmental actions through social media platforms, or spearheading fundraising campaigns for marginalized groups have become commonplace. These shifts are reflective of an educated and globally connected culture, facilitated by technological advancements and evolving societal trends. It's important to recognize that civic engagement is not a static or neutral concept; rather, it involves intricate interrelationships among individuals, communities, and society at large.

The presence of this technology has formed a new awareness of the great potential of the new media. The forms of citizen involvement are no longer carried out conventionally, such as demonstrations, boycotts, channeling opinions in the mass media, etc., which require a lot of money and energy. A person needs only to use social media on the device in his or her hand to get involved in giving opinions or just to understand the issues that are in the public discourse. Ultimately, these activities will lead to concrete actions that can be taken by good citizens. What must be addressed now is how to take advantage of advances in information technology to implement and facilitate the rights and obligations of citizens.

This represents a stark departure from the traditional model of passive citizenship characterized by one-way communication controlled by authorities (Bennett et al., 2011). The younger generation has embraced a new form of social and civic engagement within the digital sphere. As 'digital natives,' they lead the charge in promoting participatory media as a new avenue for public involvement (Jenkins, 2006). To adapt to these changes, scholars emphasize the importance of conducting civic engagement processes through online platforms such as interactive websites (Pasek et al., 2009; Raynes-Goldie & Walker, 2008), as well as leveraging social media (Bennett et al., 2011; Skoric et al., 2016; Valenzuela, 2013; Warren et al., 2014). New media has introduced a fresh 'participatory space,' fundamentally different from previous modes of engagement. This shift is particularly evident with the rise of social media, which has significantly impacted various civic activities online, including political expression and protest (Valenzuela, 2013).

Online citizen engagement activities are often referred to as online civic engagement, which entails civic involvement specifically conducted by young people and utilizing various types of digital media (Cho et al., 2020). Online civic engagement platforms serve as facilitators of offline activities, providing access to three essential components for effecting change: information, connections with others, and measurement tools (Raynes-Goldie & Walker, 2008). Consequently, online civic engagement has the potential to enhance and empower real-world actions.

The Importance of Civic Engagement

Civic engagement is crucial for several reasons:

Promotes Democratic Governance

Civic engagement is fundamental to the functioning of democracy. It ensures that citizens actively participate in the democratic process, thereby strengthening democratic institutions and practices. Voting, a primary form of civic engagement, allows citizens to choose their representatives and hold them accountable. Through political participation, citizens express their preferences, influence public policy, and ensure that their voices are heard in the governance process.

Moreover, civic engagement promotes the principles of equality, justice, and inclusivity. When citizens from diverse backgrounds participate in civic activities, it leads to a more representative and equitable society. This inclusive participation helps address systemic inequalities and ensures that marginalized and underrepresented groups have a platform to advocate for their rights and interests (Ortiz et al, 2019). Hashtags such as #BlackLivesMatter and #MeToo have sparked widespread conversations, influenced public opinion, and pressured institutions to address long-standing issues of discrimination and injustice (Earl & Kimport, 2011). Active citizen participation ensures that government actions reflect the will and needs of the people. It strengthens democratic institutions and processes by holding public officials accountable (Putnam, 2000).

Enhances Social Cohesion

Civic engagement plays a crucial role in building social cohesion and fostering a sense of community. When individuals engage in community activities such as volunteering, joining local organizations, or participating in community projects, they build relationships and strengthen social bonds. These interactions create a sense of belonging and mutual support, which are essential for a harmonious and resilient community. Civic engagement fosters a sense of community and collective responsibility. By working together on common issues, individuals build trust and cooperation, leading to stronger and more resilient communities (Skocpol & Fiorina, 1999).

Social capital, which encompasses the networks, norms, and trust that facilitate cooperation within a society, is enhanced through civic engagement. High levels of social capital are associated with greater civic participation, improved public health, lower crime rates, and increased economic development (Skocpol, 2003). By fostering trust and collaboration among community members, civic engagement contributes to the overall well-being and stability of society.

Develops Civic Skills and Knowledge

Civic engagement empowers individuals by providing them with the knowledge, skills, and confidence to participate in the democratic process. Through engagement in civic activities, individuals develop a deeper understanding of political and social issues, as well as the functioning of government institutions. This civic knowledge is crucial for making informed decisions and advocating for change.

Participation in civic activities also fosters a sense of agency and responsibility among citizens. When individuals see the impact of their contributions, whether through voting, volunteering, or community organizing, they are more likely to continue engaging in civic activities. This empowerment leads to a more active and engaged citizenry, which is vital for the health of democracy. Engaging in civic activities helps individuals develop important skills such as critical thinking, communication, and leadership. It also increases political knowledge and awareness, which are essential for informed and active citizenship (Galston, 2001).

Addresses Community Issues

Effective governance relies on the active participation of informed and engaged citizens. Civic engagement provides a mechanism for citizens to influence governmental decisions and hold public officials accountable. When citizens are involved in the policymaking process, it leads to more transparent, responsive, and accountable governance.

Participatory governance models, which encourage citizen involvement in decision-making, result in policies that better reflect the needs and preferences of the community. This collaborative approach can lead to more innovative and effective solutions to public issues. Additionally, civic engagement helps combat corruption by promoting transparency and accountability in government operations.

Through civic engagement, citizens can identify and address local problems, leading to tangible improvements in their communities. This participatory approach ensures that solutions are relevant and effective (Verba, Schlozman, & Brady, 1995).

Social Media and Civic Engagement in the Present-day Global Political Landscape

Social media has fundamentally altered the landscape of global politics, reshaping how information is disseminated, political discourse unfolds, and public opinion is formed. This section of the chapter explores the profound influence of social media on the contemporary global political landscape, examining both its opportunities and challenges.

Information Dissemination and Accessibility

Social media has emerged as a potent force for political mobilization, revolutionizing how movements organize and engage supporters. Platforms such as Facebook, Twitter/X, and WhatsApp have enabled activists to swiftly disseminate information, coordinate protests, and galvanize public opinion on a global scale. The Arab Spring uprisings in 2011 underscored social media's role in mobilizing dissent and challenging authoritarian regimes, demonstrating its power to catalyze collective action (AlSayyad & Guvenc, 2015). This point is further developed in the section below discussing examples of social media and civic engagement. Beyond protests, social media facilitates grassroots campaigns, fundraising efforts, and voter mobilization drives, democratizing political participation by providing a platform for marginalized voices and alternative narratives. However, its effectiveness in mobilization is not without challenges, including concerns over algorithmic biases, online echo chambers, and the potential for manipulation by external actors. As societies navigate these complexities, social media continues to shape the dynamics of political mobilization in profound ways, influencing the course of political movements and activism globally.

Political Discourse and Engagement

Social media has profoundly altered the landscape of political communication. It has become a pivotal tool for political actors to disseminate their messages directly to a global audience, bypassing traditional media gatekeepers. Platforms such as Twitter/X, Facebook, and Instagram enable politicians to engage directly with constituents, fostering a more immediate and interactive form of communication. Moreover, social media facilitates the rapid spread of political information and mobilization of supporters, amplifying the impact of political campaigns and movements. However, this digital realm also poses challenges, including the dissemination of misinformation and the polarization of public discourse. As social media continues to evolve, its role in shaping political communication remains complex and influential.

Social media has become a fertile ground for political propaganda, where information can be disseminated rapidly and often unchecked. Political actors and organizations leverage platforms such as Facebook, Twitter/X, and YouTube to manipulate public opinion, spread misinformation, and shape narratives to their advantage. Through targeted ads, coordinated disinformation campaigns, and the amplification of divisive content, social media has been used to sway elections, undermine trust in institutions, and exacerbate societal divisions. The viral nature of posts and the echo chambers formed by algorithms can amplify propaganda's reach, making it challenging for users to discern fact from fiction. As a result, social media platforms face increasing scrutiny over their role in facilitating propaganda and misinformation, highlighting the need for greater transparency and accountability in digital political discourse.

Social media fosters a dynamic and interactive political discourse where citizens can engage in discussions, debates, and activism. Hashtags, trending topics, and viral campaigns serve as catalysts for public engagement on critical issues such as climate change, human rights, and social justice. Politicians and political parties leverage social media to connect directly with constituents, gather feedback, and shape public opinion.

Election Campaigns and Political Strategy

Social media has transformed election campaigns and political strategy by offering unprecedented opportunities for outreach, engagement, and persuasion. Platforms such as Facebook, Twitter/X, and Instagram allow candidates to directly communicate with voters, bypassing traditional media filters and reaching diverse demographics instantly and at scale. Campaigns can microtarget specific voter segments based on demographics, interests, and online behaviors, tailoring messages to maximize impact and mobilize support. The real-time feedback and analytics provided by social media enable campaigns to adapt strategies quickly, responding to public sentiment and addressing issues in real-time. Moreover, social media facilitates fundraising efforts, volunteer recruitment, and the organization of grassroots movements, democratizing the electoral process by lowering barriers to entry for candidates and empowering citizens to participate actively. However, concerns persist regarding the influence of disinformation, algorithmic biases, and the potential manipulation of public opinion by external actors, underscoring the need for ethical guidelines and regulatory oversight in digital campaigning. As social media continues to evolve, its role in shaping election outcomes and political strategy remains a dynamic and critical aspect of contemporary democracy. However, concerns about the spread of misinformation and foreign interference have prompted debates over regulation and ethical practices in digital campaigning.

Transparency and Accountability

Social media has increased transparency in governance by providing a platform for whistleblowers, investigative journalists, and civic watchdogs to expose corruption, abuse of power, and human rights violations. Citizen journalism and user-generated content contribute to holding governments and public officials accountable, thereby promoting greater transparency and responsiveness to public concerns.

Regulation and Governance

The regulation of social media remains a contentious issue. Governments, tech companies, and civil society organizations are grappling with how to balance freedom of expression with safeguarding against harmful content and manipulation. Policies addressing data privacy, content moderation, and online hate speech are evolving as stakeholders seek to mitigate risks while preserving the benefits of digital connectivity. Interestingly, it is useful to compare how the US handles social media (issues of freedom of speech and Section 230 of the Communications Act) with international regulation and governance such as the EU's GDPR (Scheurman, 2021). In the US, social media content regulation is shaped by the First Amendment and Section 230 of the Communications Decency Act, which protects platforms from liability for user-generated content while allowing them to moderate content. Recent debates focus on whether Section 230 should be reformed to address concerns about censorship and misinformation.

In the EU, regulation is more proactive, with laws such as the General Data Protection Regulation (GDPR) and the Digital Services Act (DSA). These laws impose stricter obligations on platforms to remove illegal content and protect users, with an emphasis on transparency and accountability. The US prioritizes free speech, while the EU focuses on user protection and preventing harm.

Examples of Social Media in Civic Engagement on the Global Political Landscape

The Arab Spring, Occupy Wall Street, and the 15M movement showcased how new information technologies and networked communication are vital for enhancing organization, collective action, and the social and political influence of citizens (Gerbaudo, 2012; 2017). Undoubtedly, social media has played a pivotal role in recent social movements and political shifts, here are some examples:

1. Arab Spring (2010–2012): Social media platforms such as Facebook, Twitter, and YouTube played a crucial role in the Arab Spring uprisings, facilitating the organization of protests, dissemination of information, and coordination of activist efforts. These movements led to significant political changes in countries such as Tunisia, Egypt, and Libya (Tufekci &Wilson, 2012). Citizens used these platforms to coordinate protests and expose government corruption and human rights abuses.
2. Black Lives Matter Movement: social media has been instrumental in raising awareness and mobilizing support for the Black Lives Matter movement, which advocates against systemic racism and police brutality (Hockin-Boyers & Clifford-Astbury, 2021). The movement gained momentum through hashtags such as #BlackLivesMatter#SayHerName, and #BLM, with platforms such as Twitter and Instagram serving as spaces for sharing stories, organizing protests, and educating the public. These platforms amplify marginalized voices, provide visibility to underrepresented issues, and challenge established norms and policies (Tufekci, 2017).
3. #MeToo Movement: The #MeToo movement, which aims to raise awareness of sexual harassment and assault, gained widespread attention through social media. Survivors shared their experiences using the hashtag #MeToo, leading to a global conversation about the prevalence of sexual misconduct in various industries and institutions. Scholars such as Fileborn & Loney-Howes (2019); Liao & Luqiu (2022), Quan-Haase et al. (2021) have all commented on how this platform creates online movements with international followers.
4. Hong Kong Protests (2019): Social media platforms played a crucial role in organizing and documenting the pro-democracy protests in Hong Kong (Obar, Zube & Lampe, 2012). Protesters used platforms such as Telegram, Twitter, and LIHKG (a Reddit-like forum) to coordinate actions, share information about police movements, and raise awareness internationally.

These instances demonstrate how social media has become a crucial instrument for coordinating, rallying, and magnifying the voices of people and organizations pushing for societal transformation and political improvement.

The Advantages and Disadvantages of Social Media and Civic Engagement in the Global Political Landscape

Digital advocacy has revolutionized the landscape of activism by harnessing the power of digital tools and platforms to amplify voices, mobilize communities, and advocate for social and political change. When considering specific platforms, it's important to recognize their unique affordances in mobilizing social movements and organizing human rights protests. For instance, Facebook facilitates the formation of both covert and overt groups based on shared ideologies. Twitter/X excels in real-time organization and rapid news dissemination, allowing users to interact directly with live updates through hashtags and keyword searches. YouTube is instrumental in providing immediate evidence of human rights abuses through video documentation. Newer platforms such as Instagram and TikTok also play significant roles in mobilizing the masses, though they can also harbor hate speech. These platforms, particularly popular among younger, tech-savvy generations, serve as hubs for collective political expression. Understanding the distinct functionalities of each platform helps human rights advocates strategically maximize their impact and effectively utilize social media for advocacy.

Furthermore, the rise of digital advocacy has reshaped news and journalism. This phenomenon has led to the rise of 'citizen journalism,' where citizens actively participate in news gathering and dissemination. Social media has empowered ordinary citizens to become citizen journalists, capable of collecting, reporting, and disseminating news and information independently. Social media platforms provide citizen journalists with tools to share content widely, including text, photos, and videos, overcoming barriers faced by traditional media such as censorship or logistical constraints. Citizen journalism holds significant value, especially in regions where mainstream media may be restricted. Projects such as Syria Tracker and various newsgathering organizations have enabled the real-time documentation of human rights violations (Gregory, 2019), serving as crucial evidence for institutions such as the International Criminal Court (ICC) and the United Nations in investigative efforts.

However, digital advocacy also faces challenges such as combating misinformation, navigating algorithmic biases, and ensuring equitable access to digital resources across diverse communities. Moreover, the rapid evolution of digital technologies requires continuous adaptation and innovation in advocacy strategies to remain effective and impactful. The following section examines social media's impact on civic engagement.

Positive Impacts of Social Media on Civic Engagement in the Global Political Landscape

1 Enhanced Political Participation

Social media has been shown to increase political participation by making it easier for individuals to access information, engage in discussions, and participate in political activities. According to Boulianne (2009), social media use is positively correlated with political engagement, as it provides users with exposure to diverse political views and opportunities for political discussion. Social media platforms facilitate the dissemination of political information and enable users to engage in political discourse with a broad audience. Social media has therefore broadened the scope of political engagement beyond conventional channels, enabling individuals to exert more influence in the political sphere (Mavrodieva, et al., 2019).

With the capacity to exchange information and participate in political discourse through social media platforms, individuals are more empowered to take part in political decision-making. In this way, they can hold their elected leaders to greater levels of accountability, and champion policies that align with their beliefs and priorities. This greater engagement and involvement allow for a broader, multifaceted range of perspectives being presented and reflected within the political realm, thereby promoting policy outcomes that are more inclusive and reflective of diverse interests. Furthermore, social media has the potential to dismantle longstanding obstacles to political engagement, facilitating greater accessibility for marginalized communities to express their viewpoints and engage in democratic activities.

2 Mobilization and Advocacy

One of the most significant impacts of social media is its ability to mobilize individuals for collective action. Social media platforms have been instrumental in organizing protests, campaigns, and movements, exemplified by events such as the Arab Spring and the Black Lives Matter movement (Tufekci, 2017). These platforms allow for rapid information-sharing and coordination, enabling large-scale mobilization and advocacy efforts that transcend geographical boundaries.

3 Fostering Community Engagement

Social media also fosters community engagement by providing a space for local communities to connect, share information, and collaborate on community projects. Hampton and Wellman (2003) argue that social media strengthens community ties by facilitating communication and interaction among community members. Online community groups and forums enable individuals to engage in local issues, participate in community initiatives, and support one another.

Negative Impacts of Social Media on Civic Engagement in the Global Political Landscape

One of the most significant drawbacks is the proliferation of false information and propaganda. These platforms can be utilized to distribute misleading or entirely fabricated content, which has the potential to manipulate public opinion and erode the trustworthiness of political discussions (Zhuravskaya et al., 2020). Two good examples are the SCOTUS cases: Gonzales v. Google and Twitter v. Taamneh. In Gonzalez v. Google LLC, the Supreme Court ruled that the plaintiffs, the family of an ISIS attack victim, failed to establish that Google's algorithmic recommendations of ISIS videos could be considered aiding and abetting terrorism under the Anti-Terrorism Act. As a result, the Court did not address the issue of Section 230 immunity. Likewise, in Twitter, Inc. v.

Taamneh, the Court ruled that Twitter, Google, and Facebook could not be held liable under the Anti-Terrorism Act for providing general services that were allegedly used by ISIS. The Court found that simply providing widely available services without specific intent to aid terrorism does not constitute aiding and abetting terrorism.

Social media platforms, while facilitating connectivity and discourse, also serve as arenas where online harassment and hate speech can proliferate. The anonymity and reach of these platforms can embolden individuals to engage in abusive behavior toward others based on various factors such as race, gender, religion, or political views (Louis & Mohamed, 2024). This phenomenon not only creates a hostile online environment but can also spill over into real-world consequences, affecting individuals' mental well-being and societal cohesion. The challenge lies in balancing the benefits of free expression with the responsibility to curb harmful behaviors, ensuring that social media remains a constructive force in shaping public discourse while mitigating its potential for harm.

1 Echo Chambers and Polarization

Social media platforms have been recognized for their role in amplifying societal fragmentation and polarization (Otieno, 2024). By allowing individuals to curate their news feeds and engage primarily with like-minded peers, these platforms can create echo chambers that reinforce existing beliefs and viewpoints. This phenomenon, known as 'filter bubbles,' can lead to a narrowing of perspectives and a decreased willingness to consider opposing opinions. Moreover, the rapid spread of divisive content and sensationalized news stories on social media can exacerbate tensions within communities and contribute to heightened political and social polarization (Sunstein, 2001). Addressing these challenges requires promoting digital literacy, encouraging constructive dialogue across ideological divides, and fostering platforms that prioritize balanced information-sharing over sensationalism and division.

2 Misinformation and Fake News

The spread of misinformation and fake news on social media is a significant concern. Misinformation can distort public perception, influence political behavior, and undermine trust in democratic institutions (Guess et al., 2018). The rapid spread of false information on social media platforms poses challenges for ensuring that citizens are accurately informed and engaged in constructive civic activities.

3 Superficial Engagement

Critics argue that social media can lead to superficial forms of engagement, often referred to as 'slacktivism' or 'clicktivism.' This type of engagement involves low-effort activities, such as liking or sharing posts, that may not translate into meaningful civic action or real-world impact (Morozov, 2009). While social media can raise awareness of issues, it does not always result in sustained or effective civic participation.

4 Digital Divide

Access to digital platforms is not universal, posing challenges for equitable participation in civic engagement. Socioeconomic disparities in internet access and digital literacy may exclude marginalized communities from fully engaging in online civic activities (Mossberger, Tolbert, & Stansbury, 2003).

5 Privacy and Surveillance

Concerns about data privacy and surveillance on social media platforms raise ethical and legal questions. The collection and use of personal data by governments and corporations can infringe on civil liberties and undermine the trust necessary for meaningful civic engagement (Zuboff, 2019).

Moving Forward

Balancing the positive and negative impacts of social media on civic engagement requires a nuanced understanding of how these platforms influence behavior and public discourse. Efforts to promote positive civic engagement on social media should focus on enhancing digital literacy, encouraging critical thinking, and fostering inclusive and respectful dialogue.

Social media platforms have transformed how people communicate, obtain information, and engage in worldwide political discussions. While they provide unparalleled chances for connection and democratic participation, they also present notable challenges regarding misinformation, political manipulation, and privacy violations. As the influence of these platforms continues to grow, so does the need for comprehensive legal frameworks, independent oversight, and collaborative efforts between governments and tech companies. By adopting a multi-faceted approach that includes regulatory measures, technological solutions, and user empowerment, we can safeguard the integrity of political processes and protect individual rights in the digital age.

Establishing independent oversight bodies can enhance the accountability of social media companies. These bodies should have the authority to investigate, audit, and penalize platforms that violate regulations. They can also provide recommendations for improving platform policies and practices. Initiatives such as the Global Internet Forum to Counter Terrorism (GIFCT), a collaboration between tech companies to tackle extremist content online, demonstrate the potential of such partnerships.

Empowering users through digital literacy programs can mitigate the impact of misinformation and political manipulation. Educating individuals on how to critically evaluate online information and understand privacy settings can enhance their ability to navigate social media responsibly. Social media platforms themselves must take greater responsibility for the content they host and the data they collect. This includes implementing robust content moderation policies, investing in technologies to detect and remove harmful content, and being transparent about their data practices. Companies should also conduct regular audits of their algorithms to ensure they are not inadvertently promoting harmful content.

Conclusion

Digitalization has revolutionized our way of life by introducing advanced technologies and social networks. It shapes behavior, prompting the emergence of new collective actions known as digital-enabled social movements or digital activism. For activists, new digital technologies can certainly improve participant mobilization, expand the scale of the movement, and streamline the coordination of tactics and strategies through texting or tweeting.

Re-imagining civic engagement in the digital age involves leveraging the opportunities provided by digital technologies while addressing the associated challenges. Digital platforms and tools have the potential to enhance civic participation, foster new forms of engagement, and strengthen democratic processes. However, ensuring equitable access, combating misinformation, and protecting privacy are essential for realizing the full potential of digital civic engagement. As society continues to navigate the digital age, ongoing efforts to innovate and adapt civic practices will be crucial for fostering a vibrant and inclusive democracy.

Looking ahead, the influence of social media on global politics will continue to evolve. Emerging technologies such as artificial intelligence, augmented reality, and blockchain are poised to further transform political communication, civic engagement, and governance structures. The ongoing debate over the ethical use of data, digital rights, and the regulation of online platforms will shape the future trajectory of social media's impact on the global political landscape. Effective regulation, ethical practices, and digital literacy are essential in harnessing the potential of social media for democratic governance and global cooperation in the 21st century.

References

Adhiarso, D. S., Utari, P., & Hastjarjo, S. (2018). The impact of digital technology to change people's behavior in using the media. *Social Sciences and Humanities,* (2), 35–40.

Adler, R. P., & Goggin, J. (2005). What Do We Mean By "Civic Engagement"? *Journal of Transformative Education*, 3 (3), 236–253.

AlSayyad, N., & Guvenc, M. (2015). Virtual uprisings: On the interaction of new social media, traditional media coverage and urban space during the 'Arab Spring'. *Urban Studies*, 52(11), 2018–2034.

Anderson, L. (2011). Demystifying the Arab Spring: Parsing the Differences Between Tunisia, Egypt, and Libya. *Foreign Affairs*, 90(2), 1–3.
Beer, D. (2008). Social network(ing) sites. Revisiting the story so far: A response to Danah Boyd and Nicole Ellison. *Journal of Computer-Mediated Communication*, 13 (2), 516–529.
Bennett, W. L., Wells, C., & Freelon, D. (2011). Communicating civic engagement: Contrasting models of citizenship in the youth web sphere. *Journal of Communication*, 61 (5), 835–856. https://doi.org/https://doi.org/10.1111/j.1460-2466.2011.01588.x.
Bennett, W. L., & Segerberg, A. (2012). The Logic of Connective Action: Digital Media and the Personalization of Contentious Politics. *Information, Communication and Society*, 15(5), 739–768. doi:10.1080/1369118X.2013.782330.
Boulianne, S. (2009). Does Internet Use Affect Engagement? A Meta-Analysis of Research. *Political Communication*, 26(2), 193–211.
Boyd, D. M., & Ellison, N. B. (2007). Social Network Sites: Definition, History, and Scholarship. *Journal of Computer-Mediated Communication*, 13(1), 210–230.
Burgess, J., & Green, J. (2018). *YouTube: Online Video and Participatory Culture* (2nd ed.). John Wiley & Sons.
Carr, C. T., & Hayes, R. A. (2015). Social media: Defining, developing, and divining. *Atlantic Journal of Communication*, 23(1), 46–65. doi:10.1080/15456870.2015.972282.
Castells, M. (2015). *Networks of Outrage and Hope: Social Movements in the Internet Age*. John Wiley & Sons.
Chen, Z., Ho, P., & Chen, A. (2021). The Role of Online Media in Mobilizing Large-Scale Collective Action. *Social Media and Society*, 7 (3), 1–13. https://doi.org/10.1177/20563051211033808.
Cho, A., Byrne, J., & Pelter, Z. (2020). *Digital civic engagement by young people*. UNICEF Office of Global Insight and Policy.
Darmawan, C., Syaifullah, S., & Anggraeni, L. (2016). The development of civic engagement to empower student potential through entrepreneurial student program. 1st UPI International Conference on Sociology Education, 385–388.
Diller, E. C. (2001). *Citizens in service: The challenge of delivering civic engagement training to national service programs*. Washington, DC: Corporation for National Service National Fellowship Program.
Dhingra, M., & Mudgal, R.K. (2019). Historical evolution of social media: An overview. *International Conference on Advances in Engineering Science Management and Technology* (ICAESMT).
Dubois, E., Minaeian, S., Paquet-Labelle, A., & Beaudry, S. (2020). Who to trust on social media: How opinion leaders and seekers avoid disinformation and echo chambers. *Social Media and Society*, 6 (2), 1–30.
Earl, J., & Kimport, K. (2011). *Digitally Enabled Social Change: Activism in the Internet Age*. MIT Press.
Edwards, S. M. (2011). A social media mindset. *Journal of interactive advertising*, 12(1), 1–3.
Edwards, Mandy (2015). How Social Media Has Changed How We Communicate. *Millennial CEO*. Future of Work.
Ehrlich, T. (2000). *Civic responsibility and higher education* (American council on education oryx press series on higher Ed) (The ACE series on higher education). Rowman & Littlefield Publishers.
Ekman J., & Amnå, E., (2012). Political participation and civic engagement: Towards a new typology. *Journal of Human Affairs, 22 (3)*, 283–300. https://doi.org/10.2478/s13374-012-0024-1

Ellison, N. B., & Boyd, D. (2013). Sociality through Social Network Sites. In *The Oxford Handbook of Internet Studies*. Oxford University Press, 151–172. http://dx.doi.org/10.1093/oxfordhb/9780199589074.013.0008

Fileborn, Bianca; Loney-Howes, Rachel. (Eds.). (2019). *#MeToo and the politics of social change*. Cham: Palgrave Macmillan.

Galston, W. A. (2001). Political Knowledge, Political Engagement, and Civic Education. *Annual Review of Political Science*, 4, 217–234.

Gerbaudo, P. (2012). *Tweets and the Streets: Social Media and Contemporary Activism*. London: Pluto Press.

Gerbaudo, P. (2017). Social media teams as digital vanguards: the question of leadership in the management of key Facebook and Twitter accounts of Occupy Wall Street, Indignados and UK Uncut. *Information, Communication and Society*, 20(2), 185–202.

Gibson C. (2000). *From Inspiration to Participation: A Review of Perspectives on Youth Civic Engagement*. Carnegie Corporation of New York.

Gordon, E., Baldwin-Philippi, J., & Balestra, M. (2013). Why we engage: How theories of human behavior contribute to our understanding of civic engagement in a digital era. *Berkman Center Research Publication*, 21, 1–29. https://doi.org/10.2139/ssrn.2343762.

Goswami, M. P. (2018). Social media and hashtag activism. *Liberty Dignity and Change in Journalism*, 1, 252–262.

Gregory, S. (2019). Cameras everywhere: Ubiquitous video documentation of human rights, new forms of video advocacy, and considerations of safety, security, dignity, and consent. *Journal of Human Rights Practice*, 2(2), 191–207.

Guess, A., Nyhan, B., & Reifler, J. (2018). *Selective exposure to misinformation: Evidence from the consumption of fake news during the 2016 US presidential campaign*. [Working Paper]. Princeton University.

Hampton, K., & Wellman, B. (2003). Neighboring in Netville: How the Internet Supports Community and Social Capital in a Wired Suburb. *City and Community*, 2(4), 277–311.

Hockin-Boyers, H., & Clifford-Astbury, C. (2021). The politics of #diversifyyourfeed in the context of Black Lives Matter. *Feminist Media Studies*, 21(3), 504–509. https://doi.org/10.1080/14680777.2021.1925727.

Hu, Y., Manikonda, L., & Kambhampati, S. (2014). What we Instagram: A first analysis of Instagram photo content and user types. *Proceedings of the International AAAI Conference on Web and Social Media*, 8(1), 595–598.

Hylton, M. E. (2018). The role of civic literacy and social empathy on rates of civic engagement among university students. *Journal of Higher Education Outreach and Engagement*, 22(1), 87–106. https://eric.ed.gov/?id=EJ1175772.

Jha, Chandan Kumar, and Kodila-Tedika, Oasis. (2020) Does social media promote democracy? Some empirical evidence. *Journal of Policy Modeling* 42(2), 271–290.

Jenkins, H. (2006). *Convergence Culture: Where Old and New Media Collide*. New York University Press.

Jisha K, & Jebakumar (2014). WhatsApp: A trend setter in mobile communication among Chennai youth. *IOSR Journal of Humanities and Social Science*, 19(9):1–6.

Kiran, P., & Srivastava, A. (2018). WhatsApp and its impact on the social life of youngsters: a perspective. *Management Insight*, 14(1), 57–64.

Lee, Y., & Circella, G. (2019). ICT, millennials' lifestyles and travel choices. *Advances in transport policy and planning* 3, 107–141. Academic Press.

Liao, C.H. (2023). Exploring the Influence of Public Perception of Mass Media Usage and Attitudes towards Mass Media News on Altruistic Behavior. *Behavioral Sciences (Basel)*. Jul 26, 13(8), 621. doi:10.3390/bs13080621. PMID: 37622761; PMCID: PMC10451722.

Liao, Sara; Luqiu, Luwei R. (2022). "#MeToo in China: The dynamic of digital activism against sexual assault and harassment in higher education". *Signs: Journal of Women in Culture and Society*, 47(3), 741–764. *https://www.journals.uchicago.edu/doi/abs/10.1086/717712.*

Louis, F., & Mohamed, S. (2024). Cyberbullying and Online Harassment: A Multi-faceted Examination of Digital Platform Violence. *Journal of Sexual Aggression*, 1–15.

Mavrodieva, A. V., Rachman, O. K., Harahap, V. B., & Shaw, R. (2019). Role of social media as a soft power tool in raising public awareness and engagement in addressing climate change. *Climate*, 7 (10), 122. https://doi.org/10.3390/cli7100122.

McQuail, D. (2010). *McQuail's Mass Communication Theory* (6th ed.). Sage Publications.

Mohammadi, S. H., Norazizan, S, & Shahvandi, A. R. (2011). Civic engagement, citizen participation and quality of governance in Iran. *Journal of Human Ecology*, 36(3), 211–216.

Mohammadi E, Thelwall, M, Kwasny, M, & Holmes, K. L. (2018). Academic information on Twitter: A user survey. *PLoS one*, 13(5), 1–18.

Morozov, E. (2009). The Brave New World of Slacktivism . *Foreign Policy* 19(5). https://foreignpolicy.com/2009/05/19/the-brave-new-world-of-slacktivism/.

Mossberger, K., Tolbert, C. J., & Stansbury, M. (2003). *Virtual Inequality: Beyond the Digital Divide*. Georgetown University Press.

Mossberger, K., Tolbert, C. J., & McNeal, R. S. (2008). *Digital citizenship. The internet, society, and participation.* MIT Press.

Obar, Jonathan A., Zube, P., & Lampe, C. (2012). Advocacy 2.0: An Analysis of How Advocacy Groups in the United States Perceive and Use Social Media as Tools for Facilitating Civic Engagement and Collective Action. *Journal of Information Policy*, 2, 1–25.

O'Connor, J. S. (2006). Civic engagement in higher education. *Change*, 38(5), 52–58.

Oldenburg, Ray. (1999). *Great Good Place*. Marlow.

Olson Jr, M. (1971). *The Logic of Collective Action: Public Goods and the Theory of Groups, with a new preface and appendix* (Vol. 124). Harvard University Press.

Ortiz, J., Young, A., Myers, M., Bedeley, R. T., Carbaugh, D., Chughtai, H., & Wigdor, A. (2019). Giving Voice to the Voiceless: The Use of Digital Technologies by Marginalized Groups. *Communications of the Association for Information Systems*, 45(1), 20–38.

Otieno, P. (2024). The impact of social media on political polarization. *Journal of Communication*, 4(1), 56–68.

Pasek, J., More, E., & Romer, D. (2009). Realizing the social Internet? Online social networking meets offline civic engagement. *Journal of Information Technology and Politics*, 6(3–4), 197–215. https://doi.org/10.1080/19331680902996403.

Putnam, R. D. (1993). *Making Democracy Work: Civic Traditions in Modern Italy.* Princeton University Press.

Putnam, R. D. (2000). *Bowling Alone: The Collapse and Revival of American Community.* Simon & Schuster.

Quan-Haase, Anabel, Mendes, Kaitlynn, Ho, Dennis, Lake, Olivia, Nau, Charlotte, & Pieber, Darryl (2021). Mapping# MeToo: A synthesis review of digital feminist research across social media platforms. *New Media and Society* 23(6), 1700–1720. https://doi.org/10.1177/1461444820984457.

Raynes-Goldie, K., & Walker, L. (2008). Our space: Online civic engagement tools for youth. In W. L. Bennett (Ed.), *Civic life online: Learning how digital media can engage youth* 161–188. MIT Press.

Scheurman, T. (2021). Comparing Social Media Content Regulation in the US and the EU: How the US Can Move Forward with Section 230 to Bolster Social Media Users' Freedom of Expression. *San Diego International Law Journal*, 23, 413.

Schlosser, Ann E. 2020. Self-disclosure versus self-presentation on social media, *Current Opinion in Psychology* 31, 1–6,

Shirky, C. (2008). *Here Comes Everybody: The Power of Organizing without Organizations*. Penguin Group.

Skoric, M. M., Zhu, Q., Goh, D., & Pang, N. (2016). Social media and citizen engagement: A meta-analytic review. *New Media and Society*, 18(9), 1817–1839. https://doi.org/10.1177/1461444815616221.

Skocpol, T. (2003). *Diminished Democracy: From Membership to Management in American Civic Life*. University of Oklahoma Press.

Skocpol, T., & Fiorina, M. P. (1999). *Civic Engagement in American Democracy*. Brookings Institution Press and Russell Sage Foundation.

Stieglitz, S., & Dang-Xuan, L. (2013). Social media and political communication: a social media analytics framework. *Social Network Analysis and Mining*, 3(4), 1277–1291.

Sunstein, C. R. (2001). *Republic.com*. Princeton University Press.

Tufekci, Z. (2017). *Twitter and Tear Gas: The Power and Fragility of Networked Protest*. Yale University Press.

Tufekci, Z., & Wilson, C. (2012). Social Media and the Decision to Participate in Political Protest: Observations from Tahrir Square. *Journal of Communication* 62(2), 363–379. doi:10.1111/j.1460-2466.2012.01629. x.

Unwin, T. (2012). *Social Media and Democracy: Critical Reflections*. [Background Paper]. Commonwealth Parliamentary Conference, Colombo.

Valenzuela, S. (2013). Unpacking the use of social media for protest behavior: The roles of information, opinion expression, and activism. *American Behavioral Scientist*, 57 (7), 920–942. https://doi.org/10.1177/0002764213479375.

Verba, S., Schlozman, K. L., & Brady, H. E. (1995). *Voice and Equality: Civic Voluntarism in American Politics*. Harvard University Press.

Verduyn, P., Ybarra, O., Résibois, M., Jonides, J., & Kross, E. (2017). Do social network sites enhance or undermine subjective well-being? A critical review. *Social Issues and Policy Review*, 11(1), 274–302.

Vosoughi, S., Roy, D., & Aral, S. (2018). The spread of true and false news online. *Science*, 359(6380), 1146–1151.

Warren, A. M., Sulaiman, A., & Jaafar, N. I. (2014). Social media effects on fostering online civic engagement and building citizen trust and trust in institutions. *Government Information Quarterly*, 31(2), 291–301. https://doi.org/10.1016/j.giq.2013.11.007.

Wells, A. (2018). Telephone and Face-to-Face Communication. *The Tech Professional's Guide to Communicating in a Global Workplace*. Apress, 107–134. https://doi.org/10.1007/978-1-4842-3471-6_6.

Winder, D. (2007). Back to basics: social bookmarking. *Information World Review*, 29–31.

Zhuravskaya, E., Petrova, M., & Enikolopov, R. (2020). Political effects of the internet and social media. *Annual Review of Economics*, 12(1), 415–438. https://doi.org/10.2139/ssrn.3439957.

Zuboff, S. (2019). The Age of Surveillance Capitalism: The Fight for a Human Future at the New Frontier of Power. *Social Theory Re-wired*, Routledge, 202–213.

3

THE SEMIOTIC TRANSFIGURATION OF THE MAHĀBHĀRATA

Character Narratives and Hashtag Metaphors in Digital Microblogging

Shivani Sharma

New Media and the Turned Epic

The new media adaptation of the Mahābhārata has turned the epic tradition toward a new experimental mode, creating a digital network of interpretations. Through its tweet narrative and hashtags, the medium of Twitter has brought new contexts of reading, adding multiple semiotic layers to the epic narrative. This chapter critically analyses C. Sreedharan's two tales of the epic on Twitter (currently known as X) platform titled *Epic Retold: #Mahabharata #Twitter-Fiction #Bhima #140Characters* (2014) and *Autobiography of a Villain: Duryodhana's Story* (2019), narrated from the perspectives of Bhima and Duryodhana, respectively. Through the hashtag network of tweets, the epic has undergone a diegetic shift with new mediascapes foregrounding the new media renditions of the Mahābhārata. This study attempts to examine the semiotic transaction between the epic narrative and mediation in the Twitter adaptations of the Mahābhārata. I argue that the two Twitter retellings of the epic have (re) contextualised the narrative in the contemporary social context. While tracing the semiotic shift from graphic to digital metaphor, the chapter assesses the potential of Twitter's narrative to retell the tales of the epic in its minimalist spaces of tweeting anchored with hashtags.

This study undertakes to semiotically analyse how the format of Twitter, through the digital form of tweeting reframes the epic story and enables the character of Bhima and Duryodhana to tell their versions of narratives. Twitter retellings of the epic explore the diegetic potency of the medium and foreground the relevance of popular rendition of the epic traditions in new media. The chapter draws on the digital metaphors in the adaptation as vital cues to the process of retelling. The metaphors are embedded in the mediatic form of retelling the epic narrative. This chapter unfolds three semiotic layers as

DOI: 10.4324/9781003628910-3

follows: (a) the critical examination of the tweets as a semiotic unit in literary narration and the metaphorics of hashtags, (b) the microblogging of the hero, Bhima, and the antihero, Duryodhana, as the storytellers of the Twitter Mahābhārata narratives, and (c) tweeting the chronicles of the war. This chapter deals with the following research questions: how does the fragmented and restrictive access to the linguistic expression on Twitter capture the depth of narration without necessarily discontinuing the epic tradition? Particularly, how does the extension of characters from 140 to 280 inflect the semiotic narration in tweets? The chapter examines how the Twitter metaphors are different from the other mediatic adaptations of the Mahābhārata. In what manner does the temporality of the new media age affects the pastness of the epic?

Lev Manovich, in *The Language of New Media* (2001), highlights the popularity of new media literature and emphasises the expanding domain: "It is an ever-growing array of devices, and to the perpetual search for the one device that does everything" (Manovich, 2001, p.4). He advocates the need to initiate discussions on new media culture. He argues that the "computerization of culture" has adapted innovative techniques to recreate narratives in new cultural forms on digital mediums (Manovich, 2001, p.9). Henry Jenkins extends the discussion in *Convergence Culture: Where Old and New Media Collide* (2006). He suggests that new media serves as an "innovation, convergent, everyday, appropriate, networked, global, generational, and unequal" (Jenkins, 2006, p. 27). The convergence of old and new mediums initiates a dialogic conversation between the narratives and their adaptation on multimedia platforms, creating a new paradigm of stories.

New media has played an instrumental role in converging various mediatic forms and constructing new virtual narratives. Shakuntala Banaji discusses how convergence across mediums results in "complex interactions between particular audiences, their practices of meaning-making and use of specific texts, representations, formats or media" (Banaji, 2011, p. 1). The emergence of new media and its increasing popularity has led to the creation of mediatic cultures in India. The retellings of the Mahābhārata in the new media platforms such as YouTube, online games, and Twitter is a step toward such multi-mediatic cultures, initiating new literary forms.

This chapter explores the retellings of the Mahābhārata in the medium of Twitter. The author Sreedharan, in his work titled *Epic Retold*, shared a total number of 2,672 tweets with Twitter users from 2009 to 2014. Sreedharan's work is inspired by M.T. Vasudevan Nair's novel based on the Mahābhārata titled *Randamoozham* (1984), a tale from Bhima's perspective written in Malayalam.[1] Sreedharan artfully retells the epic in the form of tweets and builds up the narrative tension through the Twitter element of hashtags. According to its representative system, Sreedharan's narration is 'medium-specific' in the retelling and shifts with the tale.[2] Later on, the collection of these tweets was published in book format.[3] While it does make an accessible retelling in a continuous narrative form of a book text, on the other hand, it does not provide the connecting hyperlinked structure of the Twitter medium.

Later, the author extended Bhima's Twitter epic version into the novel, *I Who Killed My Brothers: A Novel Retelling of the Mahābhārata* (2019). After Bhima's tale, the subsequent version of the epic retelling from Duryodhana's perspective was initially published as a novella, *An Autobiography of a Villain*, and was released into the 'Twitterfiction' over the period of eighteen days (between November 25 and December 17, 2019) in 961 tweets.[4] Sreedharan draws on intermedial references – the visual and the textual as a collaborative narrative in order to anchor individual tweets as an extension of the narrative structure. The technique of incorporating the other narrative references functions to supply additional information about the suggested scene in a tweet. For instance, the added panel becomes the visual extension of the scene in the textual landscape of the Twittersphere. He opens the description of Duryodhana with his image depicted in the graphic narrative published by Graphic India (see Figure 3.1). The act of tweeting empowers Sreedharan as the threadbearer of the narrative. He makes a real-time conversation with the readers, inviting the reader to participate in the construction of the story.

The Twitter epic narratives traverse through different genres such as novel, novella, and a Twitterfiction, especially in the mediums of printed (book-text) and digital Twitter spaces. The non-visuality of the Twitter version of the Mahābhārata does not remain the same as the non-visuality of a book-text. The ability of re-tweeting and the use of hashtags create a network of narratives within the thread of tales. The real-time presence of the users provided instant feedback and suggestions to the author. In a conversation, Sreedharan discussed his background in journalism, which played a crucial role in creating these Twitter narratives. He mentioned the intention of testing the platform Twitter as a medium for "long-form journalism" (November 29, 2021).[5] His journalist sting motivated him to recreate the epic narrative as a sequence of tweets. His experience of reporting as a narrative technique helped him to create the story of Bhima in Twitter mode. He draws on his expertise in reportage in building the Twitter narrative of the character, Bhima. In 2009, Twitter, as a new medium with limited followership, commenced the experiment of tweeting the epic. The creatively connected blocks of tweets without obstructing the flow of narrative reflect how journalistic elements contribute to the creation of narrative space in the form of tweets. Sreedharan writes in the Author's Note of *The Epic Retold* that "this was not reimagining the Mahābhārata but reimagining the Mahābhārata for Twitter" (Sreedharan, 2014, p.5).

Chindu Sreedharan @epicretold Nov 26, 2019
So many way in which #Duryodhana has been depicted. Here's one that caught my eye today, from @Graphic India. How do we see him in our mind's eye, I wonder? Moustached? Bearded? Muscle-bound? Angry? Handsome?
#Twitterfiction #stories

FIGURE 3.1 Representation of Bhima in Graphic Novel tweeted on November 26, 2019

Jonathan Bignell, in *Media Semiotics: An Introduction* (1997), describes the significance of analysing signs in mediums: "As we become increasingly accustomed to living in a culture infused with media, semiotics is a particularly effective means of taking stock of this situation" (Bignell, 1997, p.207). In the medium of Twitter, each tweet functions as a semiotic unit which is further connected to the larger narrative structure. Tweets create a digital metaphoric network that suggests the semiotic connections between the tweets and weaves them into narrative blocks. Condensed in 140 and 280 characters, in its minimalist form, each tweet creates a story through its metaphoric underpinning in new media. Marriane Van Den Boomen, in the work *Transcoding the Digital: How Metaphors Matter in New Media* (2014), draws on Manovich's notion of "transcoding", in which the "layer of computer and culture" makes a form of metaphors (Boomen, 2014, p.18). This exchange of meaning between the medium and the culture leads to the construction of digital metaphors. Boomen's understanding of "metaphors we compute by" signifies the ways in which metaphors transcode in the new medium, as follows:

1) interfacial representation on the screen, 2) digital objects as performative material metaphors, 3) media and mediation metaphors, 4) tropes of immediacy and transparency, 5) software as mediator and metaphor, and 6) metaphors of sociality (Boomen, 2014, p.24).

Boomen argues that metaphors are located as the semiotic units in a medium. They function on distinctive levels, from a screen to software, and cultural references help disseminate a narrative through its contextual forms. Sreedharan draws on digital metaphors with their cultural transcoding to translate the selected stories of Bhima and Duryodhana into the virtual space. The process of re-scripting the epic tale on Twitter platforms becomes a 'performative material' of digital metaphor. The narration of the epic is dependent on the representational properties of the platform, specifically the hashtags as essential markers for visibility, categorising, and connecting with the users. I argue that the Twitter retellings of the Mahābhārata play a significant role in the mediatic adaptations of the epic traditions. Through the digital metaphors, the representations of the characters such as Bhima and Duryodhana, along with the episodes of the eighteen days of the war, are represented with the aspect of brevity which makes the experience of storytelling specific to the medium. Bryan Alexander, in *The New Digital Storytelling: Creating Narratives with New Media* (2017), discusses the challenges of the art of storytelling in the digital and new media age. He says, "the story is a personal, intimate, analogue thing. Therefore, cyberspace is a world apart, at its worst, a cold domain of data" (Alexander, 2017, p.4). Alexander argues that narrating a story on a web device may reduce it to a data set.

The challenge for an author and the receiver (the user) is to create an engaging space for communicating tales on Twitter. Sreedharan undertakes to create an immersive experience of storytelling with the readers of the epic twictions by engaging with them through conversations after each episode (tweet) in the retellings. Sreedharan mentions during an interview that the form of "collaborative storytelling helped transmit the stories of Bhima and Duryodhana" on the medium (November 29, 2021). This mode of 'collaborative storytelling' became a source of motivation for sustaining Bhima's epic retelling for four years on Twitter (2009 to 2013) but also affected the process of narrating the tales.[6]

The interconnected tweets organised through hashtags enable the reader to collaborate in the process of re-creating the epic. Each tweet functions as a narrative leaf of the epic and contributes to the larger framework of the Mahābhārata. The writer's task is to present the progression of the tweets with their twists leading to the resolution of the conflicts of kinship between the Pandavas and the Kauravas. The reader's visualisation of each tweet as an extension of the narrative hinges upon their understanding of the epic tradition. Thus, the Twitter narrative is a dynamic process that is enabled through active collaboration between the writer and the reader. It blends the creative and mutual readjustment between the epic tales and the modalities of the Twitter medium into a form of literary narrative.

Tweets as Literary Narrative

Twitter (X), as a new media platform, has reinvented the way narratives are created and disseminated in the public sphere. The digital space of Twitter is linguistically limited to 280 characters per tweet. Twitter serves as a site of conversations and interactions between the reader and the author. The real-time presence of the tweets provides instant responses to the narratives. The element of contemporaneity in Twitter makes the reading experience unique and distinctive from reading a book-text. Unlike the linearity and singularity of reading experience in text-reading, Twitter users have more flexibility when reading through the scattered mass of tweets. During the conversation, Sreedharan discusses the careful selection of each character to balance the process of storytelling. He says, "Usually, I think in terms of words, but here I was thinking in terms of characters. I learnt to value every character during the process" (November 29, 2021). The characters helped in creating the two literary narratives on Twitter. Moreover, the connector hashtag adds variety to the retellings by weaving the narrative structure. The fragmentary nature of Twitter does not function as a limitation but displays the creative process of weaving stories through characters. In Sreedharan's retellings, tweets create self-contained meaning(s), and the 'Twitter threads' showcase a meta-narrative structure on the medium.

Accessing the tweets on digital platforms is a significant aspect of Twitter in functioning as a distributive narrative. Virtual accessibility releases the epic narrative from the imperatives of time and space. Moreover, the hashtag function of the medium makes the narration open-ended. Placed in a flexible virtual space, the epic tradition accumulates various meanings. One of the seminal articles on Twitter Studies titled "Social Networks that Matter: Twitter Under the Microscope" (2008) says, "Social networks, a very old and pervasive mechanism for mediating distal interactions among people, have become prevalent in the age of the Web" (Huberman, Romero and Wu, 2008, p. 2). The platform has empowered its users to express their views with stories on a virtual platform. The accessibility and ease-of-use have allowed users to construct social, economic and political discourses on Twitter. It is transforming the way of perceiving stories and reinventing them in virtual spaces.

Sitaram Asur and Bernado A. Huberman, in their article "Predicting the Future with Social Media" (2010), state that through "ease of use, speed and reach, social media is fast changing the public discourse in society" (Asur and Huberman, 2010, p. 1). As part of the social media platform, Twitter is reshaping how narratives are represented in public. Jack Dorsey, one of the co-founders of Twitter, discusses the thought process behind the mega-project to bring out micro-narratives. Dorsey maintains that

> the whole bird thing: bird chirps sound meaningless to us but meaning is applied by other birds. The same is true of Twitter: a lot of messages can be seen as completely useless and meaningless, but it's entirely dependent on the recipient
>
> *(Dorsey quoted in Weller, Bruns, Burgess, Mahrt, & Puschmann, 2014, p.4).*

The symbol of Twitter, like a bluebird, signifies carrying messages and the sound of 'tweeting.' This sound can be assumed as the signals that go out in messages. The semiotics of Twitter lies in understanding how tweets function as content threads and create a Twitter structure of a story. The interconnected tweets are spread across multimodal pages of the medium.

Twitter as a social medium of communication presents a literary dimension that cannot be separated from its market imperatives. Michael Rudin, in *From Hemingway to Twitterature: The Short and Shorter to It* (2011), define the objective of Twitterature as (a) "a marketing vehicle", (b) "a revealing platform", (c) "a bite-sized form" (Rudin, 2011, p.3). Despite its marketability and commercial usage, Twitterature (Twitter and literature) has been reinvented as a mode of telling stories and has broadened the accessibility of the work to target a virtual audience. It has appeared as a digital avatar for narratives to be expressed or published in a new form and style. One of the early writers who used Twitter to express narratives is Arjun Basu. In 2008, Basu "began composing what he called 'twisters' (short stories told on Twitter), posting at least one tweet a day" (Basu quoted in Bronwen, 2014, p.73). The twisters are closely related to each other by publishing narratives as microfictions. Basu's method of tweeting led to the popularity of Twitter as a literary medium and also paved the way for the possibility of creating Twitter-fiction. In *Epic Retold*, Sreedharan mentions that "the rise of the mobile fiction in Japan" also stimulated the author to write Mahābhārata stories for Twitter (Sreedharan, 2014, p.1).

In *The New Digital Storytelling: Creating Narratives with New Media* (2017), Bryan Alexander draws our attention to the entangled narratives between old and new media. He argues that "perhaps the most powerful metaphor for thinking through successive technologies is that of tile imbrications" (Alexander, 2017, p.89). The "tile imbrications" are the digital metaphors that overlap within the mediatic form of social networking platforms. The reinvention of new media platforms functions as a successor to the old, aiming to broaden the social network. In *Social Communication in the Twitter Age* (2013), Dhiraj Murthy argues that "though restricted to 140 characters, Twitter has simple yet powerful methods of connecting tweets to larger themes, specific people, and groups" (Murthy, 2013, p.3). Tweets emerge as micro-narratives that require the technique of "aphorisms" (Ozdemir, 2024, p.63). The technique of aphorisms helps the users to create content that can engage the attention span of Twitter users. Further, the tweets connected through hashtags (expressed with the symbol '#') function as hyperlinks to intricate networking between the users' stories (Bernard, 2019, p.2).

Social networking helps create literary narratives through the dialogue between the users with the author(s). Therese Tierney, in *The Public Space of Social Media* (2013), says that "Twitter feeds represent an interactive diagram of an emerging public conversation where users not only can ascertain the cause of a debate but also learn what others are thinking about it" (Tierney, 2013, p.33). The instant feature of publishing the micro-narrative in tweets also provides room for conversations. Twitter as an "interactive diagram" builds with each tweet and retweet by the user and broadens the horizon of the Twittersphere to perceive narratives in their own way. In *Analyzing Digital Fiction* (2014), Bronwen Thomas extensively discusses the role of 'Twitterfiction' and the aspects of Twitterature (Twitter and Literature) in creating new versions of stories. She contends that

> The very notion of reading as a structured, focused, linear activity is challenged by the fact that each reader of a Twitterfiction has a unique experience shaped by his or her own choices about who or what to follow, making it impossible to predict how this surrounding content influences the interpretation of individual tweets
>
> *(Thomas, 2015, p.96).*

The non-linear form of tweets fragments the reading experience. The users curate their subjective points of view from the micro-narratives. The author discusses the readers' involvement as a critical part of creating Bhima's version (Sreedharan, 2019, p.5). Thomas adds that "Chindu has maintained a dialogue with his readers from the outset—for example, exhorting them to "read ER as a story, fiction (@epicretold, September 19, 2010)" (Thomas, 2015, p.99). As discussed earlier, the viewer's engagement with the story helps the author reinvent the epic through Bhima's and Duryodhana's characters to maintain collaborative storytelling. Sreedharan's experiment has situated the Mahābhārata in an intricate network of storytelling platforms. The work titled *New Media and Visual Communication in Social Networks* (2020) argues the notion of dialogism as a crucial aspect of creating a Twitter experience. Kir argues that "Twitter allows for dialogic communication which allows for a carnival interaction" (Kir, 2020, p.279). The communicative interaction between two users leads to dialogues, creating a form of "carnivalesque experience" (Kir, 2020 p.279). Unlike closed texts or what Barthes termed "writerly texts," Twitter is an open-ended text that allows the reader to edit its content and navigate its meaning-making through the interactive process of tweeting and creating literary narratives.

Hashtag Mahābhārata

The praxis of Twitter (X) as a medium collaborates in constructing a narrative and navigating the reading process of its readers. The form of retelling unveils the process of the medium and its cultural decoding. Sreedharan's epic narration is "medium-specific" in the retellings and narrates the tales according to its representational system. The medium of Twitter adopts the mode of "concurrent narration" (Sreedharan, 2014, p.9). The author discusses the mediation of concurrent narration that provides "the real-time nature of Twitter: the immediacy, the breathless urgency expected of every tweet" (Sreedharan, 2014, p.4). Twitter has dynamic medial properties, lends new modes of narrations, and enables the Mahābhārata to contest its space in the digital domain.

Alexander Aciman and Emmett Rensin in *Twitterature: The World's Greatest Books in Twenty Tweets or Less* (2009) argue the limitations that the Twitter avatars of classic literature may invite as the

> voice of Twitter, the social networking tool that with its limit of 140 characters a post (including spaces) has refused to its purest form the instant-publishing, short-attention- span, all digital-all-the-time, self-important after of info-deluge.
>
> *(Aciman and Rensin, 2009, p.16).*

Despite the medium-specific limitations of Twitter, it has enabled the book-text narratives to carve out their digital spaces on the medium. The *Routledge Encyclopedia of Narrative Theory* (2010) suggests that the aspect of narration as "an actual, rather than a historical, present raises the issue of when and what we read, or witness is no longer narration but rather the unfolding of events as they happen" (Ryan, 2010, p.43). Bhima and Duryodhana narrate similar incidents and events as recorded in the translations of the epic but provide a unique point of view from their perspective with the brevity of the medium. Sreedharan mentions Bhima and Duryodhana as the two sides of the same coin (November 29, 2021). Their version of the epic narrative in a series of tweets is interconnected as narrative threads through the signifier (metaphor) hashtag.

The hashtags provide alternative interpretations and connect tweets with other Twitter threads. The hashtag becomes a metaphor for a narrative space in which the reader attends to the process of weaving the narrative and decodes the tale from the perspective of Bhima and Duryodhana. It is significant to note that hashtags as a metaphor are not limited to the Mahābhārata on Twitter but as a metaphor for the medium. I argue that the hashtag operates as a digital metaphor specific to the narration of Sreedharan's Twitter retellings. His works elucidate by creating a new digital space where the epic's textual (book-text) traditions intersect with the digital retellings. However, the author discusses the careful use of hashtags to disseminate the significant episodes from the epic retellings (November 29, 2021). The hashtag is instrumental in forging a structural connection between tweets and inviting the reader to construct meaning through Twitter threads.

Epic Retold is filled with "cliff-hangers, flash-forwards, deviations design to foreshadow, to create suspense" (Sreedharan, 2014, p.5). The narration uses the flashback technique in tracing the trajectory of Bhima's and Duryodhana's life through different phases of their journey. During the discussion with the authors, he mentions, "I used cliffhangers more because my story was divided into mini-papers" (November 29, 2021). Sreedharan's version of the epic highlights the significance given to the structure. The hashtag also allows the viewers to connect each tweet and gives them the liberty to 'retweet' the threads. The process of tweeting and re-tweeting the tale creates a network through the storytellers' narration. The reader navigates through each tweet separately and collectively as one epic tale. The nonlinear nature of Twitter has reversed the storytelling tradition from the genre to the medium-specific narration. The story travels "tweet by tweet" within Bhima's and Duryodhana's storytelling narrative framework. The hashtag as a digital metaphor links the plot, the narration, and the characters in the epic Twitterature. The narration of Bhima and Duryodhana is divided into forty episodes and eighteen episodes, respectively. Each tweet succeeds in creating a personalised pattern for the users to keep the dramatic tension in the story.[7]

Murthy discusses the semiotic role of a hashtag as a digital technique for organising and categorising tweets. It works as a signpost in form of a metaphor for individual tweets and organises the narrative in a thread.[8] He argues that "hashtags are an integral part of Twitter's ability to link the conversations of strangers together. By including a hashtag in one's tweet, it becomes included into a "larger conversation consisting of all tweets with the hashtag" (Murthy, 2013, p.3). The hashtags as digital metaphors also navigate the reader's interpretations. Sreedharan mentions that "then there is the 'participation of followers, their (near) real-time feedback. There are questions, critique-nudges to read other versions" (Sreedharan, 2019, p.5). Sreedharan mentions that he "walked-away from the overuse of the hashtags" (November 29, 2021). He incorporates the hashtags to the significant places in the narratives. He builds the discussion on Duryodhana in-between tweeting the epic narrative by discussing Duryodhana's representation in other media spaces such as graphic narratives.[9] He also tweets about the temple where Duryodhana is being worshipped in South India (see Figure 3.2). Sreedharan's hashtagging situates the Twitterfiction of the epic with cross- referencing in meta-data of tweets. In the tweet, hashtags such as 'Mahābhārata' and 'Duryodhana' contextualise the narrative with a limited space of 280 characters in the Twitter avatar of the epic with other hashtags.

Sreedharan has also situated Twitter retelling in contemporary discussions. Duryodhana narrates the episode of the disrobing of Draupadi after the game of dice in the Kaurava's court. Sreedharan contextualises the act of disrobing in contemporary society and brings the question of sexual and gender violence to the fore (see Figure 3.3). The technique of hashtags, such as incorporating 'gender violence,' re-signifies Draupadi as a paragon for gender justice, and connects the narrative with other contemporary stories. He establishes an active engagement with the readers of the Twitter epic. The reader is invited to participate in the act of rereading the epic and decoding the episode of disrobing Draupadi with the possibility of subverting hierarchies of gender.

Chindu Sreedharan @epicretold Nov 28, 2019
Today's #Mahabharata trivia: there's a #Duryodhana temple in Kerala (where I come from, BTW). The only temple, if I am not mistaken, where he's worshipped. The land tax receipt of the temple is still addressed to King D. :-) Have a look.
Malanada Duryodhana Temple
The Epic Mahabharata is known to all.. The rival king Duryodhana, the eldest of the Kaurava clan is

FIGURE 3.2 Sreedharan's reference to Malanada Temple, *Autobiography of a Villain* (2019)

Chindu Sreedharan @epicretold Dec 10, 2019
Coincidentally, on the last day of the #16Days of activism for eliminating violence against women, we are at a crucial moment in the #Mahabharata: the #Draupadi vastraharan, An epic reminder, if ever there was one, of # GenderedViolence, of right and wrong. 1/3

Chindu Sreedharan @epicretold Dec 10, 2019
The #Mahabharata, one could say, present #GenderedViolence as the ultimate wrong. This is the one incident that leads to the destruction of a kingdom, a society. In that sense, you could say the epic is a story of consequence. BUT. 2/3

Chindu Sreedharan @epicretold Dec 10, 2019
But I'm not sure how to interpret the event. On one hand, it does show #Draupadi as an agent of change, an agent of correction. But she hardly comes across as empowered, particularly in the scene. Help comes from the divine, a male divine...Hm. How do you read it? 3/3

FIGURE 3.3 The Episode of the game of dice and hashtagging the gendered violence, *Autobiography of a Villain* (2019)

In the medium's participatory mode of narration, Twitter users actively attend the process of narrative formation through their responses to Sreedharan's tweets. Their reaction and interrogatory questions to a tweet add new layers of meaning to the narrative (see Figure 3.4). During the conversation, Sreedharan explained how the reader's responses had shaped the act of drafting the tweets. He argues that

> the participation of the readers through tweets impacted to a minor degree. Most writers do not get the privilege of being read while they are writing, and it was a privilege for me. It was interesting for me to see what they liked. It played a part in my mind whenever I was writing the next tweet *(November 29, 2021).*

The reader's reactions to tweets often triggered new interpretations, and their suggestions provided new insights to unraveling new twists in the narrative mode (see Figure 3.4). In response to the rewriting of the character of Duryodhna in the Twitter mode, a reader suggests renaming Duryodhana as 'Suyodhana' (see Figure 3.4). The reader's suggestion indicates both the successful communication of the Twitter retelling of the character of Duryodhana and the way the reader's active participation navigates the mode of narration and offers an alternative reading. Both Duryodhana and Bhima are interconnected in the narrative that they define each other's identity. This is the reason Duryodhana remains an important character in Bhima's narration, and Bhima in Duryodhana's narration. Another instance of the reader's collaboration in building the narrative is Hidimbi's character. Sreedharan re-tweets the responses of the readers on Hidimbi's narrative in

Niksez
@epicretold do u think he wud have been called by the name of Suyodhana, then, by everyone, including Bhima. Sun Aug 23 2009 22.56.51(GMT Daylight Time) via web

Vivekananda
@epicretold Can you please update more often! Sat Aug 22 2009 18.48.22 (GMT Daylight Time) via web in reply to epicretold

Kabra
I always loved the Mahabharata, but @epicretold's retelling is making it even more fascinating. Can't wait for Hidimbi's response! Fri Feb 05 2010 10.35.00 (GMT Standard Time) via Tweet in reply to epicretold

FIGURE 3.4 Reader's participation through tweets in *Epic Retold,* August 23, 2009 and February 5, 2010

Epic Retold. The references to her bring a new perspective on the character of Bhima. Hidimbi, as one of the central characters in Bhima's version helps the author to humanise the character of Bhima. We will discuss in the subsequent sections of this chapter how she becomes the locus of Bhima's storytelling and situates the tales in an everyday setting by being relatable to the readers.

Similarly, the readers also contribute to Duryodhana's retelling. Sreedharan mentions that he "shifted the camera angle" from Bhima to Duryodhana (November 29, 2021). Sreedharan encourages his readers to actively participate in the meaning-making process by sharing their views and feedback on the epic tales (see Figure 3.5). Their feedback functions as a semiotic extension of the narrative and enables the readers to reconstruct the text and enrich its diegetic reach. Through the digital metaphor of the hashtag 'readerswrite', Sreedharan ignites readers by providing a space for their contribution in the epic retelling. The readers collaborate in creating the beginning of the game of dice episode as an interactive exercise and storytelling. The readers emerge as an active agency of the Twitter narration and creates a semiological loop between the narrator and its readers. Thus, hashtags as digital metaphors weave the tweets into a well-knit narrative and create a space of transaction between the retellings and the reading process.

Microblogging Narrators

Bhima and Duryodhana are Sreedharan's protagonists in the two Twitter retellings of the epic. The storytellers narrate the tales from their perspectives and empower the storytellers by giving them the voice as narrators of the story. They hold the central narrative space, which enables them to manoeuvre the narrative according to their perspective. The Twitter retelling depicts Bhima and Duryodhana in a new light, challenging the reader's perception of the epic narrative. The retellings unfold the semiotic layers of the epic's characterisation and popularise the new media renditions of the epic narrative.

Chindu Sreedharan @epicretold Dec 6, 2019
@MalaSivaprasad's version:
1. Despodent Yudhisthira concedes defeat.
2. Duryodhana tells him that he's not lost everything yet & reminds him he still has Draupadi.
3. Yudhisthira then puts up Draupadi, only to lose her as well.
#readerswrite #TwitterFiction

Chindu Sreedharan @epicretold Dec 6, 2019
Thanks to all who responded to my 'challenge', and tweeted how they visualised the story will continue. Great seeing how others think of the scene to comes. Here are three versions, courtesy @MalaSivaprasad, @NinaSubraman, and @makarand_s.

FIGURE 3.5 Reader's participation through tweets in *Autobiography of a Villain*, December 6, 2019

Ruth Cecily Katz in the work *Arjuna in the* Mahābhārata (1990) argues Bhima's position in the translated works of the epic as "overwhelming that of a warrior" (Katz, 1990, p.36). In the translations, Bhima is depicted as an impulsive character who can only resolve conflicts with physical strength. Duryodhana is depicted as an epitome of evil and an antidote to what Krishna terms 'Dharma' (morality law) in the epic. Whereas in the twentieth century, writers have attempted to paint an alternate image of both the characters. Sreedharan's inspiration to portray the character of Bhima came from Nair's *Randamoozham,* which marks a departure from the interpretive setting as a warrior in the translated versions of the epic and recasts Bhima as an ordinary being with his personal struggle with his inner conflicts.

In *Epic Retold*, Sreedharan mentions that

> from Mt's powerful etching of Bhima and the recent reading of *Bhimsen*, I have seen how a pathos-filled protagonist can hook the reader. So, yes, a pathos-filled Bhima will be the protagonist in this story, too. He will live his life on Twitter, telling this story, sharing his NOW moments as they 'happen' *(Sreedharan, 2014, p.4).*

Likewise, we see a similarity in Duryodhana, who is shown as a character with strength and morality and not as a partaker in villainy (see Figure 3.6). Sreedharan says in the author's note of *Autobiography of a Villain*, "yet there is much good, much magnanimity, in him. One need only look at the way Duryodhana stood up for Karna" (Sreedharan, 2019, p.2). Duryodhana and Bhima, as pivotal characters, demand a new vantage point. However, the attempt to draw alternative views of Bhima and Duryodhana was initiated by twentieth-century

Chindu Sreedharan @epicretold Nov 25, 2019

I became fascinated with Duryodhana's character when I was halfway through Epic Retold (Harper Collins 2015), narrating the #Mahabharata from Bhima's perspective. #AutobioOfVillian

Chindu Sreedharan @epicretold Nov 25, 2019

One could argue that in that action #Duryodhana was motivated by his dislike of the Pandavas, but to me it speaks volumes in terms of equality, non-discrimination, and human rights. #AutobioOfVillian

Chindu Sreedharan @epicretold Nov 25, 2019

How many young princes would have the courage to tell their elders that the idea of barring someone from a competition based on birth is just plain wround? #AutobioOfVillian #Twitterfiction

FIGURE 3.6 The portrayal of Duryodhana in Twitter epic, *Autobiography of a Villain* (2019)

writers. It raises the question of how Sreedharan's epic retellings are different from the other twentieth-century textual retellings from the perspective of Bhima and Duryodhana. The traditional textual narratives draw their potency from lengthy descriptions and elaborative narrative threads (Ganguli, 1993, p.72).

The various translations of the epic also shaped the existing oral traditions and other visual forms of narrative, which collectively constitute the epic traditions. The Twitter retelling is based on the central storyline of the epic as popularly known. Narrated from a non-central character's point of view, the narrative deviates from the traditional narrative of the epic not only in terms of characterisation but also in terms of presentation. Sreedharan mentions that due to the limited linguistic expression of Twitter, it was pertinent to keep "the central narrative which functions as the heart of the epic" as the key incidents in the retellings (November 29, 2021). Each tweet is a semiotic unit of the narrative structure of the epic, which is invoked metaphorically in the act of reading. The reader draws on their cultural information in the act of interpreting each tweet and linking it further with other tweets. The epic is repeated by the reader in a memorial mode, more like the epic codes to decode the semiotic layers of tweets. The narration displays both discontinuation and continuation of the epic. It challenges the received interpretations of the epic and creates alternative readings of the narrative.

The Epic Retold rewrites the personal journey of Bhima. He is shown empowered and observant about the family feud (between the Kauravas and the Pāṇḍavas). Sreedharan has depicted Bhima's struggle in daily routine life. The author takes the "liberties in narration" to showcase Bhima in a close-up setting (Sreedharan, 2014, p.6). The everyday setting functions as a metaphorical layer to portray Bhima's character as cataloguing his daily events via tweets. Sreedharan also mentions his influence on tweeting Bhima on microblogging from Prem Panicker's work titled *Bhimsen* (2009) (Sreedharan, 2014, p.3). We see the keen observation of Bhima in distinctive situations, and the monologues serves as the portrayal of his dilemmas. Sreedharan focuses on humanising Bhima and Duryodhana to make them relatable to the viewers (November 29, 2021). Unlike the mighty and impulsive Bhima of the grand narrative, the avatar of Bhima in the Twitter retelling is critically aware of the conflicts and their ramifications in his life. In an interview, Sreedharan says that the character of Bhima in tweets is provided for not only overt, external conflicts but for internal ones as well. In the first-person narrative, the Twitter saga begins with Bhima's commentary on Gandhari's appearance. He mentions that "I stare at the lady with the black cloth over her eyes. I feel disturbed, scared, but I cannot look away" (Sreedharan, 2014, p.9). The tweets introduce Bhima's observant nature and the return of the Pandavas to the city of Hastinapur. Bhima's tweets reveal his perception of the Pandavas as merely a warrior. He tweeted, "I did not understand many things. Yudhishthira said I was slow and stupid. But if Father was king, why were we living in a forest lodge?" (Sreedharan, 2014, p.9). He remains in the shadow of discerning a character in the Twitter epic narrative and emerges as one of the complex storytellers.

In *Autobiography of a Villain*, Duryodhana is displayed as a character who is "no superhero. He is human, flawed, like most of us, but with a lot of good in him" (Sreedharan, 2019, p.5). Sreedharan's rewriting of Duryodhana presents him as an anti-hero (the anti-thesis of Bhima) who narrates the epic from his unique perspective. The author attempts to push the question of fatherhood from Bhima's to Duryodhana's retellings (November 29, 2021). He mentions that working on the narrative of Duryodhana served as "shifting the camera angle from Bhima" (November 29, 2021). The retelling begins with a scene on the eighteenth day of the war, and Duryodhana is waiting for his opponents to kill him. Duryodhana's narration reflects the story of a tragic hero and indicates the consequences of his impulsive actions. Sreedharan's depiction of him evokes sympathy rather than contempt for his sinful intentions, as the conventional portrayal of Duryodhana does in K.M. Ganguli's translation of the epic (Ganguli, 1993, p.427). Duryodhana receives a shorter space on Twitter with nine hundred and sixty-one tweets than Bhima's narration two thousand six hundred and seventy-two tweets, and sums up his narrative in eighteen days, calling it a "Twitter serial" (tweeted on November 14, 2019). The serialised form of tweets and the technique of flashback help Duryodhana to retell the narrative. Sreedharan's fascination with the character of Duryodhana was a result of his venture from Bhima's retelling. In the flashback narrative, Duryodhana tweets about his childhood, especially the first encounter with the Pandavas (Sreedharan, 2019, p.14). Duryodhana keenly observes the five Pandavas and refers to Bhima as "the big boy" (see Figure 3.7). Sreedharan consciously situates Bhima against Duryodhana from their first encounter and concludes with them staring at each other.

Duryodhana keeps Bhima as the locus of the tweets in his version of the narrative (2019). Similarly, Bhima's dynamic personality is viewed through his comparisons with Duryodhana and Arjuna. Bhima in *Epic Retold* introduces Duryodhana in a subtle comparison with himself "Duryodhana is taller, bigger. But I am stronger-born to the forest" (Sreedharan, 2019, p.12). In comparison, Bhima considers Duryodhana as a stronger contender in his version. Duryodhana views Bhima as his worthy opponent in his retelling. In Duryodhana's retelling, Sreedharan depicts Bhima as his arch-enemy in the mace fighting. The author highlights Duryodhana's act of selecting Bhima for the mace fighting as 'heroic' (see Figure 3.8). Sreedharan signals Duryodhana as the "superhero we are in search for" from the epic narrative (Ayyappan, 2020).

> Chindu Sreedharan @epicretold Nov 27, 2019
>
> As Father made his exit holding Sanjaya's hand, I saw the big boy staring at me again. #AutoBioVillian

FIGURE 3.7 The first encounter between Duryodhana and Bhima, *Autobiography of a Villain* (2019)

Chindu Sreedharan @epicretold Nov 25, 2019
And what does #Duryodhana do? He does the honourable thing. He picks the strongest #Pandava, his archenemy, Bhima-not #Yudhistra, whom he could have broken like a twig. #Twitterfiction #AutobioOfVillian

Chindu Sreedharan @epicretold Nov 25, 2019
Yudhistira-silly Yudhistira!-gives away all the advantage his brothers gained at Kurukshetra when he challenges Duryodhana to a duel and grandly announces that Duryodhana can pick any weapon, and any Pandava to fight-and if he won, the kingdom would be his. #AutobioOfVillian

FIGURE 3.8 The episode of the mace fight between Bhima and Duryodhana, *The Autobiography of a Villain* (2019)

In *Epic Retold*, we witness Bhima's animalistic nature appear in constant comparisons and depicted as justification for his actions. In a tweet, the young Bhima, during the training sessions with Droṇa, discusses the preference given to Arjuna. He mentions, "Arjuna is clearly Dronacharya's favorite. My brother plays up to me unashamedly, spending hours practicing archery as the master looks on" (Sreedharan, 2019, p.30). On the other hand, the author depicts Arjuna as dissatisfied with the training from Drona and believes that he is "holding back, saving his techniques for his son, Ashwatthama" (Sreedharan, 2019, p.30). As the unreliable narrator, Bhima draws comparisons between other characters and successfully portrays himself as the central character in the series of tweets.

The Twitter narrative indicates Bhima's aspirations and constant striving for equal recognition. Hidimbi remains a crucial knot in Bhima's storytelling. The author departs from the epic and reinvents the Twitter narrative through Bhima's experiences with Hidimbi. The episode "Hidimbi" is a significant marker for Bhima's quest for self-discovery. He meets Hidimbi in the forest after the Pandavas escape from the lac palace. Bhima tweets the encounter with Hidimbi as "she stands tall, almost as tall as I am, her skin the colour of copper, deerskin wrapped around her waist. Her face is young, very young" (Sreedharan, 2014, p.45). However, Sreedharan says that Hidimbi's character in *Epic Retold* remains 'underdeveloped' and 'disempowered' (see Figure 3.9). The focus on the storytellers has affected the other characters' depiction in the Twitter tales. Twitter as a medium limit detailed observations or descriptions, and the narrator's tweets function as important microblogs of interpretations. These microblogs add to the multimodal feature of the medium. The search for Hidimbi in the Twitter epic also becomes the motif for Bhima's journey. Hidimbi remains the digital metaphor for Bhima's unanswered questions about his identity and position in the epic. Sreedharan mentions "what Hidimbi was for Bhima; Bhanumati was for Duryodhana" (November 29, 2021).

Chindu Sreedharan @epicretold Nov 16, 2019
No, I would go for Hidimbi. I don't think any author has really done her justice. Much like Bhima, I have had a soft corner for her-though, like most other writers, I left her character underdeveloped-and shamefully disempowered-in @epicretold.

Chindu Sreedharan @epicretold Nov 16, 2019
Mahabharata is a vast cauldron of stories within stories, full of many, many interesting characters. So it-s difficult to pick a favourity character. But if I were to pick one, I think I would go for, no, not usual suspects, and no, not Draupadi or Gandhari or Kunti...

FIGURE 3.9 Sreedharan's tweet on the role of Hidimbi in *The Epic Retold* (2014)

In *Autobiography of a Villain*, Sreedharan tweets Karna as a significant part of Duryodhana's character development. The author argues that the act of giving a kingdom to Karna during the demonstration of skills showed Duryodhana's "quality, non-discrimination, and human rights" (Sreedharan, 2019, p.3). Duryodhana's retelling situates the relationship with Karna as a metaphor for loyalty and friendship. The central motif of Duryodhana's narration remains the claim of the "rightful heir" of the kingdom. In Figure 3.10, the tweet narrates the episode of Pāṇḍavas' return to the city from the forest Varnavarat. The debatable question of the 'rightful heir' of Hastinapur remains a contentious point in Duryodhana's retelling of the epic narrative.

The Twitter revisualisations show Bhima and Duryodhana's ethical and moral dilemmas in the episodes of the dice game. In *Epic Retold*, Bhima questions the ethical dilemma of the king, Yudhishthira playing the game of dice with Duryodhana. Bhima tweets, "my elder brother, who can recite the Vedas backward. How can he be so stupid?" (Sreedharan, 2014, p.97). Bhima expressed concern about the impulsive decisions made by his brother. In tweets, Bhima probes the ethical questions for waging Draupadi in the game. The tweets reveal Bhima's agony and guilt when he witnesses Draupadi's entry to the palace. He says, "the look on Draupadi's face burns my soul. It is a shame, more than grief or anger, that makes me turn on Yudhishthira" (Sreedharan, 2014, p.104). Sreedharan draws on the stream of consciousness technique to reveal the struggles and foregrounds his intellectual sharpness and emotional capacity to identify with others suffering. Bhima's final observation on the episode concludes with the question of making Yudhishthira their king. He mentions to Draupadi that "'this is us now – slaves!' I tell her. 'Because our king, the great Yudhishthira, wills it so. Because

Chindu Sreedharan @epicretold Dec 2, 2019
The news the spy brought made me seethe. Far from partaking in the festivities, the Pandavas were cultivating loyalists. Yudhistira held long meetings with chieftains who arrived from Madra and nearby everyday. Many were now referring to him as the 'right heir'.

FIGURE 3.10 The episode of the return of the Pandavasto Hastinapur, *The Autobiography of a Villain* (2019)

his word is above all else" (Sreedharan, 2014, p.104). Bhima rediscovers his identity as a narrator of the epic. His version of the epic indicates how the epic generates new stories; even alternative stories spun around the family feud between the Pandavas and the Kauravas.

Sreedharan portrays an alternative narrative of the game of dice in Duryodhana's retelling. In a conversation with Bhanumati, Duryodhana raises an ethical stance on Bhima's pledge after the game of dice to harm Dushasana on the battlefield. He says, "if I were you," I said, gazing up, "I wouldn't have pledged I would have killed and drank blood right there!" (Sreedharan, 2019, p.41, see Figure 3.11). His comments on the game of dice subvert the dominant reading of the epic. The traditional understanding of the episode holds only the Kauravas responsible for the act of disrobing Draupadi. Duryodhana draws the reader's attention to the Pāṇḍavas' decision to gamble their life. He explores the possibility of avoiding gambling if the Pandavas could have resisted the temptation of playing the game of dice. Through his critical suggestions on the event, he navigates the reader's views of the epic from his perspective. The Twitter adaptations of the epic serves a dual purpose. Firstly, it provides an alternative version of the grand story, and the adaptation of the epic on Twitter lends validity as an equal literary medium despite its limitation of linguistic expression. Secondly, in its limited space but a semiotically rich network of tweets, the Twitter narrative allows Bhima and Duryodhana to render their side of the story, opening the epic narrative to reinterpretations. Sreedharan's adaptation not only gives voices to Bhima and Duryodhana but also suggests the hierarchical semantic structure of the epic and the possibility of alternative readings through retellings.

Tweeting the War Chronicles

The episodes on the eighteen days of war portray a range of characters, incidents, the marching of armies, and battles in the Twitter retellings *Epic Retold* and *Autobiography of a Villain*. The description of the war conflict is stretched beyond

Chindu Sreedharan @epicretold Dec 10, 2019
None of this was meant to happen, I wanted to scream after her. No one was meant to gamble a kingdom, or brothers, or wife!

Chindu Sreedharan @epicretold Dec 10, 2019
Bhanumati looked at me for a long moment. There was anger on her face, tenderness...and more sorrow than I ever cared to see. Then, without a word, she disappeared indoor.

Chindu Sreedharan @epicretold Dec 10, 2019
"If it were you," I said, gazing up, "I wouldn't have pledged-I would have killed and drank blood right there!"

FIGURE 3.11 The conversation between Bhanumati and Duryodhana after the game of dice, *The Autobiography of a Villain* (2019)

the boundaries of a book-text and unfolds intensively with the real-time experience of the Twitter users. Unlike the spectacular textual details of the war in the print medium, the writer uses the minimalist space to depict the intensity and agony of characters involved in the conflict. Bhima's and Duryodhana's narration led to a new form of micro-epic with the interconnected web of users. In both the retellings, each episode serves as a digital metaphor for the war chronicles unveiled into the thread of tweets. Bhima and Duryodhana elaborate on the layout of armies on the battleground of Kurukshetra, which appear as visual vignettes in 140 and 240 characters, respectively (Sreedharan, 2014, p.97 and 2019, p.62). We perceive the micro-narratives of the war narrated by Bhima and Duryodhana, contrary to the traditional epic narratives in a textual format that has provided elaborate descriptions of the battlefield (Ganguli, 1992, p.3). In *Epic Retold*, the war narrative in the episode "#Kurukshetra" unfolds with the tweet, "a week after Abhimanyu's wedding, the first group of soldiers begin to march out, tasked with clearing out land for a crematorium" (Sreedharan, 2014, p.191). Bhima takes another aspect of the war by drawing our attention to the diseased warriors. Through the aspect of tweeting, Bhima creates a spatial image of the war on Twitter.

Duryodhana's narration in *Autobiography of a Villain* challenges the grand narrative description of his character as a villain. In contrast to the prejudicial depiction of his character in the traditional narrative of the epic, the Twitter retelling introduces him as a man of thinking and reflecting on the ramifications of warfare. He contemplates the outcome of the impending war, and the future for his heir. In a tweet, Duryodhana is seen as theorising the nature of war and discussing the realities of the conflict. The episode deepens the agony by foregrounding the plight of his children in the aftermath of the violent war. The writer illustrates the sympathetic sight of Laxmana sleeping with his mother (Sreedharan, 2019, p.52, see Figure 3.12). V.S. Sukthankar in work titled *On the Meaning of the Mahābhārata* (1957), discusses how the epic is the "archetype of all wars or conflicts of the past, the present or the future" (Sukthankar, 1957, p. 63). Further, the war becomes an archetype of loss.

Instead of glorifying the war as a triumph of good over evil, Bhima foregrounds the loss of human life, connecting the war with the failures and loss of ordinary people. Thomas, in "140 Character in Search of a Story: Twitterfiction as an Emerging Narrative Form" (2013), argues that "Twitterfiction destabilizes

Chindu Sreedharan @epicretold Dec 13, 2019
Will he survive?

Chindu Sreedharan @epicretold Dec 13, 2019
I looked at the slight form by the doorway. Laxmana, my gentle son with his mother's eyes-for whom war was but a game. How peacefully he sleeps!

FIGURE 3.12 The episode of the eighteen days of the war, *The Autobiography of a Villain* (2019)

the relationship between author and reader" (Thomas, 2013, p.96). There is multimodality of the war, which provides a real-time experience to the viewer/reader. Unlike the book-reader, the Twitter user is more of an equal participant in weaving the Twitter-threads. Reading a book, readers are comparatively restricted by the textual narrative. Their interpretations are regulated by the restraints forced by the text itself.

The Twitter-user is comparatively free to peruse the tweets and the interlinks between tweets. Moreover, the tweets, hashtags, and comments on tweet all convert the Twitter narrative into a dialogic network. The user has the liberty to connect the tweets and decoding the narrative beyond the given context. The active interactional mode of tweeting lends an oral dimension to the Twitter medium. Each tweet and retweet are stamped with a date that makes the user a participant in the epic war. The viewers become the participants in the micro-form of the epic battle.

The war takes a position in a non-linear narrative. The structure deploys the 'narrative hook' technique to capture the viewer's attention and maintain suspense with the progression of the story via tweets. The purpose of a 'narrative hook' is "to hook the audience and engage them with a world of audience" (Tidmarsh, 2014, p.74). Each tweet serves as a 'narrative hook' due to the non-linearity of the medium, where the tweets are a part of a narrative thread and a narrative in themselves. Duryodhana's retelling contains 'narrative hooks' with the questions asked to him by Sakuni (Sreedharan, 2019, p.54, see Figure 3.13). Duryodhana's commentary is a critical reflection on his own personality, dilemmas and conflicting decisions. The narrative unveils decision and actions of his conduct that he exercises in the serialised Twitter war. Also, Bhima, in the retelling, discusses the nomination of Shikhandi as the Commander-in-Chief for the Pandavas during the war. He narrates, "Shikhandi has the eyes of a killer. War is not duty, but joy for him. He would not waver against elder and blood relations" (Sreedharan, 2014, p.193). Bhima's introduction to Shikhandi lends variety to his storytelling and deepens the narrative. The interior monologue of Bhima creates signposts about the strategies of the Twitter war. While building the crematoriums was a priority on the battlefield, on the other hand, "minstrels and musicians who will sing our victories every night is the last to arrive. Our preparations are now complete" was also important (Sreedharan, 2014, p.193). The tweets on the war focus on navigating the formation of troops for the two armies – the Kauravas and the Pandavas.

Chindu Sreedharan Dec 17, 2019
"Could we have avoided this war? Perhaps. But could you have made peace with the fact that you have given in to the evil of Yudhistira?"

FIGURE 3.13 The dialogue between Sakuni and Duryodhana, *The Autobiography of a Villain* (2019)

The storyteller invokes other narrative knots, such as the emotional turmoil created after the meeting with his sons. Bhima recalls his meeting with the son, Soothasoma. He says, "I had seen my son Soothasoma, born of Draupadi, as I was setting out for Kurukshetra. That was the second time I saw him" (Sreedharan, 2014, p.195). Bhima's foreshadowing of the narrative further adds "yet here he is. Just a boy. But come to fight his father's war" (Sreedharan, 2014, p.195). Bhima's role as a storyteller and the character signals the reader about his take on the narrative. Bhima also takes the position in the centre of the crescent formation on the battleground (Sreedharan, 2014, p.199). The tweets of Bhima's attack on the battleground fill the tweets with sensory details. He says, "when we get close to the enemy, I let my bow clatter to the deck and jump out. Mace swinging, I plunge into the enemy troops" (Sreedharan, 2014, p.200). The visualisation of the battle is dramatic and sets the tone of tension in the narrative. Similarly, in *Autobiography of a Villain*, the narrative foregrounds the friendship between Duryodhana and Karna. The revelation of Karna's identity as a son of Kunti by Shakuni after his demise on the battlefield to Duryodhana stirs his emotions. Duryodhana tweets that

> I thought of the boy who had glowed like the Sun and decimated Arjuna in the skills of the demonstration all those years ago. I thought of his quiet words when I had stood by his side. I will not forget; Karna had said then *(Sreedharan, 2019, p.61).*

Duryodhana was overwhelmed by Karna's affection and sacrifice towards him. The progression of the tweets paves the way for warfare and arranges the chronicles as digital metaphors for the sight of loss. The narrative becomes an account of 'live-wire' Twitering in the form of the telecast. The tweet "time tears by as a chronicle of corpses. Swigging from the waterskin Visoka shoves into my hand, I continue my rampage" (Sreedharan 203). Bhima's participation in the war is experienced by the viewer in real-time space. The orality becomes an expression of reporting in the space of Twitter. There is an effect of "urgency" and "immediacy" in narrating the accounts of war which serves as a crucial marker of narrating the 'Twitterfiction' and keeping the interest of the viewers. Bhima uses metaphors to highlight the ethical and moral dilemma. He says, "in war, there are no killers, only warriors with indestructible souls. Death is the soul shedding worn-out clothes to dress in new garments" (Sreedharan, 2014, p.204). The episode "#Change of Clothes" signifies the metaphorical role of Bhima's stance on the ethical and moral plane, where the "change of clothes" is depicted as signifying the change of bodies. Therefore, the author's arrangement of the episodes and the titles also suggests the thematic layer of digital metaphors in tweets.

The multimodality of the Twitter epic provides a personalised narrative view of Bhima's and Duryodhana's life. The arrival of Ghatotkacha on the battlefield strikes the narrative chord with Hidimbi's absence. Bhima recalls his son's arrival as a "voice booms from the darkness. I have come to fight Father" (Sreedharan, 2014, p.210). The first-person narration of Bhima reveals the connections between the progression of the war and his self-discovery. The character of Hidimbi functions as a digital metaphor. Her absence weaves the narrative, and the story breathes her tweets. Bhima's part as a storyteller also invests in the emotional experience of the viewers during warfare. In the episode titled "#Bhishma", Bhima mentions that the "Bhishma will fall tomorrow. Shikhandi will not let the emotion in his way" (Sreedharan, 2014, p.217). Bhima's internal and external conflicts prevail through the tweets during the warfare, where he narrates the impending demise of Bhishma through Shikhandi. Sreedharan has carefully selected the tweets in which he doesn't clarify the unresolved issue between Bhishma and Shikhandi but flashforwards to their encounter on the battlefield.

The formation of the armies and the use of weapons are also markers of defining the battleground in the war chronicles. Bhima reports the incidents from the war about Arjuna being a crucial narrative cue. He says, "when Arjuna unleashes the fire arrows, there is panic in the enemy ranks. Our ground troops use the confusion to batter their formation" (Sreedharan 2014, p.229). The position of weapons such as the 'Gandiva', which is considered "famous for having the power to punish evil and wicked people. It made its user capable of fighting against one lakh (100,000) warriors at a time" (Williams 132). It was passed to Arjuna as one of the celestial weapons, which was used during the war. Bhima retells the story of using the celestial weapon as "the Gandiva spoke. Jayadratha fell, an arrow through his throat" (Sreedharan 2014, 232). The weapons in the war are digital metaphors. Bhima amplifies the concluding tweets by commenting on Yudhishthira. He tweets, "we have killed our flesh and blood by the foulest of means. We have lied and cheated. All of us, including you, righteous Yudhishthira!" (Sreedharan 2014, 245). The narrator revisits the scene of war and rewrites the sight as he narrators the war chronicles in the form of reporting.

In its democratic and participatory space, the medium of Twitter retells the epic tales as a digital network of narrative blocks in the form of tweets and retweets, interconnected with hashtags. In its minimalistic yet open-ended space, the narrative suggests new ways of reading the epic in its contemporary context of configuration. The chapter explores the potential of the Twitter narrative in retelling the epic in its unique modality, offering an alternative interpretation of the selected tales. The Twitter tales are an experimental remaking of the epic, placing the characters in an interactive mode with the users. The chapter demonstrates the collaboration of the journalistic praxis with Twitter in retelling the epic through tweets. Sreedharan's long-form journalistic training brings a unique perspective on retelling the epic and navigating its narrative on the medium. The appearance of the tweets as reporting codifies and novelise the Mahābhārata in the minimalistic space of Twitter. The chapter argues that the tweets operate as the literary narrative to disseminate the epic and democratise the Twitter narrative space by inviting the reader to attend the process of constructing the narrative. Tweets are formulated through the process of selection that attempts to encapsulate the epic through digital metaphors.

The selective process of the adaptation has a semiotic mode in which the entire epic is not narrativised; rather, only the narrative's epicness is indicated through tweeting. Tweets are navigated through the tool of a hashtag. The hashtags also function as an extension of digital metaphors, which determine the mode of narration and add a new framework for retelling epic tales. The representation of Bhima's and Duryodhana's narratorial voices, along with the aspect of reporting the war chronicles, are digital metaphors that facilitate the multimodal aspect of the medium in recreating the epic. Twitter retelling suggests the possibility of retelling the epic on new media platforms to recontextualise the epic traditions in contemporary digital culture.

Notes

1 Prem Panicker's *Bhimsen* (2009) is an English transcreation of M.T. Nair's retelling of the Mahābhārata.
2 TO FILL IN
3 *Epic Retold* narrates the incidents from the Pandavas and Kauravas childhood (Sreedharan, 2014, 15); the game of dice (Sreedharan, 2014, p.95), the exile of the Pandavas (Sreedharan, 2014, p.111); the eighteen days of war (Sreedharan, 2014, p.191).
4 *An Autobiography of a Villain* (2019) initially published as novella by the author.
5 November 29, 2021, refers to my interview of the author Sreedharan.
6 See Roland Barthes work *S/Z* (1970) for 'writerly text.'
7 In the interview "When Bhima Tweeted his Epic Story" (2015) appeared in the newspaper *The Hindu*, Sreedharan talks about the selection of the medium for the retelling of Bhima's story. He says "this was 2009 when Twitter was beginning to be popular. I was interested in social media and Twitter was acquiring a variety of audience and readers who engaged with it differently – more proactively" (Nathan 2015).
8 Sreedharan provides a reference to Duryodhana's visual depiction in the graphic narratives of Graphic India (@epicretold, Dec 2, 2019).
9 Twentieth-century writers refer to M.T. Nair.

References

Aciman, Alexander and Emmett Rensin. (2009). *Twitterature: The World's Greatest Books in Twenty Tweets or Less*. Penguin.

Alexander, Bryan. (2017). *The New Digital Storytelling: Creating Narratives with New Media*. Praeger.

Asur, Sitaram and Bernado A.Huberman. (2010). *Predicting the Future with Social Media*. IEEE, International Conference on Web Intelligence and Intelligent Agent Technology. (Vol. 1, pp. 492–499). IEEE.

Ayyappan, R. (2020). Duryodhana, the misunderstood hero of Mahabharata? *Onmanorama*. January 7. https://www.onmanorama.com/news/india/2020/01/07/chindu-sreedharan-duryidhana-mahabharata-epicretold-caa-protest.html

Banaji, Shakuntala. (2011). *South Asian Media Cultures: Audiences, Representations, Contexts*. Anthem Press.

Barthes, R. (1980). *S/Z: an essay*. Siglo XXI.

Bernard, Andreas. (2019). *Theory of The Has#tag*. Translated by Valentine A.Pakis, PolityPress.

Bignell, Jonathan. (1997). *Media Semiotics: An Introduction*. Manchester University Press.

Boomen, Marriane VanDen. (2014). *Transcoding the Digital: How Metaphors Matter in New Media*. Instituut Voor Netwerkcultuur.

Bronwen, Thomas. (2014). "140 Characters in Search of a Story: Twitterfiction as an Emerging Narrative Form". *Analyzing Digital Fiction*. Edited by Alice Bell, Astrid Ensslin, and Hans Kristian Rustad, Routledge.

Cecily. (1990). *Arjuna in the Mahabharata*. Motilal Banarasidass.

Ganguli, Kisari Mohan. (1993). *The Mahabharata*. Munshiram Manoharlal, New Delhi. (First published in 1883)

Huberman, B. A., Romero, D. M., & Wu, F. (2008). *Social Networks that Matter: Twitter Under the Microscope*. https://arxiv.org/pdf/0812.1045.pdf.

Jenkins, Henry. (2006). *Convergence Culture: Where Old and New Media Collide*. NYU Press.

Katz, Ruth Cecily. (1990) *Arjuna in the Mahabharata*. Motilal Banarasidass.

Kir, S. (2020). *New Media and Visual Communication in Social Networks*. IGI Global.

Manovich, Lev. (2001). *The Language of New Media*. MIT Press.

Murthy, Dhiraj. (2013). *Social Communication in the Twitter Age*. Polity Press.

Nathan, A. (2015). When Bhima tweeted his epic story. *The Hindu*. https://www.thehindu.com/features/magazine/when-bhima-tweeted-his-epic-story/article6966093.ece

Özdemir, M. (2024). The Impact of Twitter on Digital Diplomacy in the Context of International Media. In *Digital Diplomacy in the OSCE Region: From Theory to Practice* (pp. 89–100). Springer Nature Switzerland.

Panicker, P. (2009). *Bhimsen*.

Rudin, Michael. (2011). *From Hemingway to Twitterature: The Short and Shorter of It*. Michigan Publishing.

Sreedharan, Chindu. (2014). *Epic Retold: #Mahabharata #Twitter Fiction #Bhima #140 Characters*. HarperCollins Publishers.

Sreedharan, Chindu. (2019). *The Autobiography of a Villain: Duryodhana's Story*. Independent Publishing Network.

Sukthankar, V. S. (1957). *On the Meaning of the Mahābhārata*.

Thomas, Bronwen. (2015). *Narrative: The Basics*. Taylor & Francis.

Tidmarsh, A. (2014). *Genre: A Guide to Writing for Stage and Screen*.

Tierney, Therese. (2013). *The Public Space of Social Media: Connected Cultures of the Network Society*. Routledge.

Weller, K., Bruns, A., Burgess, J., Mahrt, M., & Puschmann, C. (2014). Twitter and Society: An Introduction. *Digital Formations*, 89, xxix–xxxviii.

4

THE GROWING INFLUENCE OF ICTS ON ONLINE COMMUNITIES IN THE POST-COVID ERA

Opportunities and Challenges

Vijay Kumar Chattu and Sujatha Alla

Background

The pandemic has fundamentally altered work styles, catalyzing a shift towards remote work and necessitating the formation of organization-led virtual teams. Before the pandemic, work was predominantly conducted in physical office spaces, emphasizing in-person meetings and direct supervision. The traditional work environment facilitated spontaneous interactions and collaborations but was also constrained by geographical limitations and office hours. The onset of the COVID-19 pandemic accelerated the adoption of remote work, pushing organizations to reevaluate their work models and leverage Information and Communication Technologies (ICTs) more extensively. This transition necessitated a shift from a physical to a digital workplace, where organization-led virtual teams became the norm. These teams, formed and coordinated through digital platforms, allow for work to be conducted from diverse geographical locations, offering flexibility and continuity in operations despite disruptions.

Organization-led virtual teams rely heavily on ICTs for communication, collaboration, and project management. Tools such as video conferencing software, collaborative work management platforms, and cloud-based services have become essential for facilitating the seamless functioning of these teams. The agility and responsiveness of virtual teams have been bolstered by these technologies, enabling organizations to maintain productivity and even to explore new ways of working and serving customers. The shift towards remote work and the formation of virtual teams have brought about significant benefits, including increased flexibility, reduced commute times, and the potential for a better work-life balance. However, this transition has also posed challenges, particularly in terms of maintaining team cohesion, ensuring effective communication, and fostering a shared organizational culture. The reliance on digital

DOI: 10.4324/9781003628910-4

communication tools can sometimes lead to miscommunications and feelings of isolation among team members.

In the post-pandemic era, many organizations are considering a hybrid work model, blending remote work with traditional office-based work to combine the best aspects of both. This approach acknowledges the benefits of remote work while addressing its challenges by allowing for periodic in-person interactions and collaborations. Effective communication within teams is fundamental for achieving operational excellence and fostering a dynamic and adaptive working environment. Communication ensures that informational resources are consistently shared, enhancing team coordination and project outcomes. Challenges in organizational accountability often stem from deficiencies in leadership or communication strategies. Implementing strategic communication tools and practices can rejuvenate leadership approaches and encourage a culture of openness, enabling team members to feel empowered to disclose and discuss issues (Vidgen & Wang, 2009). This environment contributes to the collective progress of the project and mitigates procrastination by encouraging continuous improvement and fostering a proactive work ethic among team members (Whitworth, 2006).

The essence of effective work performance lies in the ability to collectively critique, analyze, and address problems, enabling swift action on solutions. This collaborative problem-solving approach ensures flexibility in responding to challenges. Effective communicative strategies improve collaboration. Emphasizing constant communication and collaboration is essential for building strong, effective teams, promoting a culture of openness, accountability, and continuous improvement. The chapter flow is illustrated in Figure 1.

Section I

The Evolution of Information and Communication Technologies (ICTs) in the Workplace: Pre-Covid vs. Post-Covid Era

The integration and evolution of Information and Communication Technologies (ICTs) in the workplace have undergone significant transformations, markedly influenced by the COVID-19 pandemic. This section draws insights from the literature, focusing on the growing influence of ICTs on online communities in the post-Covid era, highlighting the opportunities and challenges presented by this technological paradigm shift.

Shift Change in ICTs

Before the pandemic, ICTs were already integral to business operations, facilitating communication, enhancing productivity, and enabling remote work to a certain extent. The pre-Covid era saw ICTs used primarily as a support tool rather than a necessity for business continuity. Technologies such as email, instant messaging, and basic enterprise software were commonplace, with remote work being more of an exception than a norm. The focus was on digital transformation, but at a controlled pace, emphasizing on-site collaboration and traditional office setups.

The advent of COVID-19 accelerated the adoption of ICTs exponentially, transitioning from a supportive to a critical role in workplace operations. This era was characterized by the emergence of self-organizing online communities, a reliance on digital platforms for collaboration, and a 'connected world' facilitated by smart technologies. The post-Covid workplace has seen the integration of sophisticated ICTs, such as cloud computing, advanced cybersecurity measures, collaboration platforms (e.g., Zoom, Microsoft Teams), and AI-driven tools, reshaping how work is conducted, monitored, and optimized. The necessity of ICTs has not only prompted capital investment but also spurred technological innovation to support a new wave of digital workflows and online community interactions.

Digital Activism

The rapid evolution of Information and Communication Technologies (ICTs) in the post-COVID-19 era has not only transformed workplaces and education but also revolutionized how individuals and communities advocate for social and political change. Digital activism, the use of digital tools such as social media, websites, and mobile platforms to raise awareness, mobilize support, and drive societal progress, has emerged as a defining feature of modern advocacy. In the context of a digitally connected world, this form of activism has become a powerful means for individuals and marginalized groups to amplify their voices, challenge systemic inequities, and foster global movements.

ICTs have played a pivotal role in creating spaces for self-forming and self-organizing communities to collaborate and advocate for change, overcoming traditional barriers such as geographical distance and limited access to mainstream media. From the widespread adoption of social media campaigns to real-time live streaming of protests, digital activism has redefined the way activism operates, allowing for unprecedented reach and engagement. However, the same technologies that empower activism also present challenges, such as the spread of misinformation, polarization, and accessibility gaps.

In the context of this chapter, digital activism serves as a crucial example of how ICTs shape not only online communities but also broader socio-political landscapes. Understanding their mechanisms, opportunities, and challenges is essential for leveraging the potential of ICTs to build equitable, inclusive, and impactful advocacy in the digital age.

Integration Level

Pre-Covid, ICTs were integrated into business operations but did not dominate them. Post-Covid, ICTs have become central to the functioning of workplaces, with a significant portion of work conducted digitally, emphasizing the importance of technology in maintaining business continuity.

Remote Work

Before the pandemic, remote work was less common and often seen as a perk. In contrast, the post-Covid era has normalized remote work, with a substantial portion of the workforce operating from various locations, supported by robust ICT infrastructures.

Technology Evolution

The rate of technological evolution and adoption has accelerated post-Covid, with businesses rapidly adopting advanced technologies to support remote work, digital collaboration, and online community building. This is a departure from the more gradual digital transformation seen in the pre-Covid era.

Challenges of Digital era

While the pre-Covid era dealt with challenges related to digital transformation at a steady pace, the post-Covid era faces unique challenges, including cybersecurity risks, digital divide issues, and the need for effective online community management to mitigate misinformation and polarization. To understand the extent of these challenges and their influence on virtual teams it is important to dwell into various types of virtual teams.

ICT Driven Changes in Global Digital Economies

The COVID-19 pandemic served as a catalyst for unprecedented changes in how societies and economies operate, particularly highlighting the critical role of Information and Communication Technologies (ICTs) in maintaining business continuity, enabling remote work, and facilitating access to services. This situation led to significant capital investment and technological innovation across various sectors. ICTs have driven these changes in the following aspects.

Promoting Capital Investment

The need to adapt to remote work and digital services rapidly increased demand for ICT infrastructure, prompting both public and private sectors to invest heavily in technological advancements. Governments around the world launched digital initiatives to support businesses and education, reinforcing the digital economy's infrastructure (World Bank, 2020). For example, the European Union's recovery plan, 'NextGenerationEU,' emphasizes digital transitions, allocating substantial funds for digitalization efforts across member states

(European Commission, 2021). Businesses, in response to the shift in consumer behavior and the need for digital transformation, increased their capital investment in ICTs. Investments were directed towards cloud computing, cybersecurity, e-commerce platforms, and digital marketing tools to support remote work, ensure business resilience, and capitalize on online markets (Kumar et al., 2020).

Facilitating Technological Innovation

The pandemic accelerated technological innovation as companies sought to adapt to new market conditions and consumer preferences. There was a notable surge in the development and adoption of technologies such as artificial intelligence (AI), machine learning (Alla, 2019), blockchain (Soltanisehat et al., 2018 & Alla et al., 2018) and the Internet of Things (IoT) (Kamuni et al., 2024; Soni et al., 2024, Alla & Pazos., 2019). These technologies have been pivotal in enhancing e-commerce, improving supply chain resilience, enabling remote healthcare services, and supporting public health measures (Sharma et al., 2020).

In the healthcare sector, for instance, the pandemic spurred innovation in telehealth (Alla & Chattu, 2021), digital diagnostics, and mobile health applications, transforming how healthcare services are delivered and accessed (Smith et al., 2020; Kumar et al., 2023; Lakshminarayan et al., 2023). Similarly, the education sector witnessed the rapid adoption and development of e-learning platforms, virtual classrooms, and digital assessment tools to ensure the continuity of education (Marinoni et al., 2020). The transition to remote work also encouraged innovations in virtual collaboration tools, cybersecurity measures, and digital workplace solutions, further pushing the boundaries of what's possible in a digital-first work environment (Kniffin et al., 2021). The post-COVID era underscored the indispensability of ICTs, driving capital investment and technological innovation across sectors. As societies continue to navigate the challenges and opportunities presented by the pandemic, the role of ICTs in shaping the future of work, healthcare, education, and commerce remains pivotal. The accelerated digital transformation witnessed during this period is likely to have lasting impacts, emphasizing the need for ongoing investment in and innovation of ICTs to support a resilient and inclusive digital economy.

Section II

Virtual teams in professional settings have become increasingly prevalent, especially in the wake of the global shift towards remote work catalyzed by the COVID-19 pandemic. These teams leverage digital communication technologies to collaborate across geographical, temporal, and organizational boundaries. There are several types of virtual teams, each serving different purposes and operational dynamics within professional settings. The range of Information and Communication Technologies (ICTs) utilized by various types of virtual teams in professional settings is diverse and expansive, designed to meet the specific needs of each team type. These technologies facilitate communication, collaboration, coordination, and project management across geographical distances. The following is an overview of the various types of virtual teams and the range of ICTs used by these teams:

a) Networked Teams: Networked teams consist of individuals who collaborate on specific projects but may not work together continuously. These teams are characterized by their flexible and dynamic nature, often forming to address a particular need or project and disbanding upon its completion (Lipnack & Stamps, 2000).

ICTs used:

- Social Networking Platforms: Tools such as LinkedIn or professional forums allow members to connect, share insights, and collaborate on specific topics or projects.
- Cloud Storage Services: Dropbox, Google Drive for sharing and accessing documents and resources flexibly.

b) Parallel Teams: Parallel teams work in tandem with the regular organizational structure and are typically formed to develop recommendations for a specific process or system improvement. They operate on a temporary basis and usually disband after providing their insights or achieving their goal (Townsend et al., 1998).

ICTs used:

- Project Management Tools: Trello, Asana, or Monday.com help in tracking progress, assigning tasks, and managing timelines.
- Idea Management Software: Platforms such as IdeaScale or Brightidea facilitate brainstorming and the collection of team inputs.

c) Project or Product-Development Teams: These teams are assembled to develop new products or projects within a limited timeframe. They often include members from various functional areas, bringing together diverse skills and expertise to achieve a common objective (Pawar & Sharifi, 1997).

ICTs used:

- Collaborative Engineering Tools: CAD and CAM software for product design and development that support simultaneous access by multiple users.
- Version Control Systems: GitHub or Bitbucket to manage and track changes in software development projects.

d) Work or Production Teams: Work teams are responsible for managing and executing day-to-day operational tasks. In a virtual context, these teams rely on digital tools to perform their functions, despite physical distances between members (Martins et al., 2004).

ICTs used:

- Workflow Management Systems: Tools such as Airtable or Zapier that automate tasks and processes.
- Enterprise Resource Planning (ERP) Systems: SAP, Oracle, or Microsoft Dynamics to integrate various functions such as sales, finance, and HR.

e) Service Teams: Service teams operate in customer service settings, providing support and assistance to clients or customers. Virtual service teams can offer round-the-clock service by leveraging members in different time zones (Zakaria et al., 2004).

ICTs used:

- Customer Relationship Management (CRM) Software: Salesforce or Zendesk for managing customer interactions and support.
- Live Chat and Virtual Call Centers: Software like LiveAgent or tools that integrate with websites to provide real-time customer support.

f) Management Teams: These teams consist of managers or leaders who coordinate across different units or departments of an organization. Virtual management teams focus on strategic planning and decision-making, often involving members who are geographically dispersed (Duarte & Snyder, 2006).

ICTs used:

- Strategic Planning Software: Tools such as Cascade Strategy or ClearPoint Strategy that assist in planning, executing, and tracking strategic goals.
- Business Intelligence Tools: Power BI or Tableau for data analysis and decision-making support.

g) Action Teams: Action teams are highly specialized and are convened to address critical, time-sensitive challenges. They are known for their ability to make rapid decisions and execute tasks under pressure, a capability enhanced by the immediacy of digital communication channels (Marks et al., 2001).

ICTs used:

- Real-time Communication Tools: Slack or Microsoft Teams for instant messaging and quick decision-making.
- Task and Incident Management Software: Jira or ServiceNow for tracking and resolving critical issues efficiently.

Each type of virtual team presents unique challenges and opportunities, particularly concerning communication, trust, and leadership. Effective virtual teamwork requires clear goals, strong leadership, and the appropriate use of technology to support communication and collaboration (Gibson & Gibbs,

2006). As organizations continue to navigate the complexities of remote work, understanding the nuances of different virtual team types is crucial for optimizing their performance and achieving desired outcomes.

Section III

The influence of Information and Communication Technologies (ICTs) on computer literacy, internet availability, and the global digital reset in the post-Covid era is profound and multifaceted. As the pandemic catalyzed a seismic shift towards remote work, education, and digital services, the role of ICTs became central, not only in facilitating this transition but also in reshaping societal norms around technology use, access, and skills development.

Computer Literacy

The rapid adoption of ICTs in the wake of COVID-19 has underscored the importance of computer literacy as a fundamental skill. With remote work and virtual learning becoming the new norm, individuals across various sectors have been compelled to enhance their digital skills. This necessity spans beyond basic computer operations to include a comprehensive understanding of cloud services, cybersecurity practices, collaborative online platforms, and digital communication tools. Educational institutions and organizations have implemented digital literacy programs to equip students and employees with the necessary skills to navigate the digital landscape effectively. Consequently, there's been an uptick in the demand for online courses and training programs focused on digital skills, highlighting a global push towards enhancing computer literacy to meet the demands of a digital economy (Van Dijk, 2020).

Internet Availability

The pandemic has spotlighted internet access not just as a utility, but as an essential service, critical for participation in the modern world. The increased reliance on ICTs for work, education, and healthcare services has amplified calls for universal broadband access, recognizing the internet as a key driver of socio-economic development. Governments and international organizations have initiated policies and investments aimed at expanding internet infrastructure, reducing the digital divide, especially in underserved and rural areas. Efforts include the deployment of 5G networks, satellite internet services, and affordable connectivity programs, aiming to ensure that no individual is left behind in the digital era (ITU, 2020).

Global Digital Reset

The post-Covid global digital reset refers to the sweeping transformations in how societies operate, catalyzed by the accelerated integration of ICTs across all aspects of life. This reset encompasses a broader acceptance and integration of digital solutions in business models, governmental operations, and social interactions. For instance, e-commerce, telehealth, and online learning have seen unprecedented growth, establishing these platforms as mainstay services beyond the pandemic. Moreover, the digital reset has propelled innovations in digital payments, AI, and automation, heralding new opportunities and challenges in data privacy, cybersecurity, and employment dynamics. The shift has prompted a re-evaluation of digital policies, with a focus on fostering digital economies that are inclusive, resilient, and sustainable (Schwab, 2020).

The influence of ICTs in the post-Covid era on computer literacy, internet availability, and the global digital reset signifies a pivotal moment in history. As societies navigate this transformed landscape, the emphasis on digital inclusion, literacy, and infrastructure will be crucial in leveraging the benefits of ICTs while mitigating potential disparities and challenges. This period of transition presents an opportunity to redefine the global digital agenda, prioritizing equity, access, and empowerment to ensure that the digital future is accessible to all.

Broader Socio-Political Implications due to Technology Shifts

Digital Divide

The reliance on ICTs has highlighted and exacerbated the digital divide. Access to high-speed internet and modern digital devices has become essential for participation in the modern workforce. This disparity affects socio-economic equality, as those without adequate access are at a significant disadvantage. A significant portion of the global population lacks access to high-speed internet and modern digital devices, which are essential for participating in the modern workforce. This gap is more pronounced in rural areas and developing countries, where infrastructure is often inadequate. According to a report by the International Telecommunication Union (ITU), nearly half of the world's population still does not have access to the internet (ITU, 2020). Economic disparities also contribute significantly to the digital divide. Lower-income households are less likely to have access to reliable internet connections and up-to-date technology. This economic barrier prevents many individuals from participating fully in remote work opportunities and online education, further widening the gap between different socio-economic groups (Robinson et al., 2015).

Changes in Urbanization and Mobility

With more people working remotely, there has been a noticeable impact on urbanization and mobility patterns. Cities may see reduced congestion and pollution, but there is also a potential economic impact on businesses that rely on commuter traffic. Suburban and rural areas might experience growth as people move away from urban centers.

Evolution of Workplace Dynamics

The shift to digital workspaces has changed workplace dynamics, with virtual teams becoming the norm. This transformation requires new skills in digital literacy, self-management, and virtual collaboration, which can be a barrier for some workers but an opportunity for others. Those without access are left behind, unable to compete for these new roles. This digital exclusion can lead to increased unemployment rates and further economic disparity (van Dijk, 2020). The digital divide also affects educational outcomes. Students in underprivileged areas with limited access to digital tools and internet connectivity face significant challenges in participating in remote learning. This gap can lead to long-term educational disadvantages and limit future employment opportunities for these students (Warschauer & Matuchniak, 2010).

Remote Work Normalization

The pandemic forced a rapid transition to remote work, which has become a permanent fixture for many organizations. This shift has led to increased flexibility for employees, allowing for a better work-life balance and reduced commuting times. However, it has also introduced challenges such as social isolation, blurred boundaries between work and personal life, and potential impacts on mental health.

Section IV

UTAUT Model

The Unified Theory of Acceptance and Use of Technology (UTAUT) is a comprehensive model developed to explain and predict user behaviors regarding the adoption and use of technology. Introduced by Venkatesh, Morris, Davis, and Davis (2003), the UTAUT framework consolidates elements from eight prominent theories that previously addressed technology acceptance and use, including the Theory of Reasoned Action, the Technology Acceptance Model (TAM), and the Theory of Planned Behavior, among others.

UTAUT posits that four key constructs: Performance Expectancy, Effort Expectancy, Social Influence, and Facilitating Conditions, are direct determinants of usage intention and behavior. Additionally, it suggests that user characteristics, such as gender, age, experience, and voluntariness of use, moderate the effects of these constructs on technology acceptance and usage.

Performance Expectancy is defined as the degree to which an individual believes that using the technology will help them to attain gains in job performance. Effort Expectancy refers to the ease of use associated with the technology. Social Influence is the extent to which an individual perceives that important others believe they should use the new system. Facilitating Conditions represent the degree to which an individual believes that an organizational and technical infrastructure exists to support the use of the system.

Recent studies have expanded and refined the UTAUT model to adapt to new technological contexts and user groups. For instance, Dwivedi et al. (2019) provided a comprehensive review and critique of UTAUT, suggesting areas for future research and refinement to better understand technology adoption in an ever-evolving digital landscape. Alalwan, Baabdullah, Rana, Tamilmani, and Dwivedi (2018) applied the UTAUT model to explore mobile banking services adoption, showcasing the model's applicability beyond its initial organizational focus to broader consumer technology interactions.

Users' perceptions and attitudes towards using Information and Communication Technologies (ICTs) in virtual environments have become a focal point of research, especially in the wake of the global shift towards remote work, education, and social interaction. These perceptions and attitudes are critical determinants of the successful adoption and effective use of ICTs, influencing user satisfaction, productivity, and overall engagement in virtual settings.

Adoption and Usage

The Unified Theory of Acceptance and Use of Technology (UTAUT) remains a pivotal framework for understanding users' adoption of ICTs. According to Venkatesh et al. (2003), factors such as performance expectancy, effort expectancy, social influence, and facilitating conditions significantly impact users' intentions to use technology. In virtual environments, these factors play a crucial role in shaping users' willingness to engage with various ICT tools, from collaborative platforms to virtual reality interfaces (Venkatesh et al., 2003).

Performance Expectancy

Performance expectancy, or the belief that using a technology will enhance job performance, is a key driver of ICT adoption in virtual environments. A study by Williams, Rana, and Dwivedi (2015) confirmed that users are more likely to embrace ICTs if they perceive a clear benefit to their productivity or the quality of their work outcomes. This finding is particularly relevant in remote work settings where efficiency and effectiveness are paramount.

Effort Expectancy

Effort expectancy, or the ease of use of a technology, also significantly influences users' attitudes towards ICTs. Technologies that are user-friendly and require minimal effort to learn and use are more readily accepted. Bala and Venkatesh (2016) highlighted that simplicity and intuitive design are critical for the adoption of virtual collaboration tools, as they reduce the cognitive load on users and enhance their overall experience.

Social Influence

Social influence, defined as the extent to which users perceive that important others believe they should use the technology, impacts the adoption of ICTs in virtual environments. In the context of virtual teams, colleagues' and supervisors' attitudes towards technology can significantly affect individual team members' willingness to use these tools. A study by Tarhini et al. (2017) found that social norms and peer influence play a crucial role in shaping users' perceptions and attitudes towards ICTs.

Facilitating Conditions

Facilitating conditions, which refer to users' perceptions of the technical and organizational infrastructure support for using a technology, are vital for ICT adoption in virtual settings. According to Maruping, Bala, Venkatesh, and Brown (2017), adequate support and resources are necessary to overcome potential barriers to the use of virtual collaboration tools, ensuring that users feel confident and supported in their technology use.

Policy Implications

The digital divide remains a significant barrier to equitable participation in the modern digital economy. Addressing this issue requires concerted efforts and comprehensive policies focused on improving access to technology, enhancing digital literacy, and ensuring economic inclusivity. Collaboration between governments, private sector companies, and non-profit organizations can lead to innovative solutions to bridge the digital divide. By tackling the digital divide, societies can move towards a more inclusive and equitable digital future.

Investment in Digital Infrastructure

Governments must prioritize investment in digital infrastructure to ensure equitable access to high-speed internet and modern digital tools. This investment is critical to bridge the digital divide and support remote work capabilities across all regions (Federal Communications Commission, 2020). Providing financial assistance and subsidies for low-income households to acquire necessary digital devices and internet connectivity can help reduce economic barriers. Programs similar to the U.S. Federal Communications Commission's Lifeline program, which offers discounted phone and internet services, should be expanded and promoted (FCC, 2020).

Regulation and Support for Remote Work

Policymakers need to develop regulations that support remote work, including labor laws that address the rights and responsibilities of remote workers. This includes guidelines on working hours, health and safety standards, and provisions for mental health support.

Cybersecurity and Data Privacy

The increased use of digital platforms for work raises significant cybersecurity and data privacy concerns. Governments must enact and enforce robust cybersecurity policies to protect sensitive information and ensure that companies adhere to high standards of data protection.

Support for Skill Development

To adapt to the new digital landscape, there should be a focus on continuous education and skill development programs, especially in federal organizations that are not used to rely much on advanced ICTs. Governments and organizations need to collaborate on initiatives that provide training in digital literacy, cybersecurity, and remote work best practices. Implementing digital literacy programs to educate individuals about using digital tools effectively can help bridge the knowledge gap.

Rethinking Urban Planning

Urban planning policies need to adapt to the changing patterns of urbanization and mobility. This includes supporting the development of smart cities, promoting sustainable transportation, and ensuring that urban infrastructure can support hybrid work models.

Health and Well-being Initiatives

Addressing the mental health impacts of remote work is crucial. Policies should encourage organizations to implement mental health and well-being programs, including providing access to mental health resources and promoting work-life balance.

Changing Attitudes

The COVID-19 pandemic has accelerated the digital transformation, reshaping users' perceptions and attitudes towards ICTs. The necessity of remote work and virtual interactions has led to a more positive outlook on the capabilities and benefits of ICTs, fostering a culture of innovation and openness to new technologies (Dwivedi et al., 2020). Users' perceptions and attitudes towards

ICTs in virtual environments are shaped by a complex interplay of factors, including performance expectancy, effort expectancy, social influence, and facilitating conditions. As virtual environments become increasingly prevalent in professional and educational settings, understanding these perceptions and attitudes is essential for the successful integration of ICTs. Future research should continue to explore these dynamics, particularly in the context of the ongoing digital transformation and the post-pandemic landscape.

Role of ICTs on Online Team Dynamics

Information and Communication Technologies (ICTs) play a pivotal role in shaping the dynamics of virtual and hybrid teams, facilitating communication, collaboration, and management in distributed work environments. The contribution of ICTs to team dynamics can be understood through several key aspects:

Enhancing Communication

ICTs provide a broad range of tools (e.g., email, instant messaging, video conferencing) that support real-time and asynchronous communication among team members. Tools such as Slack, Microsoft Teams, and Zoom allow for seamless interaction, mirroring face-to-face conversations and enabling the exchange of ideas, feedback, and updates instantly, irrespective of geographical boundaries. This continuous flow of communication is vital for maintaining team cohesion, alignment, and a sense of community within virtual and hybrid teams (Gilson et al., 2015).

Supporting Collaboration

Collaborative technologies, including shared digital workspaces and project management software (such as Asana, Trello, and Google Workspace), facilitate joint effort on projects by allowing team members to collaborate on documents, share resources, and track project progress in real time. These technologies enhance the collective capability of teams by enabling efficient division of labor, integration of diverse expertise, and timely completion of tasks (Hertel, Geister, & Konradt, 2005).

Fostering Inclusion and Participation

ICTs can democratize participation in team discussions and decision-making processes by providing platforms where every team member can voice their opinions and contribute equally. This is particularly important in hybrid teams, where there's a risk of remote members feeling isolated or less engaged compared to their on-site counterparts. ICTs help bridge this gap by ensuring that all members have access to the same information and opportunities to participate (Mazmanian, Orlikowski, & Yates, 2013).

Enabling Flexibility

The use of ICTs in virtual and hybrid teams offers unparalleled flexibility, allowing team members to work from different locations and often at times that best fit their personal and professional schedules. This flexibility can lead to an improved work-life balance, increased job satisfaction, and potentially higher productivity, as team members can work in environments that suit their preferences and productivity patterns (Allen, Golden, & Shockley, 2015).

Monitoring and Performance Management

ICTs provide tools for tracking work progress, setting goals, and evaluating performance in a transparent and efficient manner. Tools such as performance dashboards and automated reporting systems offer leaders insights into team dynamics, individual contributions, and project milestones, facilitating informed decision-making and timely interventions to address challenges or bottlenecks (Maruping, Zhang, & Venkatesh, 2009).

Section V

Challenges and Considerations

While ICTs offer numerous benefits for virtual and hybrid teams, their effectiveness is contingent on several factors, including the choice of appropriate technologies that match the team's needs, the digital literacy of team members, and the establishment of norms around technology use. Moreover, reliance on ICTs can lead to issues such as digital overload, loss of personal connection, and challenges in establishing trust and cohesion within the team. Thus, the successful integration of ICTs into team dynamics requires careful management, training, and support to maximize the benefits while mitigating the potential drawbacks (Leonardi, Treem, & Jackson, 2010).

Impact of ICTs on Virtual Teams' Work Performance

The impact of Information and Communication Technologies (ICTs) on the work performance of virtual teams has been extensively researched, especially in the context of the increasing prevalence of remote work arrangements catalyzed by the COVID-19 pandemic. ICTs have transformed how virtual teams operate, communicate, and perform, offering both opportunities and challenges that affect overall productivity and effectiveness.

Positive Impacts of ICTs on Virtual Team Performance

Enhanced Communication and Collaboration

ICTs facilitate a broad spectrum of communication and collaboration tools that enable the real-time sharing of information and seamless collaboration among team members dispersed geographically. This accessibility to information and ease of collaboration significantly boosts team efficiency and productivity (Maruping, Zhang, & Venkatesh, 2009). Tools such as Slack, Microsoft Teams, and Zoom mimic in-person interactions, fostering a sense of closeness and teamwork essential for high-performing virtual teams.

Flexibility and Work-Life Balance

The use of ICTs in virtual teams provides flexibility in work schedules and locations, contributing positively to work-life balance. This flexibility has been linked to higher job satisfaction, reduced stress, and increased productivity among team members (Allen, Golden, & Shockley, 2015).

Access to Global Talent

ICTs enable organizations to tap into a global talent pool by removing geographical barriers. This access allows for the formation of diverse teams with a wide range of skills, perspectives, and expertise, potentially leading to innovative solutions and improved team performance (Ebrahim, Ahmed, & Taha, 2009).

Challenges and Negative Impacts

Over-reliance on Technology

An over-reliance on ICTs without adequate face-to-face interactions can lead to misunderstandings and a lack of deep social connections among team members, potentially harming team cohesion and trust (Cascio & Shurygailo, 2003).

Digital Overload

The extensive use of digital communication tools can lead to information overload, making it difficult for team members to manage emails, messages, and notifications efficiently. This overload can increase stress levels and decrease overall productivity (Mark, Voida, & Cardello, 2012).

Technology Literacy and Accessibility

Differences in technology literacy and access to reliable internet connections among team members can create disparities in how effectively individuals can contribute to the team's goals. These disparities can impact team dynamics and overall performance negatively (Gilson et al., 2015).

Mitigating the Negative Impacts

The effective management and strategic use of ICTs are crucial in maximizing the positive impacts while mitigating the negative effects on virtual team performance. Training on digital tools, establishing clear communication norms, and encouraging regular check-ins can enhance the efficacy of ICTs in virtual teams (Purvanova, 2014). Additionally, integrating occasional face-to-face meetings, when possible, can strengthen team bonds and improve collaboration (Mesmer-Magnus, DeChurch, Jimenez-Rodriguez, Wildman, & Shuffler, 2011).

Negative Impacts of Advanced ICTs

ICTs have a profound impact on the work performance of virtual teams, offering tools that enhance communication, collaboration, and flexibility, which are essential for high performance. However, the challenges associated with an over-reliance on technology, digital overload, and disparities in technology literacy must be carefully managed. With thoughtful implementation and management, ICTs can significantly contribute to the success and effectiveness of virtual teams.

The development of Information and Communication Technologies (ICTs) has been instrumental in facilitating the transition to a virtual work environment, especially highlighted by the rapid shift during the COVID-19 pandemic. This transition, while offering numerous advantages such as flexibility, reduced commute times, and access to a global workforce, has also led to significant social isolation among remote workers. This section explores how the advancement of ICTs contributed to the proliferation of virtual work environments and the consequent social isolation, supported by recent research findings.

Facilitation of Virtual Work Environments

The evolution of ICTs, including high-speed internet, cloud computing, and collaborative software tools, has made remote work more feasible and efficient than ever before. Platforms such as Zoom, Microsoft Teams, and Slack have become staples in virtual communication, enabling real-time collaboration and maintaining team connectivity across distances (Kniffin et al., 2021). The scalability of cloud services has allowed for the seamless access and sharing of work resources, further blurring the lines between physical office spaces and virtual work settings (Maruping, Zhang, & Venkatesh, 2009). This technological infrastructure has provided organizations with the agility to continue operations amidst lockdowns and social distancing measures, highlighting the role of ICTs in sustaining business continuity during the pandemic (Sharma, Leung, Kingshott, Davcik, & Cardinali, 2021).

Consequences of Social Isolation

While the development of ICTs has enabled the widespread adoption of virtual work environments, it has also led to unintended consequences in workers' social well-being, primarily through increased feelings of isolation. Remote work diminishes the incidental social interactions that occur in physical office settings, such as casual conversations and team lunches, which play a crucial role in building social connections and a sense of belonging among employees (Golden, Vega, & Dino, 2021). The reliance on virtual communication can also lead to a depersonalization of work relationships, where interactions become task-focused, lacking the depth and warmth of face-to-face engagements (Morikawa, 2020).

The shift to virtual work environments has also blurred the boundaries between work and personal life, leading to longer working hours and further isolating individuals from their social circles outside of work (Eurofound, 2020). The accumulation of these factors contributes to the social isolation experienced by remote workers, which can have detrimental effects on mental health, job satisfaction, and overall well-being (Oakman, Kinsman, Stuckey, Graham, & Weale, 2020). Often it also leads to reduced work performance.

The advancement of ICTs has undeniably transformed the landscape of work, enabling the proliferation of virtual work environments. While these technological developments have facilitated operational continuity and offered unprecedented flexibility, they have also contributed to increased social isolation among remote workers. Balancing the benefits of virtual work with the need for social connection poses a significant challenge for organizations navigating the post-pandemic world. Addressing this challenge requires a conscious effort to leverage ICTs not just for work-related purposes but also to foster a sense of community and belonging among remote teams.

Mitigating Social Isolation in Virtual Work Environments

Addressing social isolation in virtual work environments requires a multifaceted approach. Organizations can foster social connectedness by creating virtual spaces for non-work-related interactions and encouraging informal video calls among team members (Choudhury, Foroughi, & Larson, 2021). Regular check-ins and virtual team-building activities can also help maintain team cohesion and mitigate feelings of isolation. Furthermore, providing employees with resources and support for mental health and well-being is essential in recognizing and addressing the impacts of social isolation (Neeley, 2021).

Recommendations to Mitigate Reduction in Performance in Virtual Settings

Establish Clear Communication Protocols

Clear and consistent communication is essential in virtual work settings. Implementing regular check-ins and using collaborative tools can ensure that team members are aligned and engaged. Gilson et al. (2015) emphasize the importance of leveraging ICTs to maintain open channels of communication and support team cohesion.

Foster a Strong Organizational Culture Virtually

Building a strong culture that transcends physical boundaries can motivate and unify team members. Leaders should focus on transmitting organizational values through virtual onboarding, team-building activities, and recognizing employees' achievements (Bergiel et al., 2008).

Provide Training and Support for Digital Tools

Ensuring that all employees are comfortable and proficient with the digital tools required for their work can significantly enhance performance. Offering ongoing training and support can alleviate frustrations and improve efficiency (Tarafdar et al., 2019).

Encourage Work-Life Balance

Virtual work can blur the boundaries between personal and professional life, leading to burnout. Encouraging employees to establish clear work-life boundaries and promoting flexibility can help mitigate this risk (Allen et al., 2015).

On the other hand, there is another problem companies face these days. Employees are not willing to come back to in-person work setting. The reluctance of online workers to return to in-person work is a phenomenon that has become increasingly prevalent in the post-pandemic world. The shift to remote work, necessitated by the COVID-19 pandemic, has led to a re-evaluation of work-life balance, productivity, and employee well-being. This part of the section explores the reasons behind this reluctance, supported by insights from published studies, and discusses the implications for organizations and the future of work.

Reasons for Reluctance

Work-Life Balance Improvements

One of the most cited reasons for the reluctance to return to in-person work is the perceived improvement in work-life balance that remote work offers. The elimination of commute times and the flexibility to manage work and personal responsibilities concurrently have been significant benefits (Allen, Golden, & Shockley, 2015). Employees have reported higher levels of satisfaction with their work-life balance, contributing to their hesitancy to give up the autonomy remote work provides.

Increased Productivity

Many online workers have reported increased productivity while working remotely. The ability to work in a personalized and distraction-free environment has led to enhanced focus and efficiency (Bloom, Liang, Roberts, & Ying, 2015). The flexibility to work during hours that align with individuals' peak productivity periods rather than a strict 9-to-5 schedule has further amplified this effect.

Health and Safety Concerns

The COVID-19 pandemic has heightened awareness and concern regarding health and safety in the workplace. Many employees are apprehensive about returning to an office environment where social distancing may be challenging to maintain, and the risk of virus transmission is perceived to be higher (Kniffin et al., 2021).

Changes in Organizational Culture and Communication

The transition to remote work has led to changes in organizational culture and communication patterns. Virtual communication tools have facilitated more focused and efficient meetings, and many employees find online communication to be just as effective as in-person interactions (Choudhury, Foroughi, & Larson, 2021). The prospect of returning to in-person work raises concerns about losing these efficiencies.

Implications for Organizations

Organizations are now faced with the challenge of addressing employees' reluctance to return to in-person work. This situation necessitates a re-evaluation of workplace policies, office design, and communication strategies to accommodate the preferences and concerns of the workforce.

Hybrid Work Models

One response to employee reluctance is the adoption of hybrid work models that combine in-person and remote work. These models offer a compromise, allowing employees to benefit from the flexibility and autonomy of remote work while still maintaining some level of in-person interaction and collaboration (Eurofound, 2020).

Reimagining the Office Space

For those returning to in-person work, organizations may need to reimagine office spaces to prioritize health, safety, and collaboration. This could include redesigning workspaces to allow for social distancing, implementing health and safety protocols, and creating collaborative spaces that justify the commute (Marinoni, Van't Land, & Jensen, 2020).

Addressing Employee Concerns

Organizations will need to actively address employee concerns regarding health and safety, work-life balance, and productivity. Transparent communication, flexible policies, and support for employee well-being will be crucial in easing the transition back to in-person work.

The reluctance of online workers to return to in-person work poses significant challenges and opportunities for organizations worldwide. As the future of work continues to evolve, it will be essential for employers to listen to their employees' preferences, adapt to the changing landscape, and create work environments that support both productivity and well-being. Embracing flexibility, re-evaluating traditional work models, and prioritizing employee health and safety can help organizations navigate this transition successfully.

Mitigating the reduction in performance due to virtual work settings and harnessing the advantages of hybrid work models have become critical areas of focus for organizations navigating the post-pandemic work landscape. Addressing the challenges of virtual work and effectively implementing hybrid models can lead to enhanced productivity, employee satisfaction, and organizational resilience. Here are recommendations based on recent publications, along with the benefits of adopting hybrid work models.

Advantages of Hybrid Work Models

Increased Flexibility and Autonomy

Hybrid models offer employees the flexibility to choose where they work best, whether at home or in the office. This autonomy can lead to increased job satisfaction and productivity (Kniffin et al., 2021).

Enhanced Work-Life Balance

The ability to work remotely part of the time allows employees to better manage their personal and professional responsibilities, contributing to a healthier work-life balance (Eurofound, 2020).

Access to a Wider Talent Pool

Organizations can recruit from a broader geographic area, not limited by the proximity to a physical office. This access can lead to more diverse and skilled teams (Choudhury, Foroughi, & Larson, 2021).

Reduced Overhead Costs

With employees splitting their time between home and the office, companies can reduce the need for large office spaces and associated costs (Bloom et al., 2015).

Sustained Productivity with Enhanced Employee Well-being

Hybrid models can maintain or even improve productivity while also enhancing employee well-being, offering a balanced approach to work that addresses the challenges of both fully remote and in-person models (Morikawa, 2020).

The network diagram illustrates the interconnectedness of key domains: ICT Technologies, Socio-Political Implementations, UTAUT Model Attributes, and Challenges in ICT Implementation. At the core, ICT technologies such as cloud computing, AI, blockchain, IoT, and collaboration platforms serve as enablers of digital transformation. These technologies directly influence socio-political implementations, including the development of the digital economy, e-governance systems, digital divide mitigation strategies, and cybersecurity policies. The diagram also integrates the UTAUT model, emphasizing attributes such as performance expectancy, effort expectancy, social influence, and facilitating conditions that drive user adoption of ICT tools. However, challenges such as digital overload, misinformation, privacy risks, and infrastructure inequality are depicted as barriers that intersect with all domains, highlighting the complexities of ICT adoption and implementation. This interconnected framework underscores the need for a holistic approach to leveraging ICT technologies while addressing their limitations and societal implications. Figure 2: Network Diagram of Interconnections of ICT Technologies, Applications, and Challenges

Mitigating the potential drawbacks of virtual work settings and adopting hybrid work models present viable paths for organizations aiming to navigate the evolving work environment. By implementing clear communication protocols, fostering a strong organizational culture, providing necessary training, and encouraging a healthy work-life balance, companies can support their employees' performance and satisfaction. Hybrid work models, with their blend of flexibility, access to talent, and cost savings, offer a compelling structure for the future of work, balancing the benefits of in-person collaboration with the autonomy and efficiency of remote work.

Conclusion

In conclusion, the COVID-19 pandemic has acted as a catalyst for the rapid evolution and integration of Information and Communication Technologies (ICTs) across various domains, transitioning workplaces, education, and social interactions from traditional settings to flexible, digital-first environments. This transformation has revolutionized how we work, learn, and connect, making ICTs indispensable for sustaining the dynamics of today's digital-centric world. Beyond enabling seamless communication, collaboration, and remote work, ICTs have also empowered the rise of digital activism, offering new platforms for organizing, advocating, and mobilizing social change across distances.

While these advancements present significant opportunities for efficiency, connectivity, and societal impact, they also introduce challenges such as digital overload, social isolation, misinformation, and access disparities. These issues necessitate strategic interventions, including setting boundaries around technology-use to prevent burnout, fostering inclusive and equitable access to digital tools and training, and leveraging ICTs to amplify underrepresented voices in digital activism.

By addressing these challenges and maximizing the benefits of ICTs, organizations and individuals can create environments that not only enhance productivity and collaboration but also support effective digital activism. This dual approach balances technological benefits with individual well-being, organizational effectiveness, and the potential to drive social progress in a connected, post-pandemic world.

References

Alalwan, A.A., Baabdullah, A.M., Rana, N.P., Tamilmani, K., & Dwivedi, Y.K. (2018). Examining adoption of mobile internet in Saudi Arabia: Extending TAM with perceived enjoyment, innovativeness and trust. *Technology in Society*, 55, 100–110.

Alla, S. (2019). A statistical analysis of surgeons' preference on robot-assisted surgeries. *Institute of Industrial and Systems Engineers Annual Conference Proceedings*, 1385–1390.

Alla, S., & Chattu, V. K. (2021). Future implications of Telehealth in post-COVID world. *Telehealth and Medicine Today*, 2–10.

Alla, S., & Pazos, P. (2019). *Healthcare robotics: Key factors that impact robot adoption in healthcare.*

Alla, S., Soltanisehat, L., Tatar, U., & Keskin, O. (2018). *Blockchain technology in electronic healthcare systems Institute of Industrial and Systems Engineers Annual Conference Proceedings*, 901–906.

Allen, T. D., Golden, T. D., & Shockley, K. M. (2015). How effective is telecommuting? Assessing the status of our scientific findings. *Psychological Science in the Public Interest*, 16 (2), 40–68.

Bala, H., & Venkatesh, V. (2016). Adaptation to information technology: A holistic nomological network from implementation to job outcomes. *Management Science*, 62 (1), 156–179.

Bloom, N., Liang, J., Roberts, J., & Ying, Z. J. (2015). Does working from home work? Evidence from a Chinese experiment. *Quarterly Journal of Economics*, 130 (1), 165–218.

Cascio, W. F., & Shurygailo, S. (2003). E-leadership and virtual teams. *Organizational Dynamics*, 31 (4), 362–376.

Choudhury, P., Foroughi, C., & Larson, B. Z. (2021). Work-from-anywhere: The productivity effects of geographic flexibility. *Strategic Management Journal*, 42 (4), 655–683.

Costa, P., Graça, A. M., Santos, C., Marques-Quinteiro, P., & Rico, R. (2021). Teamworking virtually: business as usual? *European Journal of Work and Organizational Psychology*, 30 (5), 619–623.

Duarte, D. L., & Snyder, N. T. (2006).*Mastering Virtual Teams: Strategies, Tools, and Techniques That Succeed*. Jossey-Bass.

Dwivedi, Y.K., Rana, N.P., Chen, H., & Williams, M.D. (2011). A meta-analysis of the Unified Theory of Acceptance and Use of Technology (UTAUT). In Nüttgens, M., Gadatsch, A., Kautz, K., Schirmer, I., & Blinn, N. (Eds.), *Governance and sustainability in information systems: IFIP advances in information and communication technology*, 366. https://doi.org/10.1007/978-3-642-24148-2_10.

Ebrahim, N. A., Ahmed, S., & Taha, Z. (2009). Virtual teams: a literature review. *Australian Journal of Basic and Applied Sciences*, 3 (3), 2653–2669.

Eurofound. (2020). Living, working and COVID-19. Retrieved from https://www.eurofound.europa.eu/publications/report/2020/living-working-and-covid-19.

European Commission. (2021). NextGenerationEU: Europe's recovery plan. Retrieved from https://ec.europa.eu/info/strategy/recovery-plan-europe_en.

Federal Communications Commission (FCC). (2020). Lifeline Program for Low-Income Consumers. Retrieved from https://broadbandusa.ntia.gov/resources/federal/federal-funding/federal-communications-commission-lifeline#:~:text=Program%20Overview,%2C%20family%2C%20and%20emergency%20services.

Gibson, C. B., & Gibbs, J. L. (2006). Unpacking the concept of virtuality: The effects of geographic dispersion, electronic dependence, dynamic structure, and national diversity on team innovation. *Administrative Science Quarterly*, 51 (3), 451–495.

Gilson, L. L., Maynard, M. T., Jones Young, N. C., Vartiainen, M., & Hakonen, M. (2015). Virtual teams research: 10 years, 10 themes, and 10 opportunities. *Journal of Management*, 41 (5), 1313–1337.

Golden, T. D., Vega, R. P., & Dino, R. N. (2021). Telework and the socialization paradox: The role of relative telework arrangements. *Journal of Vocational Behavior*, 126, 103518.

Hertel, G., Geister, S., & Konradt, U. (2005). Managing virtual teams: A review of current empirical research. *Human Resource Management Review*, 15 (1), 69–95.

International Telecommunication Union (ITU). (2020). *Measuring Digital Development: Facts and Figures 2020.*

Kamuni, N., Shah, H., Chintala, S., Kunchakuri, N., & Alla, S. (2024, February). Enhancing end-to-end multi-task dialogue systems: A study on intrinsic motivation reinforcement learning algorithms for improved training and adaptability. *2024 IEEE 18th International Conference on Semantic Computing (ICSC)*, 335–340. IEEE.

Kniffin, K. M., Narayanan, J., Anseel, F., Antonakis, J., Ashford, S. J., Bakker, A. B., … & Vugt, M. V. (2021). COVID-19 and the workplace: Implications, issues, and insights for future research and action. *American Psychologist*, 76 (1), 63–77.

Kumar, P., Chaudhary, B., Yadav, N., Devi, S., Pareek, A., Alla, S., & Gupta, M. M. (2023). Recent advances in research and management of human Monkeypox virus: an emerging global health threat. *Viruses*, 15 (4), 937.

Kumar, V., Dixit, A., Javalgi, R. G., & Dass, M. (2020). Research framework, strategies, and applications of intelligent agent technologies (IATs) in marketing. *Journal of the Academy of Marketing Science*, 48, 24–45.

Lakshminarayanan, V., Ravikumar, A., Sriraman, H., Alla, S., & Chattu, V. K. (2023). Health care equity through intelligent edge computing and augmented reality/virtual reality: a systematic review. *Journal of Multidisciplinary Healthcare*, 2839–2859.

Leonardi, P. M., Treem, J. W., & Jackson, M. H. (2010). The connectivity paradox: Using technology to both decrease and increase perceptions of distance in distributed work arrangements. *Journal of Applied Communication Research*, 38 (1), 85–105.

Lipnack, J., & Stamps, J. (2000). *Virtual Teams: People Working Across Boundaries with Technology*. John Wiley & Sons.

Livingstone, S., & Helsper, E. (2007). Gradations in digital inclusion: Children, young people and the digital divide. *New Media and Society*, 9 (4), 671–696.

Marinoni, G., Van't Land, H., & Jensen, T. (2020). *The impact of COVID-19 on higher education around the world. IAU Global Survey Report.*

Mark, G., Voida, S., & Cardello, A. (2012). "A pace not dictated by electrons": An empirical study of work without email. *Proceedings of the SIGCHI Conference on Human Factors in Computing Systems.*

Marks, M. A., Mathieu, J. E., & Zaccaro, S. J. (2001). A temporally based framework and taxonomy of team processes. *Academy of Management Review*, 26 (3), 356–376.

Martins, L. L., Gilson, L. L., & Maynard, M. T. (2004). Virtual teams: What do we know and where do we go from here? *Journal of Management*, 30 (6), 805–835.

Maruping, L. M., Bala, H., Venkatesh, V., & Brown, S. A. (2017). Going beyond intention: Integrating behavioral expectation into the unified theory of acceptance and use of technology. *Journal of the Association for Information Science and Technology*, 68 (3), 623–637.

Maruping, L. M., Zhang, X., & Venkatesh, V. (2009). Role of collective ownership and coding standards in coordinating expertise in software project teams. *European Journal of Information Systems*, 18 (4), 355–371.

Mazmanian, M., Orlikowski, W. J., & Yates, J. (2013). The autonomy paradox: The implications of mobile email devices for knowledge professionals. *Organization science*, 24 (5), 1337–1357.

Norris, P. (2001). *Digital divide: Civic engagement, information poverty, and the Internet worldwide*. Cambridge University Press.

Pawar, K. S., & Sharifi, S. (1997). Physical or virtual team collocation: Does it matter? *International Journal of Production Economics*, 52 (3), 283–290.

Robinson, L., Cotten, S. R., Ono, H., Quan-Haase, A., Mesch, G., Chen, W., & Stern, M. J. (2015). Digital inequalities and why they matter. *Information, Communication and Society*, 18 (5), 569–582.

Schwab, K., & Malleret, T. (2020, July). *COVID-19: The Great Reset*. Forum Publishing.

Sharma, G. D., Lijuan, W., & Alvi, A. K. (2020). Blockchain for supply chain management: A comprehensive survey. *IEEE Access*, 8, 118773–118788.

Smith, A. C., Thomas, E., Snoswell, C. L., Haydon, H., Mehrotra, A., Clemensen, J., & Caffery, L. J. (2020). Telehealth for global emergencies: Implications for coronavirus disease 2019 (COVID-19). *Journal of Telemedicine and Telecare*, 26 (5), 309–313.

Soni, A., Alla, S., Dodda, S., & Volikatla, H. (2024). *Advancing Household Robotics: Deep Interactive Reinforcement Learning for Efficient Training and Enhanced Performance*. arXiv preprint arXiv:2405.18687.

Tarhini, A., Hone, K., & Liu, X. (2017). User acceptance towards web-based learning systems: Investigating the role of social, organizational and individual factors in European higher education. *Procedia Computer Science*, 113, 568–575.

Taylor, A. K., & Alla, S. (2018). Influence of reward systems on motivation-pros and cons based on current literature. *Proceedings of the International Annual Conference of the American Society for Engineering Management*, 1–8. American Society for Engineering Management (ASEM).

Taylor, A. K., & Alla, S. (2018). Managing conflict towards improving team performance-what we know so far. In *Proceedings of the International Annual Conference of the American Society for Engineering Management*. (pp. 1–6). American Society for Engineering Management (ASEM).

Townsend, A. M., DeMarie, S. M., & Hendrickson, A. R. (1998). Virtual teams: Technology and the workplace of the future. *Academy of Management Executive*, 12 (3), 17–29.

Van Dijk, J. A. (2020). *The Digital Divide*. Polity.

Venkatesh, V., Morris, M.G., Davis, G.B., & Davis, F.D. (2003). User Acceptance of Information Technology: Toward a Unified View. *MIS Quarterly*, 27 (3), 425–478.

Vidgen, R., & Wang, X. (2009). Coordinating and Communicating in Agile Software Development Projects. *Journal of Systems and Software*, 82 (11), 1785–1795.

Warschauer, M., & Matuchniak, T. (2010). New technology and digital worlds: Analyzing evidence of equity in access, use, and outcomes. *Review of Research in Education*, 34 (1), 179–225.

Whitworth, E. and R. Biddle, (2007). "The Social Nature of Agile Teams," *Agile 2007 (AGILE 2007)*, 26–36, doi:10.1109/AGILE.2007.60.

Williams, M. D., Rana, N. P., & Dwivedi, Y. K. (2015). The unified theory of acceptance and use of technology (UTAUT): A literature review. *Journal of Enterprise Information Management*, 28 (3), 443–488.

World Bank. (2020). *The World Bank Annual Report 2020*. Retrieved from https://www.worldbank.org/en/about/annual-report.

Zakaria, N., Amelinckx, A., & Wilemon, D. (2004). Working together apart? Building a knowledge-sharing culture for global virtual teams. *Creativity and Innovation Management*, 13 (1), 15–29.

5

CONCLUSION

Fostering Synergy: The Next Chapter of Digital Engagement

Nalanda Roy

The Power of Digital Synergy

In the rapidly evolving landscape of the 21st century, digital technology has become a formidable force in shaping how communities organize, collaborate, and effect change. The concept of digital synergy—where technology enhances collective action and fosters cross-border cooperation—has emerged as a transformative phenomenon. The concluding chapter "Fostering Synergy: The Next Chapter of Digital Engagement" synthesizes the key insights on how self-organizing communities leverage digital tools to transcend geographical, cultural, and political boundaries, and explores the implications for the future of global collaboration.

In *From Epic Tales to Digital Trails: Understanding New Mediascapes in Activism*, the authors explore the transformation of activism in the digital age, highlighting how new media platforms shape narratives, mobilize communities, and influence social change. One of the central arguments is the shift from traditional, narrative-driven forms of activism—often characterized by epic storytelling—to the fragmented and instantaneous nature of digital activism. The author posits that while traditional narratives offered a cohesive understanding of social issues, digital platforms enabled rapid information dissemination, allowing movements to gain momentum quickly. However, this immediacy often sacrifices depth and context, leading to what can be termed "hashtag activism," where engagement is superficial, limited to likes and shares rather than a sustained commitment.

Furthermore, the edited volume discusses the democratizing potential of digital media, emphasizing how marginalized voices can find platforms to share their stories. Social media has empowered grassroots movements, providing tools for organization and communication that were previously inaccessible. As Howard Rheingold said, "The future of social media is not just about networks, but about creating a collective intelligence that spans the globe"

DOI: 10.4324/9781003628910-5

(Rheingold, 2009). This democratization, however, comes with a caveat; the saturation of content can dilute messages, making it challenging for movements to maintain visibility and stay on track amid a constant flow of information.

The analysis also addresses the role of algorithms and corporate interests in shaping digital activism. While platforms such as Twitter/X and Facebook provide essential tools for outreach, they also prioritize certain narratives over others, often favoring sensationalism over substantive discourse. This raises critical questions about the sustainability of digital activism, such as, are movements relying too heavily on platforms that ultimately commodify their struggles? The edited volume discusses how digital synergy leads to the harmonious interaction between various digital tools and platforms that facilitate the emergence and functioning of self-organizing communities. The chapters have demonstrated how communities, often formed around shared goals or causes, harness the collective intelligence and resources of individuals spread across the globe. Platforms such as social media, collaborative workspaces, and open-source software enable these communities to coordinate their efforts efficiently, share information instantaneously, and mobilize resources with unprecedented ease.

From Epic Tales to Digital Trails: Understanding New Mediascapes in Activism discusses the most compelling aspects of digital synergy is its ability to break down traditional barriers to participation. Geographic distance, linguistic differences, and socio-economic disparities can be mitigated through digital connectivity, allowing individuals from diverse backgrounds to contribute to and benefit from collective initiatives. The Arab Spring, climate change activism, the COVID-19 pandemic, and global humanitarian responses illustrate how digital tools have empowered self-organizing communities to address pressing issues on a global scale.

Lessons Learned from Self-Organizing Communities

The rise of self-organizing communities has provided several important lessons about the nature of modern collaboration.

Inclusivity and Diversity: Successful digital communities often thrive on inclusivity and diversity. By embracing a wide range of perspectives and expertise, these communities can develop more innovative solutions and foster a sense of belonging among members. For instance, open-source software projects rely on contributions from individuals with varying skills and backgrounds, leading to more robust and versatile products.

Decentralization and Flexibility: The decentralized nature of digital communities allows for greater flexibility and adaptability. Without a centralized hierarchy, these groups can respond quickly to changes and challenges. This flexibility is evident in grassroots movements that rapidly adapt their strategies in response to shifting political or social contexts.

Trust and Credibility: Building and maintaining trust is crucial for the success of self-organizing communities. Transparency, accountability, and effective communication are key factors in establishing credibility and ensuring that community members remain engaged and motivated.

Scalability and Reach: Digital tools enable communities to scale their efforts and reach a global audience. The viral nature of social media campaigns and the ease of disseminating information online allow for rapid mobilization and widespread impact.

Challenges and Future Directions

Despite the remarkable potential of digital synergy, challenges remain that must be addressed to fully realize its benefits.

The Digital Divide: The disparity in access to technology and internet connectivity can hinder participation from marginalized groups. Bridging this divide is essential for ensuring equitable involvement and representation in global digital communities.

Information Overload and Misinformation: The vast amount of information available online can lead to information overload and the spread of misinformation. Developing strategies for effective information management and fact-checking is crucial for maintaining the integrity of digital initiatives.

Privacy and Security: The digital realm poses risks related to privacy and security. Safeguarding personal information and ensuring the protection of digital identities are vital for maintaining trust and encouraging participation.

Sustainability and Impact: Ensuring the long-term sustainability of digital communities and evaluating their impact is essential for achieving lasting change. This involves not only sustaining engagement but also measuring the effectiveness of initiatives and adapting strategies as needed.

Conclusion

From Epic Tales to Digital Trails: Understanding New Mediascapes in Activism is not just a theoretical exploration; it is also a call to action. The edited volume urges readers, policymakers, and technologists to think critically about the direction of technological development and its implications for society. The chapters emphasize the importance of collective action in shaping a future where technology enhances rather than diminishes democratic and societal values. Overall, *From Epic Tales to Digital Trails* provides a comprehensive and insightful analysis of how technology is likely to shape the future of politics. It challenges readers to consider both the opportunities, and the risks associated with technological advancements and to engage actively in shaping a future that aligns with democratic principles and social justice.

Digital synergy represents a transformative shift in how communities come together and collaborate across borders. By leveraging the power of digital tools and platforms, self-organizing communities have demonstrated the potential for collective action on a global scale. As we move forward, it is crucial to address the challenges associated with digital synergy while continuing to harness its strengths. Embracing inclusivity, fostering trust, and ensuring equitable access to technology will be key to advancing the potential of self-organizing communities and driving meaningful global change. The future of digital synergy holds immense promise for addressing complex global issues, fostering innovation, and enhancing collective well-being. As technology continues to evolve, so too will the ways in which we organize and collaborate. By understanding and embracing the dynamics of digital synergy, we can build a more connected, equitable, and resilient world.

The future of digital activism promises to be dynamic and transformative, driven by advancements in technology and an increasingly interconnected global community. By harnessing the potential of emerging technologies, activists can enhance their ability to mobilize support, drive change, and address pressing social issues. However, navigating the evolving landscape will require careful attention to ethical considerations, inclusivity, and the challenges posed by misinformation and privacy concerns. As digital activism continues to evolve, it will be crucial for activists, organizations, and technologists to collaborate and innovate, ensuring that the future of digital activism remains vibrant, effective, and aligned with the values of justice and equity.

From Epic Tales to Digital Trails: Understanding New Mediascapes in Activism offers a nuanced examination of how new media reshapes activism. While digital platforms provide unprecedented opportunities for engagement and organization, they also present significant challenges, including the risk of oversimplification, algorithmic bias, and the need for intersectional awareness. As activism continues to evolve in this digital landscape, understanding these dynamics will be crucial for fostering meaningful and sustained social change. In conclusion, fostering synergy in digital engagement is not just an aspiration; it is a necessity for the evolution of activism in our interconnected world. As we navigate the complexities of the digital landscape, the potential for collaboration among diverse voices has never been greater.

By harnessing the strengths of technology and the collective power of communities, we can create a more inclusive and impactful approach to advocacy. Embracing this synergy allows us to transcend traditional barriers, enabling meaningful dialogue and action that resonate across borders. As we move forward, it is crucial to remain adaptable and innovative, ensuring that our digital strategies not only amplify our messages but also empower those who have historically been marginalized. Together, we can write the next chapter of digital engagement, one that champions unity, resilience, and a shared vision for a more equitable future. Afterall, as Kevin Kelly said, "The future is not something we enter. The future is something we create" (Kelly, n.d.).

References

Kelly, K. (n.d.). https://perell.com/podcast/kevin-kelly-seeing-the-future/
Rheingold, H. (2009). https://www.youtube.com/watch?v=V-92xiczDC8

BIBLIOGRAPHY

Adhiarso, D. S., Utari, P., & Hastjarjo, S. (2018). The impact of digital technology to change people's behavior in using the media. *Social Sciences and Humanities*, 2, 35–40. https://doi.org/10.29037/digitalpress.402256.

Adler, R. P., & Goggin, J. (2005). What Do We Mean By "Civic Engagement? *Journal of Transformative Education*, 3(3), 236–253. https://doi.org/10.1177/1541344605276792.

Alalwan, A.A., Baabdullah, A.M., Rana, N.P., Tamilmani, K., & Dwivedi, Y.K. (2018). Examining adoption of mobile internet in Saudi Arabia: Extending TAM with perceived enjoyment, innovativeness and trust. *Technology in Society*, 55, 100–110. https://doi.org/10.1016/j.techsoc.2018.06.007.

Alexander, A., & Resin, E. (2009). *Twitterature: The World's Greatest Books in Twenty Tweets or Less*. Penguin.

Alexander, B. (2017). *The New Digital Storytelling: Creating Narratives with New Media*. Praeger Publishers.

Alla, S. (2019). A statistical analysis of surgeons' preference on robot-assisted surgeries. *Institute of Industrial and Systems Engineers Annual Conference Proceedings*, 1385–1390.

Alla, S., & Chattu, V. K. (2021). Future implications of Telehealth in post-COVID world. *Telehealth and Medicine Today*, 21, 2–10.

Alla, S., & Pazos, P. (2019). Healthcare Robotics: Key Factors that Impact Robot Adoption in Healthcare. *IISE Annual Conference. Proceedings*, 1121–1126. https://www.proquest.com/scholarly-journals/healthcare-robotics-key-factors-that-impact-robot/docview/2511387399/se-2.

Alla, S., Soltanisehat, L., Tatar, U., & Keskin, O. (2018). Blockchain technology in electronic healthcare systems *Institute of Industrial and Systems Engineers Annual Conference Proceedings*, 901–906.

AlSayyad, N., & Guvenc, M. (2015). Virtual uprisings: On the interaction of new social media, traditional media coverage and urban space during the 'Arab Spring'. *Urban Studies*, 52(11), 2018–2034.

Allen, T. D., Golden, T. D., & Shockley, K. M. (2015). How Effective is Telecommuting? Assessing the Status of Our Scientific Findings. *Psychological Science in the Public Interest*, 16(2), 40–68. https://doi.org/10.1177/1529100615593273.

Anderson, L. (2011). Demystifying the Arab Spring: Parsing the Differences Between Tunisia, Egypt, and Libya. *Foreign Affairs*, 90(3), 2–7. http://www.jstor.org/stable/23039401.

Asur, S., & Huberman, B. A. (2010). Predicting the future with social media. *IEEE/WIC/ACM International Conference on Web Intelligence and Intelligent Agent Technology*, 492–499. https://doi.org/10.1109/WI-IAT.2010.63.

Ayyappan, R. (2020). Duryodhana, the misunderstood hero of Mahabharata? *Onmanorama*. January 7. https://www.onmanorama.com/news/india/2020/01/07/chindu-sreedharan-duryidhana-mahabharata-epicretold-caa-protest.html

Bala, H., & Venkatesh, V. (2016). Adaptation to information technology: A holistic nomological network from implementation to job outcomes. *Management Science*, 62(1), 156–179. https://doi.org/10.1287/mnsc.2014.2111.

Banaji, S. (2010). *South Asian Media Cultures: Audiences, Representations, Contexts.* Anthem Press.

Barthes, R. (1980). *S/Z: An Essay*. Siglo XXI.

Beer, D. D. (2008). Social network(ing) sites…revisiting the story so far: A response to Danah Boyd and Nicole Ellison. *Journal of Computer-Mediated Communication*, 13(2), 516–529. https://doi.org/10.1111/j.1083-6101.2008.00408.x.

Bennett, W. L., & Segerberg, A. (2012). The Logic of Connective Action: Digital Media and the Personalization of Contentious Politics. *Information, Communication and Society*, 15(5), 739–768. doi:10.1080/1369118X.2013.782330.

Bennett, W. L., Wells, C., & Freelon, D. (2011). Communicating civic engagement: Contrasting models of citizenship in the youth web sphere. *Journal of Communication*, 61(5), 835–856. https://doi.org/https://doi.org/10.1111/j.1460-2466.2011.01588.x.

Bernard, A. (2019). *Theory of the Hashtag* (V. A. Pakis, Trans.; English edition). Polity Press.

Bignell, J. (2002). *Media Semiotics: An Introduction* (Second edition). Manchester University Press. Distributed exclusively in the U.S.A. by Palgrave.

Bloom, N., Liang, J., Roberts, J., & Ying, Z. J. (2015). Does working from home work? Evidence from a Chinese experiment. *Quarterly Journal of Economics*, 130(1), 165–218. https://doi.org/10.1093/qje/qju032.

Boulianne, S. (2009). Does Internet Use Affect Engagement? A Meta-Analysis of Research. *Political Communication*, 26(2), 193–211. https://doi.org/10.1080/10584600902854363.

Boyd, A., & McEwan, B. (2024). Viral paradox: The intersection of "me too" and #MeToo. *New Media and Society*, 26(6), 3454–3471. https://doi.org/10.1177/14614448221099187.

Boyd, D. M., & Ellison, N. B. (2007). Social Network Sites: Definition, History, and Scholarship. *Journal of Computer-Mediated Communication*, 13(1), 210–230. https://doi.org/10.1111/j.1083-6101.2007.00393.x.

Bronwen, T. (2014). 140 characters in search of a story: Twitterfiction as an emerging narrative form. In Bell, B., Ensslin, A., & Rustad, H.K. (Eds.), *Analyzing Digital Fiction*. Routledge.

Burgess, J., & Green, J. (2018). *YouTube: Online Video and Participatory Culture* (2nd ed.). John Wiley & Sons.

Carr, C. T., & Hayes, R. A. (2015). Social Media: Defining, Developing, and Divining. *Atlantic Journal of Communication*, 23(1), 46–65. https://doi.org/10.1080/15456870.2015.972282.

Cascio, W. F., & Shurygailo, S. (2003). E-Leadership and virtual teams. *Organizational Dynamics*, 31(4), 362–376. https://doi.org/10.1016/S0090-2616(02)00130-4.
Castells, M. (2015). *Networks of Outrage and Hope: Social Movements in the Internet Age*. John Wiley & Sons.
Chen, Z., Oh, P., & Chen, A. (2021). The Role of Online Media in Mobilizing Large-Scale Collective Action. *Social Media and Society*, 7(3). https://doi.org/10.1177/20563051211033808.
Cho, A., Byrne, J., & Pelter, Z. (2020). *Digital Civic Engagement by Young People*. UNICEF Office of Global Insight and Policy. Digital civic engagement by young people | UNICEF
Choudhury, P., Foroughi, C., & Larson, B. Z. (2021). Work-from-anywhere: The productivity effects of geographic flexibility. *Strategic Management Journal*, 42(4), 655–683.
Costa, P., Graça, A. M., Santos, C., Marques-Quinteiro, P., & Rico, R. (2021). Teamworking virtually: business as usual? *European Journal of Work and Organizational Psychology*, 30(5), 619–623.
Darmawan, C., Syaifullah, S., & Anggraeni, L. (2016). The development of civic engagement to empower student potential through entrepreneurial student program. 1st UPI International Conference on Sociology Education, 385–388.
Dhingra, M., & Mudgal, R.K. (2019). Historical evolution of social media: An overview. *International Conference on Advances in Engineering Science Management & Technology (ICAESMT)-2019*.
Diller, E.C. (2001). *Citizens in Service: The Challenge of Delivering Civic Engagement Training to National Service Programs*. Corporation for National Service National Fellowship Program.
Duarte, D. L., & Snyder, N. T. (2006). *Mastering Virtual Teams: Strategies, Tools, and Techniques That Succeed*. Jossey-Bass.
Dubois, E., Minaeian, S., Paquet-Labelle, A., & Beaudry, S. (2020). Who to trust on social media: How opinion leaders and seekers avoid disinformation and echo chambers. *Social Media and Society*, 6(2), 1–30. https://doi.org/10.1177/2056305120913993.
Dwivedi, Y.K., Rana, N.P., Chen, H., & Williams, M.D. (2011). A meta-analysis of the Unified Theory of Acceptance and Use of Technology (UTAUT). In Nüttgens, M., Gadatsch, A., Kautz, K., Schirmer, I., & Blinn, N. (Eds.), *Governance and Sustain-Ability in Information Systems: IFIP Advances in Information and Communication Technology*, 366. https://doi.org/10.1007/978-3-642-24148-2_10.
Earl, J., & Kimport, K. (2011). *Digitally Enabled Social Change: Activism in the Internet Age*. MIT Press.
Ebrahim, N. A., Ahmed, S., & Taha, Z. (2009). Virtual teams: a literature review. *Australian Journal of Basic and Applied Sciences*, 3(3), 2653–2669.
Edwards, Mandy (2015). How Social Media Has Changed How We Communicate. *Millennial CEO*. Future of Work (fowmedia.com)
Edwards, S. M. (2011). A Social Media Mindset. *Journal of Interactive Advertising*, 12 (1), 1–3. https://doi.org/10.1080/15252019.2011.10722186.
Ehrlich, T. (2000). *Civic Responsibility and Higher Education* (American Council on Education Oryx Press Series on Higher Ed) (The ACE series on higher education). Rowman & Littlefield Publishers.
Ekman, J. & Amnå, E. (2012). Political participation and civic engagement: Towards a new typology. *Human Affairs*, 22(3), 283–300. https://doi.org/10.2478/s13374-012-0024-1.
Ellison, N.B., & Boyd, D. (2013). Sociality through Social Network Sites. *The Oxford Handbook of Internet Studies*, 151–172. https://doi.org/10.1093/oxfordhb/9780199589074.013.0008.

Eurofound. (2020). *Living, Working and COVID-19*, COVID-19 series. Publications Office of the European Union.

European Commission. (2021). *NextGenerationEU: Europe's recovery plan.* European Commission. Retrieved from https://ec.europa.eu/info/strategy/recovery-plan-europe_en.

Federal Communications Commission (FCC). (2020). *Lifeline Program for Low-Income Consumers.* Federal Communication Commission. Retrieved from https://broadbandusa.ntia.gov/resources/federal/federal-funding/federal-communications-commission-lifeline#:~:text=Program%20Overview,%2C%20family%2C%20and%20emergency%20services.

Fileborn, Bianca; Loney-Howes, Rachel. (Eds.). (2019). *#MeToo and the Politics of Social Change.* Palgrave Macmillan.

Galston, W. A. (2001). Political Knowledge, Political Engagement, and Civic Education. *Annual Review of Political Science*, 4, 217–234.

Ganguli, Kisari Mohan. (1993). *The Mahabharata.* Munshiram Manoharlal, New Delhi. (First published in 1883)

Gerbaudo, P. (2012). *Tweets and the Streets: Social Media and Contemporary Activism.* Pluto Press.

Gerbaudo, P. (2017). Social media teams as digital vanguards: the question of leadership in the management of key Facebook and Twitter accounts of Occupy Wall Street, Indignados and UK Uncut. *Information, Communication and Society*, 20(2), 185–202. https://doi.org/10.1080/1369118X.2016.1161817.

Gibson C. (2000). *From Inspiration to Participation: A Review of Perspectives on Youth Civic Engagement.* Carnegie Corporation of New York.

Gibson, C. B., & Gibbs, J. L. (2006). Unpacking the Concept of Virtuality: The Effects of Geographic Dispersion, Electronic Dependence, Dynamic Structure, and National Diversity on Team Innovation. *Administrative Science Quarterly*, 51(3), 451–495. https://doi.org/10.2189/asqu.51.3.451.

Gilson, L. L., Maynard, M. T., Jones Young, N. C., Vartiainen, M., & Hakonen, M. (2015). Virtual Teams Research: 10 Years, 10 Themes, and 10 Opportunities. *Journal of Management*, 41(5), 1313–1337. https://doi.org/10.1177/0149206314559946.

Golden, T. D., Vega, R. P., & Dino, R. N. (2021). Telework and the socialization paradox: The role of relative telework arrangements. *Journal of Vocational Behavior*, 126, 103518.

Gordon, E., Baldwin-Philippi, J., & Balestra, M. (2013). Why we engage: How theories of human behavior contribute to our understanding of civic engagement in a digital era. *Berkman Center Research Publication*, 21, 1–29. https://doi.org/10.2139/ssrn.2343762.

Goswami, M. P. (2018). Social media and hashtag activism. *Liberty Dignity and Change in Journalism*, 1, 252–262.

Gregory, S. (2010). Cameras everywhere: Ubiquitous video documentation of human rights, new forms of video advocacy, and considerations of safety, security, dignity, and consent. *Journal of Human Rights Practice*, 2(2), 191–207. https://doi.org/10.1093/jhuman/huq002.

Guess, A., Nyhan, B., & Reifler, J. (2018). *Selective Exposure to Misinformation: Evidence from the Consumption of Fake News during the 2016 US Presidential Campaign.* [Working Paper]. Princeton University.

Hampton, K., & Wellman, B. (2003). Neighboring in Netville: How the Internet Supports Community and Social Capital in a Wired Suburb. *City and Community*, 2(4), 277–311. https://doi.org/10.1046/j.1535-6841.2003.00057.x.

Hertel, G., Geister, S., & Konradt, U. (2005). Managing virtual teams: A review of current empirical research. *Human Resource Management Review*, 15(1), 69–95. https://doi.org/10.1016/j.hrmr.2005.01.002.

Hockin-Boyers, H., & Clifford-Astbury, C. (2021). The politics of #diversifyyourfeed in the context of Black Lives Matter. *Feminist Media Studies*, 21(3), 504–509. https://doi.org/10.1080/14680777.2021.1925727.

Huberman, B.A., Romero, D.M., & Wu, F. (2008). Social Networks that Matter: Twitter Under the Microscope. *Information Systems: Behavioral and Social Methods.* https://doi.org/10.48550/arXiv.0812.1045.

Hu, Y., Manikonda, L., & Kambhampati, S. (2014). What we Instagram: A first analysis of Instagram photo content and user types. *Proceedings of the International AAAI Conference on Web and Social Media*, 8(1), 595–598.

Hylton, M. E. (2018). The role of civic literacy and social empathy on rates of civic engagement among university students. *Journal of Higher Education Outreach and Engagement*, 22(1), 87–106. https://eric.ed.gov/?id=EJ1175772.

International Telecommunication Union (ITU). (2020). *Measuring Digital Development: Facts and Figures 2020.*

Jenkins, H. (2006). *Convergence Culture: Where Old and New Media Collide.* NYU Press.

Jha, C.K., & Kodila-Tedika, O. (2020). Does Social Media Promote Democracy? Some Empirical Evidence. *Journal of Policy Modeling*, 271–290. https://doi.org/10.1016/j.jpolmod.2019.05.010.

Jisha K, & Jebakumar (2014). WhatsApp: A trendsetter in mobile communication among Chennai youth. *IOSR Journal of Humanities and Social Science*, 19(9), 1–6.

Johnson, B. L. (2003). Ethical Obligations in a Tragedy of the Commons. *Environmental Values, 12*(3), 271–287. https://doi.org/10.3197/096327103129341324.

Kamuni, N., Shah, H., Chintala, S., Kunchakuri, N., & Alla, S. (2024, February). Enhancing end-to-end multi-task dialogue systems: A study on intrinsic motivation reinforcement learning algorithms for improved training and adaptability. *2024 IEEE 18th International Conference on Semantic Computing (ICSC)*, 335–340. IEEE.

Katz, R. C. (1990). *Arjuna in the Mahabharata: Where Krishna is, there is Victory* (1st Indian ed). Motilal Banarsidass.

Kelly, K. (n.d.). https://perell.com/podcast/kevin-kelly-seeing-the-future/

Kir, S. (2020). *New Media and Visual Communication in Social Networks.* IGI Global.

Kiran, P., & Srivastava, A. (2018). WhatsApp and its impact on the social life of youngsters: a perspective. *Management Insight*, 14(1), 57–64. https://doi.org/10.21844/mijia.14.01.9.

Kniffin, K. M., Narayanan, J., Anseel, F., Antonakis, J., Ashford, S. P., Bakker, A. B., Bamberger, P., Bapuji, H., Bhave, D. P., Choi, V. K., Creary, S. J., Demerouti, E., Flynn, F. J., Gelfand, M. J., Greer, L. L., Johns, G., Kesebir, S., Klein, P. G., Lee, S. Y., Ozcelik, H., … Vugt, M. V. (2021). COVID-19 and the workplace: Implications, issues, and insights for future research and action. *American Psychologist*, 76(1), 63–77. https://doi.org/10.1037/amp0000716.

Kumar, P., Chaudhary, B., Yadav, N., Devi, S., Pareek, A., Alla, S., Kajal, F., Nowrouzi-Kia, B., Chattu, V. K., & Gupta, M. M. (2023). Recent Advances in Research and Management of Human Monkeypox Virus: An Emerging Global Health Threat. *Viruses*, 15(4), 937. https://doi.org/10.3390/v15040937.

Kumar, V., Dixit, A., Javalgi, R. G., & Dass, M. (2020). Research framework, strategies, and applications of intelligent agent technologies (IATs) in marketing. *Journal of the Academy of Marketing Science*, 48, 24–45. https://doi.org/10.1007/s11747-015-0426-9.

Lakshminarayanan, V., Ravikumar, A., Sriraman, H., Alla, S., & Chattu, V. K. (2023). Health Care Equity Through Intelligent Edge Computing and Augmented Reality/Virtual Reality: A Systematic Review. *Journal of Multidisciplinary Healthcare*, 16, 2839–2859. https://doi.org/10.2147/JMDH.S419923.

Lee, Y., & Circella, G. (2019). ICT, millennials' lifestyles and travel choices. *Advances in Transport Policy and Planning*, 3, 107–141. Academic Press. https://doi.org/10.1016/bs.atpp.2019.08.002.

Leonardi, P. M., Treem, J. W., & Jackson, M. H. (2010). The Connectivity Paradox: Using Technology to Both Decrease and Increase Perceptions of Distance in Distributed Work Arrangements. *Journal of Applied Communication Research*, 38(1), 85–105. https://doi.org/10.1080/00909880903483599.

Liao C. H. (2023). Exploring the Influence of Public Perception of Mass Media Usage and Attitudes towards Mass Media News on Altruistic Behavior. *Behavioral Sciences (Basel, Switzerland)*, 13(8), 621. https://doi.org/10.3390/bs13080621.

Liao, S., & Luqiu, L. R. (2022). #MeToo in China: The Dynamic of Digital Activism against Sexual Assault and Harassment in Higher Education. *Signs: Journal of Women in Culture and Society*, 47(3), 741–764. https://doi.org/10.1086/717712.

Lipnack, J., & Stamps, J. (2000). *Virtual Teams: People Working Across Boundaries with Technology*. John Wiley & Sons.

Livingstone, S., & Helsper, E. (2007). Gradations in digital inclusion: children, young people and the digital divide. *New Media and Society*, 9(4), 671–696. https://doi.org/10.1177/1461444807080335.

Louis, F., & Mohamed, S. (2024). Cyberbullying and Online Harassment: A Multifaceted Examination of Digital Platform Violence. *Journal of Sexual Aggression*, 1–15. https://doi.org/10.48550/arXiv.2404.18989.

Luckin, R., & Du Boulay, B. (1999). The importance of the learner's perspective in the design of educational software. *Proceedings of the 9th International Conference on Artificial Intelligence in Education*, 35–42. IOS Press.

Manovich, Lev. (2001). *The Language of New Media*. MIT Press.

Marinoni, G., Van't Land, H., & Jensen, T. (2020). *The Impact of COVID-19 on Higher Education Around the World. IAU Global Survey Report*. iau_covid19_and_he_survey_report_final_may_2020.pdf (iau-aiu.net)

Mark, G., Voida, S., & Cardello, A. (2012). "A pace not dictated by electrons": An empirical study of work without email. *Proceedings of the SIGCHI Conference on Human Factors in Computing Systems*.

Marks, M. A., Mathieu, J. E., & Zaccaro, S. J. (2001). A Temporally Based Framework and Taxonomy of Team Processes. *The Academy of Management Review*, 26(3), 356–376. https://doi.org/10.2307/259182.

Martins, L. L., Gilson, L. L., & Maynard, M. T. (2004). Virtual teams: What do we know and where do we go from here? *Journal of Management*, 30(6), 805–835. https://doi.org/10.1016/j.jm.2004.05.002.

Maruping, L. M., Bala, H., Venkatesh, V., & Brown, S. A. (2017). Going beyond intention: Integrating behavioral expectation into the unified theory of acceptance and use of technology. *Journal of the Association for Information Science and Technology*, 68(3), 623–637. https://doi.org/10.1002/asi.23699.

Maruping, L. M., Zhang, X., & Venkatesh, V. (2009). Role of collective ownership and coding standards in coordinating expertise in software project teams. *European Journal of Information Systems*, 18(4), 355–371. https://doi.org/10.1057/ejis.2009.24.

Mavrodieva, A. V., Rachman, O. K., Harahap, V. B., & Shaw, R. (2019). Role of social media as a soft power tool in raising public awareness and engagement in addressing climate change. *Climate*, 7(10), 122. https://doi.org/10.3390/cli7100122.

Mazmanian, M., Orlikowski, W. J., & Yates, J. (2013). The autonomy paradox: The implications of mobile email devices for knowledge professionals. *Organization Science*, 24(5), 1337–1357. https://doi.org/10.1287/orsc.1120.0806.

McQuail, D. (2010). *McQuail's mass communication theory* (6th ed.). Sage Publications.
Mohammadi E, Thelwall M, Kwasny M, Holmes K.L. (2018). Academic information on Twitter: A user survey. *PLoS one*, 13(5), 1–18. https://doi.org/10.1371/journal.pone.0197265.
Mohammadi SH, Norazizan S, Shahvandi A. R. (2011). Civic engagement, citizen participation and quality of governance in Iran. *Journal of Human Ecology*, 36(3), 211–216.
Morozov, E. (2009, May 19). The Brave New World of Slacktivism. *Foreign Policy*. https://foreignpolicy.com/2009/05/19/the-brave-new-world-of-slacktivism/.
Mossberger, K., Tolbert, C. J., & Stansbury, M. (2003). *Virtual Inequality: Beyond the Digital Divide*. Georgetown University Press.
Mukherjee, S., & Roy, A. (2024). Worldwide protests held over Indian trainee medic's rape and murder. *Reuters.com*. https://www.reuters.com/world/india/worldwide-protests-held-over-indian-trainee-medics-rape-death-2024-09-08/.
Murthy, Dhiraj (2013). *Social Communication in the Twitter Age*. Polity Press.
Nathan, A. (2015). When Bhima tweeted his epic story. *The Hindu*. https://www.thehindu.com/features/magazine/when-bhima-tweeted-his-epic-story/article6966093.ece
Norris, P. (2001). *Digital Divide: Civic Engagement, Information Poverty, and the Internet Worldwide*. Cambridge University Press.
Obar, Jonathan A., Zube, P., & Lampe, C. (2012). Advocacy 2.0: An Analysis of How Advocacy Groups in the United States Perceive and Use Social Media as Tools for Facilitating Civic Engagement and Collective Action. *Journal of Information Policy*, 2, 1–25. https://doi.org/10.5325/jinfopoli.2.2012.0001.
O'Connor, J. S. (2006). Civic Engagement in Higher Education. *Change: The Magazine of Higher Learning*, 38(5), 52–58. https://doi.org/10.3200/CHNG.38.5.52-58.
Oldenburg, Ray. (1999). *Great Good Place*. Marlow.
Olson Jr, M. (1971). *The Logic of Collective Action: Public Goods and the Theory of Groups, with a new preface and appendix* (Vol. 124). Harvard University Press.
Ortiz, J., Young, A., Myers, M., Bedeley, R. T., Carbaugh, D., Chughtai, H., & Wigdor, A. (2019). Giving Voice to the Voiceless: The Use of Digital Technologies by Marginalized Groups. *Communications of the Association for Information Systems*, 45(1), 20–38. Article 2. https://doi.org/10.17705/1CAIS.04502.
Otieno, P. (2024). The impact of social media on political polarization. *Journal of Communication*, 4(1), 56–68.
Özdemir, M. (2024). The Impact of Twitter on Digital Diplomacy in the Context of International Media. In *Digital Diplomacy in the OSCE Region: From Theory to Practice* (pp. 89–100). Springer Nature Switzerland.
Panicker, P. (2009). *Bhimsen*.
Pasek, J., More, E., & Romer, D. (2009). Realizing the social Internet? Online social networking meets offline civic engagement. *Journal of Information Technology and Politics*, 6(3–4), 197–215. https://doi.org/10.1080/19331680902996403.
Pawar, K. S., & Sharifi, S. (1997). Physical or virtual team collocation: Does it matter? *International Journal of Production Economics*, 52(3), 283–290. https://doi.org/10.1016/S0925-5273(97)89241-9.
Putnam, R. D. (1993). *Making Democracy Work: Civic Traditions in Modern Italy*. Princeton University Press.
Putnam, R. D. (2000). *Bowling Alone: The Collapse and Revival of American Community*. Simon & Schuster.
Quan-Haase, Anabel; Mendes, Kaitlynn; Ho, Dennis; Lake, Olivia; Nau, Charlotte; Pieber, Darryl (2021). Mapping# MeToo: A synthesis review of digital feminist

research across social media platforms. *New Media and Society*, 23(6), 1700–1720. https://doi.org/10.1177/1461444820984457.
Raynes-Goldie, K., & Walker, L. (2008). Our space: Online civic engagement tools for youth. In W. L. Bennett (Ed.), *Civic Life online: Learning How Digital Media can Engage Youth* 161–188. MIT Press.
Rheingold, H. (2002). *Smart mobs: The next social revolution*. Perseus Publishing.
Rheingold, H. (2009). https://www.youtube.com/watch?v=V-92xiczDC8
Robinson, L., Cotten, S. R., Ono, H., Quan-Haase, A., Mesch, G., Chen, W., … Stern, M. J. (2015). Digital inequalities and why they matter. *Information, Communication and Society*, 18(5), 569–582. https://doi.org/10.1080/1369118X.2015.1012532.
Rosenfeld, A., Sina, S., Sarne, D., Avidov, O., & Kraus, S. (2018). WhatsApp usage patterns and prediction of demographic characteristics without access to message content. *Demographic Research*, 39(1), 647–670. https://doi.org/10.4054/DemRes.2018.39.22.
Roy, Nalanda, ed. (2022). *Nonviolent Resistances in the Contemporary World: Case Studies from India, Poland, and Turkey*. Routledge.
Rudin, Michael. (2011). *From Hemingway to Twitterature: The Short and Shorter of It*. Michigan Publishing.
Scheurman, T. (2021). Comparing Social Media Content Regulation in the US and the EU: How the US Can Move Forward with Section 230 to Bolster Social Media Users' Freedom of Expression. *San Diego International Law Journal*, 23, 413.
Schlosser, A. E. (2020). Self-disclosure versus self-presentation on social media. *Current Opinion in Psychology*, 31, 1–6. https://doi.org/10.1016/j.copsyc.2019.06.025.
Schwab, K., & Malleret, T. (2020, July). *COVID-19: The Great Reset*. Forum publishing.
Sharma, G. D., Lijuan, W., & Alvi, A. K. (2020). Blockchain for supply chain management: A comprehensive survey. *IEEE Access*, 8, 118773–118788. https://doi.org/10.3390/su12187638.
Shirky, C. (2008). *Here Comes Everybody: The Power of Organizing Without Organizations*. New York: Penguin Group.
Skocpol, T. (2003). *Diminished Democracy: From Membership to Management in American Civic Life*. University of Oklahoma Press.
Skocpol, T., & Fiorina, M. P. (1999). *Civic Engagement in American Democracy*. Brookings Institution Press and Russell Sage Foundation.
Skoric, M. M., Zhu, Q., Goh, D., & Pang, N. (2016). Social media and citizen engagement: A meta-analytic review. *New Media and Society*, 18(9), 1817–1839. https://doi.org/10.1177/1461444815616221.
Smith, A. C., Thomas, E., Snoswell, C. L., Haydon, H., Mehrotra, A., Clemensen, J., & Caffery, L. J. (2020). Telehealth for global emergencies: Implications for coronavirus disease 2019 (COVID-19). *Journal of Telemedicine and Telecare*, 26(5), 309–313. https://doi.org/10.1177/1357633X20916567.
Soni, A., Alla, S., Dodda, S., & Volikatla, H. (2024). Advancing Household Robotics: Deep Interactive Reinforcement Learning for Efficient Training and Enhanced Performance. *Journal of Electrical Systems* 20(3). https://doi.org/10.52783/jes.1510.
Sreedharan, C. (2014). *Epic Retold: #Mahabharata #Twitter Fiction #Bhima #140 Characters*. HarperCollins Publishers.
Sreedharan, C. (2019). *The Autobiography of a Villain: Duryodhana's Story*. Independent Publishing Network.
Stieglitz, S., & Dang-Xuan, L. (2013). Social media and political communication: a social media analytics framework. *Social Network Analysis and Mining*, 3(4), 1277–1291. https://doi.org/10.1007/s13278-012-0079-3.
Sunstein, C. R. (2001). *Republic.com*. Princeton University Press.

Susskind, J. (2018). *Future Politics: Living Together in a World Transformed by Tech*. Oxford University Press.

Tarhini, A., Hone, K., & Liu, X. (2017). User acceptance towards web-based learning systems: Investigating the role of social, organizational and individual factors in European higher education. *Procedia Computer Science*, 113, 568–575. https://doi.org/10.1016/j.procs.2013.05.026.

Taylor, A. K., & Alla, S. (2018). Influence of reward systems on motivation-pros and cons based on current literature. *Proceedings of the International Annual Conference of the American Society for Engineering Management*, 1–8. American Society for Engineering Management (ASEM).

Taylor, A. K., & Alla, S. (2018). Managing conflict towards improving team performance-what we know so far. *Proceedings of the International Annual Conference of the American Society for Engineering Management*, 1–6. American Society for Engineering Management (ASEM).

Thomas, Bronwen. (2015). *Narrative: The Basics*. Taylor & Francis.

Tidmarsh, A. (2014). *Genre: A Guide to Writing for Stage and Screen*. Bloomsbury Methuen Drama.

Tierney, Therese. (2013). *The Public Space of Social Media: Connected Cultures of the Network Society*. Routledge.

Townsend, A. M., DeMarie, S. M., & Hendrickson, A. R. (1998). Virtual teams: Technology and the workplace of the future. *Academy of Management Executive*, 12(3), 17–29. https://doi.org/10.5465/ame.1998.1109047.

Tufekci, Z. (2012). Social Media and the Decision to Participate in Political Protest: Observations from Tahrir Square. *Journal of Communication*, 62(2), 363–379. https://doi.org/10.1111/j.1460-2466.2012.01629.x.

Tufekci, Z. (2017). *Twitter and Tear Gas: The Power and Fragility of Networked Protest*. Yale University Press.

Unwin, T. (2012). *Social Media and Democracy: Critical Reflections*. [Background Paper]. Commonwealth Parliamentary Conference, Colombo.

Valenzuela, S. (2013). Unpacking the Use of Social Media for Protest Behavior: The Roles of Information, Opinion Expression, and Activism. *American Behavioral Scientist*, 57(7), 920–942. https://doi.org/10.1177/0002764213479375.

Van den Boomen, M. V. T. (2014). *Transcoding the Digital: How Metaphors Matter in New Media*. [Doctoral thesis 1 (Research UU / Graduation UU), Utrecht University]. Institute of Network Cultures.

Van Dijk, J. A. (2020). *The Digital Divide*. Polity.

Venkatesh, V., Morris, M. G., Davis, G. B., & Davis, F. D. (2003). User Acceptance of Information Technology: Toward a Unified View. *MIS Quarterly*, 27(3), 425–478.

Verba, S., Schlozman, K. L., & Brady, H. E. (1995). *Voice and Equality: Civic Voluntarism in American Politics*. Harvard University Press.

Verduyn, P., Ybarra, O., Résibois, M., Jonides, J., & Kross, E. (2017). Do social network sites enhance or undermine subjective well-being? A critical review. *Social Issues and Policy Review*, 11(1), 274–302. https://doi.org/10.1111/sipr.12033.

Vidgen, R., & Wang, X. (2009). Coordinating and Communicating in Agile Software Development Projects. *Journal of Systems and Software*, 82(11), 1785–1795. https://doi.org/10.1016/j.jss.2012.02.017.

Vosoughi, S., Roy, D., & Aral, S. (2018). The spread of true and false news online. *Science (New York, N.Y.)*, 359(6380), 1146–1151. https://doi.org/10.1126/science.aap9559.

Vygotsky, L. S. (1986). *Thought and Language* (A. Kozulin, Ed. & Trans.). MIT Press. (Original work published 1934)

Warschauer, M., & Matuchniak, T. (2010). New Technology and Digital Worlds: Analyzing Evidence of Equity in Access, Use, and Outcomes. *Review of Research in Education*, 34(1), 179–225. https://doi.org/10.3102/0091732X09349791.

Warren, A. M., Sulaiman, A., & Jaafar, N. I. (2014). Social media effects on fostering online civic engagement and building citizen trust and trust in institutions. *Government Information Quarterly*, 31(2), 291–301. https://doi.org/10.1016/j.giq.2013.11.007.

Webster, A., Svalastog, A. L., & Allgaier, J. (2020). Mapping new digital landscapes. *Information, Communication and Society*, 23(8), 1100–1105. https://doi.org/10.1080/1369118X.2020.1784507.

Weller, K., Bruns, A., Burgess, J., Mahrt, M., & Puschmann, C. (2014). Twitter and Society: An Introduction. *Digital Formations*, 89, xxix–xxxviii.

Wells, A. (2018). Telephone and Face-to-Face Communication. *The Tech Professional's Guide to Communicating in a Global Workplace*. Apress, 107–134. https://doi.org/10.1007/978-1-4842-3471-6_6.

Whitworth, E. and Biddle, R. (2007). "The Social Nature of Agile Teams," *Agile 2007 (AGILE 2007)*, Washington, DC, USA, 2007, 26–36, doi:10.1109/AGILE.2007.60.

Williams, M. D., Rana, N. P., & Dwivedi, Y. K. (2015). The unified theory of acceptance and use of technology (UTAUT): A literature review. *Journal of Enterprise Information Management*, 28(3), 443–488. https://doi.org/10.1108/JEIM-09-2014-0088.

Winder, D. (2007). Back to basics: social bookmarking. *Information World Review*, 29–31.

World Bank. (2020). *Annual report 2024*. https://www.worldbank.org/en/about/annual-report.

Wucker, M. (2020). *The Digital Transformation of Labor: The Role of Social Media in the 21st century*. Routledge.

Zakaria, N., Amelinckx, A., & Wilemon, D. (2004). Working Together Apart? Building a Knowledge-Sharing Culture for Global Virtual Teams. *Creativity and Innovation Management*, 13(1), 15–29. https://doi.org/10.1111/j.1467-8691.2004.00290.x.

Zhuravskaya, E., Petrova, M., & Enikolopov, R. (2020). Political effects of the internet and social media. *Annual Review of Economics*, 12(1), 415–438. https://doi.org/10.2139/ssrn.3439957.

Zuboff, S. (2019). The Age of Surveillance Capitalism: The Fight for a Human Future at the New Frontier of Power. *Social Theory Re-wired*, 98(2), 202–213. https://doi.org/10.1093/sf/soz037.

INDEX

For Product Safety Concerns and Information please contact our EU
representative GPSR@taylorandfrancis.com
Taylor & Francis Verlag GmbH, Kaufingerstraße 24, 80331 München, Germany

www.ingramcontent.com/pod-product-compliance
Ingram Content Group UK Ltd.
Pitfield, Milton Keynes, MK11 3LW, UK
UKHW021307260926
475702UK00048B/775
9781041038863

Disability & International Development

Malcolm MacLachlan • Leslie Swartz
Editors

Disability & International Development

Towards Inclusive Global Health

Springer

Editors
Malcolm MacLachlan
Centre for Global Health Group & School of Psychology
University of Dublin
Trinity College
Dublin 2
Ireland
malcolm.maclachlan@tcd.ie

Leslie Swartz
Department of Psychiatry
University of Stellenbosch
Cape Town
Tygerberg
7505 South Africa
lswartz@sun.ac.za

ISBN 978-0-387-93843-1 e-ISBN 978-0-387-93840-0
DOI 10.1007/978-0-387-93840-0
Springer Dordrecht Heidelberg London New York

Library of Congress Control Number: 2009926304

Printed on acid-free paper

Springer is part of Springer Science+Business Media (www.springer.com)

We dedicate this book to all those who by reason of their marginalization or social exclusion will not have an opportunity to read it.

Foreword

Until fairly recently, the fields of disability studies and international development were viewed as completely separate. Much of what we know about disability and contemporary approaches to disability was researched and written about in wealthier countries, and it remains true to say that the major debates about disability are dominated by people in such countries. In the international development world, furthermore, the issue of disability was almost completely ignored. Plans for economic development and empowerment of the poorest of the poor in lower-income settings rarely considered issues faced specifically by disabled people.

There is an enormous irony to this situation. We know that the vast majority of disabled people live in low and middle income countries. We also know that there are strong links between disability and poverty worldwide. Disabled people are less likely to be adequately skilled for the workplace, they are more likely to be denied access to work because of prejudice and stigma, and disability itself is costly. Particularly in countries where the state does not provide adequate services and care (and this is the case in most countries in the world), disabled people and their families bear an enormous burden of care and loss of opportunity to work because of care burdens. Many conditions in the majority world, including war, internal displacement, communicable diseases (including HIV/AIDS, malaria and tuberculosis), parasitic infections, famine and civil strife, and lack of access to clean water are all factors which may dispose people to disabilities. It is therefore crucial that the two fields of disability studies and development studies begin to talk to one another so that both can contribute to improving the lives of people (and not only disabled people) worldwide.

There are some encouraging signs emerging. The United Nations Declaration on the Rights of Disabled Persons had been promulgated after a long consultative process, and the Global Partnership on Disability and Development has recently been established. In order for such initiatives to succeed, however, it is crucial that we learn more about disability and development issues on global context. This book is especially welcome in that it covers disability issues in a range of low and middle income countries. It provides a refreshing mix of case studies of country level activities, descriptions of emerging disability research networks and initiatives, and theoretical papers looking at disability research more generally.

It is crucial that disability activists and researchers worldwide join hands to keep disability firmly on the international development agenda, and to infuse disability studies with knowledge about the way in which disability is experienced and dealt with by most disabled people in the world. This book is an important step to reaching these goals, and it is my pleasure to welcome its publication and the possibilities it encapsulates. This book is also a challenge to all of us to do more and to learn more about disability and international development and it is essential that we pay this book the compliment of taking the work of understanding disability and international development forward.

I congratulate the editors and authors of this landmark volume for their excellent and important work. May this be the start of a fundamental change in how we view disability and international development

Cape Town
March 2009

Kudakwashe Dube
Chair of the Global Partnership on Disability and Development, and CEO of the Secretariat of the African Decade for Persons with Disabilities

Acknowledgements

An edited book is a collective, but not necessarily a unified, expression of interest in a particular theme. We welcome both this collectivity and the variation within it; as it reflects a much wider community of individuals and groups who share a concern with realizing the rights of persons with disability. As researchers and practitioners we have been inspired by a range of people, especially those in civil society who have done so much to develop this area and have provided such important leadership in recent years. Especially important to shaping our own thinking have been A.K. Dube, Chair of the Global Partnership on Disability and Development, and CEO of the Secretariat of the African Decade for Persons with Disabilities, who also kindly agreed to write a forward for this book; Rachel Kachaje of Disabled People International; Alexander Phiri of the Southern African Federation on Disability; Elias Ngongondo of the Malawian Ministry of Disabled Persons and the Elderly; and Mzolisi ka Toni of Disabled People South Africa.

The production of this book has also been supported by our colleagues at Stellenbosch University's Department of Psychology and Centre for Rehabilitation Studies; and Trinity College Dublin's School of Psychology and Centre for Global Health, "especially from Michael O'Toole, Hasheem Mannan and Eilish Mc Auliffe and Marcella Maughan". Diarmuid McClean, Vincent O'Neill and David Weakliam, all in Irish Aid, encouraged the Centre's development of work in this area, as have grants from Irish Aid, the Health Research Board (Ireland), the Irish Research Council for Humanities and Social Sciences and the European Union's FP7 programme. Collaborations with Aidan Leavy of International Services (Ireland), the Dochas Disability and Development Group, and especially consortium partners on the A-PODD and EquitAble projects, have also been very important in helping to develop our work in the Centre for Global Health. Stellenbosch University generously permitted Leslie Swartz to be seconded to the South African Human Sciences Research Council (HSRC) for three years, and it was at the HSRC that he developed his interest in disability studies. Emma Sherry (of Capital Letters) provided us with speedy and professional copy editing, and Ian Marvinney and Khristine Queja at Springer have been supportive and encouraging throughout. We should also like to thank our partners and families for their patience.

Contents

List of Tables

List of Figures

List of Boxes

Author Biographies

Joanne Barratt is a speech-language pathologist and audiologist working in the Speech Therapy Department at the University of the Witwatersrand, Johannesburg, South Africa. Joanne has both clinical and research experience in a rural area, and has a special interest in disability, primary healthcare, and the interplay of contextual and cultural factors on health-seeking behaviours. Joanne is currently working on her PhD, documenting the narratives of adults living with acquired disabilities in a rural setting in order to expand on our knowledge regarding the socio-cultural processes associated with disability in rural areas and to guide the training of healthcare practitioners.

Mary Anne Burke has published widely in the areas of public policy, social conditions and human rights. She developed Gender-based Analysis (GBA) and social inclusion tools, including the "*BIAS FREE* Framework", a tool for examining and eliminating biases that derive from social hierarchies, with Margrit Eichler. She has extensive experience as Senior Policy Analyst and Statistician in the Canadian government for Statistics, Canada; Status of Women; Health Canada; and Human Resources and Social Development Canada, and internationally for UNICEF and the Global Forum for Health Research. She is President of the *BIAS FREE* Co-operative, Inc. and Assistant Professor at OISE/UT.

Arne H. Eide is Chief Scientist at SINTEF Research Institute (Norway), Professor in rehabilitation at Sør-Trøndelag University College (Norway) and Honorary Professor at Stellenbosch University (South Africa). Eide has 20 years of experience in research and research collaboration in low-income countries, in particular southern Africa. His main research fields are disability statistics, studies on living conditions among people with disabilities, community-based rehabilitation and disability and poverty. He has been responsible for a number of national studies on living conditions among people with disabilities in Southern Africa.

Petra Engelbrecht is at present Executive Dean of the Faculty of Educational Sciences, North-West University, Potchefstroom campus, South Africa. She is an acknowledged researcher in the field of inclusive education as well as research capacity development in higher education. She has led and is still leading several international research projects funded by various agencies on equity in inclusive education as well as the implementation of inclusive education in school communities.

Siphokazi Gcaza is a Senior Lecturer at the Centre for Rehabilitation Studies (CRS) at Stellenbosch University. She obtained an MSc (Occupational Therapy) from the University of Cape Town. She has worked in the area of community based rehabilitation and childhood disability, and within the disability sector where she gained in-depth knowledge and experience in advocacy and formation of collaborative networks between the disability sector, government, and universities. Siphokazi has expanded her networks throughout Africa and internationally to contribute to building constructive engagements with strategic stakeholders for the equalization of opportunities for disabled people. Ms. Gcaza is currently the Chairperson of the African Community Based Rehabilitation Network (CAN) and a board member of the Global Partnership on Disability and Development (GPDD).

Marianne Griffiths studied at Dublin Institute of Technology where she received a BA (first class honours) in International Business and Languages (Spanish and French). She has worked with people with intellectual disabilities in a community residential setting for several years, providing care, promoting self-advocacy and encouraging the independence of the service users. She also worked providing family support to children and teenagers with intellectual disabilities living at home. She completed the MSc in Global Health in Trinity College Dublin where she received the Kevany Prize for academic excellence. As part of her Masters qualification she lived in Bolivia and researched advocacy and empowerment for people with disabilities.

Ansie Elizabeth Kitching is an educational psychologist and lecturer in the Faculty of Educational Sciences, North West University, Potchefstroom campus, South Africa, since 2004. She has 10 years experience in research and teaching in inclusive education. She is currently enrolled for a PhD in Community Psychology. The focus of her research is on the co-construction of enabling social contexts in school communities.

Mitchell Loeb, Msc is an epidemiologist with research experience from Canada, Norway, the United States and several developing countries in sub-Saharan Africa and Southeast Asia. At SINTEF Health Research, in Norway, he collaborated in a series of surveys of living conditions among people with disabilities in the southern African region (South Africa, Namibia, Zimbabwe, Malawi, Zambia and Mozambique). In 2005 he consulted for the World Bank in Indonesia to supervise disability data collections in support of the Indonesia Poverty Analysis Program. He also acted as disability data consultant for the Medical Committee Netherlands Vietnam (MCNV) in 2006 where he facilitated workshops to formalize a common understanding of disability, and harmonize the collection and management of disability data in Vietnam. He is currently a health scientist at the National Center for Health Statistics/CDC in the USA and is involved with the work of the Washington Group on Disability Statistics.

Mac MacLachlan is with the Centre for Global Health and School of Psychology at Trinity College Dublin, where he established the Dublin Psychoprosthetics Group (www.tcd.ie/psychoprosthetics). He is also Extraordinary Professor of

Disability and Development at the Centre for Rehabilitation Studies, Stellenbosch University, and Visiting Professor at the Department of Social Medicine and Global Health, Harvard University. Mac wants to promote inclusive global health and has particular interest in disability, international aid and cultural influences on healthcare. He pursues these through interdisciplinary social science with a strong interest in promoting research utilization. Before moving to Trinity Mac worked as a clinical psychologist and management consultant in the UK, and then as a lecturer at the University of Malawi. He is a co-founder of AfriNEAD (www.afrinead.org) and Principal Investigator on EquitAble (www.medicine.tcd.ie/global_health/research/projects/equitable.php) and A-PODD (www.A-PODD.org). He has worked with local and international NGOs and WHO, OECD, Unicef, and GDN.

Hasheem Mannan, PhD is a Marie Curie Fellow at the National Institute for Intellectual Disability and a research associate at the Centre for Global Health, Trinity College Dublin, Ireland. His international research experience incorporates projects for WHO (Geneva, Switzerland), the National Center for Health Statistics (Maryland, USA), and the National Disability Authority (Dublin, Ireland). He obtained his doctorate in Special Education with emphasis on disability policy and family studies from the University of Kansas and his Masters in Community Disability Studies for Developing Countries on a British Chevening Scholarship at the Centre for International Child Health, University College London.

Natalie Melling-Williams is a physiotherapist and has completed her Masters in Medical Sciences in Rehabilitation through the Centre for Rehabilitation Studies at Stellenbosch University. She now does project work with the Centre, and is currently primarily focused on the AfriNEAD project. The African Network on Evidence-to-Action in Disability (AfriNEAD) aims to link people with disabilities, academics, business people, governments and civil society in order to ensure that research evidence addresses, informs and guides the development of new and existing policies, programmes and products in and for Africa, so as to improve the quality of lives of people with disabilities on the ground.

Gubela Mji is a physiotherapist working at the Centre for Rehabilitation Studies at Stellenbosch University, Cape Town, South Africa. Gubela has experience in working in rural areas and amongst vulnerable groups such as homeless disabled people. She is engaged in various collaborative disability research projects with some Disabled People's Organizations and academics at local, continental and international levels. Gubela is also the chairperson for the African Network on Evidence-to-Action on Disability. She is currently working on her PhD, exploring the indigenous health knowledge carried by older Xhosa women.

Willy Nel is an educational psychologist and lecturer in the Faculty of Educational Sciences, North-West University, Potchefstroom campus, South Africa, since 2007. Willy is active in organized psychology through the Psychological Society of South Africa (PsySSA) and he serves on the South African Journal of Psychology as an associate editor. He is currently enrolled for a PhD and his research focuses on the provision of education support services for the ‡Khomani San (a South African indigenous First Peoples grouping).

Tone Øderud is a Senior Research Scientist and MSc at SINTEF Health Research in Norway. She has conducted research and development projects within the field of disability issues, service delivery systems, assistive technology, accessibility and universal design for 18 years. Ms. Øderud is currently involved in the development of local rehabilitation workshops providing wheelchairs and services to people with disabilities in Namibia and Zimbabwe. The workshops also empower people with disabilities by providing employment. She has special interest in development of assistive technology and services for people with disabilities focusing on user involvement.

Cliona O'Sullivan is a Lecturer in the School of Physiotherapy and Performance Science, University College Dublin. Since graduating in 1997, she has worked as a physiotherapist in a variety of clinical areas in the UK, Ireland and Burkina Faso and as a lecturer in the School of Physiotherapy, Trinity College Dublin. Her main research interests are in disability and rehabilitation; including childhood disabilities in low income countries. She is currently pursuing a PhD developing novel and objective methods of measurement and rehabilitation of disabilities associated with the upper limb. The work reported in her chapter in this book was supported by the Health Research Board, Ireland and Irish Aid.

Claire Penn is a speech language pathologist and currently holds an endowed Chair of Speech Pathology and Audiology at the University of eth Witwatersrand. She has undertaken research in areas of language disability, sign language and has a particular interest in the impact of stroke and head injury on individuals and their families. She has established the Health Communication project at Wits, which examines the interaction between health professionals and patients in a variety of settings and develops training programmes to facilitate communication. Particular interests include paediatric HIV/Aids, genetic counselling and research ethics. She was awarded the Order of Mapungubwe (Silver) in 2007 and was category winner of Shoprite Checkers Woman of the Year in 2008.

John Philander, Dphil, is deputy principal at Athlone School for the Blind in Cape Town, South Africa. He is a trained educational psychologist and has 15 years of experience of working with adolescents with visual impairment. His special interest is in the area of visual impairment, HIV risk, sexuality, special needs education and disability issues. His doctoral thesis (Stellenbosch University, 2008) is the first known study to evaluate an HIV prevention intervention for youth with visual impairments.

Andrea Pupulin is an international consultant dedicated to helping the most marginalized and unfortunate peoples. Following post-graduate studies in ethics, human rights theory, political philosophy and international development, he worked with orphans and street children in Brazil and in Egypt, and with Caritas, WHO and the Global Forum for Health Research. He is working with the *BIAS FREE* Framework on a UNICEF project in the Kyrgyz Republic, assessing the situation of disabled children and developing a national strategy for an inclusive Kyrgyzstan. He is currently Database Manager for the *BIAS FREE* Co-operative, Inc., and is researching exclusion of Roma peoples.

Poul Rohleder is a Senior lecturer in psychology at Anglia Ruskin University, UK. He trained and worked as a clinical psychologist in South Africa. He completed a doctorate at Stellenbosch University looking at organizational responses to HIV/AIDS as it affects persons with disabilities. His research interests include psychosocial aspects of HIV/AIDS and critical health psychology. He is currently working on a forthcoming co-edited volume with Leslie Swartz, Seth Kalichman and Leickness Simbayi, *HIV/AIDS in South Africa 25 Years On* (to be published by Springer).

Theresa Rouger, B.A., LL.B., is an international human rights lawyer and lectures on international law at Université Catholique, Lyon and Centre d'études franco-américain (C.E.F.A.M.), International School of Business Management, Lyon, France and U.S.A. She also lectures on the humanitarian Masters programme at the Université of Lyon 2, France. She is interested in international human rights, disability rights, gender rights, child protection rights and international law including business and human rights. She is currently working on a legal comparative disability project involving child rights with the Law Society of England and Wales. Other projects include a legal and social comparative disability project involving child rights with Handicap International, which will span across four African countries, and human rights and mental health research. She works as a legal human rights consultant for NGOs.

Leslie Swartz is a clinical psychologist and professor in psychology at Stellenbosch University. He is interested in public mental health, disability studies, and issues of identity in higher education. He is currently working on a co-edited volume on HIV and the social sciences in South Africa (Springer). He project managed and co-edited the first comprehensive volume on disability in South Africa (*Disability and Social Change*, HSRC Press, 2006) and current projects include work on HIV and disability, access to health services for disabled people in sub-Saharan Africa, and research capacity training for the Southern African Federation on Disability (SAFOD).

Patricia Thornton has undertaken research on disability and development in Papua New Guinea and latterly in Guyana, as a volunteer with Voluntary Service Overseas. In Papua New Guinea, she piloted methods of surveying disabled people to help establish the prevalence of disability, undertook a review of the VSO Disability Programme there and also carried out a study of national volunteering in Papua New Guinea. Patricia's previous career was in university-based social research, notably as Senior Research Fellow at the Social Policy Research Unit, University of York. She specialises in international comparisons of policies to promote employment of disabled people and in evaluation of UK employment programmes for disabled people.

Chapter 1
From the Local to the Global: the Many Contexts of Disability and International Development

Leslie Swartz and Malcolm MacLachlan

1.1 Introduction

A few months ago, one of us participated in a disability workshop held in a southern African country. The workshop went well, and it was clear from the inputs from people at the workshop that there is an assertive and vibrant disability movement in some very poor countries, some of which are only tentatively emerging from decades of war and civil conflict, and some of which continue to face deepening economic, political and governance challenges. The meeting was held at a hotel that has conference facilities. The building was not fully accessible to wheelchair users but was the only venue the organization could find and afford in that African capital. While we were there, the leadership of the organization told the management about the difficulties in getting to and from the conference room, as there was a small step close to the entrance to the conference room that could not be negotiated by wheelchairs. We struggled with this environmental barrier, but were delighted to emerge from one of the later sessions of the meeting to find that the hotel management had arranged for a concrete ramp to be built there and then, so that wheelchair users could more easily access the conference room. The concrete would not be dry by the time our meeting was over, but the ramp would be there for later users.

The makeshift ramp that was built at the hotel was subject to no plans, no designs, no building regulations, and no local or national laws or policies complying buildings for public use to be accessible to disabled people. The fact that our meeting was held where it was, and the reaction on the part of some people to issues of impairment being made visible, tells us part – and an important part – of the story of disability and international development. Most countries in the world are poor and far from the rarefied world of high-income countries with substantial provisioning for disability. But daily activism of an almost routine nature, and receptivity to this activism, can and does make a difference.

L. Swartz (✉)
Department of Psychology, Stellenbosch University, Stellenbosch, South Africa
e-mail: lswartz@sun.ac.za

M. MacLachlan (✉)
Centre for Global Health and School of Psychology, Trinity College Dublin
e-mail: Malcolm.MacLachlan@tcd.ie

M. MacLachlan and L. Swartz (eds.), *Disability & International Development: Towards Inclusive Global Health*,
DOI 10.1007/978-0-387-93840-0_1,

After the meeting, many of us were on the same flight to a hub from which we would go our different ways to our home countries. The airline we were using was a well-known international airline, subject to international regulations. Ground staff of the airline could not have been more rude or oppressive towards those of us with visible impairments. They talked only to people with no obvious impairments, offered no help for a number of blind people and wheelchair users to navigate their way through security checks and customs, and claimed inaccurately that the airline had not been informed that disabled people would be on board, even threatening not to allow disabled people to board. There are, for good reason, international safety regulations about having disabled people on aeroplanes – there must be adequate provision so that, especially in an emergency, there is minimal danger to all passengers. Whether this was part of the concern of the airline staff we do not know, but even if it was, there was no excuse for the rude, and indeed disablist, way in which members of our group were treated. We suspect that it would be very unlikely that employees of the same airline working in high-income countries would have behaved in the same way.

These two images of how disabled people are treated and live their lives in low and middle-income countries are to an extent emblematic of more pervasive images of disability in these countries. On the one hand, we have an image of disabled people being exceptionally badly treated, locked up, shackled, and even killed in low and middle-income countries; on the other there is a view that people living rural lives far removed from the dehumanizing reaches of the global formal economy are tolerated and given meaningful roles in a world more tolerant of impairment and diversity. These images resonate through much of the literature on disability in poorer countries in general, and in the literature on specific areas, such as the literature on psychiatric disability (Swartz, 1998).

Somewhere between these two extremes of complete oppression and complete idyll, disabled people live their lives. Part of what is confusing about thinking about disability in such contexts is that, commonly, both images hold an element of truth simultaneously. There is no longer any question, for example, that poverty and disability are reciprocally related, with poor people more likely to be or become disabled and disabled people not only more likely to be poor but also to bear a burden of high costs of care and resources in countries where these are not provided (Emmett, 2006). There are cycles of impoverishment and disablement – consider for example a parent of a child with a serious mobility impairment in a low-income country. The parent may have to take off work to care for the child, and in the absence of assistive devices and free accessible transport, the parent may have to carry a growing child (even an adolescent) on her back when the child needs to go anywhere. Because of the difficulties of getting around, the child (especially if the child is a girl) may have interrupted schooling or no schooling at all, even if the school is prepared to accept disabled children. The child then loses opportunities to learn and train in order to support him/herself and the family in years to come. The parent, meanwhile, may come to have chronic back problems as a result of the sheer physical effort of caring for the child and carrying the child around, and may also develop a serious and disabling mental disorder because of the anxiety and demands of the situation. The parent may become less able, even when opportunities are presented to earn a living and support a family.

On the other hand, and equally true, we know that there are other stories. Duncan (2007) for example carefully documents case studies of how disabled people living in extreme poverty and with what seem to be no resources can and do organize their lives such that they not only find ways of surviving but also find a dignity in the way they live their lives and spend their time. In his now classic writings, Werner (1987) demonstrated how, with considerable ingenuity and at almost no cost, very poor people made their own assistive devices from what others would regard as waste or worthless materials. Local emancipatory practices have been shown to have the potential to improve people's lives and livelihoods (Lorenzo et al., 2007).

There is a real danger that we may romanticize the difficult lives of poor people, especially by drawing on idealized and unhelpful ideas about "culture" (Daniels and Swartz, 2007; Swartz, 2007, 2008; Tomlinson and Swartz, 2002). But if we look to the empirical evidence, we can see impressive examples of the ways in which in many poor parts of the world people with disabilities have taken an active role in advocating for their rights and in putting disability at the heart of the international development agenda. In southern Africa, for example, the Southern Africa Federation on Disability (SAFOD, which represents national Disabled People's Organizations (DPOs) in ten southern African countries, is internationally known as an important player on the disability and development scene. Once again, this vibrancy and effectiveness takes place against a backdrop of almost inconceivable challenges for many readers of this book. SAFOD coordinates a network of ten national DPOs, and recently launched its groundbreaking SAFOD Research Programme (SRP), groundbreaking because it is led by a Disabled Person's Organization (DPO). This programme, with significant donor support, is situated in Bulawayo, Zimbabwe, where, at the time of writing, there is a high degree of political repression, severe hunger, a cholera epidemic superimposed on the HIV/AIDS epidemic, almost total collapse of educational and health services, and no consistent supply of any basic services – including supply of water and electricity, and removal of rubbish and sewage. To say that SAFOD leadership are not suffering at present would be inaccurate, as it would be inaccurate to say that the particular struggles faced by disabled Zimbabweans are not more challenging than those faced by non-disabled Zimbabweans (for more discussion on this issue see Loeb, Chap. 2).

Under extremely difficult circumstances though – circumstances that must not be overlooked – organizations are contributing to important and exciting developments in how disability is viewed within the international development context. Key role-players in Disabled Peoples International (DPI) include disabled people from low-income countries. The African Decade on Disabled Persons, one of the offshoots of the UN Decade on Disabled Persons (Chalklen, 2006), has now become a misnomer as it has been extended (into a second decade) and it continues to link struggles for disabled people in sub-Saharan Africa with global struggles. The UN Convention on Disabled Persons was drafted in part by disabled people from low and middle-income countries. The recently established Global Partnership for Disability and Development (http://gpdd-online.org/disability) embraces not only the vibrancy of these African DPOs, but also the parallel and equally impressive developments that have taken place in South America, Asia, the Pacific and elsewhere. The GPDD statement on disability and international development is uncompromising:

> The chronic and vicious cycle of disability and poverty is a critical threat to the eradication of poverty and the enhancement of sustainable development in several of the world's poorest regions. Many poverty reduction strategies and ambitious development projects that seek to achieve the Millennium Development Goals (MDGs) and a critical reduction in poverty around the world fail to capture the necessity of incorporating the needs of people with disabilities, and their voices, in the design and implementation of these programs.
>
> Studies have shown that a majority of existing Poverty Reduction Strategy (PRS) papers fail to address the needs of people with disabilities, and often relegate disability issues to side programs without considering them within the mainstream strategies targeted at the general population. Additionally, there is a significant lack of monitoring and evaluation of benefits and outcomes of PRS for people with disabilities.
>
> Exclusion from mainstream reforms and systems has marginalized people with disabilities for generations, and it is vital that measures aiming to improve well-being and standards of living, reducing poverty, and increasing means of economic sustenance include them at every stage of the process. Development projects centred on disability issues, such as special education schools, tend to be fragmented, and mostly relegated to select ministries or departments.
>
> (Downloaded from (http://gpdd-online.org/disability January 19th 2009)

The GPDD seeks to address the devastation of disabled people's lives in poorer countries, with oppression and exclusion of disabled people being an omnipresent feature; however, once again, the fact that there is meaningful representation by people from low and middle-income countries on such a body is a cause for great optimism.

A review of the architecture or function of international development agencies is beyond the scope of this book. There are however a few issues that are particularly pertinent to disability that are therefore worth a brief mention. While there have undoubtedly been "development successes", Black argues that "Instead of creating a more equal world, five decades of "development" have produced a socio-economic global apartheid: small archipelagos of wealth, within and between nations, surrounded by impoverished humanity" (Black, p 13, 2002). We have already noted above, in the form of the quoted GPDD statement, that people with disabilities are among those groups who have been largely excluded from the benefits of "development". One of the key challenges for people with disabilities (PWDs) is therefore their empowerment, to be able to "get on" the development agenda. Barbery (2007, p 76) suggests that "Empowerment is the expansion of poor people's abilities to participate in, negotiate with, influence, control and hold accountable institutions that affect their lives." We believe that the application of the social model of disability to the challenges that many people with disabilities in low-income countries face, has in fact prepared Disabled People's Organizations (DPOs) well for this sort of struggle (see Watermeyer et al., 2006).

Many of the difficulties with "development" actually centre around the "development" institutions that "affect peoples lives." The need to reform these institutions and how they relate to each other has been recognized in major policy documents such as the Paris Declaration and the Accra Accord. The Paris Declaration sought to harmonize the activities of donor governments, institutions and agencies; align their work with those of the national governments of low-income countries; and increase a sense of ownership among the intended beneficiaries of aid. However, the Advisory Group on Civil Society and Aid Effectiveness (2008) argue that the Paris Declaration "... fails to take into account the rich diversity of social interveners in a democratic society and fails to recognize the full range of roles played by CSOs (Civil Society Organizations) as development actors and change agents" (p. ii). The Advisory Group goes on to claim that "CSOs are often particularly effective at reaching the poor and socially excluded, mobilizing community efforts, speaking up for human rights and gender equality, and helping to empower particular constituencies" (p. ii). While we would want to support these aspirations, we would also stress the need to demonstrate what is being claimed here, to be able to point to research evidence that shows this to be the case. We would also stress that a strong civil society should be a complement to, not a substitute for, strong governmental institutions and services, particularly services that are equally accessible to all (MacLachlan et al., 2010).

The chapter by Griffiths et al., discusses the importance of Poverty Strategy Reduction Papers (PRSPs) as the primary documents that outline a country's development plans, at least in the short to medium term. PRSPs are the development agenda that disability needs to be on and so it is important that the GDPP make the sort of strong and determined statements that we have quoted above. Now that the issue of disability is at the "development" table we need to understand more about how the "development world" works and some of its inherent problems and challenges. MacLachlan et al. (2010) argue that the very term "development" is problematic, as it positions one group as being superior to another, and that development is about changes in relationships between people, rather than simply about technical or material gains, even though these are of critical importance too. MacLachlan et al. (2010) also argue that the international aid system can be understood through a triangular relationship concerning the psychological, socio-political and economic dominance of some parties over others; the injustice of such relationships, of poverty and of how organizations attempt to address poverty; and the implications of dominance, injustice and social and cultural change for the identity of the recipients of aid, as well as its givers and mediators. The themes of dominance, justice and identity also of course resonate with regard to the sort of disadvantaged relationships that people with disabilities often have with "mainstream" society.

1.2 What is this Book About?

The discerning reader will have noted that this is not the first text to address issues of disability and international development. This is both true and something to celebrate. The fact that there are now a number of materials available that address disability and international development (see, for example, Albert, 2006; MacLachlan et al., 2009; Watermeyer et al., 2006; Bhanushali, 2008; Barron and Amerena, 2007) and overarching policy-oriented documents such as the GPDD website, means that our thinking about disability and international development is coming of age. Many in the disability field and in the international development field are now thinking about disability as a cross-cutting development issue, which is an encouraging sign.

It is also true, though, that there is fragmentation in the disability field itself, with debates still raging about fundamental approaches to thinking about disability (Shakespeare, 2006). Similarly, the international development world is riven with debates and disagreements, and different points of departure (Giddens, 2001). In both the disability and development fields, furthermore, there are widely differing discursive spaces. Some materials are available as resources for people who have not accessed much formal education (Conant, 2008; Maxwell et al., 2007; Werner, 1987); other texts are accessible to those with only very rarified technical skills. These issues of differences in texts – perhaps even "textures" – are magnified by the exciting, dynamic, but often very challenging overlap between the loosely bounded fields of disability studies and development studies.

This book makes no claim to be either the first or the last word on disability and international development. What we have tried to do, though, is to put between the covers a fairly short and reasonably accessible text; a series of chapters tackling the disability and international development interface from a range of perspectives, using various methods, and with foci which range from the broad and comparative to the local and specific. Some edited texts attempt to impose on all chapters (and authors) a fairly uniform approach to the topic. Indeed, some edited books have uniform headings and subheadings across all chapters. Some books, furthermore, attempt to demonstrate the "state-of-the-art" at a particular moment in the history of a field.

This is a different sort of book, and for this we make no apology. We wanted a book (and we believe we have one) which could give readers some sense of the fluidity within the field and the vitality that comes from the multiple approaches, indeed, even to thinking about what the field is and should be. At times we disagree with our own authors, or we ourselves might have taken a different approach to the topic. But in this book we have tried to embody what we believe to be fundamental to all work on disability and international development – an openness to and inclusion of other views, other voices and other approaches. Having said that, we also recognize that this book is a very particular kind of document – an academic text written largely by academics – and as such it is only one of the range of different types of document in the suite of what needs to be said about disability and international development, and by whom.

1.3 Outline of the Book

The book is divided into three sections. The first of these focuses on broad contextual issues, using selected countries as case studies. The second section looks at disability and research development, and in the final section authors discuss some specific issues and challenges.

1.3.1 Section 1: Contextual Issues

Loeb kicks off this section in Chap. 2 by going to the heart of the disability and development field. Introducing the concept of failed states and comparing and contrasting the Zimbabwean and South African cases, he shows how inextricable disability issues are from broader questions of governance. As the disability and development fields mature and begin to talk more to each other, it should no longer be possible to discuss disability without thinking about governance. Conversely, the case of disability rights forms a useful lens through which to interrogate governance issues.

Rouger (Chap. 3), looking specifically at the Ethiopian case, but with implications which are far wider than Ethiopia, shows that there is a slew of international agreements about disability in international practice, and that governments are required through various means to implement disability policies and practices. Despite this, actual on-the-ground implementation often does not occur, for a range of reasons that Rouger discusses. If realizing the rights of disabled people in global context is to be more than lip service, much more attention needs to be given to this policy-practice divide.

Focusing on Kyrgyzstan, Burke and Pupulin in Chap. 4 pull the lens in much more narrowly to focus on the process of developing policy in a newly existing state. They demonstrate the interfaces between policy and process. The process of moving the discussion on disability from one of deficits to an engagement of what it takes for a society to be inclusive is not a process that can be taken for granted world-wide, and the *BIAS FREE* Framework proves helpful in developing this process, as is illustrated in the Kyrgyzstan context.

1.3.2 Section 2: Disability Research and Development

This section opens in Chap. 5 with a discussion by Mji, Gcaza, Melling-Williams and MacLachlan of a new research partnership with a wide range of stakeholders, including DPOs, the African Decade on Disabled Persons, and academic and research institutions. AfriNEAD (the African Network for Evidence-to-Action on Disability) is designed to stimulate and collate research on disability in Africa – but research of a particular kind. Two core principles are at work here – providing information which will have a positive impact on disabled people's lives in a development context, and increasing the participation in and ownership of the entire research and dissemination process by disabled people. The authors show that though the logistical challenges of setting up and maintaining such a network are immense, even more important perhaps is a supportive and mutually empowering ethos in all the network does. They draw on the African concept of ubunt (human interrelatedness) and use this to envision new ways of thinking about local and virtual communities of practice.

Moving to the challenges of developing research capacity in new contexts, in Chap. 6 Swartz describes some of the exhilaration but also the challenges involved in this process. There is a need, he argues, to balance participation imperatives with the right of disabled people to develop stronger technical research skills. To claim that capacity building in research is an easy process is to ignore the real challenges involved, and Swartz argues that the fundamentals of basic knowledge management need to be in place as a foundation for sustained and versatile research capacity.

Griffiths, Mannan and MacLachlan in Chap. 7 consider the relationship between empowerment and advocacy, the inclusion of disability in PRSPs, and the reality of advocacy actions on the ground in the resource-constrained environment of La Paz, Bolivia. There is a need, even for poorly resourced locally focused DPOs, to invest in and contribute to including disability on the development agenda, as only such inclusion can ultimately address the needs of DPOs and of PWD more generally.

In Chap. 8, Thornton gives a reflexive account of the complex process of piloting disability surveys in Papua New Guinea. Nothing in this sort of work can be taken for granted, and researchers who wish to assist countries and international development agencies with collecting what on first impressions may seem the simplest and most uncontroversial data on disability ignore the cultural and process issues at their peril. Linking back to the chapter by Mji et al., that opens this section, Thornton shows that understanding processes and relationships is always important.

1.3.3 Section 3: Some Specific Challenges

In Chap. 9, Rohleder, Swartz and Philander discuss the complex and controversial issues associated with the disability/HIV interface in sub-Saharan Africa in particular. Though there is now great awareness about HIV issues in the disability sector, there is probably less awareness about disability in the HIV sector. We need to know much more about this life-and-death development issue and the authors suggest that part of why we do not know more can be traced to attitudes towards disability and sexuality.

In Chap. 10, Eide and Øderud discuss the huge gap between the need for assistive technology and availability of such technology in low-income countries. What may seem to be a narrow technical matter – getting technology to people who need it – is in fact a much broader organizational systems challenge. As we have seen in many other chapters, process issues and relationships amongst people also play a very important part. The potential for international agencies to waste vast amounts of money and resources on devices that will not be used or will not be maintained is enormous. We need to understand the local terrain in all senses of that word – physical, social, and relational, in order to allow technology to make the difference it can.

It is often the case that children's issues are not much considered in debates on disability and those on development. Focusing on work in Sierra Leone and Burkina Faso, in Chap. 11, O'Sullivan and MacLachlan redress this imbalance. Participatory methods are used to gain a better understanding of the needs of disabled children in these two countries. A core contribution of this chapter is to show that even in the context of fairly small scoping studies it is both desirable and possible to access and involve stakeholders from different levels, ranging from children with disabilities and their families to policy makers. Without considering the overarching human rights framework, we cannot realize the rights of disabled children and their families.

Continuing a theme that is central to child issues, Engelbrecht, Kitching and Nel in Chap. 12 provide a helpful overview of what is at stake in inclusive education, from the earliest years to tertiary level. In common with other chapters, these authors note the good quality of many policy documents but also the challenges in implementing these, and it is clear that the policy-implementation gap remains a crucial one for ongoing research and action.

In Chap. 13, Barratt and Penn also discuss work with children, this time focusing on cerebral palsy in rural South Africa. One of the most interesting features of this careful exposition, for purposes of this book, is that the chapter in some senses gives a practical example through a case study of what can happen when a disability focus is brought to development policies. Partly in order to increase access to health care, the South African government has instituted a policy whereby newly qualified health professionals have to complete a year of community service before they may be registered to practice. Understandably, this requirement for an extra year of work, often far away from home, has not met with unqualified support from trainees, but Barratt and Penn show how much can be achieved – to the mutual benefit of the trainee and the community.

We want to finish by briefly considering the relationship between disability and health. We are of course aware that health and disability are different, but also that everyone has the right to health, and that the most recent conceptions of health are, thankfully, much broader and more inclusive than heretofore. In November 2008, government ministers from some 60 countries met and endorsed the Bamako Call for Action on Research for Health. The Call adopted a reinterpretation of "health research," as "research for health". IJsselmuiden and Matlin (2006) have argued that in relation to health "the fields of interest span the relationships between health and, among many others, social, economic, political, legal, agricultural and environmental factors" (p.4). For example, major health gains have been made possible through civil engineering improvements in water quality, sanitation and housing conditions, in addition to medicines, assistive technologies and other forms of healthcare. Recognition of the intersectoral nature of health is an important part of the Bamako Call: "The nature of research and innovation for health improvement, especially in the context of the United Nations Millennium Development Goals, is not sufficiently interdisciplinary and inter-sectoral; there is a need to mobilise all relevant sectors (public, private, civil society) to work together in effective and equitable partnerships to find needed solutions" (Recognition Statement 5). This "inter-sectorality" invites a more joined-up way of thinking about and approaching a whole range of human challenges.

While not all of the chapters in this book explicitly address "health", they are all ultimately concerned with health, welfare, and the achievement of human rights to fully participate in society. We therefore make no apology for using the term "health", but we also accept its potential to be provocative.

Michael Marmot, the Chair of The Commission on the Social Determinants of Health (CSDH, 2008), recently stated that "social injustice is killing people on a grand scale" (Marmot, 2008). The CSDH provides an authoritative summary of research showing how social inequalities disadvantage people and diminish their health and welfare. The report does not, however, adequately address how many of the same processes result in disability, affect people with disability, or how the adoption of services that are universally accessible would be beneficial for all. Anticipating the forthcoming World Health Report on Disability and Rehabilitation, we hope this book will contribute to attempts to broaden people's thinking about disability, health and development, and to moving towards a more inclusive global health which foregrounds the situation of some of the most disadvantaged people, in some of the poorest countries in the world. The chapters in this volume range across South America, Asia, Africa and Europe; education, policy, research and practice, and adults and children with disabilities. We hope that this book, which lightly sketches such a vast life-scape will both delight and infuriate, excite and perplex, because it is in the debated and contested spaces that thinking can go on – and that collectively we can do better as thinking people to promote disability in international development.

References

Albert, B (ed.), (2006). *In or Out of the Mainstream? Lessons from Research on Disability and Development Cooperation*, Leeds: The Disability Press

Barron, T and Amerena, P (2007). *Disability and Inclusive Development*, London: Leonard Cheshire International

Barbery, C (2007). 'Response to Banerjee', in Banerjee, AV (2007) (ed.), *Making Aid Work*, Cambridge, MA: The MIT Press

Bhanushali, K (2008) (ed.), *Rehabilitation of Persons with Disabilities*, Hyderabad: ICFAI Books

Black, M (2002). *The No-Nonsense Guide to International Development*, Oxford: New Internationalist

Commission on the Social Determinants of Health (Final Report) (2008), *Closing the Gap in a Generation: Health Equity Through Action on the Social Determinants of Health*, Geneva: World Health Organization

Chalklen, S, Swartz, L and Watermeyer, B (2006). 'Establishing the Secretariat for the African Decade of Persons with Disabilities', in Watermeyer, B, Swartz, L, Lorenzo, T, Schneider, M and Priestley, M (eds.), *Disability and Social Change. A South African Agenda*, pp. 93–98, Cape Town: HSRC Press

Conant, J (2008). *Sanitation and Cleanliness for a Healthy Environment* (Booklet), Berkeley, CA: Hesperian Foundation

Daniels, K and Swartz, L (2007). 'Understanding health care workers' anxieties in a diversifying world', *PLoS Medicine* 4(11): e319 doi:10.1371/journal.pmed.0040319

Duncan, EM (2007). '*A Theoretical Investigation into the Occupations of Households Surviving Chronic Poverty and Psychiatric Disability*', (unpublished manuscript)

Emmett, T (2006). 'Disability, poverty, gender and race', in Watermeyer, B, Swartz, L, Lorenzo, T, Schneider, M and Priestley, M (eds.), *Disability and social change. A South African agenda*, pp. 207–233, Cape Town: HSRC Press

Giddens, A, (ed.), (2001). *The Global Third Way Debate*, London: Polity Press

IJsselmuiden, C and Matlin, S (2006). *Why Health Research?*, Geneva: Research for Health Policy Briefings, Council on Health Research for Development & Global Forum for Health Research

Lorenzo, T, van Niekerk, L and Mdlokolo, P (2007). 'Economic empowerment and black disabled entrepreneurs: Negotiating partnerships in Cape Town, South Africa', *Disability and Rehabilitation*, 29(5), 429–436

MacLachlan, M, Mji, G, McLaren, P and Gcaza, S (2009). *Realizing the Rights of Persons with Disabilities in Africa*, Special Issue of *Disability & Rehabilitation*, 1 (Whole issue)

MacLachlan, M, Mannan, H, Schneider, M, Eide, AH, Swartz, L, McAuliffe, E, Mji, G, Van Rooy, G, Amin, M, Munthali, A and Dube, AK (2008). 'Disability as a Systems Probe for Evaluating Health, Development and Equity', Dublin: Centre for Global Health Working Paper

MacLachlan, M, McAuliffe, E and Carr, SC (2009). *The Aid Triangle: The Human Dynamics of Dominance, Justice and Identity*, London: Zed

Marmot, M (2008). 'The Report of the Commission for the Social Determinants of Health', *Global Ministerial Forum on Research for Health*, Bamako, 17th–19th November, 2008

Maxwell, J Watts Belser, J and David, D (2007). *A Health Handbook for Women with Disabilities*, Berkeley, CA: Hesperian Foundation

Shakespeare, T (2006). *Disability Rights and Wrongs*, London: Routledge

Swartz, L (1998). *Culture and Mental Health: A Southern African View*, Cape Town: Oxford University Press

Swartz, L (2007). 'The virtues of feeling culturally incompetent', *Monash Bioethics Review*, 26(4), 36–46

Swartz, L and Rohleder, P (2008). '*Cultural Psychology*', in Willig, C and Stainton-Rogers, W (eds.), *Handbook of Qualitative Research Methods in Psychology*, pp. 541–553. London: Sage

Tomlinson, M and Swartz, L (2002). 'The "good enough" community: power and knowledge in South African community psychology', in Swartz, L, Gibson, K and Gelman, T (eds.), (2002). *Reflective Practice: Psychodynamic Ideas in the Community*, pp. 99–112, Cape Town: HSRC Press

Werner, D (1987). *Disabled Village Children*, Berkeley, CA: Hesperian Foundation

Watermeyer, B, Swartz, L, Lorenzo, T, Schneider, M and Priestley, M, (eds.) (2006). *Disability and Social Change. A South African Agenda*, Cape Town: HSRC Press

Chapter 2
The Effect of Failed States on the Well-Being and Lives of People with Disabilities

Mitchell Loeb

2.1 Introduction

This chapter will present documentation to describe failed states and attempt to draw a connection between state failure and the lives of people with disabilities. There is a general lack of evidence linking state failure directly with disability, either in terms of its effect on the well-being and lives of people with disabilities or as a cause of disability. However, through an examination of current literature, ancillary evidence and specific cases, the association between failed-states and disability is addressed through an assessment of the effects and ramifications of state failure on people in general; through the link between state failure and poverty; and the link between poverty and disability. Through these associations it will be shown that state failure can have significant detrimental effects on the lives of people with disabilities.

Unstable or weakened states can exist in various recognized levels or degrees of decline; they can be *fragile, crisis* or *failed states.*

- According to the Crisis States Research Centre (CSRC) at the London School of Economics "a *fragile state* is a state significantly susceptible to crisis in one or more of its subsystems. (It is a state that is particularly vulnerable to internal and external shocks and domestic and international conflicts)." (CSRC 2006). The opposite of a *fragile state* is a *stable state* – however, as will be shown, even relatively stable states may be impacted by a neighbouring fragile state in the throes of failure.
- The CSRC defines a crisis state as one under acute stress, potentially unable to manage conflict and shocks and under the impending danger of state collapse. Specific *crises* within the subsystems of the state can also exist, such as an economic crisis, a public health crisis like HIV/AIDS, a public order crisis, or a constitutional crisis.

M. Loeb (✉)
National Center for Health Statistics, Hyattsville, MD, USA
e-mail: mloeb@cdc.gov

M. MacLachlan and L. Swartz (eds.), *Disability & International Development: Towards Inclusive Global Health*,
DOI 10.1007/978-0-387-93840-0_2,

- A *failed state*, as defined by CSRC, is in a condition of collapse; that is, it no longer can perform its basic security and development functions and has no effective control over its territory and borders. A failed state is one that can no longer reproduce the conditions for its own existence (Crisis States Research Centre, Crisis States Workshop 2006).

A review of the current literature on the subject of failed states brings forth several examples of states that fall into the category *failed* or *fragile* – among them, those you might expect to find on such a list: Sudan (1)[1], Iraq (2), Somalia (3), Zimbabwe (4), Afghanistan (8), Pakistan (12), East Timor (20), and Liberia (27) (Milliken and Krause, 2002; Foreign Policy, 2007). These states fail on a national level; the entire population (or the majority of the population) indiscriminately suffers the effects of war, a corrupt, self-serving government, or perhaps a catastrophic natural or man-made disaster. Foreign Policy (2007) provides a set of criteria for the determination of state instability or vulnerability to collapse or conflict – these are outlined in Box 2.1. While these criteria are provided as determinants or predictors of impending state failure they also allow insight into the mechanisms of such failure and thereby an understanding of the broader impacts or consequences of failure on the underlying social fabric of the state.

The list of state failures, however, is not exclusive to low-income developing countries. High-income, developed countries can fail particular population sub-groups based on their ethnicity, gender, sexual orientation, geography or disability. History provides a disturbing record of state failure: in the 1930s and 1940s the map of Europe was being systematically redrawn and, among others, Jews, gypsies, homosexuals and the intellectually and physically impaired were targeted during WWII by their state; the plight of African Americans in the United States has been well documented throughout history and was given new focus in a recent speech by then Presidential-candidate Barack Obama (NY Times, 18th March, 2008); women in many western societies have fought disenfranchisement – and won their battle against states that would deny them the right to vote, and deprive them of their equality (and basic human rights); in fact the success of the women's liberation movement has informed many of the disability activists both in the west and in South Africa in particular. More recently, inhabitants of the State of Louisiana may feel that their local, state and federal governments have failed them in the aftermath of Hurricane Katrina. Finally, it seems that there is no statute of limitations on the laying of responsibility or acceptance of blame for the failure of a state to adequately provide for its citizens. For example, the government of Australia recently apologized to its aboriginal population for having failed them for generations (NY Times, 13th Feb, 2008), and the US Senate is currently negotiating legislation that will include an apology to Native Americans for years of government mistreatment and abuse (Library of Congress, 2008, http://thomas.loc.gov/Search on Bill number: S. J. Res. 4).

[1] Numbers in parentheses refer to ranking on the Failed State Index (2007) that ranks 177 countries from worst, Sudan (FSI = 113.7) to best, Norway (FSI = 17.1).

Box 2.1: Indicators of State Vulnerability (derived from: Foreign Policy, 2007)

The Foreign Policy's State Failure Index ranks are based on twelve indicators of state vulnerability – four social, two economic and six political. The indicators are not designed to forecast when states may experience violence or collapse. Instead, they are meant to measure a state's vulnerability to collapse or conflict.

Social Indicators

1. *Demographic pressures*. Including the pressures deriving from high population density relative to food supply and other life-sustaining resources; the pressure from a population's settlement patterns and physical settings, including border disputes, ownership or occupancy of land, access to transportation outlets, control of religious or historical sites, and proximity to environmental hazards.
2. *Massive movement of refugees and internally displaced peoples*. Forced uprooting of large communities as a result of random or targeted violence and/or repression, causing food shortages, disease, lack of clean water, land competition, and turmoil that can spiral into larger humanitarian and security problems, both within and between countries.
3. *Legacy of vengeance-seeking group grievance*,. Based on recent or past injustices (dating back perhaps centuries), including atrocities committed with impunity against communal groups and/or specific groups singled out by state authorities, or by dominant groups, for persecution or repression; institutionalized political exclusion; public scapegoating of groups believed to have acquired wealth, status or power as evidenced in the emergence of *hate* radio, pamphleteering and stereotypical or nationalistic political rhetoric.
4. *Chronic and sustained human flight*. Both the *brain drain* of professionals, intellectuals and political dissidents and voluntary emigration of *the middle class*; growth of exile/expatriate communities are also used as part of this indicator.

Economic Indicators

5. *Uneven economic development along group lines*. Determined by group-based inequality, or perceived inequality, in education, jobs, and economic status; may also be measured by group-based poverty levels, infant mortality rates, and education levels.
6. *Sharp and/or severe economic decline*. Measured by a progressive economic decline of the society as a whole (using: per capita income, GNP, debt, child mortality rates, poverty levels, business failures); a sudden drop in commodity prices, trade revenue, foreign investment or debt payments; collapse or devaluation of the national currency and a growth of hidden economies,

(continued)

Box 2.1 (continued)

including the drug trade, smuggling, and capital flight; failure of the state to pay salaries of government employees and armed forces or to meet other financial obligations to its citizens, such as pension payments.

Political Indicators

7. *Criminalization and/or delegitimization of the state*, Endemic corruption or profiteering by ruling elite and resistance to transparency, accountability and political representation – includes any widespread loss of popular confidence in state institutions and processes.
8. *Progressive deterioration of public services*. A disappearance of basic state functions that serve the people, including failure to protect citizens from terrorism and violence and to provide essential services, such as health, education, sanitation and public transportation; also using the state apparatus for agencies that serve the ruling elite, such as the security forces, presidential staff, central bank, diplomatic service, customs and collection agencies.
9. *Widespread violation of human rights*. An emergence of authoritarian, dictatorial or military rule in which constitutional and democratic institutions and processes are suspended or manipulated; outbreaks of politically inspired (as opposed to criminal) violence against innocent civilians; a rising number of political prisoners or dissidents who are denied due process consistent with international norms and practices; any widespread abuse of legal, political and social rights, including those of individuals, groups or cultural institutions (e.g., harassment of the press, politicization of the judiciary, internal use of military for political ends, public repression of political opponents, religious or cultural persecution.)
10. *Security apparatus as "state within a state"*. An emergence of elite or praetorian guards that operate with impunity; emergence of state-sponsored or state-supported private militias that terrorize political opponents, suspected *enemies*, or civilians seen to be sympathetic to the opposition; an *army within an army* that serves the interests of the dominant military or political clique; emergence of rival militias, guerrilla forces or private armies in an armed struggle or protracted violent campaigns against state security forces.
11. *Rise of factionalized elites*. A fragmentation of ruling elites and state institutions along group lines; any use of nationalistic political rhetoric by ruling elites, often in terms of communal irredentism or of communal solidarity (e.g., *ethnic cleansing* or *defending the faith*).
12. *Intervention of other states or external factors*. Military or Para-military engagement in the internal affairs of the state at risk by outside armies, states, identity groups or entities that affect the internal balance of power or resolution of the conflict; intervention by donors, especially if there is a tendency towards over-dependence on foreign aid or peacekeeping missions.

The effects of state failure on a population or population subgroup may, furthermore, be exacerbated by historically pre-existing conditions. I would assert, for example, that the living conditions of those most affected by Hurricane Katrina were poor at the outset, and these conditions were further worsened by the natural disaster of the hurricane. Discrimination in an emergency setting in a failed state can be life-threatening (IFRC World Disaster Report, 2007). The International Federation of Red Cross Red Crescent Societies (IFRC) World Disaster Report goes on to state that "the most marginalized and vulnerable risk not surviving the crisis or, if they do, they are then overlooked in plans to recover and regain their livelihoods." Only when aid agencies and government agencies are aware of the consequences and manifestations of discrimination during the heightened tensions brought about by emergency will minority groups, older people, persons with disabilities, and women and children become a key factor in emergency planning, relief programmes and reconstruction efforts (IFRC World Disaster Report, 2007).

Several marginalized and vulnerable groups, among them women, blacks, gays & lesbians, and people with disabilities, have fought or are still fighting their battles before the portals of governments and legislatures and the benches of the judiciary in order to be heard, to be included, to be permitted to participate on an equal basis in society. Most countries are not without their underprivileged or disenfranchised groups – and several of these groups may have been subjected to long-term, generational neglect leading them to the conclusion that their state has failed them.

One common, even natural, reaction to the failure of a state may be to take flight. When one's safety is threatened for political reasons or one's survival is threatened for economic reasons – when the basic elements of existence (e.g. food, health care) become scarce or absent, the need to protect one's self or family may become the driving force that impels one to flee. Western democracies and more stable, more prosperous borderlands are continually assailed with waves of refugees (political and other) fleeing their homelands that have failed or are on the brink of collapse.

For many, allegiance to a homeland, or national pride, represents a strong bond that is not easily broken. This sense of allegiance may also have a bred-in-the-bone quality that is culturally nurtured and at times politically exploited. And while many may find the strength to break the bonds of allegiance or the equally compelling bonds of family in order to flee or migrate from the untenable consequences of state failure, still many others choose – or have no choice but – to stay.

Solomon (1996) identified eight factors that may influence one's decision to migrate (see Box 2.2). These include socio-cultural factors, communications and technology, geographical proximity, precedent, demographic factors/population growth, environmental factors, economic factors and political factors. Apart from man-made or natural environmental disasters, state failure is most frequently associated with aspects of economic and/or political mismanagement.

Any one or any combination of the extenuating factors that may lead one to a decision to migrate also offers some insight into the potential consequences of migration – on both sides of the "migration equation" – not merely what people are escaping from and leaving behind, but also what they may be escaping to. The burdens placed on an individual, a family or a society that is required to deal

Box 2.2: Determinants of Migration (Derived from: Solomon, 1996)

1. *Socio-cultural factors*. Bosnia, Rwanda and Burundi are recent examples illustrating how people may be forced out of their homeland as a result of their specific cultural and ethnic identities; the crisis in Sudan/Darfur represents an example of domestic migration. (This effect can work both ways – in terms of a socio-cultural *pull*; Israel might be an example of such an effect, where, among the Diasporas, there are socio-cultural incentives or advantages to migrate *home*).
2. *Communications and technology*. It is claimed that the communications and technology revolution has acted to encourage population movements. Recent advancements in information technology have resulted in people having more information at their disposal and being better able to make informed decisions regarding the need and feasibility of migrating.
3. *Geographical proximity*. It has been argued that foreign populations originate primarily from the same geographical area, in part because migrants retain a certain loyalty to their country of origin. Consequently, they may wish to visit their loved ones or, if they are refugees, they may wish to return to the land of their birth once circumstances stabilize. Examples include Zimbabwean and Mozambican refugees residing in South Africa, or France's experience of migration from Algeria, Morocco and Tunisia.
4. *Precedent*. Some experts suggest that precedent plays an important role in migration. A pioneer group, who smoothly migrate, acts as a magnet for further migration: for example, most foreigners in Germany are from Turkey (34%) and the former Yugoslavia (13%).
5. *Demographic factors/population growth*. Population growth in itself does not necessarily constitute a factor that urges people to cross international borders. However, when coupled with economic decline, population growth induces migrants to cross borders in search of a better life. This results simply from fewer employment opportunities, greater stress on the social and welfare services of the state and, ultimately, social and political discontent.
6. *Environmental factors*. Increasingly, policy-makers are aware that deepening ecological damage can also foster major population movements. These environmental migrants result from two categories of catastrophe:

   - Those without an anthropogenic cause, arising from volcanic eruption, earthquakes, whirlwinds, hurricanes, drought, landslides, avalanches, floods, and forest fires
   - Those with an anthropogenic cause, including the destruction of arable and grazing land, sustained heavy flooding, and increased hurricanes, whirlwinds, hailstorms, landslides, avalanches and forest fires as the direct or indirect result of human activities.

7. *Economic factors (local/global)*. Economic considerations were the primary cause of the westward movement of people from former Eastern Bloc countries, as well as the main cause of the movement of Haitians, Mexicans and El Salvadorans into the United States, and the movement of North Africans into Western Europe. This desire for an improvement in life's chances also seems to be a prime motive for migration in Africa. For instance, between 1986 and 1990, countries in central Africa lost between 2 and 5% of their populations to eastern and southern Africa. This shift coincided with differential GDP growth rates: higher in eastern and southern Africa, with an average of 3.2%, and lower in central Africa, averaging 0.5%.
8. *Political factors*. Turmoil resulting from political rivalry, ethnic strife, socio-economic inequities or regional imbalances tends to promote south-south migration. Its roots take various forms: persecution of certain groups, denial of political rights, mass expulsions, *coups* or civil war. While the link between political instability and mass movement has ancient historical roots, more recent examples include the two to three million Iraqi Kurds who escaped persecution and repression by sheltering in neighbouring Iran and Turkey, or the case of the former Yugoslavia where disintegration, civil war and the redrawing of boundaries created an internal haemorrhaging and resulted in the release of large numbers of refugees to both Hungary and Germany. A process that began with the fall of Tito in 1980 continues today with the recent declaration of independence by Kosovo in February of 2008. In southern Africa, civil strife in both Angola and Mozambique has displaced thousands of people, and most currently it has been estimated that as many as 3 million Zimbabweans (out of a population of 13 million – about 23%) have fled the political crisis in that country for better prospects in South Africa (Economist, 9th Aug 2007).

with a "stranded" sub-population of people with disabilities, left behind by a mass exodus from the consequences of state failure, describe but one side of this migration equation. Despite the promise of greener pastures, an influx of migrants may be felt as palpable stressors to a host economy or social structure that may result in consequent failure on a larger or smaller scale. For example, the influx of Mexican migrants to the USA has had repercussions on the entire US economy, and those fleeing the oppression and economic collapse of Zimbabwe for South Africa have placed added pressures on an extant fragile social system.

Some migration scenarios may also, in and of themselves, be mitigating factors or consequential in creating a population of disabled people, most notably through acts of war and violence – but also through neglect. When armed conflict is entered into the equation, the result will always be an increase in the number of victims, many of whom will become disabled as a consequence of these actions.

The failure of states and repercussions felt by their victimized citizens continue to feed the global press and are continually the subject of global concern. Nowhere in the documentation, however, is the plight of the disabled person elucidated – neither in terms of the disabling consequences of migration nor the life situation of the disabled person left behind in a failed state. A search of the literature that combines disability and failed or fragile state brings forth nothing. Independently, disability and state failure are factors that tend to marginalize people. This general lack of awareness, or oversight, in the literature is noteworthy, especially since migration (as a component of state failure) may compound marginalization for persons with disability.

I now consider two quite different cases of how persons with disabilities are affected by state failure: the case of South Africa as it emerged from the failure of apartheid and the case of Zimbabwe and the challenges facing those struggling to survive in a failing state.

2.2 Surviving a Failed State

2.2.1 The Example of South Africa: From Apartheid to Reunification – and Disability

The history of apartheid and its downfall provides an example of the power of a failed state to suppress a people on the basis of race and to compound that suppression on the basis of disability. However, in South Africa, the commitment to the disability rights movement and the inspirational leaders who spearheaded its inception and growth ensured that the emerging post-apartheid democracy of re-unification would not neglect the lives and livelihood of people with disabilities. This is perhaps best outlined in *A history of the disability rights movement in South Africa* (Howell et al., 2006).

The authors proffer a depiction of the rise of the disability movement as it dovetails with the fall of apartheid, and in the process they also offer some insight into the disparities not only between black and white but between disabled and non-disabled.

> Under apartheid, the experiences of disabled people were also the experiences of a deeply divided people living in a profoundly unequal society. The lived experiences of black and white disabled people under apartheid were very different and reflected the general inequalities between white and black people in South Africa. For the majority of black disabled people, their lives were about struggling on a daily basis to cope with the poverty, deprivation and violence of the apartheid system, a struggle compounded by their disability. However, it is important to recognize that under apartheid all disabled people, black and white, were discriminated against and marginalized because of their disability and had very limited access to fundamental socio-economic rights such as employment, education and appropriate health and welfare services. This kind of discrimination and marginalization occurred because disabled people in general were

seen as people who were sick or in need of care, rather than equal citizens with equal rights and responsibilities (Howell et al., 2006).

The disability movement in South Africa has been pivotal in ensuring that the rights of persons with disability are included on the political agenda. At an early stage in the country's reconstruction, the National Office on the Status of Disabled Persons (OSDP) was established within the Presidency at the national level, and within the Premier's office in the nine provinces. The South African Constitution, adopted in 1996, was very clear on the issue of disability and the need to eradicate any form of discrimination on the basis of disability (Matsebula et al., 2006).

The comprehensive policy in South Africa on disability issues is founded on the Integrated National Disability Strategy (Government of South Africa, 1997). This policy document was formulated in 1997 following a participatory process in which people with disabilities were consulted throughout the country. The Integrated National Disability Strategy (White Paper) provides a blueprint for integration and inclusion of disability into every aspect of governance (Vuyiswa McClain, 2002).

Despite the long struggle for recognition and equality and these very best of intentions, disparities between disabled and non-disabled still remain. A recent research project addressed issues of poverty and disability in South Africa's Eastern and Western Cape Provinces (Loeb et al., 2008a). In this research, poverty was addressed through paradigms defined not only by income and material possessions but in terms of inclusion in the benefits that society offers to all its constituents; in particular education and employment, and these paradigms were subsequently assessed in relation to disability.

The results of this research indicated that the policies of the South African Government (ODP, 1997) in providing disability grants to members of society who have a disability have played a significant part in equalizing the living situation of these individuals. In the Eastern Cape in particular, mean monthly incomes among households with a disabled family member were not only *not* lower than households without a disabled family member, they were significantly higher, and this finding has been reiterated through the analysis of material possessions – households with a disabled family member in the Eastern Cape have more possessions than Eastern Cape households without a disabled family member.

Results in the Western Cape were less divergent and reflect, in part, the socio-economic structure particular to that area; households with a disabled family member had similar monthly incomes and similar amounts of material possessions as families without a disabled family member. However, despite the improved situation of households with a disabled family member in terms of financial resources (due primarily to the allocation of disability grants), other measures of poverty (in particular education and employment) remained divisive for those with disabilities.

Findings from this survey indicated that the improved economic status of households with a disabled family member was not the result of employment. According to the survey results, unemployment is high in the Eastern Cape, with only 6% of individuals of working age (regardless of disability status) currently employed, and in the Western Cape where similar monthly incomes between households was recorded, unemployment was significantly higher among those with a disability. Assuming equality in terms of economic status between households with and without a disabled family member, it remains alarming that access to education should remain so inequitable, with a significantly larger proportion of school aged children with a disability in both Eastern and Western Cape provinces having never attended school.

The provision of disability grants is a government initiative that clearly benefits a group of people who experience disadvantages (in terms of education and employment). This financial gain, however, has not been easily translated into social equality, and this inequality is most evident in the lower numbers of employed among those with disabilities, and the lower number of those with disability among those receiving both primary and secondary education.

Although grants do provide for an immediate solution to, at times, dire situations, the decreased access to both employment and education will exacerbate the problem and perpetuate the need for, and dependency on, these grants. A more lasting solution would be to ensure that people with disabilities are afforded access to services which would increase their self-sufficiency and make the grants themselves redundant. This is in turn dependent on the improvement of the socio-economic situation of all members of the poorest sectors of South African society.

Despite the continued challenges facing South Africa in terms of the removal of physical, legislative, social and attitudinal barriers to equitable access to basic services and rights such as education, employment and health services to people with disabilities – there are existing structures, both governmental and non-governmental, that are committed to redressing these inequities. There is a coincident obligation on the part of DPOs and will on the part of the government that, if activated in unison, would provide the impetus for progress for those who continue to fall between the gaps of state prosperity.

2.3 Failing in a Failed State

2.3.1 The Example of Zimbabwe: From Prosperity Through Deconstruction to Ruin – and Disability

Interestingly, the disability movement that began to blossom in South Africa in the late 1970s and early 1980s "was strongly influenced by the existence and success of the Zimbabwean Movement of Disabled Persons" (Howell et al., 2006). Not unlike the then current struggles in South Africa, the disability movement in Zimbabwe also sprung from a local liberation struggle in the mid to late 1970s. In 1991, the Southern Africa Federation of the Disabled (SAFOD), an umbrella organization for the national Disabled People's Organizations: in the Southern African Development Community (SADC) (SAFOD, 2008), organized a symposium on equal opportunities legislation for disabled people in Harare. The key outcome of the symposium was the ratification of the Harare Declaration on Legislation for

Equalization of Opportunities for Disabled People. Zimbabwe was especially active in taking forward the recommendations from the symposium and managed to secure the passing in 1992 of the Zimbabwe Disability Discrimination (or Disabled Persons) Act. The Act makes provisions for "the welfare and rehabilitation of disabled persons; to provide for the appointment and functions of a Director for Disabled Persons' Affairs and the establishment and functions of a National Disability Board; and to provide for matters connected with or incidental to the foregoing" (Government of Zimbabwe, 1992). The Act was last amended in 2002.

Until the late 1990s Zimbabwe was a breadbasket for southern Africa, with steady economic growth supporting strong health and education programmes. However a combination of factors has changed – and even reversed – that trend. According to a DFID report (2005), recent military involvement in neighbouring Democratic Republic of Congo, along with a combination of economic mismanagement, political instability, and poorly implemented land reforms contributed to the economy declining by 30% during the period 2000–2005. Under multiple political, economic and social burdens, including high levels of HIV/AIDS, the country has become unable to service its external debt and requires substantial humanitarian assistance, with as much as 70% of the population below the poverty line (DFID, 2005). Thus, despite a history of positive or affirmative action on behalf of people with disabilities, Zimbabwe is currently undergoing a phase of socio-economic *deconstruction* that has affected the majority of Zimbabweans, but perhaps most severely affected will be the vulnerable and marginalized – among them people with disabilities.

The media have recently described Zimbabwe's economy as *capsized* or *in free fall* and its society as *collapsed*. The result of the most current events has been a notable migration of Zimbabweans, for the most part to South Africa. Two points are worth mentioning with respect to migration and disability. *Migration* evokes *action* and thus it follows that one's *ability* to migrate is correlated to their physical (and in some cases mental or emotional) *capacity* – thus people with disabilities or functional limitations are often less able to migrate, to physically leave a failing state.

Secondly, it appears also that migration or one's ability to migrate is further dependent on one's personal socio-economic situation ('South Africa's Wealth is Luring Black Talent', UN Economic Commission for Africa as reported in NYT, February 12th, 1993) – the greater one's wealth, the further they are able to go. Evidence indicates that people with disabilities are over-represented among those living in poverty and thus with the fewest means at their disposal to migrate.

Without direct empirical evidence linking state failure and disability, simple reckoning can be used to illustrate *effect by association*. For example, evidence exists to corroborate the fact that state failure may exacerbate and spread the effects of poverty – and we have evidence that disability and poverty are inextricably linked – it follows then that there must exist a link between failed states and disability. This is further evidenced by the data presented below.

While the Zimbabwean survey of living conditions among people with disabilities was carried out in 2000–2002 at the cusp of state failure, and the South African

Table 2.1 Education and literacy among persons 5–18 years of age inclusive, South Africa and Zimbabwe Living Conditions Surveys

	SA		Zimbabwe	
Disability	Yes	No	Yes	No
School attendance				
% Never attended school	13.7	1.6	25.3	8.0
Literacy				
% Unable to write	17.5	13.3	46.4	19.2

Source: Surveys of living conditions among people with disabilities in Zimbabwe and Eastern & Western Cape Provinces, SA. SINTEF Health Research, Oslo, Norway: www.sintef.no/lc

survey mentioned above was carried out in 2004/2005 during a period of national re-construction, it is of interest to contrast the two countries (Table 2.1).

There can be no doubt of the link between poverty and disability and this is illustrated in the table above that compares school attendance and literacy rates among disabled and non-disabled children between the ages of 5 and 18 years. Non-attendance rates are significantly higher among children with disabilities in both countries (SA: $\chi^2 = 62.83$ (1), $p<0.001$; Zimbabwe: $\chi^2 = 121.35$ (1), $p<0.001$). Illiteracy rates (as measured by ability to write) were also higher among children with disabilities, but the difference was only statistically significant in Zimbabwe ($\chi^2 = 151.47$ (1), $p < 0.001$).

Reasons for regional differences are not immediately evident; however, each country has experienced social development (pre-colonial, colonial and post-colonial) differently, and the results may, in part, be a reflection of that history. For example, under colonial rule Zimbabwe experienced the development of a well-functioning social infrastructure (albeit to the exclusion of the majority black population), and in particular, the development of facilities specifically designed for those with disabilities (Jairos Jiri Association). In 1995 it was noted that an extended network of institutions still served persons with disabilities (Devlieger, 1995). That the infrastructure remains intact is a tribute to those who would continue to fight for the inclusion and rights of people with disabilities. However, under the current economic situation, the fiscal constraints placed on schools serving all children – and children with disabilities in particular – reduce both the quality and quantity of education provided. South Africa on the other hand, at the time of the survey, had the benefit of several years of re-unification policy that may have improved the situation for children with disabilities somewhat.

Unemployment in sub-Saharan Africa is high, regardless of one's disability status, and this is illustrated in Table 2.2. In the surveys presented here *working* has been operationalized as *working outside the household and bringing cash into the household.* In both countries informal employment is common and often encouraged without strict enforcement of laws and regulations governing work environments. Subsistence farming and barter trade are other important factors influencing household income. Although the way in which *working* has been defined here will also cover

Table 2.2 Employment situation among persons 15–65 years of age inclusive, South Africa and Zimbabwe Living Conditions Surveys

	SA		Zimbabwe	
Disability	Yes	No	Yes	No
Are you currently working?				
% Unemployed	91.9	87.0	78.4	78.3
Do you have a skill?				
% Unskilled	75.9	88.6	64.6	71.8

Source: Surveys of living conditions among people with disabilities in Zimbabwe and Eastern & Western Cape Provinces, SA. SINTEF Health Research, Oslo, Norway: www.sintef.no/lc

the informal economy, it is limited to the cash economy and may thus underestimate the level of activity to secure a living for the household.

The results demonstrate that unemployment, as defined in these surveys, is significantly higher among individuals with a disability in South Africa ($\chi^2 = 7.56$ (1), $p = 0.006$) though not in Zimbabwe. Recall however that the survey in Zimbabwe was carried out in 2002. Due to recent developments, including the downturn in the economy, living conditions, including access to work, have deteriorated dramatically.

Survey results are different in terms of the possession of skills. While the ranks of the unskilled are substantial, the difference between those with and those without disability are reversed; there are significantly fewer unskilled individuals among the disabled in both countries (SA: $\chi^2 = 54.07$ (1), $p<0.001$; Zimbabwe: $\chi^2 = 23.32$ (1), $p < 0.001$). This again may be a reflection and a remnant of earlier programmes and initiatives that focused on the disabled, raised awareness concerning their rights and provided them with sheltered workshops and skills-training environments.

As mentioned above, the ability to migrate is dependent on one's personal socio-economic situation. Professionals or skilled labourers, who have the economic means and are internationally mobile, will be less confined to geographical space than unskilled or semi-skilled labour. This has been borne out in a study by the United Nations Economic Commission for Africa that estimated that in 1987 an astonishing 30% of the skilled manpower in Africa was living in Europe (South Africa's Wealth is Luring Black Talent, NYT, February 12, 1993). This also seems to be confirmed by the fact that the overwhelming majority of Mozambican migrants in South Africa are unskilled (Washington Post, 26 November 1990 as cited in Solomon, 1996).

This would seem to substantiate the theory that distance migrated is proportional to education and skills level. Considering the disadvantaged, the marginalized, the vulnerable, and the disabled – they would not have the means to migrate at all. They would be among those left behind.

Deconstruction, according to Alexander Phiri, Director General of SAFOD, located in Bulawayo, Zimbabwe, seems to be a very appropriate term to use in the case of Zimbabwe, not only with reference to disability but to any people-centred development that many African leaders, including Robert Mugabe, promised their citizens when they delivered them from colonial rule. During a relatively short span of time, many African countries attained independence, with South Africa being the last one to do so in 1994. State by state Africa emerged from bondage and became a continent of freedom and hope. Phiri goes on to state, however, that "if the truth were to be told, what used to be called the Dark Continent still remains dark today to a majority of its inhabitants in terms of poverty. As Africa[n] people we are poor because we have not enjoyed freedom, and many of us are living under predatory, incompetent governments which are difficult to remove from power, and yet they promised us milk and honey when they got into power at independence. Our liberation leaders are enjoying all the milk and honey and we are not."

Many of Africa's citizens may count themselves among the ranks of the poor, and in any given situation, people with disabilities will be located on the lowest rungs of the ladder. Ironically, the very same governments that were expected to be the liberators of their people are making these citizens poorer through corruption, bad economic policies and dictatorial practices that scare off investors (Guest, 2005; Phiri, personal communication).

In the early 1980s, Zimbabwe was a prospering country; the average annual income was ZW$950 and a Zimbabwean dollar was worth more than an American dollar. By 2003, the average income was less than ZW$400, the country's economy was in freefall, and, by late 2003, inflation had reached 526% (Guest, 2005). In September 2007 Zimbabwe experienced the most severe economic collapse in its modern history. At that time, one American dollar was worth about 30,000 Zimbabwean dollars. Today income and savings have been devalued at an alarming rate, hyperinflation is running at not less than 10,000% and unemployment is standing at 82% (Phiri, personal communication). At the time of writing (07/21/08) the inflation rate is reported in the media (CNN.com) as 2.2 million% and the value of one American dollar is approximately 100 billion Zimbabwean dollars, the denomination of the newly introduced banknotes.

Phiri goes on to explain that the current plight of people with disabilities in Zimbabwe is critical on several fronts:

1. People with disabilities are among the most stigmatized and marginalized in the country, and as the situation becomes more desperate, people are becoming less and less tolerant towards those deemed to be a *burden* on their families; abuse and neglect of children with disabilities is widespread and women with disabilities in particular are highly vulnerable to sexual abuse and exploitation, and HIV and AIDS. This statement is borne out by Turnbull (1992) who claims that "Tolerance of people with disabilities has also tended to diminish sharply during periods of economic hardship" (Turnbull, 1992 – cited in Choruma, 2006).
2. Specialist services for people with disabilities have collapsed, and hyperinflation has totally eroded the value of the state disability allowance – currently just over ZW$800 per month; assistive devices (wheelchairs, crutches, etc.) are in short supply and completely unaffordable to most people who need them. State grants for devices have collapsed; special schools are struggling to function.
3. People with disabilities suffer disproportionately from Zimbabwe's crisis; the collapse of health services particularly affects people with disabilities as

they typically use health services more than non-disabled people. For example, catheters for those with spinal cord injuries are in desperately short supply and prohibitively expensive; the collapse of the water supply disproportionately affects people with disabilities as they often need to use more water for sanitation and are least able to collect water from informal sources (shallow wells, rivers); and the high cost of transport has severely impacted on the mobility of people with disabilities.

4. Focus on short-term humanitarian assistance has further marginalized disability issues and funding for organizations for and of people with disabilities has declined.

Over a period of a little less than 30 years this once prosperous country has been systematically de-constructed into a failed state. Living conditions for the hardiest are dire and, all things considered, the current economic situation has made things even more difficult for people with disabilities (Choruma, 2006).

2.4 Conclusions

We may harbour some expectations that our homelands will develop over time; that they will evolve and prosper, and provide a socio-political infrastructure that allows all citizens, regardless of gender, race or disability status, to thrive. To this end, the intentions of the international community are most honourable when issues of human rights are concerned. This has been reconfirmed in 2006 through the adoption and recent ratification of the UN Convention on the Rights of Persons with Disabilities.

The purpose of this Convention is "to promote, protect and ensure the full and equal enjoyment of all human rights and fundamental freedoms by all persons with disabilities, and to promote respect for their inherent dignity" (UN Enable, 2006).

The rights and freedoms demanded of the Conventions are dependent, however, upon a well functioning social structure that is supported by the political will and determination to ensure the equitable distribution of and accessibility to services that may benefit the lives of people with disabilities. The livelihood of people with disabilities is dependent on an open and accessible socio-political environment, free of physical, attitudinal and legislative barriers.

Several countries styled on western democracies or successful single-party states may represent examples of successful socio political structures in which the rights of all citizens are paramount. Social structures incorporating a system of health and social services have been constructed to serve the needs of the public. With few exceptions the services provided are intended to be available and accessible to all – providing people with disabilities access to not only these services but to a life that is based on social and economic equity.

The actual situation in many low-income, developing countries presents a different picture. In many such countries authorities are dealing with opposing dilemmas: to provide services with scarce resources while at the same time trying to meet the growing demands of those who need those services. The economically sound provision of services is based on existing and, at times, forecasted need for the service in question. In terms of disability, need may be based on proportion of the population that has been enumerated or counted as disabled. Disability prevalence is widely under-reported in many low-income countries (Loeb & Eide, 2006; Mont, 2007; Loeb et al., 2008b). Prevalence rates in these countries tend to reflect that proportion of the population with, for the most part, severe impairments. The exclusion of lesser degrees of disability would then suggest that the real need for services is larger than that based solely on the proportion of the population with severe impairments (Mont, 2007, Loeb et al., 2008b). This is not to underestimate the value or need for services to those with severe impairments, but full social participation requires that the needs of those with moderate and even mild disabilities be addressed.

As mentioned earlier, Zimbabwe is currently in a period of socio-economic *deconstruction*. In this phase the vulnerable and marginalized – among them people with disabilities – will more acutely feel the effects of the disintegration of the social infrastructure. As limited services become scarcer the plight of those in need becomes more desperate and the already extant poverty-disability interdependency becomes entrenched.

Disability movements at national and international levels continue to be preoccupied with the fulfilment of human potential. The rights of persons with disability have been acknowledged in a UN Convention. One might imagine that these efforts would gain support through national legislative policies that would ensure the rights of people with disabilities. But politics make strange bedfellows … and too often, policies can have a negative effect on those they are intended to serve. Entrapped citizens of a failed state become the unwitting pawns in a game that has few, if any, victors.

One particular factor has been omitted from both sides of the *migration equation*, and that is hope. Zimbabweans who flee their homeland leave often with only hope – hope for a job and the ability to send money home to family still in Zimbabwe – hope and $50 – the cost of boat transport across the Limpopo River (IRIN, 2008). And, despite dire circumstances, Zimbabwe is not devoid of its citizenry. While some may leave a failing state because they are forced to for political reasons or for reasons of survival, some remain – the party loyal, those who would remain with their family or would not abandon their country in a time of crisis, and some remain because, for them, there is no means of escape. There are those also who remain because they continue to be hopeful – those who place their hope in imminent change and in a more stable and equitable future.

Notwithstanding the relative scarcity of compelling empirical evidence, there is an important relationship between failed states, poverty and disability. The evidence that I have provided indicates that even relatively strong states (like South Africa, as it emerges from a failed past) may continue to fail marginalized people in significant ways, and more conventionally recognized failed states (like Zimbabwe) fail people, and disabled people especially, with at times dire results.

References

Choruma, T (2006). *The Forgotten Tribe*, Progressio, London

CSRC – Crisis States Research Centre (2006). Crisis States Workshop, http://www.crisisstates.com/download/drc/FailedState.pdf [accessed 16th July 2008]

Devlieger, P (1995). From self-help to charity in disability service: the Jairos Jiri Association in Zimbabwe, Disability & Society 10(1): 39–48

DFID – Department for International Development (2005). Why we need to work more effectively in fragile states, http://www.dfid.gov.uk/Pubs/files/fragilestates-paper.pdf [accessed 16th July 2008]

Foreign Policy (2007). The Failed State Index 2007, The Fund for Peace and Foreign Policy Magazine, http://www.foreignpolicy.com/story/cms.php?story_id=3865 [accessed 2nd May 2008]

Government of South Africa (1997). Integrated National Disability Strategy (White Paper), Office of the Deputy President. http://digitalcommons.ilr.cornell.edu/cgi/viewcontent.cgi?article=1144&context=gladnetcollect [accessed 2nd May 2008]

Government of Zimbabwe (1992). Disabled Persons/Disability Discrimination Act, http://www.kubatana.net/docs/legisl/disab021201.pdf [accessed 2nd May 2008]

Guest, R (2005). *The Shackled Continent, Africa's Past, Present and Future*, Pan Books, Pan Macmillian, London

Howell, C, Chalklen, S, & Alberts, T (2006). A history of the disability rights movement in South Africa, in Watermeyer, B et al. (eds) *Disability and Social Change, A South African Agenda*, HSRC Press, Cape Town

IFRC World Disaster Report (2007). Focus on Discrimination, International Federation of Red Cross and Red Crescent Societies, Geneva, Switzerland. http://www.ifrc.org/Docs/pubs/disasters/wdr2007/WDR2007-English.pdf [accessed 28th February, 2008]

IRIN - Integrated Regional Information Networks (2008). South Africa: Zimbabweans flee with hope and US$50, UN Office for the Coordination of Humanitarian Affairs, Humanitarian news and analysis. http://www.irinnews.org/Report.aspx?ReportId=76837 [accessed 3rd March, 2008]

Loeb, ME, & Eide, AH (2006). Paradigms lost: the changing face of disability in research, in Altman, B and Barnartt, S (eds) *International views on Disability measures: Moving towards comparative measurement*, Research in Social Science and Disability, 4:111–129, Elsevier Ltd. Oxford

Loeb, ME, Eide, AH, Jelsma, J, Ka Toni, M, & Maart, S (2008a). Poverty and disability in Eastern and Western Cape Provinces, South Africa, Disability & Society 23(4): 311–321

Loeb, ME, Eide, AH, & Mont, D (2008b). Approaching the measurement of disability prevalence: the case of Zambia, ALTER: European Journal of Disability Research 2(1): 32–43

Matsebula, S, Schneider, M, & Watermeyer, B (2006). Integrating disability within the government: the Office on the Status of Disabled Persons, in Watermeyer, B et al. (eds) *Disability and Social Change, A South African Agenda*, HSRC Press, Cape Town

Milliken, J, & Krause, K (2002). State failure, state collapse, and state reconstruction: Concepts, lessons and strategies, Development and Change 33(5): 753–774 Institute of Social Studies 2002, Blackwell Publishers, Oxford

Mont, D (2007). 'Measuring Disability Prevalence', SP Discussion Paper No. 0706, The World Bank. http://www.wds.worldbank.org/external/default/WDSContentServer/WDSP/IB/2007/04/18/000090341_20070418142907/Rendered/PDF/395080Disability0SP070601PUBLIC1.pdf [accessed 29th April 2008]

ODP (1997). 'White Paper on an Integrated National Disability Strategy', Pretoria, Office of the Deputy President

SAFOD (2008).http://www.safod.org [accessed 18th April 2008]

Solomon, H (1996). 'Strategic Perspectives on Illegal Immigration into South Africa', Human Security Project, Institute for Defence Policy, African Security Review, 5: 4. http://www.iss.co.za/ASR/5No4/StrategigPerspectives.html

Turnbull B (1992). Cognitive style and ability in art related tasks, Educational Insights 1(1): 60–66

United Nations Enable (2006). 'Final report of the Ad Hoc Committee on a Comprehensive and Integral International Convention on the Protection and Promotion of the Rights and Dignity of Persons with Disabilities'. http://www.un.org/esa/socdev/enable/rights/ahcfinalrepe.htm [accessed 18th April 2008]

Vuyiswa McClain, C (2002). 'Governance and Legislation in South Africa: a contemporary overview', Disability World, Issue 12, January–March 2002. http://www.disabilityworld.org/01–03_02/gov/southafrica.shtml

Chapter 3
The Impact of International Human Rights Law on the National Laws of Ethiopia from a Gender Rights and Disability Rights Perspective

Theresa Rouger

3.1 Introduction

As the importance of disability as a human rights issue is recognized more consistently internationally, the question arises as to whether this international interest transfers to practices at local country levels. To what extent do international agreements and treaties make a difference at local level? With reference to the situation on the African continent as a whole, it has been suggested that the question of disability rights and the realization of these rights can easily be separated from more general question concerns about governance at country and regional level. This chapter takes the situation of Ethiopia as a case study and after a brief introduction examines the links between policy in Ethiopia and international codes and conventions. The particular lens of the analysis will be through a gender rights and disability rights approach. As may be expected, there are some disjunctions between Ethiopian practices and international prescriptions, and some suggestions for changes in approach to the field are made.

3.2 Introduction to Ethiopia and Disability

Tirrusew Teferra (2005) wrote that the most commonly known causes of disability in Ethiopia are the presence of diversified pre and post natal disabling factors like the health of prospective mothers, difficulties relating to delivery, childhood infectious diseases, lack of proper child management, traditional and harmful practices, malnutrition, civil strife, periodic episodes of drought and famine and the absence of early primary and secondary preventative services at large.

The International Labour Organization has pointed out in a study made in 2004 that the 1994 Census is acknowledged to have underestimated the number of

T. Rouger (✉)
International Human Rights Lawyer

M. MacLachlan and L. Swartz (eds.), *Disability & International Development: Towards Inclusive Global Health*,
DOI 10.1007/978-0-387-93840-0_3, © Springer Science+Business Media, LLC 2009

disabled persons in the country. In 2003, it was estimated that there were over 5 million children, adults and elderly persons with disabilities in Ethiopia, representing 7.6% of the population.

Teferra has further argued that persons with disabilities have neither equal participation nor equal opportunity to health and education. In Ethiopia, many women with disability serve domestically but are still not recognized as "productive" citizens. Furthermore, children with mental retardation and severe disability are often kept indoors for fear of social and community condemnation and denied rights to happiness through play, social interaction and schooling.

Other factors that increase the vulnerability of persons with disabilities were also identified at the 2007 Handicap International planning workshop:

- *Poverty*. It is widely recognized that poverty is directly related to HIV risk, and worldwide people with disability are over-represented among the poor. Ethiopia is no exception, where food, money and material goods may be exchanged for sex by disabled women who have no alternative means of generating income.
- *Physical dependency*. Visually impaired persons might be led to unsafe areas where they can suffer sexual violence. An adolescent with motor impairment cannot resist sexual advances from an aggressor, who may well be a family member. Others living in institutions are highly susceptible to aggression from caregivers or other residents without means for recourse in the event of sexual abuse.

Legal obstacles that deny persons with mental disability basic rights, such as the right to bear witness in a court of law, the right to make decisions for oneself (autonomy), and the right to information about HIV, serostatus, etc.

3.3 International Law, National Law and Local Cultural and Traditional Practices

3.3.1 The United Nations and the African Regional Human Rights Standards

The United Nations has been the primary actor engaged in efforts to promote human rights since 1945 and right up to the present day, culminating in the recent twenty-first century Convention on the Rights of Persons with Disabilities 2007. International human rights law focuses on the protection of the inherent dignity and equal and inalienable rights of all people, including women, children and persons with disabilities.

The United Nations methodology has been to promote human rights from the top down, typically done through cooperative strategies such as creating human rights norms, raising awareness about human rights and monitoring human rights performances. International states rarely use force as a means to promote international human rights.[1] Generally speaking, States, including Ethiopia, have not willingly relinquished sovereignty in order to give the United Nations and international organizations the legal right to use enforcement measures for human rights. There are other regional human rights standards, such as the African Charter's Protocol on women's human rights and disability rights that strengthen the legal framework of their human rights entitlements.

3.3.2 Does International Human Rights Legislation Have an Impact on Domestic Law?

Today, almost every area of national legislative concern is affected in one way or another by international and/or regional treaty standards. Over 20 years ago, concrete constitutional and legislative commitments to women's rights and disability rights were practically non-existent. Today, we see some countries, including Ethiopia on some level, responding to the worldwide call for protection of minority groups and adopting laws against domestic violence and female genital mutilation, strengthening social protectionist policies for disability workers and basically moving into the private sphere (harassment, battery, marital rape, incest, female genital mutilation, etc.) that traditionally affects women. As noted by many feminist activists in Ethiopia, both the formal and informal justice systems have often failed to take gender and disability rights into account. In many instances the challenge to the barriers between the public and private spheres in the formal and informal justice systems has proved and continues to prove to be an uphill struggle.

Philip Allot (1992) argues that International Human Rights legislation is important but one should not disregard the importance of national legislation, an essential and fundamental link in the fulfilment of international law-making.

Compared to previous Constitutions of Ethiopia, the Constitution of the Federal Democratic Republic of Ethiopia (FDRE) 1995 has made progress in terms of addressing the concern of persons with disabilities and gender and child rights. A national country's constitution is a country's legal "birth certificate". A constitution can provide courts with a useful tool for the elaboration of standards on gender equality and disability rights. Article 41(5) of the FDRE sets out the States responsibility for the provision of necessary rehabilitation and support services for persons with disabilities: *The state shall, within its available means, allocate resources to provide rehabilitation and assistance to the physically and mentally disabled.*

The Constitution states in Article 9.4 that all International Human Rights instruments ratified by Ethiopia are considered to be an integral part of the law of the land.

[1] Force has been used against sovereign states but it has usually been used against weak states that do not have the power to protect its sovereign interests. Critics argue that when some states intervene in other countries on human rights grounds, it is unclear whether the state in question is genuinely concerned by human rights abuses or are only trying to further their own national/foreign policy interests.

The integration of human rights instruments to Ethiopian law means that the Ethiopian government is duty bound to respect, protect and fulfil the specific obligations as set out in the various conventions. Depending on the specific conventions, the Ethiopian government will be held responsible at the international and domestic level when violating a declared right.

The FDRE states in Article 35(4) that women have the right to be protected from practices that are harmful to them. This is in obvious contrast to previous constitutions that had no provisions protecting women from customs and traditions that are harmful to them.

The Ethiopian Penal Criminal Code 2005 further emphasizes the domestic legalistic move towards gender and child rights including persons with disabilities, thus displaying an obvious impact of International Human Rights Conventions. Many national labour laws providing rights to persons with disabilities have also been enacted in response to international labour law such as the ILO Convention concerning Vocational Rehabilitation and Employment (Disabled Persons) No. 159 (1983). But while the move is obviously a positive one, Ethiopia has a long way to go in offering the type of protection desired or aspired to by the international and national community.

Giorgis et al. (2004) point out that Article 564 in the New Criminal Code states that harmful traditional practices, which result in the death of a pregnant woman or a young child, are punishable under criminal law. Local practices such as smearing the umbilical cord of a newborn baby with animal dung or prevention of the child from having an injection will also be considered as crimes under this provision.[2]

Giorgis et al. further point out that the New Criminal Penal Code contains a provision declaring that traditions like Female Genital Mutilation (FGM) are now considered as a criminal offence. Prior to 1995, FGM was not even recognised as a criminal offence. Now, according to Article 568 circumcising a girl/woman of any age is punishable. The penalty provided is from 3 months to 3 years imprisonment or a fine not less than 500 Birr.

3.3.3 *Local Customs and Traditions: Informal Justice Systems*

While the justice system, both nationally and internationally, is being used more and more by women to claim their legal rights, many women or persons with disabilities will never come into contact with the formal justice system. The term "informal" or traditional justice institutions describes customary or religious norms that deal with a wide range of issues, including resolving marriage disputes,

[2] Article 566 states that in pronouncing penalties for such acts, the court will take into consideration the age, educational level and social background of individuals who committed the act. So while the punishment may in some cases range from 6 months to 1-year imprisonment, it can sometimes result in a strong warning to the accused.

recording births and marriages, allocating land ownership and land use rights and in some instances rape cases.

While one cannot over-emphasize the importance of international or national legislation, one should not underestimate the impact of local justice, culture and traditions on the everyday lives of these vulnerable groups.

In Ethiopia, disputes are often resolved at the district or local level (woreda or kebele) by religious or customary courts, in accordance with religious or customary laws, which might have discriminatory consequences for members of some ethnic groups. In some instances, local culture and tradition is a lot more powerful than any national or international law. Are constitutional human rights' standards provided to those seeking justice at local/district level? Probably not. As Nyamu-Musembi points out, in many African countries the application of customary or religious law in matters of family is generally exempt from constitutional scrutiny. Even where such constitutional scrutiny exists, in practice it can be difficult to enforce the constitution's reach to those customary and religious forums. Many of the laws are made and enforced locally with the higher officials turning a very convenient "blind eye" to decisions that should otherwise shock. Women can of course appeal the decision but many do not, fearing reprisal from family or the community.

The World Bank points out that many women (and this would undoubtedly include persons with disabilities) opt for the traditional methods of justice because they tend to be closer, cheaper and more often more efficient than formal justice systems. The decisions may enjoy greater legitimacy among the local community. The negative aspect of the local justice system is that they are barely answerable to women. Critics say that the decisions (more often than not made by the male members of the population called elders) are often made based on entrenched traditional views of gender roles where the perpetrators (usually male) are often given reduced sentences or warnings because of lack of evidence on the part of the victim or simply lack of sympathy for the female viewpoint.

Many international and local NGOs have carried out tremendous and painstaking work on trying to educate the local population on the negative impact of certain life-threatening practices. Change has not come easily and has been met with hostility in some areas but in order to appreciate the work done by the international community and the local community, critics argue that traditions and local customs should be respected even if they appear peculiar to those of us coming from the developed world. In some instances, certain traditions have existed for centuries and are associated with marriage chances or coming of age and the removal of those create confusion for those marginalized groups such as persons with disabilities. However, I would argue that any culture or tradition that can kill/injure or maim requires action, such as was provided both by the Ethiopian community itself as well as local and international NGOs when faced with the many horror stories associated with FGM.

Gender based violence is often embedded in the traditional and cultural power relations in which men dominate women. Many Ethiopian women, through fear, embarrassment, confusion and ignorance of their legal rights, remain silent. Silence in Ethiopian society (at domestic, community and even at state level) in the face of sexual abuse or rape is the price paid for the family's reputation and honour, sometimes at the risk of the individual woman's interest.[3]

This is one of the many reasons why rape and other acts of domestic violence are highly under-reported crimes in Ethiopia. The reverence of female virginity until the consummation of marriage is still deeply felt amongst many Ethiopians (particularly in rural areas) and it puts tremendous cultural pressure on girls' societal and cultural behaviour.[4] Many children with disabilities are "hidden away" from public view as they are sometimes seen to bring shame upon the family and those that suffer physical abuse are allegedly "protected" by this shroud of silence; they simply do not know who to turn to.

3.4 International Human Rights Instruments in Relation to Global Health and Disability

3.4.1 Global Health and Disability

The human right to health has been specifically mentioned in several international human rights treaties and instruments, and in each of the major regional human rights systems. In the past decade, the right to health has seen an unprecedented level of interpretation, expanding both its normative scope and identifying specific responsibilities of governments. Ethiopia has adopted several international agreements and conventions that have great importance for the protection and promotion of special needs and human rights concerning health and persons with disabilities.

The general concept of the right to health made its first appearance in Article 25.1 of the Universal Declaration of Human Rights (UDHR) in 1948. The UDHR represents the normative basis that led to formulating the standards concerning persons with disabilities that exist today. Article 25 (1) specifically mentions the socio-economic rights of people with disabilities: the right to an adequate standard of living, including food, clothing, housing and medical care and social services, and the right to security in the event of unemployment, sickness, disability, widowhood or old age. Article 7 guarantees equality before the law and equal protection by the law for all people, including against discrimination.

The idea of the right to health was then isolated and defined somewhat more precisely in the International Covenant on Economic, Social and Cultural Rights (1966 – ICESCR Article 12). This includes steps related to the treatment and control of epidemic diseases (Article 12.2 (c)), such as access to affordable

[3]Discussions held between writer and the Ethiopian Women's Lawyers Association. June 2007.

[4] The police make separate classification of rape of virgins and non-virgins in their investigations, although the law does not require such classifications. Information obtained from several interviews held between writer and various members of the Ethiopian police force in June 2007.

HIV-related medications, and the creation of conditions which would ensure to all medical services and medical attention in the event of sickness (Article 12.2 (d)).

While the Covenant does not explicitly refer to disability, disability can be included under "other status" in Article 2(2), which calls for non-discrimination on any grounds such as race and colour, and "other status". At its 53rd meeting in 1995, the U.N. Commission on Human Rights subsequently concluded that "discrimination on the basis of AIDS or HIV status, actual or presumed, is prohibited by existing international human rights standards" in that the term "or other status" in international human rights instruments (including the ICCPR and the Convention on the Rights of the Child) "can now be interpreted to cover health status."

The UDHR proclaims people's right to a standard of living adequate for their health and well-being that includes medical care and other basic necessities like food, clothing and housing. Thus, while the right to health is an important free-standing right, it is closely linked to many other human rights protections contained in international treaties and domestic constitutions, including rights to life, non-discrimination, privacy and freedoms of association, assembly and movement.

Other important core Human Rights Conventions ratified by Ethiopia include the International Convention on the Elimination of All Forms of Racial Discrimination (CERD) 1966, which is monitored by the Committee on the Elimination of Racial Discrimination (1966); the Convention on the Elimination of All Forms of Discrimination against Women (CEDAW) 1979[5] which is monitored by the Committee on the Elimination of Discrimination against Women; the Convention against Torture and Other Cruel, Inhuman or Degrading Treatment or Punishment (CAT) 1979,[6] CAT is monitored by the Committee against Torture; the Convention on the Rights of the Child (CRC) 1989, which is monitored by the Committee on the Rights of the Child.[7]

The Ethiopian government has acknowledged that international human rights norms give persons with disabilities the "judicial right and the human right to be treated equally, to have the same rights as everybody else." To date Ethiopia has ratified all of the above conventions with the exception of the International Convention on the Protection of the Rights of All Migrant Workers and Members of Their Families (MWC).

While many of the above mentioned international conventions do not refer explicitly to disability rights, except Article 23 of the Convention on the Rights of the Child, it has been understood that disability rights are certainly inherent in all of the conventions and Ethiopia, as a ratifying member state to the conventions, is expected to adhere to all rights contained in the respective international conventions. Gerard Quinn and many other renowned academic experts point out that it is by

[5]Ethiopia ratified the Convention on the 10th October 1981.Ethiopia is not a signatory to the optional protocol.

[6]Ethiopia ratified (without signing) the CAT on the 13 April 1994.

[7]Ethiopia ratified the CRC on the 13 June 1991 without any reservations. However, it has not ratified the Optional Protocol on the sale of children (OPSC), child prostitution and child pornography nor the Optional Protocol on the involvement of children in armed conflict.

now clear that disability is covered by the term "other status" in Articles 2 and 26 of the ICCPR. The ICESCR Committee has taken this view in interpreting the comparable non-discrimination provisions of that treaty so when studying national legislation, it can also be inferred that persons with disabilities can be included under the term "other status".[8]

Recent years have witnessed the development body of international law relating specifically to HIV/AIDS related discrimination. United Nations resolutions have now clarified the term "or other status" to be interpreted to include health status, such as HIV/AIDS. In 2001 the UN Commission on Human Rights (UNCHR) adopted a landmark resolution declaring that "access to medication in the context of pandemics such as HIV/AIDS is one fundamental element for realising the right to health." Other resolutions call upon States to "pursue policies that would promote the availability and affordability of medicines". The ILO Code of Practice on HIV/AIDS and the World of Work has developed the Code of Practice containing fundamental principles for policy development and practical guidelines for prevention of HIV/AIDS, management and mitigation of the impact of HIV/AIDS on the world of work, care, support of workers affected and infected by HIV/AIDS.

3.4.2 Ethiopia with Particular Reference to HIV/AIDS

Kumsa Mekonnen has documented that in Ethiopia, women and girls are disproportionately "infected and affected by HIV/AIDS". He argues that there are many conditions that contribute to the vulnerability of Ethiopian women and girls to HIV/AIDS. For example (a) Physiological vulnerability compounded by what Human Rights Watch call "the risks borne from subordination, discrimination and inequality under the law", (b) Socio-economic disparities and limited bargaining power for women who, because of social and cultural norms (for example submission to their husband's sexual needs), have little or no control over their sexual relations.

Rape is a punishable offence under the amended criminal code Article 623. However, rape must occur outside of wedlock for any legal process to occur. Marital or spousal rape is not recognized as a crime under the amended law. Women have little or no control over their sexual lives in marital relationships. Because of socio-cultural, religious norms and attitudes, many of the women's husbands engage in extramarital high HIV-risk sexual behaviour without any legal repercussions for the husbands.[9] (d) Barriers of access to treatment – many women believe that they need their husband's permission to visit health care services and in a society where HIV-positive women may be beaten or ejected from their homes and communities, the prospect of visiting a clinic is an extremely frightening one. Added to that the poor literacy rate amongst

[8] Ibid.

[9] Sexual violence appears to be on the increase as documented by the Ethiopian Women's Lawyers Association (EWLA) – (a local Ethiopian NGO for women's rights). EWLA are also very active in campaigning for marital rape to be criminalised.

Ethiopian women, usually the primary care providers for children with disabilities, makes any treatment practically impossible. (e) Harmful Traditional Practices (HTP)) such as FGM, early marriage and abduction makes girls susceptible to vaginal tearing and thereby makes young adults and children with disabilities vulnerable to HIV/AIDS.

Another traditional custom such as polygamy (a practice whereby both men and women can have extramarital relationships) exposes women even more to contracting HIV/AIDS. ETHARC, a local Addis Ababa organization has said that many women, for economic reasons, have been forced into high-risk sexual activities such as prostitution or commercial sex. Such high-risk sexual activity also leads to a high prevalence of HIV/AIDS amongst the commercial sex community.[10]

3.4.3 *Ethiopian National Law and HIV/AIDS*

Ethiopia does not have HIV/AIDS law. The FDRE Constitution and the recent Criminal Penal Code make indirect reference to HIV/AIDS but they do not address HIV/AIDS directly or the related problems encountered by HIV/AIDS victims. The amended Labour proclamation 377/2003 provides provisions pertinent to HIV/AIDS. The Articles speak specifically about HIV testing but again the proclamation seems to be very much employer versus employee biased. Apart from it being very narrow in scope one can argue that it may even lead to discrimination. In Article 12/6 of the proclamation, it is provided that the employer has a duty to keep a record of the health status of its employees. It prohibits mandatory testing, however pursuant to Article 14/2 mandatory HIV testing is justified when required by law or required by the employer by "reasonable cause," whatever that means. Almost all other labour regulations do not have any specific HIV/AIDS provisions to deal with employment relationships in both governmental and non-governmental organizations.

3.4.4 *The Impact of the International Convention on the Rights of Persons with Disabilities*

Despite the Convention being the most groundbreaking treaty of the twenty-first century, and the immense pressure at domestic level, Ethiopia has not yet ratified the Convention.[11] Like many other State Parties, Ethiopia tried to appease the

[10] A study by Etharc found that the HIV prevalence rate amongst Addis Ababa prostitutes was 73% as of 1999.

[11] Many observers have attributed this to the preoccupation and intense preparations within government circles and elsewhere of the Ethiopian New Year, which was celebrated (according to the Ethiopia calendar) in September 2007.

international community and its own nationals keen on Ethiopia ratifying the convention, by signing the Convention on 30 March 2007.[12] However, Ethiopia opted not to sign the Optional protocol, much to the chagrin of local disability groups and international NGOs.

Now that the Convention has received its 20th ratification on 3 April 2008, triggering the entry into force of the Convention and the Optional protocol, it remains to be seen the impact of the Convention on a domestic level.

The United Nations state on their website devoted to the Convention that the purpose of the 50-Article Convention is "to fight discrimination in relation to a wide range of rights that are often not accorded to persons with disabilities, either deliberately or through neglect." Pursuant to the Convention, persons with disabilities now have clear specified rights to education, health, work, adequate living conditions, freedom of movement, freedom from exploitation and equal recognition before the law. The Convention also addresses the need for persons with disabilities to have access to public transport, buildings, and other facilities and recognizes the capacity of persons with disabilities to make decisions for themselves.[13]

The Optional Protocol now gives persons with disabilities the right to petition an international expert body in case of the violation of the rights as set out above. Traditionally, persons with disabilities have had little recourse to the legal system both at domestic level and at international level. Many citing fear of the unknown and just pure lack of knowledge of the justice system, not to mention the feelings of intimidation involved, as reasons for not pursuing their respective cases. It is hoped that these issues will be addressed when the various state parties set about implementing the Convention at domestic level.

3.5 Ethiopia and its Relationship with the International Human Rights Treaty Committees

3.5.1 Ethiopia in Context

Ethiopia has a poor reporting record, hence resources are scarce and are drawn from many different committees. The poor reporting is due in no small way to the internal unrest within the country and the various conflicts with neighbouring States in the past years. This has subsequently resulted, inter alia, in very large numbers of displaced persons and refugees. Adverse climatic conditions have also contributed

[12] Signing indicates the intention of a State to take steps to express its consent to be bound by the Convention and/or Optional Protocol at a later date. Signing also creates an obligation, in the period between signing and consent to be bound, to refrain from acts that would defeat the object and purpose of the treaty. Ratification legally binds a State to implement the Convention and/or Optional Protocol, subject to valid reservations, understandings and declarations.

[13] Further UN analysis can be found on the UN website/ http://www.un-ngls.org/site/article.php3?id_article = 469

to serious economic hardship in recent years. Ethiopia has experienced several famines and a significant part of its population has suffered and continues to suffer from extreme poverty as a result.

3.5.2 *Study of the International Human Rights Committee Reports*

The object of this analysis was simply to derive some sense of how Ethiopia as a state party saw themselves as discharging their obligations in the specific context of disability. Indeed, no criticism is intended of the treaty monitoring bodies either; it is well documented by Gerard Quinn and others that there is a heavy backlog of work and much discussion has been advanced on how to improve the monitoring system.

A total of 36 periodic reports ranging from 1995 to 2008 concerning all references to Ethiopia were examined.[14] However, out of all the reports studied, few made reference, if any, to persons with disabilities. I have opted to focus on those few reports that deal specifically with the issues as discussed in this chapter. The reports were selected on the basis of the availability of documentation.[15] Many of the reports deal with the observations made by the relevant committees; over the 13-year period, there were very few direct reports from the Ethiopian government despite repeated demands made by the respective committees to provide detailed, written replies.

Two of the 36 reports deal specifically with The International Convention on the Elimination of All Forms of Racial Discrimination (CERD). Nine of the 36 reports deal specifically with The Convention on the Elimination of All Forms of Discrimination against Women (CEDAW). 25 of the 36 reports dealt specifically with the Convention on the Rights of the Child (CRC). The first initial report of the State Party was submitted in 1995, 2 years after the due date of 1993, and the final concluding observations submitted on the 1st November 2006.

> This begs the question, why is there such a high concentration on the CRC? Why are there no reports or any documentary evidence on the following committees: Committee on Economic, Social and Cultural Rights, the Human Rights Committee and the Committee against Torture. There are no clear responses to these queries except to note that Ethiopia has not made international reporting a priority. Unfortunately, the various committees have no real way of "forcing" state parties to co-operate. It is really left up to the goodwill of the state party itself to decide to cooperate. Financial sanctions or international embarrassment techniques may work to a point. Resources are so limited that there is no guarantee that the state party would react, if at all. The committees have adopted a conciliatory approach and on analysis it may be the best option under the circumstances.

---

[14] The number is quite low when compared to other African state parties.

[15] Unfortunately, not all of the reports were accessed online, particularly those reports dating between 1995/1996. The author will discuss only those reports that were accessed online.

3.5.3 Committee on the Elimination of Racial Discrimination (CERD)

It was noted that Ethiopia had not reported to the committee since it submitted its sixth periodic report, which was considered by the Committee at its 871st and 872nd meetings, held on 10 and 13 August 1990.[16]

> Ethiopia clearly violates the obligation under Article 9 of the convention by not submitting a report. It is clear that the non-compliance of the Ethiopian government in this regard creates serious obstacles to the effective functioning of the system set up to monitor the implementation of the Convention at the national level and highlights the difficulties of imposing international law on member states at domestic level.

The committee is obviously in a difficult position.[17] In the absence of a report or direct information from the Ethiopian government, the committee is forced to adopt concluding observations based on information received from other sources.[18]

Throughout the report, the committee expressed clear concern about the lack of application of the Convention at national/domestic level and the lack of information on adequate measures and programmes to disseminate information about the Convention to the public at large (Article 7 of the Convention). It was hoped that the Ethiopian government would provide information on human rights and information on the training of law enforcement officials in the protection of human rights. This information has not been provided to date.

The committee did not mention persons with disabilities at any stage.

> The committee noted that according to the information received, disputes are often resolved at the district or local level (woreda or kebele) by religious or customary courts, in accordance with religious or customary laws, which might have discriminatory consequences for members of some ethnic groups (Article 2 of the Convention). Again, while the Committee did not refer to persons with disabilities, one can infer that persons with disabilities were included in the minority groups.

The committee recommended that the state Party provide, in its overdue report, information on the status of religious and customary laws, including vis à vis the federal legislation, and on the measures undertaken by the State Party to ensure the public authorities and officials, including those at the level of local religious and customary courts, act in conformity with Article 2 of the Convention.

The Committee recommends that the state party provide, in its overdue report (to have been submitted no later than 31st December 2007) information on the status of the Convention in domestic law, the possibility of invoking its provisions

---

[16] Ibid.

[17] Local and international NGOs provide a wealth of valuable information in these instances of non-compliance.

[18] The committee noted the establishment of the Ethiopian Human Rights commission and the Office for Ombudsman in 2000, as provided for under article 55 of the Constitution, as well as the appointment of the Human Rights Commissioner and Chief Ombudsman in 2004. However, despite exhaustive research by the writer, there does not seem to be any real evidence of change since the appointment of the ombudsman and Human Rights Commissioner.

directly before national courts and on the existence of specific legislation implementing the provision of the Convention. To date, the Ethiopian government has not submitted any report.

3.5.4 The Committee on the Elimination of Discrimination Against Women (CEDAW)

Consideration was made on the 17 February 2004 of the fourth and fifth reports to the Committee on the Elimination and Discrimination of Women submitted by Ethiopia.

> The only meagre reference made by the Ethiopian government in this report to persons with disabilities was that the Government and the active community of non-governmental organizations provided tremendous support (emphasis added by writer) for disabled groups, including war veterans. No clarification of the "tremendous support" was provided.
>
> In the concluding comments of the report, the Chairperson did point out and it may be understood within the context of women with disabilities that "there was a need for a more aggressive approach to policy-making in the area of women's human rights, and gender main streaming and gender budgeting... All Ethiopian citizens needed to be informed about their human right."
>
> The Government was urged to conduct surveys and to collate gender-disaggregated data. To date nothing has been received regarding the rights of Women in Ethiopia since this report, four years ago.

3.5.5 Committee on the Rights of the Child

The Ministry of Women's Affairs (MoWA) provided information in reply to the feedback of the CRC Country Report previously submitted to the CRC Committee in Geneva. The replies were based on the information obtained from various organizations working in different sectors.

There was a very brief uninformative mention of the programmes and services for children with disabilities. They said that these associations include services for adults as well as children with disabilities; that means there are no separate national associations for children with disabilities.

It is worth listing the programmes undertaken on persons with disabilities (which also include children) including:

- Awareness raising
- Information and education on HIVAIDS
- Production of orthopaedic appliances – including provision of new ones and maintenance of old ones, especially for children

Most of the programs and services for children with disabilities are undertaken by non- governmental organizations. The Government of Ethiopia explained that the services are limited compared with the number of beneficiaries and the demand for the service.

The Government of Ethiopia then went on to provide a very optimistic view of the Convention on the Rights of the Child saying that it has been implemented without any discrimination (author's emphasis) among all children of the country.[19] They said that it was based on the premises that the Constitution of the country considers/treats all children of the country, irrespective of their ethnic backgrounds, religion or the status of their families, equally.

In a further report, the Government of Ethiopia stated that it had adopted a number of initiatives to improve children's rights. While the report did not specifically refer to children with disabilities, one can infer that these initiatives included them.

In particular, Article 36 of the Federal Constitution of 1996 related to the protection of children's rights, and the Family Code, the Penal Code, the Civil Code and the Code of Criminal Procedure dealt with specific aspects of those rights. The Family Code had been amended to bring it into line with the Convention on the Rights of the Child.

The government also said that a lot of efforts have been made to disseminate the convention at various levels by various governmental and non-governmental organizations using various media.[20] Various training and awareness raising activities on the Convention on the Rights of the Child have been undertaken by various organizations – governmental and non-governmental organizations and the UN agencies for various target groups; namely, children, CRC clubs, teachers, social workers and professionals working for and with children. In addition to the manual prepared by the Ministry of Labour and Social Affairs, a training manual has been prepared by Save the Children Norway – Ethiopia.

However, despite the above positivism, to date there are no new bills or enacted legislation as part of CRC implementation.

3.6 Recommendations from an International Level

3.6.1 The Problems with International Law

In order for real implementation of international human rights treaties at domestic level, the United Nations needs to develop a system whereby it can guarantee at least some response at State level. Inefficiency of the convention committees has

[19] From discussions the writer had with several commanders at police level, knowledge about the CRC proved to be very limited. In the police manual used in Addis Ababa police stations, only one half page is devoted to the CRC. There is no mention as to how children with disabilities should be treated within the justice system. This would be in direct contrast to the information the Ethiopian government provided in their report.

[20] Handicap International have held several workshops on international human rights law with a particular focus on the rights of persons with disabilities.

been well documented, but they appear to be doing the best they can under the circumstances. Change needs to come from the top down and some overhaul of the current UN committee would appear to be necessary.

3.7 Legislative Gaps in the Domestic Laws of Ethiopia

3.7.1 The Problems Within Domestic Law

As indicated earlier, all international instruments ratified by Ethiopia such as the Bill of rights are part of the law of Ethiopia and hence persons with disabilities are entitled to exercise their rights guaranteed in these instruments. Their rights can now legally be enforced by local judicial and other justice organs. The local enforcement of these rights in practice, however, is difficult. Many courts do not decide cases on the basis of international Human Rights provisions not necessarily because they have chosen not to, but sometimes out of pure lack of knowledge of the existence of these international conventions.[21]

Cases are only decided upon the basis of the laws and provisions published in the law gazette, *Negarit Gazeta.*[22] Many international instruments have not been published and translated into the local language "Amharic" and those that have been published usually only indicate that the international instrument has been ratified but do not provide detailed substantive and procedural provisions. A person with a disability for instance cannot lodge his claim to a local court alleging the violation of his rights recognized under an international instrument ratified by Ethiopia where such an instrument is not ratified because courts are required to take notice of laws published by the *Negarit Gazeta.*

Further problems relate to implementing international instruments, which fulfil conditions, ratification and publication. As indicated, Ethiopia has ratified the international bills of human rights and other important human rights instruments such as the Convention on the Elimination of All Forms of Discrimination Against Women – CEDAW and the Convention on the Rights of the Child (CRC), and these instruments are also published by the proclamation (the *Negarit Gazette*). The ratification proclamations, however, commonly contain few provisions indicating the designation of the instruments ratified and their entry into force, and lack detailed substantive and procedural provisions necessary for the enforcement

---

[21] Discussions held between the writer and human rights lawyers /local NGOs in Ethiopia, June 2007.

[22] Some reject this argument saying that the publication by the 'Negarit Gazeta' is for publicity reasons and the courts can interpret international instruments as long as the legislative body, the House of people's representatives ratified them even if the laws are not published (Ethiopian Women's Lawyers Association).

by courts and other justice organs. It is difficult, for instance, for a person with disability to make claims of violation of his rights based on the ratification proclamation of one of the international instruments because such a proclamation in almost all cases doesn't state his rights or the procedures to enforce them at local level even though the rights are outlined in the original international instrument.

Though one can argue that one can base his/her claims using the provisions of the original instruments, in such cases the situation is no better because of the problem of language and the generality of the provisions in the original instruments. All ratified and published instruments are not translated into Amharic, the working language, by the legislature and obviously unofficial translations of such instruments or their provisions may not be used by courts. Judges do not have the authority to apply the articles by translating them into Amharic.[23]

Putting aside this problem of language and assuming that the original instruments can be used again, there is a difficulty. The provisions are general and lack necessary details to apply them locally. The rights of persons with disabilities to receive special measures for instance are recognized under the United Nation Standard Rules on the Equalization of Opportunities for Persons with Disabilities. A person or group of persons may allege that they have this right since the international convention on the rights of the child is ratified and published. That the right is recognized under Ethiopian law is no question but enforcing the right poses a problem even assuming that the provisions of the CRC can be used to resolve the dispute. Deciding when a person is entitled to receive such measures, when the government is said to have violated the right and what procedures apply to resolve such a dispute at court level, etc … are difficult questions to answer under the relevant provision of the Convention on the Rights of the Child.

The Ethiopian constitution provides fundamental human rights principles that also cover the rights of persons with disabilities and rights specifically dealing with persons with disabilities such as the right to special measures. The power of interpreting the constitution in Ethiopia is given to the Federation Council and thus the provisions in the constitution cannot be enforced at court level. If for instance, a person with disability claims the violation of his rights guaranteed in the constitution (such as Article 4 Sub-Article 5 which entitles him the right to special measures), such a complaint is dealt with by the council. Putting aside problems related to impartiality and independence of the council, resolving such a case becomes very difficult because of the generality of the provisions. It is difficult for the council to interpret the provision; the problem begins with defining what disability means, and is exacerbated by further lack of clarity in the constitution. The provisions in the constitution dealing with the rights of persons are useful as guiding principles for the protection of the rights of persons with disabilities but are too general to protect persons with disabilities in practice.[24]

---

[23] Ibid.

[24] Ibid.

As indicated above, constitutional provisions dealing with the rights of persons with disabilities are general guiding principles and do not provide adequate protection for persons with disabilities because of the difficulty of applying them in practice. The provisions can be useful insofar as they are implemented by a subordinate legislation. However there is no such legislation that affects the rights of persons with disabilities. Particularly the absence of an implementing legislation to enforce the rights of persons with disabilities to special measures is a serious obstacle.[25]

Another issue that arises is the recognition of sign language in the constitution as a language. In relation to persons with hearing impairments the fact that they are not allowed to apply for a driving license is another issue. There are those who advocate for persons with hearing impairments to be able to drive a car and use the employment opportunity available in the transport sector.

Some of the laws operating in Ethiopia, like the civil code, are enacted four decades ago, are not harmonized with the current notion of the rights of persons with disabilities and contain provisions that lack conformity with relevant international standards, which has a negative impact on the protection of the rights of persons with disabilities. For instance a person with visual impairment can have a permanent sign or a mark for his or her identification.[26] However, in Ethiopia, in every bank transaction a visually impaired person is obliged to bring a sighted person who has an identification card with them and to give a thumb print as their signature This is not clearly indicated as compulsory in the Civil Code but bank officials are using the provision of the civil code, which states that the signature of thumb mark of a person with visual impairment or illiterate person shall not bind him unless it is authenticated by a notary, registrar or judge acting in the discharge of his duties.[27]

The Ethiopian judiciary, in general, carries out its duties under difficult conditions and lacks basic resources to perform its functions. There is a shortage of judges both in terms of number and professional qualifications, modern management and operational systems are not practical, and court and office supplies such as furniture, equipment, buildings such as courts, offices and libraries and vehicles are inadequate.[28] With such a poor inadequate national system in place, how can one conceive of the international human rights legislation working?

---

[25] Supra note 31.

[26] There is no law that forces the National Bank of Ethiopia to print Birr notes holding Braille patterns that would help persons with visual impairment to easily distinguish the notes.

[27] Supra note 31.

[28] In Ethiopia a university graduate can immediately become an assistant to a judge. After a 2-year apprenticeship he himself can become a judge. After 5 or 6 years some judges then use the experience to become practicing lawyers and earn far better salaries as a result. In Ireland and the UK it is exactly the opposite way round. (Information also confirmed in discussions held between the writer and APAP, Ethiopian NGO) in June 2007.

3.8 Conclusions and Recommendations

The domestic legal system should be subjected to a thorough reform process. Studies should be made of other African states/Western world countries with similar legal systems and changes should be implemented at domestic level even before advancing on the international sphere. Resources are clearly an obstacle; efforts should be made by the international community/NGOs, etc, to assist Ethiopia in developing a relatively up-to-date legal domestic system.[29]

I would strongly advocate the development and implementation of new laws and policies to protect the rights of persons with disabilities – policies and legislation such as affirmative action that are disability sensitive to ensure certain positions be reserved for people with disabilities.

Here particular emphasis should be given for the incorporation of detailed rules on the rights to affirmative measures in conformity with the constitution and relevant international instruments. Enactment of a comprehensive legislation is particularly important considering the length of time amendments of most, if not all, existing laws of Ethiopia might take, and the availability and efficient use of resources.

The protection of the rights of persons with disabilities does not only depend on the willingness of the government but on the resources available at its disposal. This is particularly true in resource-strapped countries like Ethiopia. The protection of the rights of persons with disabilities cannot meet the desired ends, particularly merely because the rights are stated in domestic or international legislation. The protection of the rights, particularly the protection of the right to special measures is effective mainly where sufficient financial and other resources are available for implementation. Therefore measures should be taken by the government and non-governmental actors to draw adequate resources to improve the protection of the rights for persons with disabilities.[30]

The disability community should try and ensure the participation and representation of people with disabilities in the civil service and the parliament. Persons with disabilities should be given the opportunity to participate in all areas of life and to speak on behalf of others. Persons with disabilities need to be involved in the decision-making process including being nominated to parliament.

There should be renewed pressure on the Ethiopian government to ratify the Convention. The ratification instrument should then be published in Amharic, the official working language of the country.[31] The Ethiopian government needs to respect

---

[29] Many international donors like the Oak Foundation have contributed to positive change within the Ethiopian criminal legal system. They have placed cameras in the Child courts, very pertinent particularly in areas of sexual abuse, where the child does not have to be subjected to the arduous trial process and can now give evidence in front of a camera. The evidence is provided in the presence of a trained psychologist. The system has proved to be very effective to date.

[30] Supra note 31.

[31] Information obtained from discussions held with management staff at the Handicap International offices in Hune 2008 as well as local NGO's and disability organisations in Ethiopia, June 2007.

international law; it needs to respond when requested to the various human rights committees on issues of disability. It would be very advantageous for Ethiopia if Ethiopia elected a country representative to be a member of the Convention's disability committee, which should be part of the lobbying ratification process.

References

Handicap International: 'Report of the proceedings on capacity building workshop for the judiciary and law enforcement agencies', (unpublished) February 25th 2007

Philip Allot (1992). Concept of International Law, European Journal of International Law 1999, 10(1): 31–50, doi:10.1093/ejil/10.1.31

Teferra, T (2005). Disability in Ethiopia: issues, insights and implications. Printed at Addis Ababa University Printing Press.

Chapter 4
Building an Inclusive National Strategy for Disabled Children in Kyrgyzstan Through an Application of the *BIAS FREE* Framework

Mary Anne Burke and Andrea Pupulin

4.1 Introduction

The *BIAS FREE* Framework (Burke & Eichler, 2006) is an innovative, rights-based tool for identifying and eliminating biases deriving from social hierarchies in research, legislation, policies, programs, service delivery and practices. ***BIAS FREE*** stands for ***B***uilding an ***I***ntegrative ***A***nalytical ***F***ramework for ***R***ecognizing and ***E***liminating In***E***quities. The *BIAS FREE* Framework addresses the intersection of biases deriving from hierarchies based on gender, disability, age, class, caste, socio-economic status, religion, sexual orientation, geographical location and immigrant/refugee status, among others, and how these play out in the overall health and well-being of people. The Framework is a tool for building equitable, more inclusive societies based on respect, equality, human rights and the full participation and benefit of all people.

This chapter gives further details about the *BIAS FREE* Framework and how it can be used. Specifically, it reports on one application of the Framework and how it was used to assess the situation of disabled children in Kyrgyzstan and to build momentum for the development of a National Strategy to build a fully inclusive Kyrgyzstan.

4.2 What is the *BIAS FREE* Framework?

The *BIAS FREE* Framework is an essential tool for getting at the power structures within society that serve to reinforce and maintain hierarchies and reinforce the oppression of vulnerable populations. The Framework guides users through a rights-based approach to their work, and to the treatment of all people with dignity and respect.

M.A. Burke (✉)
BIAS FREE Inc. and OISE, University of Toronto, Toronto, ON, Canada

M. MacLachlan and L. Swartz (eds.), *Disability & International Development: Towards Inclusive Global Health*,
DOI 10.1007/978-0-387-93840-0_4,

4.2.1 Addresses Multiple Biases

The Framework addresses the multiple biases that some people experience because of their position in different social hierarchies. It explores how these biases intersect and compound one another. People may be women or men, boys or girls. They can be disabled, of colour, of a particular religion, gay, poor and sometimes all these at once. The human rights abuses they experience cross many "isms", from ableism to sexism to racism and more. Understanding their situations in terms of human rights is complex.

In describing where people fit within a given hierarchy, and to facilitate the integrative approach to the various social hierarchies, the Framework uses abstract language applicable to all hierarchies. For example, the term "dominant group" is used to mean people at the top end of a hierarchy – those with the most power and ability to access and use the resources that accrue to them because of their position in a hierarchy. The term "non-dominant group" is used to refer to people whose position is further down the hierarchy and who are not as easily able to yield power and access and accrue resources. The terms *dominant* and *non-dominant* are always understood in relation to each other, within a given socio-political context.

Historically, women, disabled people, and others belonging to certain classes or ethnic, racial, linguistic or religious groups have tended to be disadvantaged relative to men, to non-disabled people, and other dominant groups in their society (Rossides, 1996; Schriner, 2001). Membership in more than one non-dominant group compounds the discrimination that people experience, and increases social, political, economic and other inequities. A disabled woman living in a low-income country in Africa or Asia, for example, would likely have access to fewer social, economic and community resources than would a white non-disabled woman living in a high-income country. Her experience, however, might not be so different from that of a disabled Aboriginal woman living on a remote "Indian" reserve in Canada.

4.2.2 Exploring Common Roots of Domination and Social Inequality

Bringing each of the hierarchies into a single framework has helped to shed light on common roots of domination and social inequality. The *BIAS FREE* Framework exposes the logic of domination faced by disabled peoples, and how it is the same for all disenfranchised communities. It thus guides the way systematically to begin to dismantle the machineries of oppression so that societies can be transformed to be fully inclusive of all people and ensure their human rights, development and overall well-being.

A common manifestation of all hierarchies is a tendency to locate "the problem" in the individual and to construct non-dominant groups as pathologically different from the dominant group (Amiot and Bouris, 2005). Rather than locating problems within the individual, the *BIAS FREE* Framework recognizes the hierarchy as problematic while, at the same time, acknowledging that personal experience is important – but without pathologizing it.

The Framework calls attention to the need at times to treat people *differently* to accommodate their differences and at other times to treat them the *same* to avoid double standards. It also helps people to identify situations of structural violence within their own cultural and historical contexts and to challenge the hierarchy in which it is rooted.

4.2.3 19 Thought-Provoking Questions

The *BIAS FREE* Frameworkconsists of a set of 19 thought-provoking questions clustered under three main problem types: *Maintaining a hierarchy*, *Failing to examine differences* and *Using double standards* (see Appendix). The questions alert the user to the presence or absence of biases deriving from social hierarchies in any given socio-historical context. The Framework points to solutions to overcome the identified problems.

4.2.4 3-Dimensional Matrix

The Framework's 3-D Matrix consists of the *type of hierarchy* examined (gender, disability, race/ethnicity, class, caste, age, religion, sexual orientation, geographical location, socio-economic status, etc.), the *type of application*, e.g. research, legislation, policy, programme, service delivery or practice, and the particular *type of bias problem* identified by the 19 questions.

4.2.5 Multiple Forms of Discrimination

The *BIAS FREE* Framework addresses multiple forms of discrimination people experience based on the intersection of biases deriving from social hierarchies and how these play out in their overall health and well-being.

The Framework helps to identify when social hierarchies are at work in a way that violates human rights and provides guidance on how to go about dismantling the power structures that serve to reinforce and maintain them. It shows the way to embed human rights and social inclusion at each step of the way, improving the health, well-being and security of all peoples.

4.2.6 Rights-Based

The *BIAS FREE* Framework is premised on the equal entitlement of all people to be treated with respect and on the inviolability of human rights. The Framework derives from the understanding of health as a human right and uses a rights-based model of health and well-being. Health (physical, mental, social and spiritual well-being) is fundamentally tied to human rights and social equality (Burke et al. 2000). The *BIAS FREE* Framework is designed to draw the users' attention to the structural and organizational determinants of health, to assist them in identifying biases in health research that derive from various social hierarchies, and in removing them, insofar as is possible.

4.3 How Does the *BIAS FREE* Framework Work?

The *BIAS FREE* Framework's set of 19 thought-provoking questions are aimed at discovering if social hierarchies are at work in research, and if so, if they are producing bias. The questions in the Framework probe the particular nature of the problem so that appropriate solutions can be applied to the identified problem. If hierarchies are not found to be at work, or if no bias is found, the researcher, policy-maker or community member can proceed to the next stage of their work. If bias is found, the Framework points to appropriate solutions that may be taken to address the particular bias problem identified.

The 19 questions stimulate discussion and soul-searching among people using the Framework. As people apply the Framework, they begin to be able to identify biases in their institutions and lives and to put a name to them. Once they identify the correct problems, they can begin to work towards resolving them. The "solutions" pointed to in the Framework help people to identify their own solutions and to address the identified problems within their particular situation and cultural settings.

In the process, people using the Framework begin to see the world through "new eyes", begin to internalize the values that underpin the Framework, and to change their attitudes and practices. This in turn leads to a more thoughtful and critical reflection on attitudes and practices, and ultimately to a process of personal and structural transformation and broad social change focused on human rights and equity.

4.4 An Application of the *BIAS FREE* Framework in Kyrgyzstan

In the Spring of 2007, UNICEF approached Mary Anne Burke to assist them in undertaking a situational analysis with regard to disabled children in Kyrgyzstan. It was to be the beginning of a process of exploring what would be needed to change the situation of disabled children to bring it in line with what was being called for by the new UN Convention on the Rights of Persons with Disabilities (UNCRPWD, 2007).

UNICEF had contracted with a local consultancy agency, EXPERT, to conduct some preliminary national research on the situation of disabled children in the Kyrgyz Republic. Mary Anne Burke followed the research from Geneva analysing research tools, legislations and results using the *BIAS FREE* Framework. Andrea Pupulin, who worked with Mary Anne in Geneva, went to the Kyrgyz Republic for four months to work directly with the researchers under the direction and supervision of Mary Anne Burke.

When Andrea Pupulin arrived in the Kyrgyz Republic the research team had already developed a set of survey questionnaires for children, parents, institution staff, etc. As well as this they had lined up a team of medical doctors to administer the surveys. So, the first task was to work with the research team applying the *BIAS FREE* Framework to both the research instruments and methodology. Working with the researchers to apply the *BIAS FREE* Framework allowed them to see for themselves the nature of the bias problems that were uncovered and consequently to find solutions to reformulate both the questionnaires and methodology to avoid the biases.

All three main problems identified by the *BIAS FREE* Framework were uncovered in the research instruments: the *H problems*: Maintaining an existing hierarchy; the *F problems*: Failing to examine differences; and the *D problems*: Using double standards. Below we describe the application of the *BIAS FREE* Framework to improving the research process, so that the products of the research can more effectively be used to promote the human rights of its intended beneficiaries. While some of the problems identified will be recognisable to researchers familiar with the area of disability, our exposition helps to link these problems to broader issues of social inclusion. Throughout the next sections we refer to problems identified, according to their characteristics as described in Table 4.1.

4.5 Questionnaire Content

H Problems: Maintaining an Existing Hierarchy

Overall, the research instruments were rooted in the "medical model" of disability, which focuses on individual deficiencies. This is an example of a *H4 problem: Pathologization*. It is opposed to the rights-based model of disability that focuses on deficiencies in the community in which the person lives and in its ability to support and provide services for disabled persons and their families. In other words, the questionnaires were designed to assess whether the disabled children could be included in society rather than trying to determine the preparedness of society for being fully inclusive, and the steps taken towards building an inclusive society where all children can enjoy equal rights and opportunities.

A number of questions were asking about the limitations of the disabled child. The nature of the questions and the way they were formulated lead to the belief that it was the child who was deficient and somewhat broken. As a result the child was

Table 4.1 The *BIAS FREE* framework for research

Type of hierarchy	Main problem type	Nature of problem	Solution	Research element
 • Gender • Disability • Race/Ethnicity • Age • Class • Caste • Socio-economic status • Religion • Sexual Orientation • Geographical Location • Health status • (among others)	*H – Maintaining an existing hierarchy* *Is dominance of one group over the other in any way justified or maintained?* *Situate the problem within a human rights framework, in which equality is an underlying value. Point out the discrepancy between this value and the inequalities among groups of people that result from the hierarchy*	*H1 Denying hierarchy*. Is the existence of a hierarchy denied in spite of widespread evidence to the contrary?	*The existence of a hierarchy is acknowledged; its validation is questioned and rejected*	• Request for proposals • Research proposal • Literature review • Ethical review • Research question & design • Research hypothesis • Description of population to be studied • Staffing • Concepts • Theoretical framework/ model • Research methods/ instruments • Recruitment of participants • Data analysis and interpretation • Conclusions • Policy recommendations • Identification of audience • Abstract/ Executive Summary • Language • Visual representations • Communication of Results
		H2 Maintaining hierarchy. Are practices or views that are based on a hierarchy presented as normal or unproblematic?	*Expressions of hierarchies are questioned and problematized*	
		H3 Dominant perspective. Is the perspective or standpoint of the dominant group adopted?	*The perspectives of non-dominant and dominant groups are respected and accepted*	
		H4 Pathologization. Is the non-dominant group pathologized when it differs from the norms derived from the dominant group?	*Challenge the norm and address the reasons given for pathologizing the group*	
		H5 Objectification. Is stripping people of their intrinsic dignity and personhood presented as normal or unproblematic?	*Recognize that every human being has intrinsic dignity and human rights that are inviolable and must be protected, and conduct the activity accordingly*	
		H6 Victim-blaming. Are victims of individual and/or structural violence blamed and held accountable?	*Victims are not blamed; individual and/or structural violence is identified and those responsible are held accountable*	
		H7 Appropriation. Is ownership claimed by the dominant group for entities that originate(d) in or belong to the non-dominant group?	*Original ownership is acknowledged and respected*	

• Gender • Disability • Race/Ethnicity • Age • Class • Caste • Socio-economic status • Religion • Sexual Orientation • Geographical Location • Health Status • (among others)	*F – Failing to examine differences* *Is membership in a non-dominant/dominant group examined as socially relevant and accommodated?* *Establish the relevance of group membership within a given context. Once relevance is established, accommodate differences in ways that reduce the hierarchy*	*F1 Insensitivity to difference*. Has the relevance of membership in dominant/non-dominant group been ignored?	*Relevance of dominant/non-dominant group membership must always be determined; group membership must be included as an analytical variable throughout the activity and only then can its relevance be assessed*	• Request for proposals • Research proposal • Literature review • Ethical review • Research question/ hypothesis • Research design • Description of population to be studied • Staffing • Concepts • Theoretical framework/ model • Research methods/ instruments • Recruitment of participants • Data analysis and interpretation • Conclusions • Policy recommendations • Identification of audience • Abstract/ Executive Summary • Language • Visual representations • Communication of results
		F2 Decontextualization. Has the different social reality of dominant and non-dominant groups explicitly been considered?	*The context with respect to dominant/non-dominant group membership is explicitly examined and differences following from this are identified, analyzed and taken into account*	
		F3 Over-generalization or universalization. Is information derived from dominant groups generalized to non-dominant groups without examining if it is applicable to the non-dominant groups?	*Information about the dominant group is acknowledged as such, and efforts are made to obtain information about the non-dominant group or conclusions are limited to the dominant group*	
		F4 Assumed homogeneity. Is the dominant or non-dominant group treated as a uniform group?	*Differences within dominant and non-dominant groups are acknowledged and taken into account*	

(continued)

Table 4.1 (continued)

Type of hierarchy	Main problem type	Nature of problem	Solution	Research element
 • Gender • Disability • Race/Ethnicity • Age • Class • Caste • Socio-economic status • Religion • Sexual Orientation • Geographical Location • Health Status • (among others)	*D – Using double standards* *Are non-dominant/ dominant groups dealt with differently?* *Identify the double standard that leads to different treatment of members of dominant and non-dominant groups and how this maintains a hierarchy; then, devise means to provide the same treatment to both groups*	*D1 Overt double standard.* Are non-dominant and dominant groups treated differently?	*Provide the same treatment to members of dominant and non-dominant groups whenever this increases equity*	• Request for proposals • Research proposal • Literature review • Ethical review • Research question/ hypothesis • Research design • Description of population to be studied • Staffing • Concepts • Theoretical framework/ model • Research methods/ instruments • Recruitment of participants • Data analysis and interpretation • Conclusions • Policy recommendations • Identification of audience • Abstract/Executive Summary • Language • Visual representations • Communication of Results
		D2 Under-representation or exclusion. Are non-dominant groups under-represented or excluded?	*Non-dominant groups are included whenever relevant*	
		D3 Exceptional under-representation or exclusion. In contexts normally associated with non-dominant groups, but pertinent to all groups, is the dominant group under-represented or excluded?	*Dominant groups are appropriately represented in issues of relevance to them that have been stereotyped as being important only for a non-dominant group*	
		D4 Denying agency. Is there a failure to consider non-dominant/dominant groups as both actors and acted upon?	*Examine ways in which dominant and non-dominant groups are both acting as well as acted upon*	
		D5 Treating dominant opinions as facts. Are opinions expressed by a dominant group about a non-dominant group treated as fact?	*Opinions expressed by dominant groups about non-dominant groups are treated as opinions, not fact*	
		D6 Stereotyping. Are stereotypes of non-dominant/ dominant groups treated as essential aspects of group membership?	*Treat stereotypes as stereotypes, not as truths*	

	D7 Exaggerating differences. Are overlapping traits treated as if they were characteristic of only non-dominant/dominant groups?	*Document both the differences and the similarities between members of non-dominant and dominant groups*
	D8 Hidden double standard: Are different criteria used to define comparable facts with the effect of hiding their comparability?	*Ask whether there might be a hidden double standard by looking for non-obvious parallels. One way of achieving this is by asking what form the phenomenon identified within one group might take within another group*

Source: Eichler and Burke (2006)

viewed as in need of "fixing" and this explains the strong medical emphasis of the questionnaires and on the rehabilitation of the child. An entire section of the parents' questionnaire was on medical rehabilitation services and the disabled children were referred to as "invalid".

This is a case of pathologization of the child: the inherent condition of the child is seen as the problem rather than the community where they lived (infrastructure, public attitudes, services, etc.). If the child could not be included it was because of the way he/she was – unable to study, to move, etc.

Here are some specific examples of pathologization from the questionnaires:

Question 1: What communication skills does your child have?
One variant of the answer is possible.

Does not understand anything	1		Can read	4
Understands some words	2		Can read and write	5
Can speak and understand words	3		*Refuse to answer (do not include)*	99

A child is able to communicate but other people are not always able to understand him/her.

Question 2: What estimation can you give to the quality of the care, development and education of disabled children in specialized institutions?

The quality of care in institutions is not an issue here. The focus should be on the preparation of the outer world to include disabled children. Assessing the work of institutions is to recognize it as a legitimate living space for disabled children who are unable to live in society, thus pathologizing them.

Question 3: Does he (she) have other chronic diseases?
It is possible to indicate several variants of the answer.

Blood diseases	1		Condition appeared in perinatal period	6
Endocrine diseases	2			
Tuberculosis	3		There is no other illnesses	55
Cancer	4		Other (Indicate the kind of diseases)	
Hydatid disease	5			

These questions asked parents about the type of pathology of the children. This is problematic for two reasons:

Firstly, the parents do not always know the medical condition of their child and we observed that even the doctor's diagnosis is often wrong, as the different commissions for disabled children frequently disagree and re-diagnose children. Consequently the results would be inaccurate.

One section of the parent's questionnaire, to be filled by the interviewers, also included questions on the physical appearance of the mother, the state of the house, etc. (see Table 4.2). The questions aimed to find out how competent the parents were in taking care of the child and to reveal practices of neglect. If the mother appeared unhealthy, the house was not clean, or the family lived in poverty, the family was blamed, rather than trying to understand the failure of the social system to provide adequate income and other supports to the family. This is an example of a

Table 4.2 The Form completed by the interviewer after visiting the household

Question 6: Please describe the amenity of the household		
	Estimate in accordance to the 5 ball scale	Notes (describe the condition)
25.1 The condition of the house on the outside (only for the private sector)	1____2___3___4___5, Where 1 is very bad condition, the house demands the complete overhaul and 5 the excellent condition	
25.2 The condition of the house/apartment inside	1____2___3___4___5, Where 1 is very bad condition, the house demands the complete overhaul and 5 the excellent condition	
25.3 The clearness in the rooms	1___2___3___4___5, Where 1 means very dirty, and 5 means very clean	
25.4 Lighting	1___2___3___4___5,Where 1 means very bad lighting, it is very dark in the rooms, and 5 means very light rooms and the lighting is very good	
25.5 Furniture	1___2___3___4___5, Where 1 means very bad furniture the lack of the furniture, and 5 the excellent condition, the presence of furniture, carpets	
25.6 The appearance of the mother	1___2___3___4___5, Where 1 means untidy, dirty cloth and 5 means accurate, clean cloth, well-groomed nails and hair	
25.7 The appearance of the child	1___2___3___4___5, Where 1 means untidy, dirty cloth and 5 means accurate, clean cloth, well-groomed nails and hair	

H5 problem: Victim-blaming. There were no follow-up questions to ask the parents what kind of difficulties they faced with their children and what support they received in overcoming them. For example, no questions were asked on whether their children were accepted in schools or whether the parents could benefit from flexible working hours to be able to look after their children. In any case a messy house is not indicative of how well children are treated. There was no recognition that having a disabled child in a community that is not inclusive adds to the expenses and work of the whole family, and can also have a negative impact on parents' ability to work and on their overall income.

F Problems: Failing to Examine Differences

Secondly, these questions are irrelevant and misleading for determining the needs of disabled children. One cannot use this data to inform policies or programmes for disabled children without assuming that children with the same pathology have the same needs. This is an example of an *F4 problem: Assumed homogeneity*. In reality children with the same condition could have completely different needs and require completely different levels of support. For instance a child with cerebral palsy may be perfectly able to walk and write on his/her own while others may need supportive equipment.

D Problems: Using Double Standards

Many of the questions were biased against disabled children because they accepted the premise that disabled children do not have the same rights as other children. This is an example of a *D1 problem: Overt Double Standards.*

Intentionally or inadvertently, the medical model advocates for disabled children to be segregated in special classrooms or institutions, and it legitimizes practices of exclusion. This is an example of a *D2 problem: Under-representation or exclusion.* The attention of the medical model is on rehabilitating the individual rather than adopting a holistic approach to improve the wider social and economic environment in which people live, which has the greatest impact on their quality of life.

The Convention on the Rights of the Child, ratified by the government of the Kyrgyz Republic, guarantees the rights of all children to full inclusion in their society and to enjoy equal rights and opportunities regardless of gender, race, or disability. The Convention clearly specifies that all children have the right to an inclusive education and to live with their families. Nonetheless, the original research questionnaires cast doubt over these rights and did not use them as their initial premises as they should have. Below are some examples from questionnaires that failed to problematize the view that all disabled children cannot be fully included in Kyrgyz society – to attend their community schools or to live with their families.

Question 4: How do you think, could your child now, or in the future, study in an ordinary school?

One variant of the answer is possible

Yes	1	
No	2	
He (she) had graduated from studies in the ordinary school	3	*These variants of the answers are suitable only for children aged 16 or older*
He (she) had been studying in the ordinary school for some years (months)	4	
He (she) has never studied in the ordinary school	5	

This question addressed to parents of disabled children inquires if in their opinion it is possible or desirable for their child to ever go to an ordinary school. There were no further questions on how their child could be included in school. Parents were not given the opportunity to explain why their child could not go to school and what needed to change in the schools and communities for him/her to be included.

A question in the questionnaires for social workers, institution staff, and members from the ministries asked:

Question 5: What do you think, how applicable is a program for deinstitutilization of disabled children in our country?
The question aimed to find out if, in the opinion of these "professionals", it is realistic, in the context of the Kyrgyz Republic, to reunite all disabled children living in institutions with their families. Living with a family is a fundamental right of every child protected by the Convention of the Rights of the Child. The research should be exploring the conditions necessary for disabled children to enjoy their right to live with their family.

Once the problems in the questionnaires were uncovered, the *BIAS FREE* Framework was used to develop new questionnaires, drawing on questionnaires that had been developed by The Roeher Institute (Burke et al., 2002a–d; Burke & Pegg 2003; Burke et al., 2003) using the *BIAS FREE* Framework, reshaping them to fit the situation and context in Kyrgyzstan. Rather than pathologizing the disabled children by trying to enumerate a long list of pathologies they have and things they can't do, the new questionnaires were refocused on trying to understand what barriers the children and their families experienced in their communities and at school. For example, instead of asking how many children could not walk, the questions were changed to ask if the child used any mobility or assistive devices to help them to move around. If they reported that they did, then the questionnaires probed to find out what was needed, whether or not the family had access to the needed devices, whether they could afford them, and if there were barriers to their child using them in their home, in the community and school, and the nature of the barrier, such as negative attitudes and behaviours by neighbours or teachers, or broken sidewalks, curbs, stairs, etc. Instead of focusing on what they could not do, the questionnaires focused on what their hopes and dreams are and what they needed to achieve them.

The questionnaires for teachers and principals were reformulated to understand what they needed in the way of training, supports, equipment and infrastructure to accommodate and fully include all children and their learning needs in their classrooms and schools. Instead of asking if disabled children could go to their local community schools, and if institutions could be shut down, the questionnaires focused on what changes were needed in the community and what additional resources parents needed so that all children could live in their families and go to their local schools with their siblings and peers.

4.6 Data Collection

The proposed methodology for administering the questionnaires was questioned. Having medical doctors administer the questionnaires was pointed out as problematic, given that their opinions would hold sway due to their elevated position in society, and because they had a vested interest in ensuring that the medical model of disability would prevail. This is an example of a *H5 problem: Dominant perspective.* Not having disabled people and their families involved in conducting the research was also an example of a *D2 problem: Under-representation or exclusion.* This is a violation of the principle of inclusion upheld by the Convention as voiced by the Disabled Peoples International (DPI) slogan: "Nothing about us without us".

Collecting data only through survey questionnaires also was cited as problematic. In a fairly authoritarian system it is unlikely that parents, who already feel disadvantaged and who are blamed for their failings as parents, would be willing to disclose more than absolutely necessary to answer the questions to people who could be seen as intimidating to them. This is an example of an *F1 problem: Insensitivity to difference.* The solution was to engage parents, disabled people and others from community-based NGOs in the data collection process, rather than to use medical doctors. In this way, the process of inclusion was modelled right from the start.

A decision was also made to hold a number of focus groups and key informant interviews so that families would feel more comfortable discussing the situations they experienced. Training sessions were held for the interviewers and guidelines were developed for focus groups with parents, teachers and disabled youth. Table 4.3 shows an excerpt from the facilitators' Discussion Guide for Parents' Focus Groups that were focused on the child's education.

Data collected through the focus groups and interviews were triangulated with data collected through surveys and secondary data. Having the information that was generated through the revised research questionnaires and focus groups rather than a list of the number of children with cerebral palsy, for example, which would have been what had been generated by the original research questionnaires, was much more useful for policy and planning purposes. Rather than identifying the number of "defective" children, the data were able to provide a picture of the degree to which there was openness in society towards inclusion of disabled children,

Table 4.3 Facilitators' discussion guide for parents' focus groups that focused on the child's education

Every child has the right to attend a community school regardless of his/her mental or physical condition. It is the duty of the schools to implement any changes needed to enable every child to access the class, follow the program and participate in every school activity. In other words, the schools need to accommodate the needs of every child and guarantee his/her full inclusion in the educational system

Objectives: to assess the degree of inclusion of disabled children in their local community schools and to identify the barriers to their inclusion

Note for facilitator. Invite the participants to think about how their child could be fully included in the community school (full inclusion means she/he can follow the lessons in class, do everything other children in the class can do)

- If the child does not go to school or goes to a specialized school ask them to think about what stops him/her from going to the local community school
- If the child goes to regular school ask them to think about what problems he/she faces in school and what he/she needs to do better and be happier. What does he/she need to be able to participate in all the activities as other children in the class (play, go on school trips, eat in the cafeteria, physical education, etc.)?
- If some parents do not want to send their child to school find out why? What prevents them from sending their child to school? Are there things of which they are afraid? If yes, what are they?
- If the child is too young to go to school ask the parents about kindergarten or if they foresee problems for their child in school. If so, why? What problems do they foresee?

Ask the parents to talk about their experiences – not to give general answers the specific support needs of disabled children and their families and teachers, and the specific barriers that existed within a child's home, community or school.

4.7 Research Findings

The research findings demonstrated that in many instances communities are not inclusive of disabled children and their families. The research identified many violations of the rights of disabled children and the physical and social barriers faced by disabled children and their families.

Some of the findings of the research:

- The medical model of disability still prevails and influences those caring for disabled children.
- Most disabled children do not go to their community schools due to the social and physical and attitudinal barriers they face.
- Stigma and discrimination towards disabled children are still widespread, especially the view that disabled children are "diseased" and need to be fixed.

4.8 Workshops

Once the preliminary research findings were available, a 2-day workshop was held in Kyrgyzstan to share the findings with a broad range of stakeholders and to explore the *BIAS FREE* Framework and its usefulness as a tool for the development of a national strategy to move towards a more inclusive Kyrgyzstan. Workshop participants consisted of representatives of parents of disabled children organizations, disabled youth organizations, NGOs, different government ministries and staff from UNICEF. Participants expressed great interest in undertaking further work to improve the situation for disabled children. Workshop participants began to constitute an informal working group and this generated a momentum for the development of a National Strategy for building an inclusive Kyrgyzstan, with a common vision and objectives shared by all the stakeholders.

As a result of the Workshop, UNICEF decided to launch a follow-up initiative in 2008 as its priority project, for which support from the Prime Minister's office has been secured. It was agreed that work would begin to create a National Steering Committee under the Prime Minister's Office. The National Steering Committee would include representatives from:

- Child Protection Department
- Ministry of Education
- Ministry of Labour and Social Welfare
- Ministry of Health
- Parents Association of Disabled Children

Table 4.4 Revised objectives

- To establish a Steering Committee to guide the process of building an inclusive Kyrgyzstan, Working Groups to develop a National Strategy and Action Plans to achieve this goal and the high level political support necessary to make the vision a reality
- To provide tools and training in equity analysis using the *BIAS FREE* Framework to those involved in the initiative
- To initiate a process of identification and elimination of all physical, social and attitudinal barriers to the full inclusion of children
- To align all legislation, policies, programmes, service delivery, social and built environments, research and practices with the vision of a truly inclusive society
- To enable families and communities to fully include and care for all children
- To end all practices involving the segregation of disabled children and close segregated residential institutions
- To serve as an incubator of ideas, methods and tools for moving towards inclusive societies that can serve as a model for other countries

- Disabled Youth Association
- Save The Children, UK
- UNICEF

It was also agreed to organize a workshop and convene a National Working group to develop the National Strategy, and that UNICEF would provide technical support to the National Working Group. A common vision, goals and objectives were also set. The overall project goal was stated to be to create a fully inclusive Kyrgyzstan that values, welcomes and treasures diversity and provides the conditions in which all people may grow, develop and contribute to society to their fullest potential, enjoy equal rights within their communities and society and achieve physical, mental, social and spiritual well-being; the associated objectives are shown in Table 4.4.

4.9 National Working Group

The National Strategy would be developed though the joint work and coordinated action of a National Working Group. The National Working Group will consist of representatives from the Ministry of Health, Ministry of Education, Ministry of Labour and Social Protection, and the Department of Child Protection. It will also be made up of representatives from Parents of Disabled Children associations, disabled youth and adults, disabled people's organizations, community members, officials from schools, institutions, the business community, human rights lawyers and other human rights experts, the media, and local, national and international organizations and NGOs who are committed to the project goal and objectives.

The National Working Group would be subdivided into teams, each working on different aspects and issues of inclusion. Separate teams would be formed to focus on each of the following: national legislation, infrastructure, education, health, social welfare, labour, and sports and recreational activities. Teams would decide on priority areas to be addressed in each area and would take decisions jointly and democratically on specific actions and activities to be undertaken.

Each team would be responsible for identifying the specific strategies that would need to be undertaken in its area of interest, identifying an Action Plan for work over the next five to ten years, including key stakeholders, activities to be undertaken, related budget requirements, and potential funders.

Each team would be chaired by a member of the National Steering Committee. Chairs will guide the process, ensuring that each team works towards the project goal and objectives and produces an Action Plan. Chairs would be responsible for pulling all the Action Plans together into a coherent National Strategy.

4.10 Conclusion

Kyrgyzstan is a relatively young country and, like many other countries in the region, it is still shaking off the legacy of the Soviet model of care of disabled children. The medical model of disability still prevails and influences those caring for disabled children including teachers, parents and medical personnel. Using the *BIAS FREE* Framework helped to shift the emphasis and direction of the research over the course of the research. A paradigm shift occurred from the medical to the social model of disability, from focusing on "repairing" the disabled child to focusing on building inclusive communities for everyone. As such, the *BIAS FREE* Framework was a very useful tool in identifying and analyzing the problems experienced by disabled children and their parents and teachers and in finding real solutions to those problems. The Framework provided a *theoretical* understanding that promoted engagement in a research *methodology* that empowered them to participate in a *process* of challenging and transforming the social hierarchies around them. It helped participants to become profoundly aware of their *rights* and injustices around them and to take action to solve injustices that they and others experience.

References

Amiot, CE, & Bouris, RY (2005). 'Discrimination between dominant and subordinate groups: The positive-negative asymmetry effect and normative process', *British Journal of Social Psychology*, 44, 289–308

Burke, MA, & Eichler, M (2006). *The BIAS FREE Framework: A Practical Tool for Identifying and Eliminating Social Biases in Health Research*, Geneva, Switzerland: The Global Forum for Health Research. http://www.globalforumhealth.org/filesupld/Bias%20free/BIASFree_References.pdf

Burke, MA, & Pegg S (2003). *Analysis of Special Needs Education Policies in Canada Using an Inclusion Lens*, North York, ON: The Roeher Institute. http://www.cacl.ca/english/priorityresouces/incedu/index.html

Burke, MA, Bach, M, Coleman, R, McKie, C, & Stewart, G (2000) *Dynamic Model of Health*, http://www.cwhn.ca/resources/health_model/Dmodel.pdf [accessed 14th February 2007]

Burke, MA, Bach, M, & Crawford, C (2001). *Striking a New Balance: Proposal for a Joint Federal-Provincial/Territorial Disability Supports Investment Strategy*, North York, ON: The Roeher Institute

Burke, MA, Bach, M, & Crawford, C (2002a). *Moving in Unison Into Action: Towards a Policy Strategy for Improving Access to Disability Supports*, North York, ON: The Roeher Institute

Burke, MA, Crawford, C, & Pegg, S (2002b). *A Tool for Assessing Child Care/ECD Programs*, http://www.cacl.ca/english/priorityresouces/childyouth/resources.html North York, ON: The Roeher Institute

Burke, MA, Crawford, C, & Pegg, S (2002c). *Community Profile Tool: Measuring Inclusivity of Early Childhood Resources*, http://www.cacl.ca/english/priorityresouces/childyouth/resources.html North York, ON: The Roeher Institute

Burke, MA, Crawford, C, & Pegg, S (2002d). *Early Childhood Development Policy Analysis Tool*, http://www.cacl.ca/english/priorityresouces/childyouth/resources.html North York, ON: The Roeher Institute

Burke, MA, Pegg, S & Stewart, C (2003) *Inclusivity of the Child Care Policy Environment in Canada: Much Work to Be Done*, North York, ON: The Roeher Institute. http://www.cacl.ca/english/priorityresouces/childyouth/Docs/Much%20Work%20rev_sed%20Sep1_041.pdf

Eichler, M, & Burke, MA (2006) The *BIAS FREE* Framework. A new analytical tool for global health research. Canadian Journal of Public Health:63–68, Ottawa, Global Health Issue, Jan –Feb 2006.

Rossides, DW (1996). Social stratification: The interplay of class, race, and gender (2nd ed.). Upper Saddle River, NJ: Prentice Hall

Schriner, K and Scotch RK (2001) *Disability and Institutional Change: A Human Variation Perspective on Overcoming Oppression*. Journal of Disability Policy Studies VOLUME 12, NUMBER 2, Fall 2001

UNCRPWD (United Nations Convention on the Rights of Persons with Disabilities) (2007), New York: United Nations

Chapter 5
Networking in Disability for Development: Introducing the African Network for Evidence-to-Action on Disability (AfriNEAD)

Gubela Mji, Siphokazi Gcaza, Natalie Melling-Williams, and Malcolm MacLachlan

5.1 Introduction

This chapter argues for the importance of networking to promote the human rights of persons with disability. The nature of relationships between people in a community can be seen as a key indicator of the well-being of that community. The global village can try and maintain the distant and sometimes difficult relationships between vulnerable groups through the imaginative use of networking, thus providing not just an opportunity, but an obligation to use such technologies to promote social capital, social inclusion and social participation. Networks offer a means of supporting and achieving these aspirations for persons with disabilities. We introduce the African Network for Evidence-to-Action on Disability (AfriNEAD) and argue for its timeliness.

Central to our approach is the concept of *ubuntu. Ubuntu* is a South African term but the concept is not uniquely South African by any means and has resonance in other African countries. In Malawi, for example, a very similar concept to *ubuntu* is that of *umunthu* (Sharra, 2005, 2006). There are various interpretations of the *ubuntu* concept, but at the heart of the concept is the idea that people are human only in relation to others[1] – the proverb "uMntu ngumntu ngabantu" (a person is a person because of other people) is commonly cited as core to the *ubuntu* concept. The concept has sparked considerable debate and difference of opinion (Bewaji and Ramose, 2003; Farland, 2007; Metz, 2007; Van Niekerk, 2007) but for the

G. Mji (✉)
Centre for Rehabilitation Studies, Stellenbosch University, Stellenbosch, South Africa

[1] *Ubuntu*: "The heritage of the philosophy that comes to us through our traditional African roots is *Ubuntu*: morality, compassion, care, understanding and empathy. It is one of share and hospitality, of honesty and humility. Simply put, it is the ethic and interaction that occurs in the extended family. In Africa, it draws in all people. In the "family" there is a community of shared values and equality" (Boon, 1996).

M. MacLachlan and L. Swartz (eds.), *Disability & International Development: Towards Inclusive Global Health*,
DOI 10.1007/978-0-387-93840-0_5, © Springer Science+Business Media, LLC 2009

current chapter it is sufficient to note two things: First, we hold the principle of interdependence as central to the way we should think about developing disability work in Africa (and in adhering to this interdependence, or *ubuntu*, concept, we are at some distance from a number of European approaches to disability which very strongly emphasize independence). Second, the *ubuntu* concept of interdependence or interrelatedness does not have to been seen as either archaic or as uniquely African. Indeed, contemporary possibilities for electronic communication in a global village enhance the opportunities for networking and mutual interdependence, all of which can further the possibilities for a global approach to disability work consonant with *ubuntu* principles.

In keeping with a community-based, *ubuntu* approach, persons with disabilities have raised disability as a human rights and a development issue indivisible from other human rights issues. It is within this context that they have tried to show how persons with disabilities have been marginalized by society at different levels. They have tried to work as a group and to network disability issues at local, regional and global levels. They have tried to combine their voices to reach the highest offices that handle global human rights issues. As a response to these initiatives, in some countries disability policies have been developed in an attempt to include the needs of persons with disabilities amongst the needs of all citizens of those countries. These attempts in some areas have started to give a sporadic positive impact to the lives of some persons with disabilities. However, it seems that the quality of life for most persons with disabilities may not be changing as rapidly as has political awareness (Ingstad and Whyte, 2007:5).

Despite the high priority given to the needs of persons with disabilities at an international level, when one looks at the picture, especially in countries that are struggling to see that a greater percentage of their citizens have food on their tables, there is minimal activity directed towards making an impact on the lives of persons with disabilities, especially those who live in rural environments.

This reality gives rise to a dilemma for disability activitists. Should disability networking be isolated to an agenda that deals exclusively with disability issues, or should persons with disabilities join up with other concerned advocates who are challenging those systems that marginalize vulnerable citizens, including persons with disabilities? Related to this dilemma is a further question: If disability advocates network with other concerned advocates, will this dilute the voices of these disabled advocates? What guarantees are there to ensure that the needs of persons with disabilities take the same prominence as those of other vulnerable citizens? [2]

Unfortunately, there are indications that other groups interested in development and human rights do not always offer prominence to disability issues in their struggles. It is a sad but common experience that many a time when White Papers, policies and conventions are debated, persons with disabilities are consulted only at

---

[2] This dilemma is not unique to disability activism. In the history of struggles for national liberation there have been debates, for example, as to whether the advancement of equality for women or for sexual minorities should be delayed in the service of the broader national liberation agenda.

the eleventh hour of the discussions; sometimes they would have been completely forgotten had it not been for their own initiatives. As a result of this negligence, questions are being asked regarding the wisdom of mainstreaming networking for disability issues both at local, regional and international levels. Also there is the historical perspective that comes with networks in relationship to how the world has developed and been shaped, especially for vulnerable groups such as persons with disabilities.

5.2 Global and Historical Aspects of Networking

The industrialized world has moved ahead in matters of genomics, service delivery and biotechnology (Lau, 2004; De Bont et al., 2007). Different action strategies have been implemented to translate knowledge from existing theory in order to guide planning and practice innovations. Decision makers have been encouraged to consider a multifocal approach that effectively incorporates networks both at physical and technological levels as well as including a social capital approach in the planning and evaluation of programmes that hasten equity (De Bont et al., 2007; Mozunder and Marathe, 2007). These may range from information communication networks to actual physical meetings of network membership from time to time to resolve certain problems and put in place specific strategies (Lau, 2004; De Bont et al., 2007; Mozunder and Marathe, 2007; Daar et al., 2007).

For these reasons the term "network" is defined as a "compressed term" that represents a perspective of hope for forward movement and as a facilitator of conducive democratization and successful cooperation, including professional optimization to those affiliated to professional bodies or organizations. As a term used almost as universally as the term "system", "network" has very nearly come to be mythologized (Weber, 2005). Networking also facilitates close forms of cooperation in a regional context, often initiated by support programmes and generating research interest in evidence-to-action (Weber, 2005). Gnahs (2003:100) in Weber (2005:40) maintains that networking is about dealing not only with a clear accentuation of the term "network", but with a "school of thought, a line of orientation, "a warmth metaphor" including an accentuated demand for initiative: regions shall be guided out of their passive role, taking on an active part in dealing with their concerns". As part of the regional networking processes, intermediary agencies for regional learning networks are created which are supposed to tie different fields together, to give creative support and to serve as bridges for the initialization of regional processes by defining needs and giving orientation of what needs to be achieved.

There has been a general perception that networks can substantially scale up the effectiveness of the existing resources and achieve equitable distribution of such resources (Lau, 2004; De Bont et al., 2007; Mozunder and Marathe, 2007; Daar et al., 2007). For example, Wilkinson and McCarthy (2007) were able to show that it was possible to reach more than three million cancer patients through cancer management network teams for the dissemination of information related to palliative management. Friedman et al., (2007) suggest that the network aspect of social capital is also useful to best understand the active, on-the-ground processes by which people of some countries, beset with poverty, racial/ethnic subordination and internal divisions (arising from inequalities at different levels), defend their own and others' safety and health. Within these discussions and innovative strategies scholars such as Boneham and Sixsmith (2005) are calling for the inclusion of the voices of older women. They perceive that these women are innovative networkers with reservoirs of prior knowledge in activities that require non-linear patterns (such as social capital) for problem-solving. These are some of the assets they have used to sustain their families during different challenges in their lives (Boneham and Sixsmith, 2005; Baum, 1997; Scott and Wenger, 1995).

The concept of networking is as old as humankind. Early on, humanity recognized the need for networking and co-opting the strengths and potential of other human beings in their day-to-day existence for survival, progress and development. The old adage "the whole is greater than the sum of its parts" also recognizes this. In the past this maxim would sometimes involve moving from one's own environment to be closer to those whom you perceive could enhance your human existence; for example, when those you were living with are no longer able to do so. The networking concept was also applied by early traders who saw the exchange of goods and human bodies as a way of enhancing their own trading vocation and skills; on the other hand, those persecuted by religious or political dogmas saw moving to other environments as a means of saving their own lives. It is interesting to note that the very oppressive approaches they were running away from in their own countries were carried at an unconscious level as the template that would at a later stage be used to subordinate and subjugate those whom they found living in their new environments (Mkhize, 1973).

It appears then that the world as we see it today has been shaped by these early networkers. From these early activities, a myriad of networking activities and exchanges started happening. People and goods migrated along with knowledge and technologies, initially slowly and later with increased pace and speed. This was influenced by industrial and technological revolutions that further facilitated and enhanced the rate and pace of networking. The result was the development of national, regional and international seaports, airports, information networks, and even scholars disseminating information; all of these constitute important potential nodes of communication and exchange.

Today we have the most extensive network of all humankind and that is the "global village". The "globalization philosophy" sees the world as one centre stage where myriads of networks, like electric wires, join individuals, organizations and systems to the global stage and to each other. As access to different commodities improves for some people, many human rights activists recognize the exclusion that continues to persist for the greater part of the world's population. For this reason they continue to lobby and network for a global village where access transgresses boundaries and is improved for all.

5.3 Perceived Culture of Global Networks

Much as there has been rapid growth and development in networking and globalization, concerns have been expressed about how the globe has become increasingly unsafe to live in, and at the widening of the gap between the poor and the rich. Health and its services has in many instances become an exclusive commodity for the rich (Rasool, 1997). Hunger, in certain parts of the world, has escalated to epidemic levels, and it is estimated that the number of undernourished in sub-Saharan Africa, for example, will treble between 1990 and 2080(von Braun, 2007). All "our children"[3] have become unsafe at all layers of our globe, irrespective of socio-economic status. They are at risk of being trafficked like goods, from south to north, from east to west, by those requiring instant gratification. The responsibility for some of these ills has been laid at the doorstep of modern technology in that it facilitates networking and makes it easy to form a family of "all sorts" depending on your interests and your networking skills.

On the other side of the coin, the interpretation of human rights and strategies to unlock equity and develop a "true global village" has taken another turn of events (Werner, 1997). The new economic order, led by those who have learnt from the architects of the old hegemony and who want to maintain the separatist exclusive gains achieved in the past, manipulates global dynamics by continually changing the goal posts for what is required to achieve global equity and to alleviate poverty and human suffering (CDRA, 2004/2005). New institutions and networks such as the G8 have been developed and accepted, depending on the extent to which you or your country is compliant with their development scale (Korten, 2003; Chossudovsky, 1997). Terms and language such as "developed" and "underdeveloped" regions, "scientific" and "non-scientific" knowledge are being loosely used in the description of some human development (Werner, 1997). We need to ask whose yardstick is being used in order to classify a whole country/ continent and its people as being "underdeveloped" and what is the impact of that term on the people of those worlds, including the new generation of those worlds? In our view, "development" should be understood to be about groups of people in a reciprocal relationship that represents improving the circumstances of all involved. It is not something that one country or group does to another country or group; it is something they help each other with. All countries should be developing countries; the process of improvement should not be claimed as an end-state by some and as a target for others (MacLachlan, Carr and Mc Auliffe, in press).

At these highly charged networking activities, you see the concerned advocates and networkers waving placards that highlight the plight of the poor (Werner, 1997; Chossudovsky, 1997). They call for a revision of laws that govern exports and subsidies to smallholding farmers (Shiva, 1997). They taunt the giants of the First World regarding the privatization of natural resources and destruction of the natural environment for profit. They ask, "Since when do shrimps and flowers fill stomachs?"

[3]Within African culture, children belong to and are the responsibility of all adult village people.

And they end warning that even the air that we breathe will soon be sold at a price (Shiva, 1997; Davies, 1997; Bond, 1997; Werner and Sanders, 1997). Is this not already happening in life-saving institutions such as health care facilities? In the so-called developing countries, if you require critical care and you do not have money for private care, you could well land up in a public hospital where the balance between supply and demand dictates your chance of access to what may be seen as 'luxury' equipment, though this equipment is necessary to save life (Marmott, 2007; Rasool, 1997; Werner, 1997; Sambo, 1997; Sanders et al., 1997). For persons with disabilities these issues might imply a shift from not only focusing on equity concerns but to paying more attention to attaining their rights in a market place where gains achieved in equity could be translated into policy and action.

5.4 The Emergence of Voices of Concerned Advocates

On the ground, another group of concerned activists and advocates has started to emerge both at regional and international levels (Sanders et al., 1997). They have recognized the plight of the poor and the inequities that continue to exist for poor people, with devastating impacts on health and well-being (People's Health Movement, Medact and Global Equity Gauge Alliance, 2008). Much as their activism is driven by the general concern for human rights neglect, at the core of their struggle is the understanding that there is a strong link between those classified as developed and the poor, and that a truly healthy global village cannot be achieved amidst such inequity (Werner, 1997; Korten, 2003; Sambo, 1997). They infer that socio-economically disadvantaged persons more often report poor social networks and social support systems. This is either often due to the scramble for meagre resources or broken family units as a result of key family members having left to look for work elsewhere (Scott and Hofmeyer, 2007; Dragon et al., 2008).

These supporters of human rights are calling for collaboration through national, regional and international networks – survey and capacity building based on proven models through education, training and needs assessment (McGorry et al., 2007). They are calling for expanded information and communication networks that will widen the avenues for community-based "participatory development" that encourages the use of local information, knowledge and decision-making (Cololizza et al., 2007). They perceive that integrated service hubs and networks across nations, community awareness, workforce training and evidence-based resource material can reduce inequities across nations. They see as essential that there should be service cohesion and synergistic planning that includes health and social outcomes for all population groups including persons with disabilities. They are concerned about regulatory mechanisms that form frameworks for commercialization and the interface to industry and the impact of these for small and medium enterprises as well as intellectual property and land rights. Discussions have taken centre stage regarding ethical, societal and cultural issues that may hamper accessibility and the need to strengthen leadership support at the political level to develop capacity to address these issues (McGorry et al., 2007; Cololizza et al., 2007; Beasley et al., 2007).

They are calling for the globalization of human and political rights to answer the issues of social justice. They see the emergence of the new class that is created from swift exchange of the latest information and how certain countries are being left behind due to lack of access to this information.

Caution is extended to these fellow advocates regarding both resources and the yardsticks they will use as they charge forward to join hands with the poor and the disenfranchised. Writers such as Montegut (2008) are commenting on how difficult it has been for organizations like WHO to meet the expectations created by its programmes, as core issues that relate to equity and human rights have not been met as yet. They further comment that this might be due to the fact that the current promulgation of the Millennium Development Goals has again tried to improve health in developing countries through a focus on disease-orientated (vertical) programmes. Suggestions are made that as these professionals are building their careers they need to take cognisance of implementing positive steps for building cooperation in the regions they enter. They invite discussions that centre on roles that professionals can play in building "cooperation networks" for underpinning health and food security, conflict resolution and global health promotion (Skinner and Sriharan, 2007). They recognize that at the core of these challenges is the need to develop cohesive strategies that will eradicate poverty and human suffering.

Our view is that the argument needs to be stretched beyond poverty to the consequences of poverty. The South African Integrated National Disability Strategy of 1997 has recognized the strong link between poverty and disability. Hence, in countries beset by poverty, such as Africa's countries, there is a high disability prevalence (South African Integrated National Disability Strategy White Paper, 1997). Early on, persons with disabilities recognized the need to come together as a group to network strategies that will address the discrimination that is entrenched in systems and relationships and that have robbed persons with disabilities for many years of the possibility of attaining the status of equal citizenship. They have coined the expression "Nothing about us without us". Judge Albie Sachs (2008) of the Constitutional Court of South Africa, describes this expression as persons with disabilities reclaiming the space of "democracy and human rights" not only for themselves but for "the whole of humanity", especially those who have been marginalized. "Nothing about us without us" is about all of us as we are struggling to find our humanity and gain an understanding regarding how some can have so much while others are struggling to put just one meal on the table. So, returning to our previously described dilemma, the question is: Should concerned advocates not join hands with persons with disabilities in challenging those systems that marginalize vulnerable citizens including persons with disabilities, and network for a global village and the rest of humanity?

5.5 Drawing Experiences from the Disability Movement

Persons with disabilities, through their resilience and networking, have chalked up some notable achievements. These include the creation of the Union of the Physically Impaired against Segregation (UPIAS), which in 1976 gave impetus to disability issues by the publishing of *The Fundamental Principles of Disability*. One of their core statements was related to the acknowledgement of the role of society in further disabling persons with disabilities when they stated that:

> In our view it is society which disables physically impaired people. Disability is something imposed on top of our impairments by the way we are unnecessarily isolated and excluded from full participation in society (Oliver 2004:19).

Another landmark networking event was the walkout of persons with disabilities from the Rehabilitation International (RI) conference in Winnipeg, Canada, in 1980 and the subsequent formation of Disability People International (DPI). This move saw persons with disabilities challenging the dominance of health professionals in the disability agenda. The establishment of DPI led to other important world initiatives that challenged marginalization and oppression of persons with disabilities. These included a declaration by the United Nations of 1981 as the International Year of the Disabled Persons (IYPD). This was followed by the World Programme of Action Concerning Disabled Persons that outlined a universal approach to tackling and overcoming discrimination and creating equal opportunities throughout the world, and was followed by the proclamation of the Decade of Disabled Persons (1982–1992) that resulted in the formulation of the Standard Rules on Equalisation of Opportunities for People with Disabilities, and the creation of an increased number of organizations for persons with disabilities (DPOs) (Howell et al., 2006:49).

More recently, the UN Convention on the Rights of Persons with Disabilities (UNCRPD, 2007), which as of 2008 has entered into international law, is perhaps the most significant – moral and practical – step towards realizing the rights of persons with disabilities. The Convention seeks to address discrimination, to change perceptions and to combat stereotypes and prejudices. Article 32 of the Convention states that "Countries are to provide development assistance in efforts by developing countries to put into practice the Convention" (UNCRPD, 2007:62). Article 32 places an obligation on people in high-income countries not only to put the Convention into practice in their own country, but also to ensure that their country assists in it being put into action in low-income countries as well.

The above gains achieved by persons with disabilities in highlighting the plight of persons with disabilities as a human rights and a development issue illustrates the sophisticated networking skills that persons with disabilities have used to tackle the years of discrimination and oppression that they have experienced. Disabled people have used networks for consultation as a group when seeking to improve accessibility, or simply a tool to voice opinions, perceptions and concerns. For this group, networks have offered vital peer support. Disability networks are a vital method of sharing disability best practice. These best practices had become valuable not only for disabled people but also for others that experience marginalization; hence disabled people are increasingly being valued for their experience and innovation in this regard.

Networks can be used to build a disability community where connections are used to share resources; networks can be used to build the reputation of disability networks where they use the connections to communicate their key values to members and the wider world; and lastly, networks can be utilized to build resources where connections are used to gain resources and strengthen DPOs (Poland, 2008). There are wider disability networks with connections between various networks at different levels for various purposes and there are big networks at a high and strategic level. These networks span from international, regional and disability local networks.

Table 5.1 presents some examples of international and national disability networks. These networks have been built up over many decades and are to be found in Africa at national, regional and global levels.

Though the disabled people are commended for their networking efforts, disability networks based in the so-called developing countries appear to be weaker as they are impacted on by not having sufficient resources to sustain themselves. Again the notion of *ubuntu* and developing synergistic effects between weaker and stronger disability networks becomes an attractive option. It appears that many challenges still lie ahead.

Despite the many progressive statements promulgated in recent years, the extent of meaningful change in the actual quality of life of persons with disability in Africa remains limited. Even in a country with relative wealth like South Africa, with its internationally acclaimed and inclusive Constitution and its established national strategies and policies (for instance, the Integrated National Disability Strategy White Paper of 1997 and the South African Employment Equity Act 1998) the possibilities for persons with disabilities to have "equal rights and dignity" remain distressingly elusive. In South Africa the majority of persons with disabilities are not yet experiencing meaningful change in their quality of life, in access to equal rights and in levels of community integration, despite a favourable policy environment and a limited, but supportive, research evidence base. Thus, the historical exclusion of persons with disabilities from society still persists. Real change and social development are still required to realize a truly inclusive society.

Research in itself will never be enough. Furthermore, there is a danger that the research community – injected with the "cash" of international aid – may simply accumulate evidence without developing practicable solutions to address the ways in which society can become more responsive to and more inclusive of persons with disability. The challenge is clear: it is not just more research that is needed; it is "improved" research and research that can be translated into policy and practice. Translating research into evidence-based advocacy, policy, practice and products – particularly in the pan-African context – needs to be systematically addressed in a coordinated, coherent and consistent fashion. A wide range of stakeholders need to be included in the process, ranging from asking the appropriate research questions through to utilizing the research outcomes – that ultimately feed back into asking further relevant research questions.

It has become clear that different groups of people all over the globe have used networks as a form of strengthening interdependence and drawing from each other's experience and expertise. Society has tried to position persons with

Table 5.1 Examples of disability networks

Organization	Membership	Goals
Disabled Peoples International (DPI, 2008) http://www.dpi.org/	National organizations or assemblies of disabled people A majority of the members as well as the governing body are persons with disabilities. Respresentatives to include all races, sex, religion, language, geography, etc	To promote the human rights of disabled people through full participation, equalization of opportunity and development To promote the economic and social integration of disabled persons To develop and support organizations of disabled persons
Christian Blind Mission (CBM) http://www.cbmi-de/	International, 700 partner organizations in developing countries throughout the world	To improve the quality of life of the world's poorest persons with disabilities and those at risk of disability in the most disadvantaged societies To support and develop local partner organizations, rather than implement projects To transfer knowledge and skills, both professional and managerial, in order to contribute to development of these partners
Handicap International (2008) CAHD – Community Approaches to Handicap in Development http://www.handicap-international.org.uk/	International, 55 countries worldwide	Focus on the causes of impairment, disability and handicap and the link to able-bodied people To create social change and inclusion as citizens with equal opportunities and full access to participation
African Community-based Rehabilitation Network (CAN) http://www.afri-can.org/	Based in Uganda.Disabled persons in Africa and their families	To benchmark best practices and research with regard to disability To make information about disability issues accessible worldwide through conferences, writer's workshops, the formation of CBR national organizations, maintaining a website and publishing To promote the equalization of opportunities, social integration and rehabilitation of persons with disabilities in Africa

Disabled People South Africa (DPSA, 2008) http://www.dpsa.org.za/	South Africa, national movement	To advocate for a paradigm shift away from seeing disability as a health and a welfare issue. Instead to emphasize disability as a human rights and development issue To assist in policy making e.g. the National Integrated Disability Strategy (1997); Inclusive Education; Employment Equity; the Rehabilitation Policy
Global Partnership for Disability and Development (GPDD, 2008). http://www.worldbank.org/disability/gpdd	International, persons with disabilities and their families, including those born with disabilities and those disabled through wars, violence, traffic or work injuries, disease, disasters and other causes	To mobilise resources through fostering relationships between North and South disability NGOs and co-operations To accelerate the inclusion of persons with disabilities and their families into development policies and practices To increase collaboration amongst development agencies and organizations to reduce the extreme poverty and exclusion of a substantial number of children, women and men with disabilities who are living in poor countries
The Secretariat of the African Decade of Persons with Disabilities (SADPD, 2008) http://www.africandecade.org.za/	Africa, governments, Decade Steering Committees (DSCs), Disabled Persons' Organizations (DPOs), development organizations	To empower African organizations to work in partnership to include disability issues and persons with disabilities in policies and programmes in all sectors of society in Africa To strengthen DSCs in at least 20 African countries by 2009. To assist the most vulnerable disability groups, e.g. persons with mental disabilities, deaf or blind persons, persons with albinism to build strong African DPOs To accelerate the inclusion of persons with disabilities and their families into development policies and practices

disabilities as being the "others"; perhaps that was the starting point for change. Lately, ideas have been challenged regarding who is disabled and who is not disabled, including fundamental definitions of disability. Questions have also been asked regarding the impact of the activities of the previous decades including the information that has been used to inform decision-making. Further concerns have been raised about the lack of cohesion between different layers (persons with disabilities, academics, civil society, business and policy makers) from those that say they are the voice of persons with disabilities. It is this context that gave birth to the African Network on Evidence-to-Action in Disability (AfriNEAD).

5.6 Background to the African Network on Evidence-to-Action in Disability (AfriNEAD)

As has been mentioned, it is now recognized that persons with disabilities are amongst the poorest and that disability is both a cause and a consequence of poverty (South African Integrated National Disability Strategy White Paper, 1997). Society has begun to recognize that disability limits access to education and employment, and leads to economic and social exclusion. For the poor, this is exacerbated as they are caught in a vicious cycle of poverty and disability. James Wolfensohn (2002), former President of the World Bank, argued that if development is about bringing excluded people into society, then persons with disabilities belong in schools, in legislatures, at work, on buses, at the theatre and everywhere else that those who are not disabled take for granted… Unless persons with disabilities are brought into the development mainstream, it will be impossible to cut poverty in half by 2015. The extent of meaningful change in the quality of life, health, access to equal rights, decent work and full community integration for persons with disabilities throughout Africa remains limited.

The Millennium Development Goals (MDGs) and strategies such as the development of Poverty Reduction Strategy Papers (PRSPs), in conjunction with the recent ratification of the United Nations Convention on the Rights of Persons with Disabilities (UNCRPD), set the stage for the development of policy, products, advocacy and practice which can improve the quality of lives of persons with disabilities in Africa.

What these lofty and worthy initiatives will actually achieve will be influenced by many factors. Their chances of success will be strengthened if they are powered by an evidence base that reaches into policy decisions and practical actions, which engages with persons with disabilities, being for them, and through them, not only about them, and, where possible, being undertaken by them. There is a need for strong evidence to support and inform new developments and to monitor and evaluate outcomes. The African Network on Evidence-to-Action (AfriNEAD) intends to be part of this solution.

5.6.1 Why AfriNEAD Now?

It is time to capitalize on the impetus that has been created by international initiatives and to further strengthen the efforts of advocates and lobbyists as well as policy makers, programme developers and businesses who are genuinely trying to address the needs of persons with disabilities in their fields.

For this reason the Centre for Rehabilitation Studies in the Faculty of Health Sciences at Stellenbosch University in South Africa has promoted the development of AfriNEAD. In this it has been supported by its African civil society partner, the Secretariat of the African Decade for Persons with Disabilities, and its northern research partner, the Centre for Global Health, at Trinity College, Dublin, in Ireland.

The vision of the African Network on Evidence-to-Action (AfriNEAD) is to improve the quality of life of persons with disabilities in Africa and throughout the world by translating new and existing disability-related research into relevant and meaningful policy, practice, advocacy and products. It is a network that is uniquely African in nature and it is well positioned to link the issues of disability, poverty reduction and development with evidence and research. It seeks solutions to its own obstacles within an African context and as such it could be a significantly unique player in research and policy-making with the key objective of increasing the participation and inclusion of the persons with disability (PWDs) in all aspects of society.

We believe that there is an urgent need for evidence

- To accurately describe the situation of persons with disabilities in Africa
- To highlight gaps in evidence
- To support new policy development
- To give credibility to advocacy for policy changes
- To inform programme development
- To monitor and evaluate existing projects
- To inform further research

There is also a need for *quality* evidence that can be of real use to end-users. This requires a strategy for the training of potential researchers and capacity building amongst DPOs, but also for all researchers in disability-related fields to find common ground in concepts such as the human rights framework, the emancipatory research approach and to move away from charity-based thinking or only a participatory approach.

There is a need to learn from one anothers' experience in the developing world so as to speed up service provision in ways that are sustainable and that address the real needs of PWDs. There is also a need to accelerate and support policy changes to help develop an enabling environment in each African country. Mutual exchanges of experiences of failure and success can strengthen the case for advocates and lobbyists.

There is a need for the integration of programmes and products as well as policy with the real needs of persons with disabilities, including the right to decent work. AfriNEAD provides a link with business people with the intention of creating mutually beneficial relationships where persons with disabilities can access meaningful work in a way that is of value to all partners. AfriNEAD can also act on a consultancy basis to the business sector to advise on issues of access and reasonable accommodation for persons with disabilities in the workplace.

5.6.2 What is AfriNEAD?

AfriNEAD's vision is to become a significant contributor to and facilitator around the needs of persons with disabilities in Africa, by assisting in translating existing and new research in the disability arena into meaningful evidence-based advocacy, practice, products and policy.

Translating research into evidence-based outcomes – particularly in the pan-African context – needs to be systematically addressed in a coherent and consistent fashion. Ongoing dialogue with all stakeholders is needed to address barriers to this integration.

Thus, the network explicitly aims to facilitate an integrated, intersectoral, multiperspective and interdisciplinary approach to realizing the rights of persons with disabilities in South Africa and throughout the African continent. AfriNEAD is proposing a range of activities commencing with the establishment of Working Groups which are tasked with identifying action pathways and producing Best Evidence-to-Action Research Practice Guidelines. This will include working with member countries to develop a methodology for profiling their own local situation regarding persons with disabilities and the services and opportunities available to them, the existing available research, research that is currently being undertaken and research that is required. An important aspect will be to identify facilitators and barriers for turning this research evidence into action. To further the work done by AfriNEAD the plan is to run a biannual symposium – to keep planting the "seeds" – every second year.

The First Stellenbosch Symposium on Evidence-to-Action in Disability (SSEAD 07) was held in November 2007 and was attended by a range of international delegates, many of whom were persons with disabilities. Delegates came from 14 different African countries, as well as from North America and Europe representing governments, institutions of higher learning, and persons with disabilities organizations (DPOs), non-governmental organizations (NGOs), businesses and research funders. A significant proportion of the speakers were persons with disabilities. Debate was positive, constructive and vigorous and affirmed the need for just such a medium of interaction. For this first symposium, we invited papers around the general theme of "realizing the rights of persons with disabilities in Africa." Several of the papers that were presented at the conference, or inspired by it, are to be published in a special issue of *Disability & Rehabilitation* early in 2009.

5.6.3 How Will AfriNEAD Measure its Success? Some Reflections Regarding the Quest for Relevancy and Sustainability in Networks

The creation of a network centres on the perception that there is a problem at hand that requires a collective generation of knowledge to develop solutions. The development of new knowledge is a prerequisite for the success of a network. At the core of a network is the understanding that people with similar and sometimes opposing ideologies have come together to stimulate and continue the ongoing generation of knowledge that will assist in giving direction on the core concern of the network.

Weber (2005) maintains that monitoring and evaluation become of central importance for network development. In the past, evaluation designs in the context of the complex structures of decision-making often predetermined the evaluation direction. It is within this context that Weber (2005) suggests alternative approaches that might be suitable for a network to evaluate if it is reaching its goals. These are:

- *Between "technocratic feasibility" and "systemic irritation"*:

The idea is to move away from pre-planned evaluation models that are driven by intentional design and seek to influence conditions with already assumed results. It is suggested that even the most advanced and differentiated instruments of planning eventually cannot "handle" social reality. Thus, there is a need for open, dynamic approaches to planning and evaluation, approaches that can evolve to match the social context.

- *Between legitimization of the past and planning for the future*:

Here networks run the risk in conducting parallel activities at all levels which do not give feedback to each other, which are directed towards network goals and which see themselves as strategically orientated. Some of the evaluation designs are embedded in a "planning culture" where the emphasis is on diagnosis, feasibility studies and conditions for success, thus leaning more towards future orientation on numbers and cost benefits. The most effective interventions are those that harmonize with visions and strategies of the system of reference, in this case the network. The aim is not the realization of individual activities but a strategic feedback relationship of all measures that is supposed to create equality in the directedness of all activities.

- *"Expert objectivity" or subject participation*:

In the past it was held that some of the challenges facing those with subjective knowledge stem from a lack of the skills that were held by those with utilitarianistic rationalist models of action. The tendency then is to hand over decision-making and responsibility to experts who have the skills. During these moments, the participants bow their heads and allow themselves to become objects of analysis instead of systemic partners in the collective efficiency of examining whether the network's goals are being realized. During this process, democratization and the production of knowledge that is relevant for action has to work with network knowledge. If this does not happen, there are distinct risks of interest-guided dominance and colonization on the one hand, with a lack of acceptance and inner emigration by the network partners on the other (development of networks within the network). Knowledge production in networks thus has to rely on the cooperative structures of participatory research. The efficiency of the solution of material problems depends on the participation of those concerned, on openness to criticism, on horizontal structures for stability and democratic procedures for implementation as expressed in the disability movement's maxim of "Nothing about us without us".

- *Completeness of what is known or the processing of what is not known/uncertain*:

When members of a network congregate around a specific concept, they are not starting from a point of knowing, but from a cup that is not yet full, and the degrees of not being full vary from member to member. There are also other spaces of the network regarding concepts that might be completely empty. The starting point is to accept this and not be threatened by it. Through dialogue and debate, osmosis of ideas happens including the germination and sprouting of completely new ideas. This suggests that the network is suspended in its planning and development through a process-orientated ideology that is driven and facilitated by communication. For networks to function and move forward there should be minimal neutrality regarding communication of the core goal of the network. This communication approach is integral for bridging the gap between philosophy and concept to action. The strength of being able to play out this function is related to the ability of the network to allow "multiple, conflicting and evolving processes and purposes". By allowing these conflicting ideologies, lessons and learning occur. We live in a world that tends to say that you are either with us, and this implies you are our friend, or against us and implying that you are our enemy. The authors of this chapter are of the opinion that networks do not work like that. If a network is allowed to operate like this, then the opportunity for learning is completely stifled, thus leading to the network's own demise. Networks should therefore guard against a tendency towards "group thinking" (Janis, 1972).

- *The space in-between as the space of uncertainty about the future and rich with possibilities for growth and development*:

As human beings, we have the past, the in-between and the future. Our perception is that the space in-between is the most critical space for developmental work. Many plans have fallen flat on their face due to how the space in-between has been managed. Network members come together laden with stories of failure and success in the past. They are unsure and concerned about the future and they put their hopes in the space in-between. Trust is put on the communication debate model of the network to bring the fruits of the membership together and to weave them into a matrix that will lead into the future. Intended or unintended qualities of learning will find their space and through an integrative discussion possibilities for new epistemologies and transdisciplinary perspectives emerge. This learning will be happening at different levels of individual, dyads and groups of actors.

Network knowledge is always social; it is created and embedded in social practice, with its individual and collective elements. Whole network relationships are based on exchange, which is, in turn, based on stable expectations and norms of reciprocity and underpinned by the concept of *ubuntu*. Trust is also seen as a *sine qua non* (important and integral) for the successful undertaking of projects. This trust is not absolute and complete; it is floating and growing, always becoming and is as dynamic as the learning and knowledge of the network. To expect trust of network members to be absolute and solid would be naïve and would put the network under undue strain and at high risk of dissolving once this absolute trust is questioned with the unfolding of the network events. If the network is about the in-between space and learning and creating new knowledge for the future, one hopes that working through each other's contribution through the communication dialogue model will contribute to the development of trust. Also working through specific projects as a group and being challenged during these processes to reveal attributes that enhance trust will further contribute to the ongoing development of trust.

It is within this context that the authors are reminded of Tuckman's 1965 classic model of group formation:

(a) Initially noncommittal and friendly encounters – the *forming* phase.
(b) Followed by the struggle for space, social status and power within the social structure – the *storming* phase.
(c) Identification of whether the group is capable of working and performing into the future – the coming together of the group into a functional whole – the *norming* phase.
(d) A "performing group" – the *performing* phase. Networks do not, however, evolve along a linear pattern. Questions arise regarding who should be part of the membership of the network as well as the selection of the "actors". Following that, clarity should be given regarding how the network will be regulated, with knowledge being integrated as well as the constitution of borders and the prioritizing of activities, including the allocation of resources for these activities as well as outcomes. Table 5.2 represents a suggested framework for network cooperation.

Since networks represent dynamic rather than static arrangements of relations and cooperation, networking has to be read as a learning process. Networks do not produce a complete agenda; continuous creation is an integral component of the network using the group "thought of the moment" – or the "new thought". Consequently, networks escape the constraints of technocratic feasibility and embark on a journey of collective and continuous creation of knowledge that denounces fear of the unknown. The network constitutes itself in time and space via social practices, as a collective social setting. It regulates itself systematically and contextually.

In this chapter we have described the historical and contemporary aspects of networking to promote the human rights of persons with disabilities. We have also sought to highlight, rather than to resolve, some of the dilemmas that marginalized groups have to face in advocating for their rights. We conceive of an international network embodying the *ubuntu* village community philosophy;

Table 5.2 Framework for network design of cooperation[4]

Design elements	Function of design elements
Variety – unity	How can a balance be reached between the variety of participating actors and their integration to some kind of unity?
Flexibility – specificity	How flexible is the network in terms of its goals and self-image, how specific is it? There needs to be a balance between these two integrals
Autonomy – dependency	How much autonomy is possible and what does it consists of, how much dependency exists and what does it consist of?
Trust – control	How much trust and what kind of trust is there; what is regulated by control mechanisms and how?
Cooperation – competition	What roles do cooperation and competition play? What relationship is created between them?
Stability – fragility	What roles do stability and fragility play? How are they created? What regulation mechanisms are there to manage these?
Formality – informality	How is the relationship between formality and informality regulated; what relationship do they have?
Economy – power	What relationship is there between arrangements of functionality and power? How are power patterns generated?

helping people "be all they can be" through their participation in a collective effort and we invite you to join with us in AfriNEAD to promote this vision (AfriNEAD@sun.ac.za).

References

African Community Based Rehabilitation (CAN) [Home page online]. 2008 [cited Sept 18th 2008]. Available from: http://www.afri-can.org/

Baum, F (1997). 'Social capital and health development: Rethinking Primary Health Care and health promotion. Lighten the Burden of Third World Health: The New World Order: A Challenge to Health for All by the Year 2000', International Conference, Cape Town South Africa. 29th–31st January 1997

Beasley, JW, Starfield, B, van Weel, C, Rosser, WW, & Haq, CL 'Global health and primary care', *J AM Board Fam Med*, 20(6): 518–26

Bewaji, JAI, & Ramose, MB (2003). The Bewaji, van Binsbergen and Ramose debate on ubuntu, *South African J Philos*, 22(4): 379–415

Bond, P (1997). 'The new world order: A challenge to health for all by the year 2000. Lighten the Burden of Third World Health', International Conference, Cape Town, South Africa, 29th–31st January 1997

Boneham, A, & Sixsmith, JA (2005). 'The voices of older women in a disadvantaged community', *Soc Direct – Soc Sci Med*, 62(2): 269–279

Boon, M (1996). *The African Way – The Power of Interactive Leadership*, Johannesburg: Struik Publishers

[4] Weber (2005) quoting Sydow (1999)

CDRA (2004/2005). *Horizontal Learning: Engaging Freedom's Possibilities*, Annual Report 2004/2005

Chossudovsky, M (1997). 'The globalization of poverty and ill health – assessing the IMF/World Bank Structural Adjustment Programme. Lighten the Burden of Third World Health: The New World Order: A Challenge to Health for All by the Year 2000', International Conference, Cape Town, South Africa, 29th–31st January 1997

Christian Blind Mission (CBM) [Home page online] 2008 [cited Sept 18th 2008]. Available from http://www.cbmi-de/

Cololizza, V, Barrat, A, Barthelemy, M, & Vespignani, A (2007). 'Predictability of disease and epidemic pathways in global outbreaks of infectious disease SARS', *BMC Med*, 5:34

Daar, AS, Berndtson, K, Persad, DL, & Singer, PA (2007). 'How can developing countries harness biotechnology to improve health?', *BMC Public health*, 7:346

Davies, R (1997). 'The implications of the new macro-economic framework (GEAR) for development in South Africa. Lighten the Burden of Third World Health: The New World Order: A Challenge to Health for All by the Year 2000', International Conference, Cape Town, South Africa, 29th–31st January 1997

De Bont, A, Stoevelaar, H, & Bal, R (2007). 'Databases as policy instruments. About extending networks as evidence-based policy', *MBC Health Serv Res*, 7th Dec 2007, 7:200

Disabled People International (DPI) [Home page online]. 2008 [cited Sept 18th 2008]. Available from: http://www.dpi.org/

Disabled People South Africa (DPSA) [Home page online]. 2008 [cited Sept 18th 2008]. Available from: http://www.dpsa.org.za/

Dragon, SS, Mobus, N, Beck, S, Stang, EM, Mobhlenkamp S, Joeckel, KH, Erbel, R, & Siegrist, J (2008). 'Low socio-economic positions are associated with poor social networks and social support: Results from the Heinz Nixdorf Recall Study', *Int J Equity Health*, 5(7):13

Farland, D (2007). 'African intuitions and moral theory', *South African J Philos*, 26(4): 356–363

Friedman, SR, Mateu-Gelabert, P, Curtis, R, Maslow, C, Bolyard, M., Sandoval, M, & Flom, PL (2007). 'Social capital or networks, negotiations and norms? Neighbourhood case study', *Am J Prev Med*, 32(6 Suppl): S160–70

Gnahs, D (2003). Indikatoren- und Messprobleme bei der Bestimmung der Lernhaltigkeit von Regionen. In. Brödel, Rainer; Bremer, Helmut; Chollet, Anke; Hagemann, Ina-Marie (Hrsg.): Begleitforschung in Lernkulturen. Berlin: Waxmann. Verlag. pp. 92–106

Handicap International [Home page online]. 2008 [cited Sept 18th 2008]. Available from: http://www.handicap-international.org.uk/

Howell, C, Chalklen, S, & Alberts, T (2006). 'A history of disability rights in South Africa', in Watermeyer, B, Swartz, L, Lorenzo, T, & Priestley, M (eds), *Disability and Social Change – A South African Agenda*, Cape Town: HSRC

Ingstad, B, & Whyte, SR (eds) (2007). *Disability in Local and Global Worlds*, Berkaley, CA: University of California Press

Ingstad, B, & Whyte, SR (2007). 'Disability connections', in Ingstad, B & Whyte, SR (eds), *Disability in Local and Global Worlds*, Berkeley, CA: University of California Press

Janis, IL (1972). *Victims of Groupthink*, Boston, MA: Houghton Mifflin

Korten, D (2003). 'The Great Turning: From Empire to Community', Available online at www.ycarmagazine.org/greatturning for book. Accessed on 8th October 2008

Lau, F (2004). 'Towards a conceptual knowledge management framework in health', *Perspect Health Inf Manag*, 1:8

MacLachlan, M, Carr, SC, & Mc Auliffe, E (2010) *The Aid Triangle: The Human Dynamics of Dominance, Justice and Identity*, London: Zed

Marmott, M (2007). 'Achieving health equity: From root causes to fair outcomes', *Lancet*, 9593, 1153–1163

McGorry, PD, Tanti, C, Stokes, R, Hickie, IB, Carnell, K, Littlefield, LK, & Moran, J (2007). 'Headspace: Australia's National Youth Mental Health Foundation – where young minds come first', *Med J Aust*, 187–97 supplement: S68–70

Metz, T (2007). 'Ubuntu as moral theory: reply to four critics', *South African J Philos*, 26(4): 369–387

Mkhize, N (1973). 'Psychology: An African perspective', in Hook D (ed.), *Critical Psychology*, Cape Town: UCT Press

Montegut, AJ (2008). 'To achieve "Health for all" we must shift the world's paradigm to "primary care access for all"', *J Am Board Fam Med*, 21(2): 169–70

Mozunder, P, & Marathe, A (2007). 'Role of information networks in malaria survival', *Malaria J*, 6: 136

Oliver, M (2004). 'The Social Model in Action: If I had a hammer', in: Barnes, C & Mercer, G (eds), *Implementing the Social Model of Disability: Theory and Research*, Leeds: Disability Press, pp. 18–31

People's Health Movement, Medact & Global Equity Gauge Alliance (2008). *Global health watch 2: An alternative World Health Report*, London: Zed Books

Poland, F (2008). 'Philosophy of Social Networks'. Presentation to African Community Based Rehabilitation Network (CAN) Executive Meeting, Winneba, Ghana, 19th–20th July 2008

Rasool, E (1997). Conference Opening Address, 'Lighten the Burden of Third World Health: The New World Order: A Challenge to Health for All by the Year 2000', International Conference, Cape Town, South Africa, 29th–31st January 1997

Sachs, A (2008). Keynote speaker for Friday Mavuso Lecture, School of Health and Rehabilitation Sciences, Faculty of Health Sciences, University of Cape Town, 31st July 2008

Sambo, A (1997). 'The Nigerian health and human rights situation in the context of structural adjustments. Lighten the Burden of Third World Health: The New World Order: A Challenge to Health for All by the Year 2000.' International Conference, Cape Town, South Africa. 29th–31st January 1997

Sanders, D, Bijlmakers, LA, & Basset, MT (1997). In rural and urban Zimbabwe. 'Lighten the Burden of Third World Health: The New World Order: A Challenge to Health for All by the Year 2000', International Conference, Cape Town, South Africa. 29th–31st January 1997

Scott, C, & Hofmeyer, A (2007). 'A networks and social capital: A relational approach to primary health care reform.' *Health Res Policy Syst*, 5:9

Scott, A, & Wenger, GC (1995). 'Gender and social support networks in later life', in: Arber, S and Ginn, GC (eds), *Connecting Gender and Aging*, Buckingham: Open University Press

Secretariat of the African Decade of Persons with Disabilities (SADPD) [Home page online]. 2008 [cited Sept 18th 2008]. Available from: http://www.africandecade.org.za/

Sharra, S (2005). 'From entrepreneurship to activism: Teacher autobiography, peace and social justice in education', *Curr Issues Comparative Educ*, 8(1): 7–17

Sharra, S (2006). 'Breaking the elephant's tusk: Teacher autobiography and methodology in teacher education', *J Stellar Educ*, 1(3): 1–13

Shiva, V (1997). 'Globalisation of agriculture and the growth of food insecurity. Lighten the Burden of Third World Health: The New World Order: A Challenge to Health for All by the Year 2000', International Conference, Cape Town, South Africa, 29th–31st January 1997

Skinner, HA, & Sriharan, A (2007). 'Building cooperation through health initiatives: An Arab and Israeli case study', *Conflict Health*, 1:8

South African Employment Equity Act. (1998). Available online at http://www.labourguide.co.za/EE.pdf. [accessed 28th August 2008]

South African Integrated National Disability Strategy White Paper. (1997). Available online at http://www.info.gov.za/whitepapers/1997/disability.htm [accessed 9th October 2008]

Tuckman, BW (1965). 'Developmental Sequences in Small groups', *Psychol Bull*, 63, 384–399

UN Convention on the Rights of Persons with Disabilities (UNCRPD) (2007), in: *Core for International Human Rights Treaties*, United Nations, New York and Geneva pp. 3–66

Van Niekerk, J (2007). 'In defence of an autocentric account of *Ubuntu*', *South African J Philos*, 26(4): 364–368

Von Braun, J (2007). 'The world food situation: New driving forces and required actions', Washington, DC: International Food Policy Research Institute

Weber, S (2005). 'Network evaluation as a complex learning process', *J Multidiscip Eval*, (2): 39–71

Werner, D (1997). Keynote Address, 'Lighten the Burden of Third World Health: The New World Order: A Challenge to Health for All by the Year 2000', International Conference, Cape Town, South Africa, 29th–31st January 1997

Werner, D, & Sanders, D (1997). 'Questioning the solution: The politics of Primary Health Care and child survival (with an in-depth critique of oral rehydration therapy)', Cape Town: Health Wrights CA in association with The International People's Health Council, Third World Network and Partners in Health

Wilkinson, DL, & McCarthy, M (2007). 'Use of comparative data for integrated cancer services', *BMC Health Serv. Res.* 17th December 2007, 7:204

Wolfensohn, JD (2002). 'Poor Disabled and Shut Out', *Washington Post*, 3rd December

World Bank, Global Partnership for Disability and Development (GPDD) [Home page online]. 2008 [cited Sept 18th 2008]. Available from: http://www.worldbank.org/disability/gpdd

Chapter 6
Building Disability Research Capacity in Low-Income Contexts: Possibilities and Challenges

Leslie Swartz

6.1 Introduction

The history of disability research is a vexed and highly politicized one. There is a long history of research conducted by able-bodied people on disabled people, some of it with the very best of intentions, but often at the exclusion of voices of disabled people themselves. With the development of the social model of disability and the "Nothing about us without us" approach, disabled people have waged (and won) struggles to take control of disability research, and it is now true to say that much of the best and most influential research is conducted by and for disabled people themselves.

Commenting on what he sees as what he terms an "impasse" (p.11) in British disability studies, and in the context of his view that the disability movement has stagnated since 2000, Tom Shakespeare wrote in 2006:

> While I value the achievements that have been won through the close alliance of disability politics and disability research, I believe that the weaknesses of the British approach now outweigh the benefits. Translation of ideas and ideologies from activism to academia has not been accompanied by a sufficient process of self-criticism, testing and empirical verification. The social model of disability that has successfully inspired generations of activists has largely failed to produce good empirical research, because it relies on an overly narrow and flawed conception of disability.
>
> (Shakespeare, 2006: 11).

Shakespeare takes issue with a totalizing view of disability and disability politics, a fragmented world in which, to put his argument somewhat crudely, there are "good guys" and "bad guys," and claims made, explicitly or implicitly, for an essentialist reading of disability. He believes that without a more nuanced approach to understanding the complexities – including the political complexities – of disability issues, our ability to generate useful knowledge which will forward the

L. Swartz (✉)
Department of Psychology, Stellenbosch University, Stellenbosch, South Africa
e-mail: lswartz@sun.ac.za

M. MacLachlan and L. Swartz (eds.), *Disability & International Development: Towards Inclusive Global Health*,
DOI 10.1007/978-0-387-93840-0_6,

rights agenda for disabled people will be compromised.[1] If Shakespeare is correct about the magnitude of challenges facing disability studies in Britain, it is the case that disability studies faces even greater challenges in the context of low and middle-income countries, where there are vast gaps between the rich and poor, enormous governance challenges, and numerous threats to livelihood, health, safety and stability, and environmental sustainability.

In this chapter I focus on the impact of these larger issues on what at first blush may seem a straightforward task – building research capacity for disabled people in lower-income contexts, drawing on my own work in this field in southern Africa. I begin by locating the politics of disability within broader debates in identity politics and the politics of exclusion. I then examine the way in which criteria set for disability research may be influenced by disability politics in ways that are not always helpful. I then discuss an example of research capacity building as a way of building a case for a broader discussion of knowledge management issues in disability work in lower-income contexts. The brief conclusion makes some recommendations for further work.

6.2 Disability, Exclusion and the Politics of Knowledge

The story of disabled people being excluded from knowledge produced about them is not a unique phenomenon. We know, for example, that racism and colonialism, just like disablist research, depended on a process of "othering" – black and colonized peoples became objects of research, their voices excluded, their bodies objects of interest (Butchart, 1998; Swartz, 1998). This interest was sometimes well intentioned and paternalistic and sometimes aimed more clearly at naked oppression and control. The Nazi holocaust is probably the twentieth century genocide that made most overt claims to the authority of "science," including "medical science." It is no coincidence that amongst the objects of this "science" were people seen as racially inferior (Jews and gypsies, for example), those described as degenerate (homosexuals, for example) but also people whose bodies and minds were thought to defile the purity of the nation – people with disabilities (Lifton, 2000). All these groups were tortured in the name of "medical research"; all these groups were murdered in large numbers.

In the international development of knowledge and technology, then, it is not only disabled people who have historically been excluded from expertise in the knowledge economy or who have been objects of study. This fact is especially important when we begin to consider issues for disability research in postcolonial contexts. Not only have disabled people in these contexts, like many disabled people in higher-income countries, been excluded from active ownership of research processes, it is also the case that disabled people in lower-income countries

[1] Shakespeare's particular engagement with the social model of disability is not a central issue for this chapter, but his frank appraisal of what he sees as both good and bad in disability politics and research certainly is.

generally share a history with their compatriots of having been colonized and having been excluded, commonly by reason of race and/or indigenous status, from having access to the best education available. Not surprisingly, there is a widespread suspicion of science as a whole in many postcolonial contexts, and certainly in Africa, as a recent review of media approaches to HIV/AIDS in Africa has shown (Bolognesi and Swartz, 2008).

In South Africa, a combination of factors including a mistrust in science has led to tragic consequences – a president and health minister vulnerable to AIDS denialism, a resultant crisis in provision of much-needed antiretrovirals, leading to approximately 330,000 deaths (Chigwedere et al., 2008; Nattrass, 2007). On the other hand, it is also true that the refusal to accept being othered by racist or colonialist or disablist science has led to enormous vitality, especially in the social sciences. There can be no question that the core recognition that knowledge production excludes people on the basis of their identities has led to interesting, exciting and innovative thinking, both in the postcolonial context (see, for example, Mbembe, 2001; Said, 1979; Spivak, 2006) and in the context of disability studies (see, for example, Felstiner, 2007; Lorenzo, 2003; Mairs, 1997; Oliver, 1995). Clearly, things have gone wrong as a consequence, or a partial consequence, of objections to racist, sexist, colonialist and disablist control of knowledge (witness the needless loss of life in South Africa) but much has also gone right (the importance of insider voices in the literature and in shaping the research agenda cannot be overemphasized).

Before we can begin to understand the specific challenges associated with capacity development in disability research in low-income contexts, it is important that we get to grips with what is at the heart of the tensions between the successes and the failures in contemporary critiques of dominant research modes. Disability studies is at the centre of a raft of critiques of dominant social and medical science, on a number of grounds including the following:

1. Scientists and researchers commonly treat oppressed or "other" groups as objects, and do not take into account the perceptions held by oppressed groups as valid data.
2. Research on the "other" often furthers the needs of the already powerful, and does not forward the needs of those who remain objects of science.
3. Information that is gained from research into oppressed groups is not used to their benefit and may in fact be used better to oppress them in the future.
4. Actual research participants ("subjects") often hear nothing about the results of the data they have provided, and gain nothing from the process.

6.3 Disability Politics and Research Criteria

The consequences of these important insights can be seen in the criteria developed by the UK Department for International Development (DFID) Disability Knowledge and Research (KaR) Program for researchers wishing to contribute to the DisabilityKaR program. In the research prospectus provided for potential research bidders, the following were the criteria by which applications were judged:

- Does the outlined method represent meaningful and genuine consultation with disabled people in the South? (10 points)
- Does the outlined method allow for consultation/involvement with a wide range of disabled people, including, particularly, disabled people's organizations, disabled women and people with different impairments? (10 points)
- Does the research team include disabled researchers? (10 points)
- Does the applicant provide evidence of capacity/track record in work of this nature? (5 points)
- Does the applicant demonstrate understanding of the social model of disability? (5 points)
- Does the applicant have experience of mainstreaming from other sectors? (2 points)
- Does the applicant outline a range of empowering and/or emancipatory research methods and have experience of using them? (5 points)

Source: http://disabilitykar.net/docs/odg_research_pros.doc, [accessed 12th January 2009]

Almost all of these criteria address important process issues. Of the total of 47 points used in ranking proposals, in fact, all of the points, with the possible exception of the 5 point criterion "does the applicant provide evidence of capacity/track record in work of this nature?" are designed to ensure that whichever team does research on disability for DisabilityKar program will not only understand the importance of inclusion of disabled people in research but will also provide evidence of this inclusion in all aspects of the program and methods used.

For the sake of comparison, consider DFID criteria for evaluating expressions of interest from research program consortia, for work not in the disability field *per se*:

The principal selection criteria for Expressions of Interest will be:

- *Originality and importance* of the research
- Likelihood of research contributing to poverty eradication, relevance to Millennium Development Goals and potential for policy impact
- *Quality of proposed organizations*, researchers and Director
- Quality of *research approach*, including dissemination strategies
- Adequacy of *collaborative arrangements and capacity building*.

(source:http://www.dfid.gov.uk/research/eoiresearchprogconsort260504.asp [accessed 12th January 2009]).

There is an enormous difference between the DFID criteria for research consortia and for the DisabilityKar criteria, and it is not really fair to compare them directly as the purposes of the calls for work were of very different magnitudes. It is also almost certainly the case that in the DisabilityKar assessment these types of considerations were brought to bear – they must be implicit in any research procurement process. But the fact that they were not formally part of the process is instructive and important, and indicative, I believe, of a broader trend in disability research. Central to much of how we see disability research these days, including in lower-income contexts, are the two key issues of identity and participation. There is a strong belief that it matters whether the person doing the research is disabled or not, and it matters who participates in research processes and who does not.

It cannot be stressed strongly enough how important these twin issues of identity and participation are, indeed, to contemporary disability research, but where matters become fuzzy is that these issues are by no means unique to disability research. At the heart of the social model of disability as a whole is the belief that disabled people must be centre stage, defining the agenda, on all issues to do with promoting the rights of disabled people. This should apply no less to disability research, and indeed, the chapter by Mji and colleagues in this volume (Chap. 5) emphasizes very clearly the importance of process and identity issues to building credible and viable disability research networks. Solidarity, self-representation, and speaking with one voice are all crucial aspects of developing networks of any kind, especially for oppressed groups. The problem though is that research requires something else as well, and this is the ability to be sceptical about data, and to allow data to change one's mind.

6.4 An Example of Research Capacity Development Issues

The easiest way to explicate both the advantages provided by and the challenges raised by a particular form of emancipatory disability politics for research capacity development in lower-income countries is by way of example. I have been fortunate to be involved in a number of disability research capacity initiatives.

My experience with a very strong DPO network in southern Africa at first pleasantly surprised me, though in retrospect I should not have been surprised. My work was with a group of highly experienced and articulate activists who are accustomed to daily struggles of living, often in contexts of great poverty. A fairly senior person in the organization, for example, feels rather lucky to live in an apartment in an African capital city, but every day she has to be carried up and down the stairs to her apartment, as the only building in which she can find a place to live is inaccessible to wheelchair users like herself. Other struggles include those of discrimination and overt disavowal by some able-bodied compatriots. It may be difficult for disabled people (or any people) in wealthier country contexts where there is some accommodation in the physical environments and where disability rights are protected in a context of overall good governance to grasp fully what many disabled people in poorer countries still live with – a combination of lack of resources, ignorance, stigma and discrimination. There are some encouraging signs that things are changing in many contexts, but the core point I wish to make here is that as a colleague and I began research capacity training with this particular network, there was no question that we were working with people who viscerally understood what it means to be excluded and not to have one's needs met, to be viewed as an outsider and even at times to be feared and avoided.

I have considerable experience of teaching research issues to university students from relatively privileged backgrounds, and with good academic histories. In this group of activists, some had tertiary education but many had not completed high school. One might have anticipated that this group, therefore, far less academically prepared than my students, would struggle more than my students with basic research concepts. Though to some extent this was true with technical concepts, it was not so with what may be regarded as one of the fundamentals of research-mindedness. In order to be a researcher and to understand the research process, one has to be able to question things, to "make strange," as the anthropologists put it, aspects of life and the world which are commonly taken for granted. Many of my students, well schooled to give "right" answers, or the answers their teachers want, in examinations, struggle with the fundamental spirit of non-acceptance – indeed, of enquiry – that makes a good researcher. They are often authoritarian about their sources, believing that if something appears in a book, it is their job to be able to memorize this and to repeat what the author has said. This lack of research-mindedness, lack of understanding of the scepticism that is at the heart of much good research, is a common phenomenon, discussed by many commentators in the higher education field (Stanovich, 2007).

This problem of lack of research-mindedness that I experience with my students was largely absent in this group of disabled activists. Why? I believe that because the group with whom my colleague and I were working were accustomed to being unfairly forced to the periphery in society, because they dealt with having to question taken for granted assumptions about disability day after day, they already had considerable experience of what is for me at the core of being a researcher – the ability to question things. There may of course be a range of other explanations for what I observed, but it is certainly the case that a group of experienced disability activists, most of whom had no research training, were easily able to grasp some key concepts of what research is and does – and that they had been applying these long before my colleague and I were there to "teach" them.

There were many other encouraging features of this particular training group. As is suggested in the literature (and, indeed, this is one of the DisabilityKar criteria, as mentioned above, though our work was not part of DisabilityKar) we used a number of participatory techniques to build research capacity. Though this is not often discussed, many participatory techniques are heavily visually loaded, requiring people to draw, to make charts and so on.[2]

One of the exercises we wished to do with our research trainees was a community mapping exercise which would assist the participants, who came from a number of different countries and contexts, both to think systematically about researchable issues in their own communities and to communicate these in an accessible way to their fellow-participants. We planned carefully for a more accessible version of community mapping for participants who were blind or had severe visual impairments, making use of story telling. After the exercise was complete and we were discussing it in the larger group, one of the blind participants said what to us was a surprising thing: "Don't be so sure," he said, "that blind people don't know about what places look like. In fact we are the best geographers." All the blind people in the group

[2] The very useful "TOOLS TOGETHER NOW! 100 participatory tools to mobilize communities for HIV/AIDS" put together by the Aids Alliance and downloadable for free from www.aidsalliance.org, for example, is a treasure-trove of participatory techniques useful for any training and not just in the AIDS field. Many of the wonderful techniques included in this manual depend heavily on visual materials.

immediately knew what he meant and a lively discussion developed on this topic. Blind participants pointed out that they all live in inhospitable environments, where there is poor road upkeep, where traffic is heavy and often very fast, where there are no pedestrian crossings which indicate it is safe to walk by the sounding of a bell, where people live and trade on pavements which were designed for pedestrians but no longer serve that function, or they live in rural areas where there are no tarred roads and it can be muddy, with pathways barely accessible. As a result of this, they are acutely aware of the physical environment, of how many steps it takes to go here or there, of road surfaces changing, of where it is (comparatively) safe to cross a road. The blind participants were amused to tell the rest of the group that whenever they get together, they discuss the physical environment in great detail and that they know more, therefore, about what places look like than the rest of us do!

This discussion in our workshop helped re-emphasize the important contribution of the social model to all aspects of disability work – if we create an environment in which people can draw on multiple knowledges, we will find useful and sometimes surprising positive outcomes. Any project which would have viewed these blind participants as objects of study and looked at them only from the outside would probably not have learnt what we all as a group learnt on that day. There is no question from this experience and many others that a participatory approach which draws on existing knowledge is a very helpful one – part of the job of the person involved in building research capacity is simply to help participants find out the ways in which they are already researchers.

Though this point is clearly true, another aspect of that training workshop illustrates some of the challenges we face in participatory research capacity development processes. After a few days of good, hard work on basic research principles, I was facilitating a session close to the end of this particular process on systematic collection of data. First, we just went round the room and asked for some basic demographic information by which people identified themselves. We captured these data on a grid, and we played around with organizing the material according to different categories – for example, we could divide the group by gender, by country of origin, by current home country, by impairment type, and so on. For the next stage of the work I wanted to introduce the participants to the basics of organizing material according to categories developed by the researcher – categories inferred from data. As it was important in any event to get some feedback from participants about their experience of the workshop, I asked them to fill in a feedback form and then as a group we would categorize the responses. The form was designed in such a way as to introduce participants to what can and cannot be learned from asking questions in a range of ways (e.g., open/closed questions, forced choice answers, etc.).

When I looked over the forms over the tea break prior to our session analyzing the data, I could see that I would have a problem with our data categorization session. The responses were uniformly positive and I would not have a range of responses easy to differentiate from one another. I should have anticipated this, as responses to workshops are commonly very positive at the time, but in the interests of building capacity about data categorization I slipped in a dummy feedback sheet that was very negative about the work we had done. We went through the responses and

I slipped in the "dummy" negative response approximately two-thirds down. When we reached this response the initial reaction from some group members was that there must be a mistake – the data must be wrong. A senior member of the group, clearly embarrassed at what he feared my colleague and I might experience as a slur on our good work, said, "We must find this person and we must discipline – he cannot be allowed to say this thing!"

We were able to use this response to discuss the nature of research and to make the point that whatever our data we cannot simply ignore data which do not fit in with what we would like our data to be. We were able to talk about the difference between the dictates of unity in activism and the fundamental research principle that there is no point in collecting any data at all if that data will not have the potential to change your views. What we did not discuss, I realize in retrospect, was the degree to which the reactions to the negative response – widespread disbelief, followed by a threat of "discipline" from a senior member of the organization to the participant who was out of line – could help us to think about the question of response set and validity of data. There was clearly a strong ethos in this group that the facilitators must be treated with kindness, and we were treated with kindness. Given this ethos, though, we must call into question the validity of the uniformly positive feedback. It is conceivable that all participants did in fact enjoy and value the training (we did, in fact, gain this impression) but in terms of developing a more nuanced understanding of the value of our work and its pitfalls, another method of collecting feedback would be required. Had we had time we would have discussed this more with participants, and there will be other opportunities for this discussion. The point for the current argument, though, is a more serious and far-reaching one, and I shall discuss this in the following section.[3]

6.5 Research Capacity and the Knowledge Management Challenge

What can we learn from the fact that in a relatively research-naïve group, and a very polite and supportive group, people were uncomfortable with negative feedback on a research capacity workshop that they themselves had probably experienced as positive? In one sense, very little – people are polite, they like to stand together, and they value input from researchers committed to helping them. There is another sense though in which our experience from this workshop, and especially the comment that the (bogus) dissenter needed to be "disciplined," reveals a deeper challenge for research capacity building for disability research in lower-income contexts.

One of the key achievements of the disability rights movement has been that disabled people have stood together and have convinced others, many of whom

[3] We did in fact reveal to participants that we had constructed a bogus response and we did have a discussion about how researchers may report on data where there are outliers, but this discussion is not germane to the present argument.

have no interest in disability issues, and in fact may even hold prejudices against disabled people, that the collective voice of disabled people cannot be ignored. International agencies have responded to this collective action. The DisabilityKar initiative has been one of a host of initiatives which have correctly emphasized two key points central to international development: first, that disability issues are in fact core to the reaching of development goals (see, for example, Albert, 2004) and second, that a core value which should underlie the mainstreaming of disability is the full participation of disabled people in processes which affect their own lives.

One of the places where these two incontrovertible values become more complex, though, is precisely in the area of disability research. Critiques of mainstream approaches to research in general and disability research in particular are commonly well put (Oliver, 1995) but particularly in the context of poorer countries there is a serious danger of a basic principle of research being overlooked. Sophisticated critiques of crude empiricism, some of which come from the disability studies field itself, correctly point out that data do not exist "out there" and that there are commonly many interpretations of the same data (Denzin and Lincoln, 2007), but making this claim is not the same as claiming that data do not matter at all.

Many disabled people in lower-income contexts who have the ability to develop substantial research skills are unaccustomed to thinking about the importance of data as a source of information that can change one's views on the world. There are two obvious reasons for this. First, many of these people, though they have excellent research potential, as I have argued, have had relatively little education, and/or have been schooled in rather authoritarian education systems, where the authority of the "expert" is privileged over a robust engagement with issues. Second, many people (most people in the world, in fact) live in circumstances where governance and policy decisions are made not on the basis of data and information but on the basis of the relative power of different groups of people (see Chalklen et al., 2006, for a discussion of the implications of this for the African Decade on Disability). Data-driven policy making is in fact quite rare internationally. When we take these two factors into account, it is not surprising that a senior participant in our research capacity workshop wanted to "discipline" a view which potentially could be seen to undermine a group view. The issues at stake in our workshop were, in the grand scheme of things, trivial, but they point to much more far-reaching questions about what disability research is and does in lower-income contexts.

It is hardly surprising, nor is it inappropriate, that calls for more disability-related research in lower-income countries tend to be couched in pragmatic terms (Turmusani, 2003) – we need to change policies and practices which affect the lives of disabled people world-wide. Nor is it a problem, as we have seen with the DisabilityKar criteria mentioned earlier, that there should be such a strong emphasis on participation by disabled people in research processes. But there is something that may be obscured in the confluence of these trends towards pragmatism and participation in disability research in lower-income countries. This is simply the need for good knowledge management as a fundamental prerequisite for research endeavors, and the understanding that data, even crude data, do matter.

Once again, an example will well illustrate the issue at stake, an issue which if ignored can leave unchallenged calls for "disciplining" or ignoring information which does not immediately or obviously fit a collective or emancipatory agenda. Some time ago, a colleague and I were interested in finding out what policies DPOs in South Africa had, or did not have, regarding HIV/AIDS (see Rohleder et al., 2009). As a first step we approached the Office on the Status of Disabled Persons (OSDP), which is a government office and resides in the highest echelon of government in the land, the Presidency, to give us a list of DPOs and organizations serving disabled people. The OSDP did not have this information, but gave us a list they themselves believed to be inaccurate and outdated. We approached government departments, who were similarly unable to help. National DPOs also did not have up-to-date lists available and were often able to supply us with outdated lists provided by consultants at some time in the past.

Clearly, all these groups – government departments and national DPOs – were able to conduct their business in the absence of up-to-date information even on formal organizations with whom they are mandated to consult. At another level, I have worked with many DPOs and other organizations that are not able to give me any estimation of the number of people they serve. Records are simply not kept and are certainly not maintained. Forms that have been devised by the organizations themselves or by consultants may be filled out, but data are not collated and are not kept up to date. When I have questioned colleagues from DPOs about this issue, they are often very articulate, and correctly so, about how difficult it is to define disability, how data may change over time, and about the dangers of labeling. All these issues are valid and very important, especially for disabled people, who have for so long been the victims of oppressive and crude forms of data gathering. It is encouraging, furthermore, to hear from the sceptical answers about data how successful the disability movement has been in sensitizing its members to the politics of knowledge – a key issue for anybody concerned with realizing the rights of excluded groups who have been the objects of oppressive study and bureaucracy. But there is a world of difference between knowing that data are subject to political influence and are difficult to collect in meaningful ways, to not having systems of data collection at all. It is important that an organization that collects complex information is aware of the complexity of that information and the limits to its validity; this does not, however, lead to the conclusion that there is no point to data collection at all.

This issue links to the question of research capacity development in two ways. First, as we have seen, the success of the critical edge of the social model of disability in alerting disabled people to the politics of disability knowledge may have had, as a partial consequence, a situation in which the old authority of the able-bodied "experts" has been replaced by a new authority of the disability activists. This can be seen not only in the example I have given from our capacity-building workshop but also from numerous other experiences where research data (whether produced by able-bodied or disabled people) are simply rejected as not true in participatory meetings. In South Africa, in this regard, it is not uncommon to hear people claiming that the data we have on disability prevalence "must be wrong" because people feel there must be more disabled people than the statistics say, but without any discussion or engagement with the methods by which statistics are generated and collated. Though in terms of empowerment of disabled people it is an important victory that disabled people feel confident to question dominant knowledges (including statistics collected by governments and other agencies), this is not enough. Disabled people need to be able to engage with issues of method and to do more than to offer broad brushstroke critiques, critiques that are fundamental but once established have limited capacity to facilitate change.

This point leads to the second issue about data and research capacity development. If we are serious about capacitating disabled people's organizations in lower-income contexts to take charge of research processes, there is a danger that we have begun this process taking insufficient account of the current knowledge management context of many such organizations. On the one hand, a sophisticated critique of oppression of disabled people is in place; on the other, many DPOs do not have a tradition of collecting data (however mindful we may be of the limitations of that data) in a systematic and sustained way. Calls for disability research in lower-income countries commonly focus on big questions on issues, for example, like HIV/AIDS, inclusive education and economic empowerment. All these issues, and many more, are indeed important.

But if DPOs continue to be involved in sophisticated and large-scale research in which data are collected in exemplary ways, and these research processes (often led or driven by consultants or international funders) are at odds with the day-to-day management of the DPOs themselves, the possibilities for research capacity to be developed and sustained in a meaningful way are much reduced. If research is seen as somehow separate from being systematic about knowledge within the day-to-day running of organizations, the opportunity will be lost to develop DPOs in the South optimally as "thinking organizations." The key issue for developing research capacity for DPOs may be less whether these DPOs can work with outsiders who have considerable research experience and infrastructure in producing research outputs (and there are some examples of excellent collaborations of this type in this book), than whether DPOs can be assisted to regard everything they do in the most mundane as producing knowledge and data. If, to use another example, DPOs in Zimbabwe had for many years been in the habit of collecting routine information on their members and on their work, it would now, with the tragic collapse of much infrastructure in that country, be possible to extract data, however limited but more than anecdotal, on trends in what Zimbabwe's political and humanitarian crisis means for disabled people in particular. DPOs in Zimbabwe have indeed been involved in research endeavors, and good ones, over the past 20 years and previously, but there are gaps in basic knowledge about information that is not very difficult to collect.

Increasingly, government and other agencies are asking for data to inform policy and practice, and though anecdotes are important, these have their limits in convincing people far from where difficulties occur to change how they do things. Capacity building in the disability research field has until now been successful as regards issues to do with the politics of participation and the politics of research knowledge. It has been less successful in developing ways in which basic information can be routinely collected by DPOs and in developing disciplined (but technically not very complex) ways of collating and interrogating data. The challenge for the future, if we are serious about sustainable capacity building, therefore, may be rather unglamorous. While the performance of participatory processes remains important, we should perhaps be focusing less at this stage on engagement with large-scale research projects than on developing knowledge management systems and cultures within DPOs. It is from this basis of manipulating everyday "mundane" knowledge that sustainable capacity in research data collection, management and interpretation can be built. It is not possible, in short, to separate research capacity development from the broader field of organizational knowledge management.

6.6 Concluding Comments

It is impossible to overstate the achievements political processes around disability have had in advancing the strength and sophistication of DPOs in lower-income countries. Paradoxically, though, the crucial and necessary emphasis on performative and participative aspects of involvement of disabled people in research processes may have obscured some fundamental challenges that now need to be taken forward. Part of the problem with these challenges for systems of knowledge management is that such systems look in many ways similar to systems of control by which disabled and other oppressed and colonized people have been excluded and reduced to ciphers within a politics of domination. It is important for us to understand why it is no mistake that many colonial governments were very good at record keeping, for example. What is important for the sustainable development of disability research in postcolonial contexts, however, is to go beyond critique to using some methods that may look embarrassingly unemancipatory, that involve sheets of information routinely collected, and not always collected through participatory workshops. Lorde (1984) famously said that "The master's tools will never dismantle the master's house" and she was correct in this. But if we wish to build a new house in a new order in which we control resources, we should not fear applying a range of tools that have formerly been denied to oppressed people. Without due attention to the development of basic skills and technical competencies, there is a real danger of the stagnation of the kind Shakespeare (2006) describes.

Participation and inclusion are key to realizing rights for disabled people. In the field of disability research, though, these are not nearly enough. Disability research is both less than and more than disability activism – disability research could not be where it is today without activist and participatory agendas. In lower-income countries where technical and knowledge management skills lag behind research-mindedness and political acumen, however, we need to address these lags. There are many ***knowledges, many ways of seeing the world, many worthwhile perspectives. This fact should lead us to the conclusion not only that we deserve a critique of dominant ***knowledges but also that disabled people have a right of access to as many tools for knowledge development as possible.

References

Albert, B (2004). 'Is disability really on the development agenda? A review of official disability policies of the major governmental and international development agencies', http://disabilitykar.net/karreport/summer2004/disabilityagenda.html [accessed 13th January 2008]
Bolognesi, N, & Swartz, L (2008). 'The media management of HIV/AIDS in Sub-Saharan Africa with particular reference to South Africa: A window to developing communication strategies for the epidemic in the region', in: Mansell, R.E. (ed.), *Reports prepared for UNESCO for the International Association of Media and Communication Research (IAMCR) 50th Anniversary Conference 2007. Media, Communication and Information: Celebrating 50 years of theories and practice* (pp. 3–33), Paris: UNESCO
Butchart, A (1998). *The Anatomy of Power: European Constructions of the African Body*, London: Zed books
Chalklen, S, Swartz, L, & Watermeyer, B (2006). 'Establishing the Secretariat for the African Decade of Persons with Disabilities', in Watermeyer, B, Swartz, L, Lorenzo, T, Schneider, M, & Priestley, M (eds.), *Disability and Social Change. A South African Agenda* (pp. 93–98), Cape Town: HSRC Press
Chigwedere, P, Seage, GR, Gruskin, S, Lee, T, & Essex, M (2008). 'Estimating the Lost Benefits of Antiretroviral Drug Use in South Africa', *JAIDS, Journal of Acquired Immune Deficiency Syndromes*, 49(4): 410–415
Denzin, N, & Lincoln, Y (eds.) (2007). *Collecting and Interpreting Qualitative Materials* (3rd ed.), Engelwood Cliffs, NJ: Sage
DFID (2008). 'Research strategy 2008–2013: Working Paper Series: Capacity Building', http://www.research4development.info/PDF/Outputs/Consultation/ResearchStrategyWorkingPaperfinal_capacity_P1.pdf
Felstiner, M (2007). *Out of Joint: A Private and Public Story of Arthritis*, New York: Bison Books
Lifton, RJ (2000). *The Nazi Doctors: Medical Killing and the Psychology of Genocide*, New York: Basic Books
Lorde, A (1984). *Sister Outsider: Essays and Speeches, Trumansburg*, New York: Crossing Press, p.110
Lorenzo, T (2003). 'No African renaissance without disabled women: a communal approach to human development in Cape Town South Africa', *Disability & Society*, 18(6), 759–778
Mairs, N (1997). *Waist-High in the World: A Life Among the Nondisabled*, Boston, MA: Beacon Press
Mbembe, A (2001). *On the Postcolony*. Berkeley, CA: University of California Press
Nattrass, N (2007). *Mortal Combat: AIDS Denialism and the Struggle for Antiretrovirals in South Africa*. Pietermaritzburg, South Africa: University of KwaZulu Natal Press
Oliver, M (1995). *Understanding Disability: From Theory to Practice*, London: Palgrave Macmillan
Rohleder, P, Braathen, SH, Swartz, L, & Eide, AH (2009). 'HIV/AIDS and disability in southern Africa: A Review of relevant literature', *Disability & Rehabilitation*, 31, 51–59
Said, E (1979). *Orientalism*, New York: Vintage
Shakespeare, T (2006). *Disability Rights and Wrongs*, London: Routledge
Spivak, GC (2006). *In Other Worlds: Essays in Cultural Politics*, New York: Routledge
Stanovich, KE (2007). *How to Think Straight About Psychology* (8th ed.), New York: Addison-Wesley
Swartz, L (1998). *Culture and Mental Health: A Southern African View*, Cape Town: Oxford University Press
Turmusani, M (2003). *Disabled People and Economic Needs in the Developing World: A Political Perspective from Jordan*, London: Ashgate Publishing

Chapter 7
Empowerment, Advocacy and National Development Policy: A Case Study of Disabled Peoples' Organizations in Bolivia

Marianne Griffiths, Hasheem Mannan, and Malcolm MacLachlan

7.1 Introduction

This chapter describes the concepts of empowerment and advocacy and considers their relevance to promoting the inclusion of people with disabilities (PWD) in development policy. We begin by considering the "big picture" of development policy instruments, focusing on Poverty Reduction Strategy Papers (PRSPs) as an ultimate target for the inclusion of disability on the development agenda. We then consider some pertinent theory concerning empowerment and advocacy. Next we look at what actually happens, on the ground, by presenting a case study of disability advocacy and empowerment activity by disabled peoples' organizations (DPOs) in La Paz, Bolivia. There are considerable challenges in moving from valuable but often opportunistic and unstructured local advocacy and empowerment initiatives to less immediately rewarding inclusion in national development policy instruments. In considering what policy rhetoric says, what theory suggests and what happens in practice, our fundamental concern is with how to link daily localized advocacy activities of DPOs to longer-term strategic interests of inclusive national development.

The issue of disability is one of great importance within the development context. People with disabilities make up 10% of the world's poorest people, about 650 million in total (WHO, 2005). If this 10% of the world's population, "including an estimated 400 million disabled people living in the developing world" (400 Million R, 2008) all lived in the same place they would make up the third-largest country on earth, a country about the same size as the European Union. Despite these statistics, people with disabilities are frequently ignored by policy makers and public health programmes. The Millennium Development Goals, agreed by world leaders in 2000, do not specifically mention disability; however this is an issue that affects each and every one of the existing goals (Lynn, 2007). In order to achieve the Millennium Development Goals it is imperative to address the issues of disability in low-income countries. Within this context it needs to be highlighted that during the launch of the

M. Griffiths (✉)
Centre for Global Health, Trinity College Dublin
e-mail: mgriffith@ tcd.ie

M. MacLachlan and L. Swartz (eds.), *Disability & International Development: Towards Inclusive Global Health*,
DOI 10.1007/978-0-387-93840-0_7, © Springer Science+Business Media, LLC 2009

MDGs there was not a standardized measure available on disability. In contrast, the health-related MDGs are monitored using an internationally harmonized and standardized measure, i.e. mortality rates. Most importantly, the need to address the issue of disability within the development agenda through international cooperation is now enshrined in international law, through the UN Convention on the Rights of Persons with Disabilities (UNCRPD,2007). While the Convention gives greater weight to moral and humanitarian arguments for the increased participation of persons with disabilities (PWD) in society, there is also a strong economic argument: not only are PWDs massively overrepresented amongst the poorest in developing countries, but they also constitute a valuable resource for economic growth, if their economic potential can be unlocked.

7.2 Disability on the Development Agenda and National Development Plans

The World Bank has contributed significantly to putting disability on the development radar due to its recognition of the double imperative – human rights and economic potential – in the context of the MDG(s). The MDGs prioritize poverty reduction in developing countries and are targets for galvanizing countries and communities into action but they do not set out strategies for achieving these goals or targets. Translating them into action requires an operational framework at the national level. In more than 70 low-income countries, this operational framework is increasingly being provided by a country-led process of developing "Poverty Reduction Strategy Papers" (PRSPs). The World Bank and International Monetary Fund have established various aid instruments to contribute to this. PRSPs, are one such instrument, and these enable countries to obtain debt relief and to access World Bank/IMF credits. PRSPs have become the main multi-lateral mechanisms for providing development aid to the world's poorest countries. In effect, they are national plans to reduce poverty. The idea is that a variety of stakeholders participate in the drawing up of the paper, with the paper reflecting stakeholder consensus and outlining priority actions to be taken.

PRSPs should outline the process that led to the formation of the PRSP; outline the poverty profile of the country; set targets and priorities within the proposed policy measures; and provide a plan for monitoring and evaluation. In designing PRSPs individual countries incorporate those aspects of the MDGs that fit their own situations and reflect the aspirations of a broad range of the country's citizens. After several cycles of PRSPs there is, however, scant evidence of disability being meaningfully incorporated into national plans. Where disability has been included in the PRSP processes, this inclusion has tended to revolve around the concept of charity; however where DPOs have been involved, the inclusion of disability has referred instead to education, training, employment, and to broader participation as well as access to services (Handicap International, 2006). Nonetheless, in some African countries disability has a higher profile than in others, including Ministries specifically addressed to disability issues. However, even where this is the case, disability has not necessarily permeated into PRSPs in a satisfactory way. In some situations Disabled People's Organizations (DPOs), whose participation in the PRSP consultation may have served to legitimize the process, have been frustrated by little or no subsequent inclusion of disability in the resulting PRSP (Dube, 2006). Elsewhere this consultative process has not even been undertaken or considered.

The PRSP process is meant to be country-driven and country-owned, results-orientated, comprehensive, partnership-orientated, based on a medium and long-term perspective, and have participation of a broad range of stakeholders (World Bank, 2008). The PRSP is not an isolated tool, but rather linked to other national and international strategies and policies (for instance, Sector Wide Approaches and Sector Investment Programmes – SWAPs & SIPs). The PRSP is now in use in over 70 countries (Handicap International, 2006). Unfortunately, disability issues have, on the whole, been poorly served by PRSPs (Dube, 2006). This raises the question of whether empowerment of persons with disabilities, and their representative organizations, and their role in advocacy, actually enables disability issues to be adequately and appropriately addressed.

7.3 Empowerment and Advocacy

We believe that in our efforts towards getting disability on the development agenda, two key elements should be addressed: the empowerment of persons with disabilities, and the strengthening of their role and the role of DPOs in advocacy. Empowerment is an imprecise concept; as explained by Rappaport (1985), the absence of empowerment is easy to notice but its presence is difficult to define. This is due to the fact that empowerment takes different forms in different contexts. Although many interpretations exist, the one we will adopt for the present purposes is that empowerment is: "a multi dimensional social process that helps people to gain control over their own lives" (Page and Czuba, 1999, p. 2). These authors correctly identify that in order to understand "empowerment" it is necessary to gain an insight into "power". Fasil et al. (2004) differentiate between structuralist and human agency approaches to power. The structuralist approach explains that powerlessness is a consequence of structural inequalities. Empowerment arises when the social, economic and institutional barriers that restrict individuals and communities from achieving their full potential are dismantled (ibid.). The human agency view of empowerment focuses upon the individual's capacity to act consciously and autonomously. This approach offers potential for immediate change on an individual basis. We believe that, in many instances, empowerment arises through a reciprocally reinforcing and virtuous circle between enabling structures and beliefs in personal efficacy.

As most people with disabilities in low-income countries find themselves in situations of disadvantage (DFID, 2000), empowerment has a role to play in order to reduce poverty and improve quality of life. Stressing personal agency, Stainton (2005, p. 291) defines empowerment as "enhancing, securing and/or legitimizing the power of oneself, another or of a collective", and sees the main aspect of empowerment being capacity. The first element of capacity is to support the choice-making process. It is not the choice itself that matters, he argues, but that people with disabilities have the tools to make that choice for themselves. Stainton sees the second element of empowerment as the ability to act on the choices available. Telling someone that they are free to attend a mainstream school but failing to provide them with the means to act on such a choice is not a choice at all (ibid.). Stressing structural issues, Ramcharan (2005, p. 283) argues that "empowerment in everyday life cannot happen unless the structures and institutions of civil society are themselves empowering rather that constraining". Both the personal agency and structural perspectives may be needed if we wish to advocate effectively for human rights.

The World Health Organization defines advocacy as "simply the process of influencing people to create change. Its lifeblood is good strategic communication – educating people about a need and mobilizing them to meet it" (2006, p. 17). McColl and Boyce (2003) describe disability organizations as having a purpose of service provision or advocacy. Their research found that most organizations began primarily for the purpose of providing a service to their members; others existed with a mandate to advocate for their members, while some groups provided a mixture of both service provision and advocacy. Some organizations were formed with a single mission in mind, whereas others dealt with a broad range of issues including (the five they identified as being most important) housing, education, employment, transportation and human rights. Other groups advocated more on philosophical or theoretical issues with the purpose of creating an inclusive environment for people with disabilities. McColl and Boyce also highlighted two important themes for DPOs: one concerned organizational tactics, cooperative or confrontational; the other how a group views those it represents as members of, or as recipients of, a service.

Newbigging and McKeown (2007) explain that advocacy is open to the criticism that it is poorly defined and lacks a theoretical basis. They claim that advocacy is "usually thought of as a process or intervention that ensures that vulnerable people have a voice within services characterized by power inequalities between providers and users". Atkinson (2000) identifies four key *elements* of advocacy: (1) empowerment (ideally people speak for themselves), (2) promotion of autonomy (enabling people to have control in their lives), (3) citizenship (ensuring rights and entitlements are met), and (4) social inclusion (addressing the exclusion of people who are marginalized in society).

Carlisle (2000) outlines four different *types* of advocacy:

1. *Representational advocacy* operates at the level of individual cases and may have traditionally prescriptive goals or represent the rights and needs of those unable to speak out for themselves.
2. *Community development*, with goals of participation and empowerment, tends to focus more on enablement rather than protection.

3. *Community activism* moves beyond facilitating communities to take enabling action, towards encouraging individuals and groups to challenge the causes of poor health more directly at policy-making level.
4. *Social policy reform* occurs where the advocate or advocacy organization has some degree of "expert" knowledge and seeks to redress health inequalities at the level of social structure. The goal of this type of advocacy is to influence governments and large organizations in order to change their policies and practices.

Although the aim of each strategy may not be explicitly to engage in advocacy, one or several of these practices may be engaged in by an organization while they simultaneously are providing a service or information to, or representing, people with disabilities.

It will be obvious from the above that advocacy and empowerment are related, and that both conceptualizations and practices of these often do, and perhaps should, overlap. While the intellectual distinction between these activities is not without practical importance for achieving impact and change in the real lives of PWD, we now consider in more detail how organizations concerned with disability actually engage in and understand these types of activities. We consider the specific example of disability advocacy in Bolivia, where there is a scarcity of research on such issues.

7.4 Disability Advocacy in Bolivia

In this section we present an exploration of the utilization of advocacy and empowerment strategies among a variety of organizations concerned with PWD in La Paz, Bolivia, including governmental and non-governmental organizations (see Griffiths, 2008, for a fuller account). Bolivia is one of Latin America's poorest countries. It has a population of 9.2 million people and an infant mortality rate of 49 deaths per 1,000 live births. Life expectancy at birth is 66.53 years (CIA, 2008). In 2006 almost 40% of the population were living in extreme poverty and the average annual income per capita was 1,153.00 USD. According to the World Bank (2008), currently 65% of the Bolivian population lives in poverty. According to the Instituto Nacional de Estadística (National Institute for Statistics), the city of La Paz has a population of 839,168 inhabitants. Using semi-structured interviews with key informants, Griffiths (2008) gained some insight into the issues that affect people with disabilities in La Paz. Participants were all decision makers from a variety of civil society and government organizations working with PWDs. Table 7.1 summarizes the advocacy actions that were described by the participants as having been undertaken in Bolivia (see also Griffiths et al., 2009, for a qualitative analysis of the key informant interviews that identified these actions).

It is noteworthy that none of those interviewed explicitly mentioned "advocacy" as one of their organizations' roles; nonetheless a wide range of advocacy-related actions were identified and are discussed below.

Table 7.1 Advocacy actions undertaken in Bolivia

Advocacy action	Example
Workshops	
(a) General skills training	Self-esteem and leadership
(b) Specific themes	Inclusive education and disability prevention
(c) Work-related skills training	To train people with disabilities in practical work-related skills to enhance their employability
Letter writing and lobbying	Contacting relevant authorities to make positive changes for and defend the rights of people with disabilities
Production of printed materials	To change the society's opinions of people with disabilities and to make people with disabilities aware of their rights
Cinema series	To show the reality of life as a person with a disability and raise awareness of the issue
Billboard campaign	Showing people with disabilities in a positive light
Meetings	To allow information exchange and give people with disabilities opportunities to self-advocate
Young leaders	Providing young people with the skills to advocate for themselves and their peers
Festivals and fund-raising activities	To raise awareness around disability and change societal attitudes

7.5 Influencing People to Create Change

The aims of these actions varied but the main ones were to sensitize Bolivian society regarding disability and to improve conditions for PWDs. The main issues that the disability movement advocated for were similar to those outlined by McColl and Boyce (2003): education, employment, human rights, transportation and housing. The achievement of improved conditions for people with disabilities regarding each of these was considered to be a source of empowerment. Advocacy actions (lobbying, education around the topic, publicity) were necessary to bring about this change. Within the Carlisle model of four different types of advocacy, it was evident that at least one of each of the groups interviewed fitted into each of the types involved. Most participants felt that a lack of resources prevented them from carrying out further advocacy actions, this is perhaps understandable given the fact that pure advocacy actions were not a major aim of any of the groups involved. It emerged during the course of the interviews that other issues, seen as more pressing, such as work and education, were much more likely to receive scarce resources. Nonetheless, most participants reported that they wished to see a change in society's attitude towards people with disabilities and acknowledged the part that advocacy actions played in this.

Each of the respondents undertook some advocacy actions but the lack of resources meant that large-scale long-term advocacy campaigns do not exist. Some groups and organizations worked together in order to change perceptions around disability, however poster campaigns and cinema seasons that operated on a city level only lasted a short time (several weeks). Only one organization incorporated "social political advocacy" into regular activities; this sought to make changes and improvements at a community level. In all, it seemed that communication between groups representing people with disabilities and government organizations was quite open. Regular meetings, the existence of the disability network and a willingness of the parties involved to take on board the opinions of their colleagues meant that information was communicated and exchanged with ease. Within the disability network, most members acknowledged that it was easier to achieve their objectives by working within a network in a collaborative manner.

7.5.1 Government as an Agent of Change

The government plays an important role in advocacy and it was usually the case that civil society groups attempted to influence the government in order to create change. Due to the fact that civil society groups have very limited resources in Bolivia, they frequently looked to the government as the only authority with the means to provide real and lasting change. The government also has a responsibility to empower it's disabled citizens by reducing the barriers that exist and enabling them to make choices and act on these choices accordingly. While participants were not directly critical of government under-funding of disability services, there was a lot of criticism regarding the fact that the most recent laws had not been enforced. The existence of the laws was viewed as a positive step. Government Decree 27477 explicitly states that 4% of the employees of public institutions should be people with disabilities. The reality seems to be far from this. Part of the reason that this law is not enforced is due to the fact that there is no authority with coercive powers to enforce it. CONALPEDIS (Comité Nacional de la Persona con Discapacidad/ National Committee for Persons with Disabilities) can demand that a public institution grant employment to a certain number of people with disabilities, but cannot fine or impose legal penalties on an organization that does not comply with the rules.

The situation within the private sector was considered to be even more difficult. There are no obligations for businesses or academic institutions to employ people with disabilities. Consequently it appears very difficult for disabled people to obtain employment in the private sector. As explained by various respondents, the attitude of business owners towards the employment of people with disabilities is extremely negative. A large part of the Bolivian economy is based on the informal market, the nature of which would make any sort of quota regarding the employment of people with disabilities impossible. While certain programmes do exist to implement the laws within the public sector, evidence from the ground suggests they are not hugely effective. The respondents who informed the authors of these successes worked for each of these authorities; none of the respondents from civil society groups referred to such successes. One positive action taken by the government, however, was to train a small number of people with disabilities in vocational skills such as plumbing and carpentry.

The government received criticism regarding the recent project of registering people with disabilities. This was considered to be a waste of time by one respondent. It was also viewed as divisive and perhaps contributing to discrimination against people with disabilities by highlighting the differences between disabled and non-disabled people. The mother of a young Bolivian man with an intellectual disability explained that he did not want to "register as disabled" as it would immediately make him more visible and thus more marginalized within society. Some channels do indeed exist to enable civil society groups representing people with disabilities to communicate their wishes, the most important of these being the Municipal Units established by CONALPEDIS (although only 30% of municipalities have these up and running at present) and the Vice Ministry for Coordination of Social Movements. Despite the existence of these authorities, anecdotal evidence would suggest that little actually changes as a result of the needs that are communicated.

There seems to be no lack of will to improve things and to listen to the needs of the people. However, it is the inability to turn requests and suggestions into actions at a government level that appears to prevent these actions from becoming a reality. Despite this, it is important to highlight the actions of the civil society groups themselves in changing attitudes, improving services and advocating on behalf of people with disabilities.

7.6 Means of Empowerment: Education and Employment

The theme of empowerment, helping people to gain control over their own lives, was presented by the participants in several ways. The principal methods of empowerment addressed were those of education and employment. The issue of education was viewed as the most important by parents of children with disabilities. Educating children with disabilities was considered to empower them to change their lives in the future, to allow them to gain an understanding of living within a society and to integrate them into the community. Inclusive education was seen as the ultimate goal. Opinions on how this should be attained were rarely expressed and respondents with experience of the education system seemed to acknowledge that a certain amount of training and resources are necessary in order to integrate children with disabilities into educational establishments. Inclusion has largely replaced the use of the word "integration" and in fact represents a different concept. While integration may be seen as the child adapting to the setting (normally a school), inclusion refers to the school or organization adapting to the needs of the students or potential members (Lindsay, 2007).

Eleweke and Rodda (2002) cite a number of authors explaining that the rationale behind inclusion is to give a child with a disability the opportunity to learn how to cope in the "real world" by learning to adapt to school at an early age. The authors echo the sentiments of one study respondent reporting that for inclusive education to work in a meaningful fashion the diverse needs of the students must be met. Programmes to make this possible must be put in place, barriers to accessing schools and universities must be removed and other students and their parents should be educated on the importance of inclusive education. These authors explain that inadequate facilities and services, a lack of teacher training programmes and few relevant materials make this difficult to achieve in any relatively poor country.

In order to become empowered, the issue of work was considered to be extremely important by all of the discussants. The fact that it was so difficult for people with disabilities to find employment was considered disempowering. The fear of not being able to cover basic living costs and the inability to support one's family fed into the desire for increased employment opportunities. Empowerment of the disability movement is difficult if people with disabilities constantly live in poverty.

In order to achieve this, integration into the workplace is of paramount importance. This issue becomes doubly important when viewed in the context of political changes. The proposed provision of social security payments to people with disabilities is much debated. All participants working for civil society organizations were against the provision of such payments stating that this would only add to the isolation of people with disabilities, preferring instead the more empowering possibility of increased employment opportunities.

7.7 Barrier Removal as Empowerment

The "social, economic and institutional barriers" (Fasil et al., 2004) that restrict individuals from achieving their full potential were addressed on various levels. At the most basic level, the attitude of Bolivian society to disability can be considered to be a social barrier. Similarly, the lack of unity and sense of mistrust that exist in the disability movement can also be considered as a social barrier. Participants reported that a huge amount of stigma exists around having a disability and being the parent of a person with a disability in Bolivia. Local myths and folklore have added to this stigma, and to a tradition of hiding people with disabilities away. Service provision in isolating institutions has meant that society has not had a chance to accept and integrate its people with disabilities. The strength of this attitude is such that it prevents many people with disabilities from reaching their full potential in the workplace, in education and in living full and happy lives. Advocacy was seen as having an important role to play in changing this culture. Improving society's attitude to disability would empower people with disabilities, reduce discrimination and allow them the same choices as people without disabilities.

The culture of the disability movement itself plays a role in the effectiveness of advocacy for and empowerment of PWDs. A culture of negative attitudes towards the disability community has contributed to feelings of suspicion of change and of "outsiders" (non-disabled people). It seems that the societal "victim" label given to people with disabilities has been internalized and that developing the confidence and the abilities to change things for the better will take work and effort; this is not something that will happen easily for many people. A lack of unity in the disability community was also evident. Bickenbach et al. (1999) outline some differences amongst PWDs, which arise as a result of a lack of commonality of experience, between people with very varied disabilities. Thus there is no unifying culture or experiences that people with disabilities share, perhaps unlike other minority groups.

A lack of resources allocated to disability can be considered to be an economic barrier, often preventing people with disabilities from reaching their full potential and the theme of money was crosscutting throughout each of the other themes. This lack of resources was cited as a reason for inadequate programmes to integrate children into schools or adults into the workplace. Resources seemed to be over-stretched in every area and a lack of continuous funding from government sources meant that activities and coverage were frequently constricted as groups relied on fundraising to pay their bills. The Bolivian government, while committed to fighting poverty, finances many worthwhile causes including that of vulnerable children and extreme rural poverty. Although a priority, it must be understood that disability is just one of many causes deserving of scarce government resources.

7.8 Advocacy and Empowerment: Practical Uses in Disability Movement

Empowerment and advocacy have an important role to play in improving the quality of life of people with disabilities. The many laws that exist indicate that people with disabilities have a level of "legal" empowerment. However, it must be acknowledged that there are still limited mechanisms in place to ensure that they are "enabled". There are very few practical means available to make choices and actualize national plans by implementing actions. Stainton (2005) would not consider people with disabilities in La Paz to be empowered. These citizens with disabilities are lacking in power as the social, economic and institutional barriers that exist prevent them from achieving their full potential.

There is much scope for advocacy actions to improve this. Each of the types of advocacy outlined by Carlisle (2000) have the potential to improve things for people with disabilities in Bolivia: individual case advocacy, improved enablement on community development, challenging health inequalities and total social policy reform would all assist in empowering PWDs in La Paz. McColl and Boyce's (2003) study of Canadian disability organizations illustrated that the issues of education, employment and human rights are of huge importance to the disability movement in Canada as well as in Bolivia. They explain that with strong leadership, adequate human and financial resources and correct tactics an organization can successfully advocate for its members and change things accordingly.

As explained by Ramcharan "It is entirely possible for a multitude of empowerment practices to be implemented without empowerment being achieved" (2005, p. 283); this seems to be the case in Bolivia. If the aspired to "National Plan" is to be put into action then it is necessary to influence the government and non-government authorities to take action. It is only by influencing those with the necessary resources to put the plan into action that real and practical empowerment can become a reality for people with disabilities in La Paz.

7.9 Recommendations

PWDs, and organizations that represent them, should address empowerment, advocacy and inclusion in national policy development instruments, as distinct but overlapping and interlocking goals. This means that DPOs should articulate which of their activities are targeted at achieving which of these kinds of goals. The further development of networks or alliances (see also Mji et al., this volume) may be one means of collectively achieving this, although such collaboration can itself of course offer challenges (Forsyth and MacLachlan, 2008). Ultimately, however, each representative organization should be cognisant of what it is purposefully contributing to empowerment, advocacy and inclusion in national development instruments. Our case study of La Paz illustrates that, despite the fact that none of the agencies identified advocacy as one of their roles *per se*, there was considerable advocacy-related activity going on. Becoming more aware of this and thinking through how such activities can influence important development processes, such as PRSPs, is a critical step towards achieving greater social inclusion and participation for PWDs.

Understanding cultural attitudes towards disability is vital in order to foster real and lasting change and facilitate genuine empowerment. We need to understand the nature of stigma, prejudice and discrimination towards PWDs if they are to be meaningfully part of the design, drafting and implementation of the PRSP. Each country and culture is unique in its approach to disability (Groce, 1999). Social networks, family, friends and the community in which a PWD lives, each have an impact on their life; similarly myths and folklore surrounding disability may affect the success or failure of a PRSP, at least from the perspectives of PWDs.

While existing legislation may provide for 4% of the employees of public institutions to be PWDs it was noted that failure to abide by this cannot be penalized, and no such requirement exists among private employers. Legal empowerment that cannot be enforced, or enabled, is ultimately undermining of the rights of PWDs. This is just one of the areas where strong leadership is required, in this case, perhaps by several DPOs coming together undertaking targeted advocacy actions and perhaps even a legal class action providing a test case for public sector employment.

A common theme throughout the interviews reported above was a lack of human and financial resources to address the immediate and pressing needs of PWD. Clearly diverting scarce resources away from such needs, to try and influence government policy regarding the much broader issue of development, is questionable. It is, however, probably the case that unless collectively DPOs can contribute something to this cause, they may continue to be caught in a "poverty of resources" trap. Ultimately the enhancement of local resources may only be achieved in a meaningful and sustainable manner if the rights of PWD impact in a real way on the drawing up of development policy documents, such as PRSPs. This may require the direction of a modest level of resources, by many different organizations, to achieve this.

We would also call for greater use of evidence-based advocacy as well as recognition that good evidence alone is not enough and that many non-evidential factors also influence decision making in PRSP processes (see for instance African Policy on Disability and Development: www.medicine.tcd.ie/globalhealth/research/projects/aPODD.php. However, these non-evidential factors may well be susceptible to the results of well-coordinated and well-targeted advocacy campaigns, as well as learning from the experience of DPOs in other countries regarding PRSP inclusion and outcomes and the avoidance of pitfalls.

Acknowledgement We are very grateful to the staff from International Services (Ireland) and other local, national, international and governmental organisations who kindly facilitated the research described in this chapter.

References

Atkinson, D (2000). *Advocacy: A Review*, York: Joseph Rowntree Foundation

Bickenbach, JE, Chatterji, S, Badley, EM, & Ustun, TB (1999). 'Models of disablement, universalism and the international classification of impairments, disabilities and handicaps', *Social Science and Medicine*, 48, 173–1187

Carlisle, S (2000). 'Health promotion, advocacy and health inequalities: A conceptual framework', *Health Promotion International*, 1(4), 369–376

CIA (2008). The World Factbook, https://www.cia.gov/library/publications/the-world-factbook/geos/bl.html#People [accessed 8th July]

DFID (2000). Disability, Poverty and Development. DFID, downloaded February 2000, www.dfid.gov.uk/pubs/files/disability.pdf

Dube, AK (2006). 'Participation of disabled people in the PRSP/PEAP process in Uganda', in Albert, B (ed.) (2006) *In or out of the mainstream? Lessons from research on disability and development cooperation*, Leeds: The Disability Press. 119–133

Eleweke, CJ, & Rodda, M (2002). 'The Challenge of Enhancing Inclusive Education in Developing Countries', *Inclusive Education*, 6, 113–126

Fasil, Q, Wallace, L, Singh, G, Ali, L, & Bywaters, P (2004). 'Empowerment and advocacy: Reflections on action research with Bangladeshi and Pakistani families who have children with severe disabilities', *Health and Social Care in the Community*, 12(5), 389–397

Forsyth, C. & MacLachlan, M. (in press) "You just don't open the doors and say 'Come on in and take away all my ideas'": NGO attitudes toward sharing organisational learning. *Knowledge Management for Development*

Four Hundred Million R (2008). http://www.400millionr.org/accessed on 8th July

Griffiths, M (2008). Disability advocacy in Bolivia. MSc Thesis, Centre for Global Health, Trinity College Dublin

Griffiths, M, Feliza, AR, & MacLachlan, M (2009). "I don't need what you think I need, I need something else": Advocacy and empowerment strategies used by organisations representing people with disabilities in Bolivia. Dublin: Centre for Global Health Working Paper

Groce, N (1999). 'Framing disability in local issues, concepts and beliefs', *Asia Pacific Disability Journal*, 10(1), 51–53

Handicap International/CBM (2006). *Making PRSP Inclusive*, Munich: Handicap International

Instituto Nacional De Estadística (INE) http://www.ine.gov.bo/indice/visualizador.aspx?ah=PC2031002.HTM [accessed 8th July 2008]

Lindsay, G (2007). 'Educational psychology and the effectiveness of inclusive education/mainstreaming', *British Journal of Educational Psychology*, 77, 1–24

Lynn, E (2007). 'Disability in development', Thesis as partial completion of MSc Development Studies, University College Dublin

McColl, MA, & Boyce, W (2003). 'Disability advocacy organizations: A descriptive framework', *Disability and Rehabilitation*, 25(8), 380–392

Newbigging, K, & McKeown, M (2007). 'Mental health advocacy with black and minority ethnic communities: Ethical implications', *Current Opinion in Psychiatry*, 20(6), 558–593

Page, N, & Czuba, CE (1999) 'Empowement: What is it?', *Journal of Extension*, 37(5), 1–5

Ramcharan, P (2005). 'Special issue on empowerment and advocacy', *Journal of Intellectual Disabilities*, 9(4), 283–287

Rappaport, J (1985). 'The power of empowerment language', *Social Policy*, 16, 15–22

Stainton, T (2005). 'Empowerment and the architecture of rights based social policy', *Journal of Intellectual Disabilities*, 9(4), 289–298

UNCRPD – United Nations Convention on Rights of Persons with Disabilities (2007). New York: United Nations

WHO (2005). World Health Organization Report WHA58.23; Fifty Eighth World Health Assembly; Disability, including prevention, management and rehabilitation, 9th Plenary Meeting 25th May 2005

WHO (2006). 'Stop the Global Epidemic of Chronic Disease: A Practical Guide to Successful Advocacy', Geneva: World Health Organization

World Bank (2008). http://web.worldbank.org/WBSITE/EXTERNAL/COUNTRIES/LACEXT/BOLIVIAEXTN/0,,menuPK:322289~pagePK:141132~piPK:141107~theSitePK:322279,00.html [accessed 8th July 2008]

Chapter 8
Cultural Challenges in Piloting Disability Surveys in Papua New Guinea

Patricia Thornton

8.1 Introduction

This is a reflexive account by a naïve researcher from the United Kingdom (UK) of the experience of piloting disability surveys in a developing country. I arrived in Papua New Guinea in July 2005 with long experience of disability-related social research but none in a developing country. In fact, I had never lived outside the UK. My task, as a Voluntary Service Overseas (VSO) volunteer, was to pilot survey methods as a first step towards establishing the prevalence of disability in Papua New Guinea, and to report within 12 months. While concerned about the likely mismatch between local conceptions of disability and internationally recognized definitions, about researching something that Papua New Guineans might not see as a priority or even as a problem and about scope for disabled people to take an active part in research production, I arrived with worries about how survey methodology might be made to work. The main problems I anticipated were reaching people to interview, dealing with aversion to taking part, communicating the purpose of the research, managing expectations of returns to participants, achieving informed consent and other familiar aspects of ethical social research. Many of these difficulties occurred and unsuspected problems arose. But what had barely crossed my mind was the possibility of difficulties with the field research personnel. Whilst I had realized that Papua New Guinea had no cohort of professional interviewers to employ, and I expected to train inexperienced local people, I had no idea of the extent of the challenge that interviewers would present in the research process.

The advantage of pilot studies in virgin territory is to report frankly on what works well and not so well. The originator of the project, a church organization promoting community-based rehabilitation services in Papua New Guinea, genuinely wanted to learn. Unlike in the policy-related social research environment I

P. Thornton (✉)
Social Policy Research Unit, University of York, Heslington, York, United Kingdom
e-mail: Trish.Thornton@yahoo.uk.co

M. MacLachlan and L. Swartz (eds.), *Disability & International Development: Towards Inclusive Global Health*,
DOI 10.1007/978-0-387-93840-0_8,

was used to back home, I felt no inhibitions in exploring what might turn out to be methodological failures. This chapter expands on the report I wrote with technical support from a Papua New Guinean research assistant (Thornton and Pirpir, 2008). The report was written as a "how to" guide for Papua New Guineans carrying out further disability surveys, including a template questionnaire developed in the pilot studies. Fully exploring the body of literature on conducting social research, and specifically disability research, in developing countries was impractical while on the job due to very poor internet connections and difficulties sourcing publications, and this chapter draws on literature I accessed after my return to the UK.

While some of the difficulties discussed in this chapter may apply to social survey research in many developing countries, others are peculiar to the Papua New Guinea context and a brief description of that follows. The chapter focuses on selected issues faced in the research process: deciding on a definition of disability; limitations on involvement of disabled people in research production; and cultural influences on the process, with particular reference to expectations of benefit and consequent effects on the quality of data collected.

8.2 The Papua New Guinea Context

Papua New Guinea is a young nation in the South Pacific, one of the last places in the world to come under colonial administration and to undergo decolonization. In the 1880s a permanent European presence was first established in coastal and island areas but inland highland dwellers had no contact with Europeans until the 1930s or later. Following Australian administration from the early twentieth century, independence came in 1975. Economically and in terms of social development, the post-independence years have seen mostly disappointing results. Economic growth has barely kept pace with population growth, despite rich natural resources and considerable external financial and practical assistance from Australia and other donors.

According to the UN Human Development Index, Papua New Guinea is now one of the poorest developing countries in terms of life expectancy, adult literacy, births attended by health professionals, number of physicians and access to safe water, with growing rates of HIV and TB. Deteriorating transport routes, grossly inadequate budgets, bureaucratic corruption and mal-administration block delivery of depleted health services. Corruption has worsened since independence, with Transparency International ranking Papua New Guinea as the 16th most corrupt out of 179 countries surveyed in 2007. The great majority of the population, 87%, lives on subsistence farming sometimes supplemented by cash cropping, forestry and fisheries. The formal employment sector is very small and stagnating. Crime and disorder is an ongoing problem: youth migrate to urban areas in search of scarce employment and fall into crime, and clan-based hostility erupts into open warfare, notably in highland regions.

Papua New Guinea is a diverse country. It has 800 or more languages, associated with tight-knit clan-based social groupings that protect their territories and cultures. While English is the language of education, Melanesian pidgin (Tok Pisin) is the *lingua franca* for people who have contacts outside of their home community. Tok Pisin is not much found in a written form, with the notable exception of the pidgin Bible that is disseminated through the work of the many missionaries and faith-based organizations that have led the great majority of the population to Christianity. Proclaimed Christianity goes hand-in-hand with supernatural beliefs, including beliefs about causes of impairment and illness.

8.3 Defining Disability

The first challenge for the project was reaching a consensus on the definition of disability to be used in the pilot surveys. Well prior to my arrival, in addition to VSO and the church-based promoter of community-based rehabilitation, representatives of one disability service organization, two research institutions, two university departments and two government departments had met to map out a research strategy. In their planning they had adopted a medical model of disability. This reflects the limited engagement in Papua New Guinea with concepts of disability. The definition in the national disability strategy is an uneasy compromise between paternalism and the WHO interactionist approach (adoption of the latter encouraged by UN regional advisers).

> Disability refers to people with special needs who require special attention, care and support in their families and communities, and encouragement to determine the full potential in life and refers to the needs created by the interaction between a person with an impairment and the environmental and attitudinal barriers he/she may face.
>
> (Department for Community Development, 2005, p8)

When, as a first step, I reviewed the limited literature reporting disability surveys in Papua New Guinea, I found a fair degree of conceptual and terminological muddle, and limited justification for the selection of the definitions adopted. These surveys variously asked about a mix of health conditions and impairments; impairments alone; impairments and activity limitations separately; activity limitations generally; a selected range of activity limitations; and a very narrow range of activity limitations. Only one work had collected additional data on participation restrictions, using the WHO categories then current of impairment, disability and handicap.

Not all members of the original planning group for the research project were fully familiar with the WHO use of "disability" as an umbrella term covering impairments, activity limitations and participation restrictions linked to a health condition. The concept of disability as a continuum was unfamiliar and dichotomous disabled/non-disabled and severe/mild categorizations were taken for granted. It seemed that disability was seen as an individual deficit rather than as a product of the environment in which one lives. Understandably in a country where much impairment is preventable, there was strong interest in the group in collecting data on health conditions and impairments to support the case for preventive and remedial interventions. Ambitious plans had already been mooted for teams specializing in different types of impairment and health conditions to advise and to support fieldwork, presumably to assist with diagnosis. I soon realized the impracticality of these plans. The specialists were scarce or almost non-existent, and in any case had many more pressing demands. The alternative of asking survey respondents to name their health condition was equally impossible in a country with five physicians per 100,000 population, where conditions are rarely diagnosed and people seldom use medical labels. Translation to and from Tok Pisin and indigenous languages would be a further barrier. Relying on unskilled fieldworkers to record impairments also would result in highly unreliable data.

The project steering group, put in place on my arrival, agreed that it was my role to review the plans so far and propose a manageable and coherent research strategy. They accepted a proposal to pilot questions on activity limitations, using a screening question derived from the ongoing development work of the Washington Group on Disability Statistics and employing a four-point scale of perceived difficulty for each activity from “no difficulty” to “cannot do at all”. The key point in support of this approach was that it is important for Papua New Guinea’s international standing that its disability data can be compared with that of other countries. Although not recommended by the Washington Group at that time, we also agreed to pilot interview questions on participation restrictions, tailored to the Papua New Guinea cultural context. Isolated from much of the internet-based literature, I did not realize at the time how courageous these decisions were and that a review of data and statistics on disability in developing countries (Eide and Loeb, 2005) was finding that screening in low-income countries to a large extent continued to be impairment-based.

The project did not want to lose sight of the original aim to understand causes of disability and it was considered useful to explore respondents’ perceptions of causes, including supernatural beliefs. Further question sets were developed to ask about service use, aids and adaptations used and unmet needs.

8.4 Outline of the Pilot Survey Methods

Table 8.1 outlines the methods of a series of three pilot surveys. Survey 1 involved asking informants in the rural highlands site to identify for interview people with one or more specified activity limitations. Here it had already been decided to use local community-based rehabilitation volunteers to interview the individuals listed. As discussed in Sect. 8.6 below, in practice some deviations from the plan were forced upon this pilot: community leaders also acted as interviewers; and self-referred people were also interviewed. Survey 2 tested an activity limitation screening question and a limited range of follow-up questions put to household

Table 8.1 Survey areas and methods

Site	Interviewers	Household data	Identification method	Data on people with difficulties
Survey 1 Rural Highlands Eastern Highlands Province	Local community-based rehabilitation volunteers Community leaders	None	Listed by local informants and Self-referral	Data from interviews with 495 people with difficulties • Socio-economic • Type, extent and duration of difficulty • Perceived causes • Help sought, aids used • Unmet need • Type and extent of participation restriction
Survey 2 Rural Coastal Madang Province	University students (non-local)	1,142 households 7,309 members Data from household representative: • Number in household • Socio-economic characteristics	Screening question to household representative	Analysis of data from household respondents on 2,153 household members with difficulties • Extent of difficulties overall • Type and duration of difficulty • Type and extent of participation restriction
Survey 3 Urban Highlands Eastern Highlands Province	Local community-based rehabilitation volunteers Selected community based rehabilitation volunteers from Survey 1 Local youth	940 households 5,717 members Data from household representative: • Number in household • Ages and sex	Screening question to household representative	Data from interviews with 722 people with difficulties • Socio-economic • Type, extent and duration of difficulty • Perceived causes • Help sought, aids used • Unmet need • Type and extent of participation restriction

representatives in a rural coastal site. Here the questions were "add-ons" to a survey of household wealth conducted by the Papua New Guinea Institute of Medical Research for James Cook University, with non-local university students as fieldworkers. My involvement in Survey 2 was limited to question design, interviewer training and analysis; that is, I had no supervision responsibilities in the survey site. Survey 3, in an urban highlands site, built on the previous two surveys. It used a slightly revised household screening question, followed up by interviews with household members identified as having activity limitations. Here the interviewers were a mix of well-performing interviewers brought in from Survey 1, local community-based rehabilitation volunteers and local unemployed youth. The data collected also are listed in Table 8.1.

Under the auspices of the project, two follow-up studies were carried out with sub-samples of respondents in Surveys 1 and 3. One follow-up qualitative study, not referred to further in this chapter, explored cultural aspects of disability. The other, carried out in conjunction with a university department of physiotherapy, focused on people with moving difficulties. Here physiotherapy students conducted the interviews, which conjoined qualitative and quantitative methods.

8.5 The Missing Role of Disabled People in the Research Process

My background in disability research in the UK, reinforced by VSO's pre-departure training, made me acutely aware of critiques of the traditional top-down research and development paradigm in which groups that are intended to benefit, such as disabled people, have no control or active role. In the UK, several research funders now specify involvement of disabled people in disability research so that disabled people participate as lead (co)researchers, advisers, fieldworkers, analysts and disseminators. Some funding bodies demand that disabled people or organizations of disabled people themselves have identified the agenda and control production. The disability movement advocates emancipatory research as opposed to participatory research.

At the time of the pilot surveys no platform for emancipatory research controlled by disabled people existed in Papua New Guinea. The emancipatory research model typically presumes that organizations of disabled people exist and desire control. In Papua New Guinea, organizations of disabled people at the time of the research were nascent and fragile, some brought into being via a few disabled individuals in touch with disabled people's movements and disability-aware funding organizations outside the country. Some province-wide organizations claimed scores of members but typically only a handful of office-holders met. A limited road and boat system, prohibitively expensive air travel and poor telecommunications thwarted a well-functioning nation-wide organization. Most effort went into establishing organizations with presidents, treasurers and so on, and into obtaining accreditation and funding to support the organization *per se*. Sustainability was a major problem as groups divided or collapsed through rivalry for status, financial mismanagement and corruption. A small number of representatives raised the profile of disabled people through the press but otherwise it was unclear what the organizations of disabled people stood for. During nearly two years, I heard from them almost no mention of disabled people's rights, discrimination or environmental barriers. Against this background, it was hard to see disabled people's organizations in Papua New Guinea as ready to share the aspirations of DPOs in Zimbabwe and Zambia: that disabled people should have the leading role in determining and implementing research (Albert and Harrison, 2006; Albert, n.d.).

It is widely recognized in Papua New Guinea that the capacity of organizations of disabled people needs to be built. Latterly, there have been some encouraging developments. An Australian disability organization supported a national meeting of "women with disabilities" in 2006, attracting disabled women who had never before travelled outside their home areas. This meeting inspired at least one participant to establish back home an association of disabled women and a mixed gender association, meeting in her backyard with a total of 97 members and rising (Lombange, 2008). In 2007, a Japanese disability organization held a national event to build the capacity of organizations of disabled people, attended by disabled people from most parts of the country. The National Assembly for People with Disabilities is working with support from a VSO volunteer to strengthen its capacity. A quarterly national disability magazine, supported by VSO volunteers, aims to raise consciousness by featuring disabled people's stories and promoting aspects of national policy.

The few organizations of disabled people centre on a few urban areas and rarely reach the rural areas where the great majority of the disabled population lives. Here, engaging people whom we categorise as "disabled" is a huge challenge, as is attempting participatory disability research in which disabled people are active in the process. The major obstacle here is little mutual recognition of communality amongst people with impairments or activity limitations. Disability as an identity is not an explicit cultural concept (Whyte and Ingstad, 1995). The word "disabled" has no equivalent in indigenous languages and Tok Pisin refers to an individual's non-functioning body parts as "broken" or "no good" (such as "man with no good eyes"), with no collective term other than the recently introduced and by no means widespread "disable". Common beliefs are that impairments and illnesses stem from breaking taboos, from offending evil spirits and especially from provoking sorcery by offending social norms or arousing jealousy. The impairment itself does not necessarily affect social acceptance in all Papua New Guinea societies. Rather, in our highlands sites stigma could result from the shameful behaviour that provoked sorcery. Consequently, there was not the sense of oppression or discrimination linked to impairment that brings solidarity amongst disabled people in the North. Considerable consciousness-raising in communities is essential to enable participatory research.

Because of these factors and the short time frame for the pilot project, the role of disabled people was very limited. That said, the National Assembly of Disabled Persons had played a part in setting the agenda by calling for a disability question in the next national census, and representatives of organizations of disabled people supported the new disability policy of the Department for Community Development that involves promoting the collection of disability data. The National Board for Disabled Persons (a grant-aided association of service-providers, organizations of and for disabled people and other stakeholders in the disability field) had called for standardized disability surveys. There was a clear consensus that data is power.

However, in the communities where the research took place there was no involvement of disabled people in the production of the research.

8.6 Cultural Influences on the Research Process: Expectations of Material Benefit

An anxiety I brought to the fieldwork was about how to explain the purpose of the research to meet the threefold aim of not raising unrealistic expectations, achieving informed consent and reducing non-response rates. I knew that the results of the research project would not benefit participants or their communities. Rather, the findings were intended to inform disability policy and service planning. Yet the arrival of researchers asking questions about activity limitations, service use and unmet needs was bound to prompt unrealistic expectations of material benefit. It is of course a common tendency for top-down research by outsiders to raise local people's expectations of solutions to problems, and an elementary step in fieldwork is to make clear the purpose of research and whether or not any action might result (Bulmer and Warwick, 1983b; Pratt and Loizos, 1992).

Our attempts to forestall false expectations paralleled those set out in fieldwork for development textbooks. In sessions with community leaders and interviewers we explained that the purpose of the research was to assist the government and other agencies to improve planning in the country. The preamble to the interview spelt this out, and during training the interviewers practised using the prescribed form of words to make it as clear as possible that the interview was not a route to the solution of immediate problems. The message probably was not reinforced enough. No doubt it was hard for the majority of local people to understand what a survey is and what it is for, especially if they have never encountered a survey (Bulmer and Warwick, 1983b). Even "good practice" examples found local people hoping the research would lead to immediate benefits (Pratt and Loizos, 1992). In retrospect, it was unhelpful in introducing the research to say that it aimed to benefit other people in the future (a common appeal to boost participation in research in the UK). The idea of benefiting some unknown others was alien and culturally inappropriate because social relationships in Papua New Guinea are ruled by the *wantok* system. Literally meaning people who speak the same language, wantoks are in-groups of people from the same community or clan who observe strong obligations towards reciprocal help. For them, benefiting non-wantoks is a foreign and unacceptable notion.

There are a number of reasons why community leaders, interviewers and respondents were not persuaded that material benefits would not flow from the research project. It is already documented that foreign researchers are likely to be perceived as representatives of international donors or other similar agencies, and respondents may participate in the belief that the researcher will bring tangible benefits to the community (Devereux and Hoddinott, 1992). Top-down research by outsiders leads to assumptions that money inevitably will be spent locally (Pratt and

Loizos, 1992). In Papua New Guinea the influences of development are especially unhelpful in this respect. In the 1970s, around the time of independence, local level organizations, such as village associations, emerged as people sought local participation in development. But disillusionment set in amongst grass-roots organizations when aspiring politicians used them for personal advancement and profit. Community development projects have been supported by an array of external donors. Top-down development initiatives bringing money or "cargo" to communities have shaped expectations of material benefits and cash. So, when an outside organization appears on the local scene, especially when represented by a white-skinned person, the assumption is that material benefits will follow. This "handout mentality" obstructed the research in more ways than one.

The questions put to respondents are likely to have fuelled expectations of individual benefit. The theoretical concept of unmet need used in the questionnaire was hard for interviewers to explain and respondents to grasp. Having been asked if there was anything they needed for their difficulty and did not currently have, some respondents not surprisingly believed that their needs would be met. Some time after the fieldwork was completed, a complaint was relayed to me that the wheelchair a respondent wanted had not been forthcoming. In planning the project, we had been keen to give something back to the people who took part. Paying respondents was out of the question. Even if the budget had allowed, giving money or presents to individuals would have been culturally inappropriate and divisive as well as fuelling escalating expectations (Devereux and Hoddinott, 1992). What was decided upon in Survey 1 and Survey 3 was to offer sight and hearing tests to all participants and a referral to a clinic if a deficit was detected. This may have encouraged a misunderstanding that other health-related services would follow from the project.

Rather to my surprise, refusal to take part was minimal. It has been commented that rural people in developing countries like being interviewed far more than might be thought (Heyer, 1992) and that refusal rates are comparatively low in rural areas of developing countries (Hershfield et al., 1983). There were no issues over accessing women for interview; indeed an impulse to protect women is not in the Papua New Guinean psyche. And in the relatively classless social structure there was no holding back through beliefs of being unworthy for interview found elsewhere (Bulmer, 1983). Despite the demands of subsistence farming and cash cropping in Papua New Guinea rural societies, there was generally no financial sacrifice attached to giving time for an interview, and people appeared to welcome a novel event. Heyer (1992) also notes that people frequently asked to be interviewed if they were not on the list. This was our experience too, and it may be that people were motivated by concerns not to miss out on presumed returns to them; just being on a list raises expectations. In Survey 1, where the sample was supposed to be provided by local informants only, the strategy was wrecked by fieldworkers accepting for interview other people who put themselves forward. It was impossible to interview everyone within the time and budget available, leading to reported dissatisfaction amongst those left out.

The expectation of gains from taking part had important consequences for the reliability of the data. In sharp contrast to the North where under-reporting of disability is problematic, there are indications that our Papua New Guinean respondents exaggerated the degree of difficulty with activities. Evidence is available for seeing and hearing. As noted above, in two surveys people were offered optional sight and hearing tests, administered by the interviewers. These were simple tests involving identifying the direction of a shape on a chart and indicating hearing a sound from a noisemaker. The results were compared with responses to subjective questions about extent of seeing and hearing difficulty. While numbers are small because not everyone with a hearing or seeing difficulty accepted the test, and bearing in mind that the measures are not strictly comparable, analysis showed that considerable minorities who claimed they were unable to see or hear at all, or had a lot of difficulty, were found in the tests to have normal vision or hearing. In comparison, few people who reported no seeing or hearing difficulty were found to have one in the tests. It is hard to avoid the conclusion that people expected to gain something, presumably money, by claiming a difficulty they did not have. There are parallels here with the problem of enumerating households in Ghana, where the expectation that researchers would bring free or subsidized food aid meant that over-reporting of households was standard practice (Devereux, 1992).

8.7 Payment Issues

It had not occurred to me that the expectation of gains would be problematic in relation to community leaders. I had quickly learnt that it would be essential to engage them to gain their acceptance of the research and assistance in smoothing the path to respondents. The textbooks emphasize that establishment and maintenance of community goodwill is crucial (Christensen, 1992) and that the ethics of fieldwork insist that local customs be respected (Hoddinott, 1992). In the parts of highland Papua New Guinea where the fieldwork took place, the "bigman" commands the social scene. Each hamlet has one or more of these influential figures. Not a hereditary position, status as a bigman arrives through accumulation of wealth (such as pigs) and wives (who rear the pigs) and demonstration of leadership. Little can happen in their domain without reference to them.

In our first survey, in the rural highlands site, we invited bigmen to join the first interviewer training day, intending to ensure that both local interviewers and bigmen received the same messages about the purpose and conduct of the research. The unintended outcome was that the bigmen assumed that they too would conduct interviews. In the course of that training day it became apparent that they were motivated by the prospect of payment, not simply that they assumed their status naturally qualified them for the task in the same way that community leaders feel that they deserve to be interviewed (Mitchell, 1983). Indeed, many went on to conduct interviews, something that the field supervisors could not prevent due to the social unacceptability of challenging a bigman. The consequences were disastrous. The local interviewers were community-based rehabilitation volunteers who had been selected because they had secondary education and knowledge of English as well as experience with disabled people, attributes lacking in the community leaders who failed to master the questionnaire. Many of the community leaders' returned questionnaires were too poorly completed to be included in the analysis.

Payment of interviewers was a particularly thorny issue, eventually handled without pain in the final, urban survey. Our initial suggestion in the first rural highlands survey, that a lump sum be given to be spent on local community-based rehabilitation efforts, was received with silent hostility by community leaders and interviewers at the first training day. This reaction may be associated with the low profile of community-based rehabilitation in the locality and, as mentioned in the previous section, with the unfamiliar concept of people with impairments or activity limitations as a social group, let alone a deserving community group. It was only much later that we realized that the proposal was unacceptable because of suspicions about the financial probity of the main field supervisor, a local man, who would have access to any lump sum and power over its distribution. The planned questionnaire practice sessions were effectively derailed until a piece-rate method of payment was agreed upon. The field supervisor was charged with distributing payments along with monies to cover travel and subsistence expenses, but irregularities in the distribution caused discontent which later deterred several fieldworkers from any further association with the project during the follow-up study. Here the project undoubtedly escalated tensions in relationships and caused conflicts that may well have persisted long after the research was completed (ESRC, 2004).

Interviewers sharing recompense equally, regardless of number of interviews completed, might have made the payments more transparent and less open to manipulation. The university student interviewers in the Survey 2 chose to pool and share equally the agreed per interview fees. Fabrication of completed questionnaires was an unfortunate consequence of the piece-rate payment system in the first survey. In Survey 3 this problem was eliminated by much tighter supervision and checking of returned questionnaires prior to payment.

The overall impression gained from the first survey was that community leaders, the field supervisor and interviewers sought to exploit the project. For them it was a moneymaking opportunity. "Sucker bias" where outsiders are seen as fair game for deception (Mitchell, 1983) is not just a respondent phenomenon. The project was expected to pay highly inflated costs for use of a rural resource centre and for catering during training. Our explanation that the budget was extremely limited, and by no means a bottomless pit, was met with disbelief. Those who knew of the instigator of the research, the promoter of community-based rehabilitation, pointed to instances where money had been forthcoming when asked for. Even physiotherapy students who were to undertake field interviews in the follow-up study as part of their course, with credits attached, attempted to negotiate upwards their daily fee. Indeed, a subgroup of these students withdrew from the fieldwork because they perceived the payment to be too low. Their attitude surprised me because the purpose of the follow-up study was to reach a better fit between the content of the physiotherapy course and the needs of physically disabled people, in turn equipping qualified physiotherapists with the appropriate skills. To my chagrin, one student accused me of being motivated to do the research only to obtain a publication (having already over one hundred publications this could not have been further from my mind). There are echoes here of the comment, reported by Wilson (1992), by a member of a much researched community to the effect that it is justifiable for local people to exploit researchers because they use local people to further academic success and fame.

It would be a mistake to characterize Papua New Guineans as grasping, self-interested individuals. The role of money in Papua New Guinean societies is complex. Wealth is not accumulated for one's self and money is important less for its economic purchasing power than for its social currency value. Money is shared with the community, put towards bride price payments or funerals for example. By doing so, people "buy" status. Another factor is customary reciprocal giving, fundamental to the wantok system, in which help is given in expectation of being helped in return. We knew it was essential to give something back to the community members and were careful to lay on lavish meals during training and an end of fieldwork feast for interviewers and community leaders with a ceremony to give out certificates of participation. It may be that our gifts did not weigh equally in the scales of reciprocity. Also relevant is that in some societies, especially in the highlands regions, the notion of compensation is deeply embedded. If a community member is harmed by an out-group, the transgressors must compensate the community for that harm, in kind or, increasingly, in cash. For example, inter-clan warfare will be suspended if someone is killed or injured until appropriate compensation (pigs, cash, even women) is paid. Without satisfactory compensation, ancestral lands and garden plots are fiercely defended against encroachment by electricity or fresh water supply pipes and roads intended to benefit the community. It may be that the highland communities in Survey 1 were seeking compensation from us for some perceived harm.

8.8 Other Cultural Influences on the Data Collected

Section 8.6 shows how expectations of material benefit affected not only the production of the research but also the quality of the data collected, including its reliability and validity. This section considers some other cultural influences on the data.

8.8.1 Lexical Equivalence

A lack of lexical equivalence is often cited as a problem affecting the quality of data collected in cross-cultural research (see several chapters in Bulmer and Warwick, 1983). It was to the project's great advantage that the word "difficulty" in the English language version is equivalent to the commonly used Tok Pisin word *hevi* and to the term in the Yagaria language in the rural highlands site. Thus the questions about difficulty with specified activities were easily understood by interviewers and respondents alike. We encountered a few problems with terms to describe the activities themselves, as the vocabulary of Tok Pisin is limited. The literature on research in developing countries notes that interviewers may shorten questions or simplify the language through on-the-spot adaptations (Bulmer and Warwick, 1983a). Reports of seeing and hearing difficulties may have been exaggerated if interviewers referred to eye and ear problems rather than seeing and hearing difficulties. To reduce room for miscommunication, the follow-up study with sub-samples of people with moving difficulties deployed photographs alongside verbal descriptions of activities. Bulmer and Warwick (1983b) cite an objection to using this device on the grounds that many peoples have no experience of seeing their own image but photographs appeared to work well in the rural highlands as well as the urban highlands site.

Asking about extent of difficulty on a four-point scale from "no difficulty" to "cannot do at all" worked well, capturing mild to moderate activity limitations which seem to have gone unreported with disability prevalence measures used in English-speaking African nations (Loeb and Eide, 2006). Loeb and Eide (2006 p.115) speculate that people do not acknowledge a limitation if they are unaware of the possibility of improving the situation with relatively simple technical aids but in our Papua New Guinea pilot surveys non-acknowledgment of limitations did not appear to be associated with lack of awareness of remedial aids.

8.8.2 Conceptual Equivalence

A further concern for surveys in developing countries is that of conceptual equivalence (see several chapters in Bulmer and Warwick, 1983b). The literature observes that the idea that individuals have views of their own is a cultural value, and that in some societies there is a greater likelihood that respondents regard themselves more as part of a community or kinship group than as individuals (Bulmer, 1983). The primacy of the individual can seem alien (ESRC, 2004). While the pilot surveys seem to have been successful in eliciting self-perceptions of difficulties with activities, it appeared hard for some interviewers to understand or accept the concept of subjective, individual judgement. This stems in part from the novelty of the concept of the individual in Papua New Guinean societies. But where interviewers were community-based rehabilitation volunteers there were also external influences: it was hard for them to put aside their training which had led them to see themselves as experts in identifying difficulties their disabled clients faced. As these volunteers already knew the people they were interviewing, they saw no point in asking questions if the answers were already known to them. In considering sources of interviewers, Bulmer (1983) concludes that use of insiders is best avoided because of the difficulty of the local interviewer in achieving the necessary detachment from known respondents.

8.8.3 Status Equivalence

The last point relates to the issue of status equivalence between interviewers and respondents. The literature contains many warnings that the status gap is likely to be wider in developing countries than in the North and that the veracity of the data collected is likely to be affected if relationships between researcher and researched are asymmetrical (see several chapters in Bulmer and Warwick, 1983b; ESRC, 2004). The prevailing assumption is that well-educated interviewers are perceived by respondents as having higher status, class, power and privilege; such asymmetries may result in acquiescent response styles and give rise to spurious results (ESRC, 2004). In surveys 1 and 3 the community-based rehabilitation volunteers and unemployed youth who served as interviewers had no more than grade 10 education, in line with the suggestion in Bulmer (1983) that interviewers with only primary or secondary education are more suitable in rural surveys. It might be assumed that community-based rehabilitation volunteers have acquired a privileged status but in Papua New Guinea volunteers are not necessarily respected, because they do not bring in financial rewards that can be shared with their communities in the customary way (Millar, 2004; Thornton, 2007).

The status gap is even greater where a European is the interviewer and I was advised that respondents would simply tell me what they thought I wanted to hear. Wuelker (1983 p.165) warns that a non-Asian interviewing an Asian would be “a fiasco” because Asians are far too polite to tell a foreigner something they might not like to hear. Melanesians are not Asians, and my impression is that their interview behaviour is more influenced by notions of right and wrong answers than by politeness or deference. For this reason, as well as risk to personal safety to me and my research assistant, who was an outsider from a distant province, I was strongly advised not to be present during interviews in Survey 1, effectively devolving the local management of research to the fieldwork supervisors. As ESRC (2004) notes, this action endangers proper conduct of field research.

8.8.4 Respondents’ Frames of Reference

The literature warns survey researchers to think about whether respondents have an adequate frame of reference for answering their questions, with particular relevance to opinion questions (Bulmer and Warwick, 1983a). Bulmer (1983 p.213) notes that articulating an opinion requires sufficient self-awareness to see that custom and tradition are not the only source of ideas and beliefs. Without an appropriate frame of reference a high proportion of “don’t know” answers to opinion questions can be expected (Mitchell, 1983). Our first and third surveys asked respondents, for each reported difficulty, if there were any kinds of help they needed for that difficulty and if so what that was. Not surprisingly, quite high proportions said they did not know, up to one in three in the cases of difficulties remembering and communicating, though well under one in ten in the cases of seeing, hearing and moving difficulties.

The question followed on from two questions on use of human sources of help and practical aids in which answer options were read out by the interviewer. The aim was that prior listing of sources of help and aids would stimulate people's thinking about what might be possible, given very limited exposure to personalized services and aids and adaptations, but this device appeared to have little effect. The overall impression is of people holding a narrow, medicalised view of what would help them. For most difficulties, an expressed need for medical advice, treatment or medicine emerged very strongly. The aids people said they needed were almost exclusively spectacles, hearing aids and sticks or crutches. It did not seem to occur to people that difficulties they had cited could be eased by environmental accommodations. For example, poor light to read by was reported as a cause of seeing difficulties but nobody said large-print materials or proper lighting was what they needed. The overall project left the strong impression that improving and accommodating living conditions is a foreign concept in Papua New Guinea.

8.8.5 Non-comprehension

Bulmer and Warwick (1983a p.145) comment that data are only rarely collected and reported about the full extent of non-comprehension. It was only in Survey 3 (the urban highlands survey) and in the fieldwork for the follow-up study that I saw first-hand the degree of comprehension. Otherwise, an impression of respondent non-comprehension is derived from that of the interviewers. Interestingly, a question set that presented difficulty to the interviewers was taken from the national census, about the main work that the respondent did in the last week. This may reflect the limited primacy of the concept of work in Papua New Guinea societies or the difficulty of identifying a single main type of work. Most problematic were questions about participation restrictions. The project tried out ways of asking people about the effects of their activity limitations on taking part in aspects of life present in Papua New Guinea societies. (Note that we did not attempt to ask about the effects of impairment on participation.) Five participation areas were chosen, with verbal examples, and respondents were asked to say how far their participation was restricted on a four-point scale from "not at all" to "all of the time". Because people might not do one or more of these things if they had no difficulty, it was made possible for them to say that an area of participation did not apply to them. This answer option proved very hard to make work, even after refinements. The subtleties got lost in Tok Pisin. The questioning is quite complex: first the interviewer had to find out if the area of participation was something that the respondent did not currently do; then they had to find out if it was something they would do if they did not have a difficulty. Some interviewers found it hard to understand the concepts involved; hypothetical questions are notoriously difficult. Our recommendation was that further surveys should focus on questions about extent of restriction on participation in the community (exemplified by going to market and church and joining in village get-togethers), activities that most people do or aim for, and, with a filter question, activities at school.

8.8.6 *Privacy*

The necessity for private interviews is debated in the literature on survey research in developing countries. Hershfield et al. (1983 p.248), for example, comment that personal privacy is neither common nor highly valued in rural areas in most developing countries and that usually the interview takes place in the presence of family and other bystanders. Our Papua New Guinea experience was that interviewers were not invited inside dwellings (hospitality is not a noticeable feature of many Papua New Guinea societies) and that curious bystanders congregated around the outdoor interview locations. Mitchell (1983 p.233) notes reports from the field suggesting that responses are influenced by overheard answers by local opinion formers. This did not seem to be the case in our pilot surveys, in part because the people interviewed tended not to have high status. While Hershfield et al. state that privacy is preferable, they acknowledge that third party presence can be helpful in obtaining factual information. The impression in our research was that on-lookers other than close family members did not intrude but rather served as silent witnesses, helping to keep the respondent honest (Mitchell, 1983). When, in a conference on our draft findings, the perennial question was raised about possible under-representation of children and disabled children being "hidden away", it was helpful to point out that the presence of bystanders inhibited dishonest responses.

8.9 Conclusion

In Papua New Guinea there has been a real desire across a range of stakeholders to obtain well-founded data on the prevalence of disability and characteristics of disabled people, to aid planning and advocate for improved services for the disabled population. Solid data are essential to compete for the attention of politicians and international development organizations and to attract the level of investment required to meet needs. Encouragingly, organizations of disabled people recognize that numbers are strength. The purpose of this chapter has not been to report the prevalence estimates obtained through three pilot surveys in selected sites in Papua New Guinea; these estimates are tentative and vary due to differences in the survey populations and in methods tried. The intention is that the recommended method and questionnaire template be used in other carefully selected parts of this heterogeneous country to arrive at a national prevalence estimate.

The thrust of the chapter has been to draw attention to cultural constraints on gathering disability data, from the perspective of an outsider doing acknowledged top-down research. Some of the methodological problems reported here are common to efforts to undertake surveys in developing countries; indeed it is claimed that problems in survey methodology in the North are merely writ large in developing countries (Bulmer and Warwick, 1983b). Other problems met have a special Papua New Guinean flavour. Groce (2006 p.43) now argues that "unique" influential cultural practices might be organized into recognizable patterns that can be anticipated and addressed in disability research. Along with Groce, I hope that insights from research in specific cultural settings might be helpful for those collecting data about disability in any community. Yet, although well-founded disability research among Melanesian populations is as yet rare, this contribution may prove to test Groce's proposition.

References

Albert, B (n.d.). *Lessons from the disability knowledge and research programme*, Disability Knowledge and Research Programme, http://www.disabilitykar.net/learningpublication/contents.html

Albert, B, & Harrison, M (2006). 'Changing the social relations of research – managing a disability research programme', in Albert, B (ed.) *In or out of the mainstream? Lessons from research on disability and development cooperation*, pp. 13–23, Leeds: The Disability Press

Bulmer, M (1983). 'Interviewing and field organization', in Bulmer, M and Warwick, P (eds), *Social research in developing countries: surveys and censuses in the third world*, pp. 205–217, Chichester: Wiley

Bulmer, M, & Warwick, P (1983a). 'Data collection', in Bulmer, M, & Warwick, P, (eds), *Social research in developing countries: surveys and censuses in the third world*, pp. 145–160, Chichester: Wiley

Bulmer, M, & Warwick, P (1983b). (eds), *Social research in developing countries: surveys and censuses in the third world*, Chichester: Wiley

Christensen, G (1992). 'Sensitive information: collecting data on livestock and informal credit', in Devereux, S and Hoddinott, J (eds), *Fieldwork in developing countries*, pp. 124–137, Hemel Hempstead: Harvester Wheatsheaf

Department for Community Development (2005). 'Papua New Guinea national policy on disability 2005'. Draft 3 (October 2005). Boroko: Department for Community Development Government of Papua New Guinea

Devereux, S (1992). '"Observers are worried": learning the language and counting the people in northeast Ghana', in Devereux, S & Hoddinott, J (eds), *Fieldwork in developing countries*, pp. 43–56, Hemel Hemstead: Harvester Wheatsheaf

Devereux, S, & Hoddinott, J (1992). 'The context of fieldwork', in Devereux, S & Hoddinott, J, (eds), *Fieldwork in Developing Countries*, pp. 3–24, Hemel Hempstead: Harvester Wheatsheaf

Eide, A, & Loeb, M (2005). *Data and statistics on disability in developing countries*, Disability Knowledge and Research Programme, http://www.disabilitykar.net/research/thematic_stats.html

ESRC (2004). 'Social science research ethics in developing countries', Research Ethics Framework Project, Discussion paper 3, April 2004 (v2), http://www.york.ac.uk/res/ref/docs/REFpaper4_v2.pdf

Groce, N (2006). 'Cultural beliefs and practices that influence the type and nature of data collected on individuals with disability through national census', in Altman, B & Barnarrt, S (eds), *International views on disability measures: moving toward comparative measurement*, pp. 41–54, Oxford and Amsterdam: Elsevier

Hershfield, A, Rohing, N, Kerr, G, & Hursh-César, G (1983). 'Fieldwork in rural areas', in Bulmer, M and Warwick, P (eds), *Social research in developing countries: surveys and censuses in the third world*, pp. 241–252, Chichester: Wiley

Heyer, J (1992). 'Contrasts in village-level fieldwork: Kenya and India', in Devereux, S & Hoddinott, J (eds), *Fieldwork in developing countries*, pp. 200–216, Hemel Hempstead: Harvester Wheatsheaf

Hoddinott, J (1992). 'Fieldwork under time constraints', in Devereux, S, & Hoddinott, J (eds), *Fieldwork in developing countries*, pp. 73–85, Hemel Hempstead: Harvester Wheatsheaf

Loeb, M, & Eide, A (2006). 'Paradigms lost: the changing face of disability in research', in Altman, B, & Barnarrt, S (eds), *International views on disability measures: moving toward comparative measurement*, pp. 111–127, Oxford and Amsterdam: Elsevier

Lombange, B (2008). 'Enga empower women with disability', *The Network* (Papua New Guinea National Disability Magazine), 14, 6

Millar, M (2004). *Volunteerism in Papua New Guinea: case study of ADRA PNG's use of local volunteers*, Lae, Papua New Guinea: Adventist Development and Relief Agency Papua New Guinea

Mitchell, R (1983). 'Survey materials collected in the developing countries: sampling, measurement, and interviewing obstacles to international and international comparisons', in Bulmer, M, & Warwick, P (eds), *Social research in developing countries: surveys and censuses in the third world*, pp. 219–239, Chichester: Wiley

Pratt, B, & Loizos, P (1992). *Choosing research methods: data collection for development workers*, Oxford: Oxfam

Thornton, P (2007). 'VSO Papua New Guinea and national volunteering: a feasibility study', draft report to VSO Papua New Guinea, (unpublished)

Thornton, P, & Pirpir, L (2008). *Discovering disability in Papua New Guinea: prevalence, perceived causes, service use and unmet needs*, Goroka, Papua New Guinea: Melanesian Institute

Wilson, K (1992). Thinking about the ethics of fieldwork, in Devereux, S, & Hoddinott, J, (eds), *Fieldwork in developing countries*, pp. 179–199, Hemel Hempstead: Harvester Wheatsheaf

Whyte, S, & Ingstad, B (1995). 'Disability and culture: an overview', in Ingstad, B, & Whyte, S (eds), *Disability and culture*, pp. 3–32, Berkeley, CA: University of California Press

Wuelker, G (1983). 'Questionnaires in Asia', in Bulmer, M, & Warwick, P (eds), *Social research in developing countries: surveys and censuses in the third world*, pp. 161–172, Chichester: Wiley

Chapter 9
Disability and HIV/AIDS: A Key Development Issue

Poul Rohleder, Leslie Swartz, and John Philander

9.1 Introduction

Despite the severity of the HIV epidemic globally, and particularly in southern Africa where the epidemic is concentrated (UNAIDS, 2007), persons with disabilities have until recently been generally overlooked with regards HIV prevention and HIV care (Groce, 2003a, 2004, 2005). This is a serious omission, as it is well established that vulnerable groups, such as young women in southern Africa, are most at risk for HIV. Persons with disabilities and particularly youth with disabilities are "among the poorest and most marginalized of all the world's young people" (Groce, 2003b; p. 3). The majority of persons with disabilities live in the "developing world" (World Bank, 2004), countries which also have some of the largest HIV epidemics in the world.

9.2 HIV/AIDS and Persons with Disabilities: What are the Risks?

Groce's (2004) seminal work, the World Bank/Yale University Global Survey on HIV/AIDS and Disability, has reported that persons with disabilities may be at increased risk for HIV infection, yet have generally been excluded from general HIV prevention campaigns, and face numerous barriers to accessing appropriate HIV prevention resources. A review of the literature in southern Africa (Rohleder et al., 2009) similarly suggests that persons with disabilities in this region are at significant risk for HIV infection. Some of the more significant risk factors include:

- *Poverty*: Persons with disabilities are more likely to earn lower incomes or be unemployed and live in conditions of poverty than the rest of the population in

P. Rohleder (✉)
Department of Psychology, Anglia Ruskin University, Cambridge, UK
e-mail: poul.rohleder@anglia.ac.uk

M. MacLachlan and L. Swartz (eds.), *Disability & International Development: Towards Inclusive Global Health*,

DOI 10.1007/978-0-387-93840-0_9,

countries throughout the world (Elwan, 1999), and women with disabilities may be particularly disadvantaged (Hanna and Rogovsky, 1991; Collins et al., 2001). This may place women with disabilities at risk for HIV infection through the need to turn to prostitution or transactional sex as a means of financial and material support (McCarthy, 1993; Smith et al., 2004). Persons with disabilities in South Africa are also reported to be disproportionately unemployed and poorer than the rest of the population (Emmett, 2006; Schneider et al., 1999; Statistics South Africa, 2005). Poverty may act as a barrier to accessing health care (Saloojee et al., 2007; Smith et al., 2004).

- *Lack of education*: Persons with disabilities worldwide have lower levels of education than the rest of the population (Elwan, 1999). Literacy levels among persons with disabilities have been found to be lower than the rest of the population, in a study conducted in Malawi (Munthali et al., 2004). Part of the reason for this is that education may be seen as unnecessary or problematic for children and adolescents with disabilities as they may be perceived as being unable to learn, or a disruption to the rest of the class (Groce, 2003b, 2004). In low-income countries, the lack of financial resources may persuade parents to invest in their non-disabled child, rather than their disabled child, with few disabled children then attending schools in poor areas (Groce, 2003b; Saloojee et al., 2007). Lack of education may act as a barrier to accessing HIV prevention information.
- *Vulnerability to sexual abuse*: It is well established in the international literature that persons with disabilities are at increased risk for sexual abuse. Review studies have indicated that persons with disabilities may be up to three times more likely to be abused, including sexual abuse, than persons without disabilities (Groce, 2004; Sullivan and Knutson, 2000), with women being particularly vulnerable to sexual abuse, although men with disabilities are more likely to be sexually abused than men without disabilities (Sobsey et al., 1997; Sullivan and Knutson, 2000). In many cases, vulnerability to abuse occurs both at home and in environments that disabled people encounter as a result of their disability (Crossmaker, 1991; Hassouneh-Phillips and Curry, 2002; Furey et al., 1994; Sobsey and Doe, 1991). In a review study of sexual assault cases of persons with learning disabilities in South Africa, it was found that in the majority of cases the perpetrator was known to the victim (Dickman and Roux, 2005).

  One factor contributing to the increased vulnerability for sexual abuse of persons with disabilities is the lack of education and knowledge about abuse (see, for example, McCabe et al., 1994). Persons with disabilities (particularly learning disabilities) may also be perceived as unreliable witnesses or are simply not believed, and the perpetrator may feel he or she will not be discovered (Andrews and Veronen, 1993, cited in Nosek et al., 2001). As a result, few cases of sexual abuse of persons with disabilities reach conviction (Brown and Turk, 1994; Sobsey and Doe, 1991; Pillay and Sargent, 2000).
- *Unsafe sex*: Persons with disabilities, particularly learning disabilities, have historically been regarded as asexual (Craft, 1987; Milligan and Neufeldt, 2001), and thus sex education is seen to be unnecessary. This however is a myth and many studies have shown that persons with disabilities are sexually active (for example, Blanchett, 2000; Blum et al., 2001; Cheng and Udry, 2002; Nosek

et al., 2001; Peinkofer, 1994). As with non-disabled people, persons with disabilities may engage in unsafe sex; sex without a condom (Blanchett, 2000; Cook, 2000; Nosek et al., 2001; Mulindwa, 2002; Munthali et al., 2004). International studies have reported sexually transmitted diseases among persons with disabilities (Jackson and Wadley, 1999; Mulindwa, 2002; Nosek et al., 2001), a further indication of unsafe sex and a risk for HIV infection.

- *Lack of sex education and HIV awareness*: Despite the evidence that persons with disabilities are sexually active, and as with non-disabled persons, also may engage in unsafe sex, persons with disabilities reportedly have received little or no sex education (Berman et al., 1999; Heyman and Huckle, 1995; McCabe, 1999; Milligan and Neufeldt, 2001; Pueschel and Scola, 1988). With little or no education about sex, and as a result of barriers to accessing HIV prevention information (Groce, 2004; Rohleder, 2008), knowledge about HIV and HIV prevention, including safe sex, is low (Bat-Chava et al., 2005; Munthali et al., 2004; Yousafzai et al., 2004). In South Africa, low levels of HIV knowledge have been reported for persons with visual disabilities (Philander and Swartz, 2006) and youth with physical disabilities (Wazakili et al., 2006). Where sex education is provided, the extent to which the topic of HIV/AIDS is covered may vary among disabilities (Getch et al., 1998; Howard-Barr et al., 2005; Kelly et al., 2002), and according to the severity of the disability (Birch et al., 2002; Yousafzai et al., 2005). Furthermore, persons with disabilities may face numerous barriers to accessing general HIV prevention information, for example accessing information that is available in sign language or in Braille formats, or health care services that are inaccessible for wheelchair users, or accessing information that is in a format that persons with learning disabilities may be able to understand (Munthali et al., 2004; Yousafzai and Edwards, 2004; Yousafzai et al., 2004; Yousafzai et al., 2005).

The myth that persons with disabilities are asexual (Craft, 1987; Milligan and Neufeldt, 2001), or alternatively sexually uninhibited and inappropriate (Craft, 1987), has resulted in a reluctance on the part of carers to provide sex education, as it is either perceived as being unnecessary or potentially dangerous (Craft, 1987; Heyman and Huckle, 1995). Carers may also feel anxious about providing sex education, as they may feel inadequately trained to do this (Bratlinger, 1992; Christian et al., 2001; Howard-Barr et al., 2005; Parritt and O'Callaghan, 2000).

Other risk factors for HIV infection include substance abuse, where the use of substances during sex may increase the likelihood of the occurrence of unsafe sex. Substance abuse has been suggested as being a serious issue for persons with disabilities (Bachman et al., 2004; Blum et al., 2001; Li and Ford, 1998). Some studies have reported the use of substances by persons with disabilities during sex (Blanchett, 2000; Kelly et al., 1992). Persons with disabilities may use substances as a means to cope with their identity as a disabled person (Njoki et al., 2007).

Associated with this then is the experience of stigma and social isolation for many persons with disabilities. Stigma is reported as a significant concern for men and women with disabilities, who may perceive themselves as sexually unattractive and undesirable (Potgieter and Khan, 2005; White et al., 1992, 1993). This may lead some persons with disabilities to engage in or remain in potentially unsafe sexual relationships, out of a need for affection and attention, or as a result of low self-esteem (Becker et al., 1997; Yousafzai and Edwards, 2004). In South Africa, Wazakili et al. (2006) found that among some youth with physical disabilities, the need to be loved was reported to be more important than having to practice safe sex. Very similar findings were reported by Philander (2007) in his study on adolescents with visual impairments in South Africa, and Joseph (2006) reported that a group of South African male adolescents claimed that because their chances to have sex were much diminished by virtue of their status as disabled people, they would take every opportunity they could to have sex.

As a result of the myths around the sexuality of persons with disabilities, and common perceptions of disabled people as either asexual and sexually inappropriate or incompetent, and the stigma and isolation associated with being disabled, talking about sexuality may be difficult for persons with disabilities themselves, as it makes one have to face the emotional pain that such stigma about "disabled sexuality" carries. As Shakespeare (2000) states:

> Sexuality, for disabled people, has been an area of distress, and exclusion, and self-doubt for so long, that it was sometimes easier not to consider it, than to engage with everything from which so many were excluded. Talking about sex and love relates to acceptance on a very basic level – both acceptance of oneself, and acceptance by significant others – and forces people to confront things which are threatening, given the abuse and isolated lives of many disabled people (p. 160).

9.3 HIV Interventions and Persons with Disabilities in Lower-Income Countries

Whereas a few years ago there was very little discussion about HIV prevention in lower income countries, there is now increasing interest in the topic. For the first time in South Africa, for example, persons with disabilities have been included in the HIV and AIDS and STI Strategic Plan for South Africa 2007–2011 (Department of Health, 2007). Hendrietta Bogopane-Zulu, a South African Member of Parliament who has a visual impairment, has been central to these developments and has also networked vigorously on HIV/AIDS and disability issues in a range of other countries. The South African Strategic Plan identifies persons with disabilities as a vulnerable group, and calls for HIV preventions that are customized and focused on such vulnerable groups. In South Africa, HIV/AIDS prevention education is included as part of the national curriculum for secondary schools. However, an evaluation of this education on implementation (Visser et al., 2004), indicated that not all schools had successfully implemented the programme. Little is known about the provision of HIV/AIDS prevention education in schools for persons with disabilities in particular.

In a study exploring the response to HIV/AIDS by organizations and schools working with persons with disabilities in South Africa (Rohleder, 2008), it was found that although there was a high awareness of the risk for HIV infection for persons with disabilities, there was a general view that there was a lack of appropriate sex education and HIV prevention. Although many disabled people's organizations had some form of HIV policy on their books, close scrutiny of their reports of what was actually taking place at selected organizations suggested a range of practices, and considerable discomfort around the topic of sexuality of persons with disabilities.

A range of publications are now available on HIV and disability in low and middle income countries. There is also a vibrant African campaign on disability and HIV, which met in Kampala, Uganda, recently, for the second time. The next issue of the magazine *Exchange*, which is funded by the Royal Netherlands Embassy and is based in Zimbabwe and focuses on HIV, sexuality and gender (due in early 2009 but not yet available at the time this book went to press) was slated to focus on HIV and disability. The organization AIDS-Free World has collated on its website a wide range of available literature on HIV/AIDS and disability (see http://www.aids-freeworld.org/content/view/114/66/). The materials collated by AIDS-Free World all in different ways focus on the need for inclusion of disabled people in HIV programmes, for elimination of discrimination against disabled people, especially on the grounds of sexuality. Mgwili and Watermeyer (2006), for example, movingly describe the experiences Mgwili has had as a disabled woman in her interaction with reproductive health services. Health workers held discriminatory and stigmatizing views on sexuality for persons with disabilities, and this must have implications for an epidemic which is spread largely through sexual contact.

What is markedly lacking on the literature on HIV and disability in both lower income and wealthier nations is that though there is consensus on the importance of the issue, and there has been much innovation in the area largely through the work of NGOs and DPOs, there are few reports of evaluated interventions of any kind. Dickman and her colleagues (Dickman and Roux, 2005; Dickman et al., 2006) report on an innovative programme run by psychologists and social workers working for a Cape Town, South Africa-based NGO to prepare intellectually disabled complainants in sexual abuse cases for court appearances, alongside training and support on issues of disability for court officials and law enforcement personnel. A review of 10 years of the programme (Dickman and Roux, 2005) showed a conviction rate for perpetrators of sexual assault against disabled complainants equal to the rate of conviction for those who sexually assaulted non-disabled people. Though the authors mention a number of caveats to the interpretation of their data, it does appear that in the context of this programme, intellectually disabled people who are sexually abused are no longer discriminated against in the justice system on grounds of disability and perceived inability to provide credible evidence, if the conviction rate is taken as the key criterion of assessment.

Philander (2007) reports on the only known formally evaluated HIV prevention intervention for adolescents with visual impairment that we have been able to find, using a control group and a 6-month follow up. The outcome of this quasi-experimental study showed a rather depressing similarity to many other studies of HIV prevention in non-disabled populations – the intervention did not show an impact on behavioural measures though some of the null findings could be attributable to small sample size. Nonetheless, part of the strength of the study lies in its rich qualitative data and very careful description of the interventions implemented.

9.4 Concluding Comments

Though there has been some progress in the field of HIV/AIDS and disability, there is a long way to go, and the issue is urgent in sub-Saharan Africa in particular. It is interesting to speculate on why, given the excellent work that has been done on outlining risk factors persons with disabilities face for HIV, we have very few data on actual rates. The only two known studies from Africa – Cameroon (Touko, 2008) and Kenya (Taegtmeyer et al., 2009) compared prevalence rates after voluntary counselling and testing among Deaf persons to hearing persons testing for HIV, or national prevalence rates. Results from these studies suggest that prevalence rates, for the Deaf, may be similar to the general population. There can be no doubt that good data showing the relative risk persons with disabilities face for HIV infection compared with non-disabled people would be helpful for example. This information would provide an evidence base for further work and if it were found that persons with disabilities were at equal or increased risk for infection this would provide an important basis for lobbying for increased funding to this neglected area. In the unlikely event that the risk were lower for disabled people, this could also be helpful for rational future use of resources.

Some time ago, a group of concerned disability activists and scholars (we know from anecdotal account) did plan a case control study to begin the process of developing evidence on HIV risk on the basis of disability. There has also been vigorous lobbying with designers of a number of large-scale HIV surveys to include questions about disability. As regards the case control study, some disability activists were very concerned that a study focusing on assessing seropositivity for HIV amongst persons with disabilities would be politically explosive and the study did not go ahead. In the case of the surveys, people running these, who had no particular interest in disability, could not be convinced that disability might be an important variable to understand in the context of the epidemic. There were also concerns that able-bodied people might be upset by the questions on disability and less inclined to participate in the surveys. The questions on disability status were omitted.

Space does not permit us fully to unpack the complex politics surrounding these decisions about research into HIV/AIDS and disability; suffice to say that the two examples both show how intertwined the area remains with issues of stigma, fear and discrimination. Clearly, the discomfort around systematically researching disability and HIV issues needs to be faced and dealt with if we are to move beyond the current (very important but not sufficient) phase of a great deal of descriptive and anecdotal knowledge.

The challenge is not minor. The issue of disability, and working with persons with disabilities may cause anxiety for many, as they are required to face issues of vulnerability, "damage" and "abnormality" (Marks, 1999; Sinason, 1992; Watermeyer, 2006). Similarly, with sex and HIV/AIDS, anxieties are raised about issues of deviance and risk (Joffe, 1999), with people drawing on metaphors of HIV/AIDS as sin, punishment and evil (Sontag, 1991), to draw a distinction between "us" and "them" (Joffe, 1999; Rohleder, 2007). For those who are tasked with the provision of sex education for persons with disabilities, this may cause some tension between the recognition of the rights of persons with disabilities to lead full sexual lives, and a need to impose a sense of morality and a need to restrict the expression of sexuality in a manner that is considered moral and acceptable (Rohleder and Swartz, 2009; Rohleder, 2008). For researchers who need to provide a research base for interventions, it may be easier to avoid the issue altogether. In the meantime, disabled people are being infected with and affected by HIV in the context of the most serious epidemic the world (and the poorer parts of the world in particular) is facing. We need to do better.

Afterword At the time this book was going to press, new data were released from the Human Sciences Research Council in South Africa from their third national HIV survey (Shisana et al., 2009), which, for the first time, invited survey participants to respond to questions about disabilities including sensory, physical, intellectual, and mental disabilities. Results of the survey mention that persons with disabilities have a higher prevalence rate of HIV (14.1%) compared to the prevalence rate among the general population (10.9%), though the confidence intervals overlapped, and the confidence interval for disabled people was very wide, which suggests a difficulty in accuracy of the estimate. This confirms suspicions that persons with disabilities may be considered at least as at risk as the general population and may even be more at risk for HIV infection than the general population. These data provides us with a suggestive evidence base for further work to be done.

References

Aids-Free World (2008). *Resource Guide: AIDS and Disability* (compiled by Myroslava Tataryn), http://www.aids-freeworld.org/content/view/114/66/ [accessed 14th January 2009]

Bachman, SS, Drainoni, M-L, & Tobias, C (2004). 'Medicaid managed care, substance abuse treatment, and people with disabilities: Review of the literature', *Health & Social Work*, 29(3), 189–196

Bat-Chava, Y, Martin, D, & Kosciw, JG (2005). 'Barriers to HIV/AIDS knowledge and prevention among deaf and hard of hearing people', *AIDS Care*, 17(5), 623–634

Becker, H, Stuifbergen, A, & Tinkle, M (1997). 'Reproductive health care experiences of women with physical disabilities: A Qualitative study', *Archive of Physical Medicine and Rehabilitation*, 78(Suppl 5), S26–S33

Berman, H, Harris, D, Enright, R, Gilpin, M, Cathers, T, & Bukovy, G (1999). 'Sexuality and the adolescent with a physical disability: Understandings and misunderstandings', *Issues in Comprehensive Pediatric Nursing*, 22, 183–196

Birch, DA, Angermeier, LK, & Gentsch, DK (2002). 'HIV Prevention education for students with mental retardation', *Rural Special Education Quarterly*, 21(3), 15–20

Blanchett, WJ (2000). 'Sexual risk behaviors of young adults with LD and the need for HIV/AIDS education', *Remedial and Special Education*, 21(6), 336–345

Blum, RW, Kelly, A, & Ireland, M (2001). 'Health-risk behaviors and protective factors among adolescents with mobility impairments and learning and emotional disabilities', *Journal of Adolescent Health*, 28(6), 481–490

Bratlinger, E (1992). 'Sexuality education in the secondary special education curriculum: Teachers' perceptions and concerns', *Teacher Education and Special Education*, 15(1), 32–40

Brown, H, & Turk, V (1994). 'Sexual abuse in adulthood: Ongoing risks for people with learning disabilities', *Child Abuse Review*, 3, 26–35

Cheng, MM, & Udry, JR (2002). 'Sexual behaviors of physically disabled adolescents in the United States', *Journal of Adolescent Health*, 31(1), 48–58

Christian, L, Stinson, J, & Dotson, LA (2002). 'Staff values regarding the sexual expression of women with developmental disabilities', *Sexuality and Disability*, 19(4), 283–291

Collins, PY, Geller, PA, Miller, S, Toro, P, & Susser, ES (2001). 'Ourselves, our bodies, our realities: An HIV prevention intervention for women with severe mental illness', *Journal of Urban Health*, 78(1), 162–175

Cook, JA (2000). 'Sexuality and people with psychiatric disabilities', *Sexuality and Disability*, 18(3), 195–206

Craft, A (1987). 'Mental handicap and sexuality: Issues for individuals with a mental handicap, their parents and professionals', in Craft, A (ed.), *Mental handicap and sexuality: Issues and perspectives*, pp. 13–33. Kent: Costello

Crossmaker, M (1991). 'Behind locked doors – Institutional sexual abuse', *Sexuality and Disability*, 9(3), 201–219

Department of Health (2007). *HIV and AIDS and STI strategic plan for South Africa, 2007–2011 (Draft 9)*, Pretoria: Department of Health, http://www.doh.gov.za/docs/hivaids-progressrep.html [accessed 8th September 2007]

Dickman, BJ, & Roux, AJ (2005). 'Complainants with learning disabilities in sexual abuse cases: A 10-year review of a psycho-legal project in Cape Town, South Africa', *British Journal of Learning Disabilities*, 33, 138–144

Dickman, B, Roux, A, Manson, S, Douglas, G, & Shabalala, N (2006). 'How could she possibly manage in court?' An intervention programme assisting complainants with intellectual disability in sexual cases in the Western Cape, in Watermeyer, B, Swartz, L, Lorenzo, T, Schneider, M, & Priestley, M (eds.), *Disability and social change: A South African agenda*, pp. 116–133. Cape Town: HSRC Press

Elwan, A (1999). *Poverty and disability: A survey of the literature*. Washington: World Bank, Social Protection Unit, http://siteresources.worldbank.org/DISABILITY/Resources/Poverty/Poverty_and_Disability_A_Survey_of_the_Literature.pdf [accessed 24th February 2006]

Emmett, T (2006). 'Disability, poverty, gender and race', in Watermeyer, B, Swartz, L, Lorenzo, T, Schneider, M, & Priestley, M (eds.), *Disability and social change: A South African agenda*, pp. 207–233. Cape Town: HSRC Press

Furey, EM, Niesen, JJ, & Strauch, JD (1994). 'Abuse and neglect of adults with mental retardation in different residential settings', *Behavioral Interventions*, 9(4), 199–211

Getch, YQ, Young, M, & Denny, G (1998). 'Sexuality education for students who are deaf: Current practices and concerns', *Sexuality and Disability*, 16(4), 269–281

Groce, NE (2003a). *Adolescents and youth with disability: Issues and challenges*, http//www.dcdd.nl/default.asp?action=article&id=2150 [accessed 14th March 2006]

Groce, NE (2003b). 'HIV/AIDS and people with disability', *The Lancet*, 361, 1401–1402

Groce, NE (2004). *HIV/AIDS and disability: Capturing hidden voices*, Report of the World Bank Yale University Global Survey of HIV/AIDS and Disability, Washington: World Bank, http://siteresources.worldbank.org/DISABILITY/Resources/Health-and-Wellness/HIVAIDS.pdf [accessed 12th March 2005]

Groce, NE (2005). 'HIV/AIDS and individuals with disability', *Health and Human Rights*, 8(2), 215–224

Hanna, WJ, & Rogovsky, B (1991). 'Women with disabilities: Two handicaps plus', *Disability, Handicap & Society*, 6(1), 49–63

Hassouneh-Phillips, D, & Curry, MA (2002). 'Abuse of women with disabilities: State of the science', *Rehabilitation Counseling Bulletin*, 45(2), 96–104

Heyman, B, & Huckle, S (1995). 'Sexuality as a perceived hazard in the lives of adults with learning difficulties', *Disability & Society*, 10(2), 139–155

Howard-Barr, EM, Rienzo, BA, Pigg, RM, Jr, & James, D (2005). 'Teacher beliefs, professional preparation, and practices regarding exceptional students and sexuality education', *Journal of School Health*, 75(3), 99–104

Jackson, AB, & Wadley, V (1999). 'A multicenter study of women's self-reported reproductive health after spinal cord injury', *Archive of Physical Medicine and Rehabilitation*, 80, 1420–1428

Joffe, H (1999). *Risk and 'the other'*. Cambridge: Cambridge University Press

Joseph, LLW (2006). 'The construction of visually impaired adolescent masculinity', Unpublished masters thesis, University of KwaZulu Natal, Pietermaritzburg, South Africa

Kelly, JA, Murphy, DA, Bahr, GR, Brasfield, TL, Davis, DR, Hauth, MA, Morgan, MG, Stevenson, LY, & Eilers, MK (1992). 'AIDS/HIV risk behaviour among the chronically mentally ill', *American Journal of Psychiatry*, 149(7), 886–889

Kelly, K, Ntlabati, P, Oyosi, S, van der Riet, M, & Parker, W (2002). *Making HIV/AIDS our problem: Young people and the development challenge in South Africa*. Centre for AIDS Development, Research and Evaluation (CADRE), www.cadre.org.za/pdf/Making AIDS our problem.pdf [accessed 12th March 2005]

Li, L, & Ford, JA (1998). 'Illicit drug use by women with disabilities', *American Journal of Drug and Alcohol Abuse*, 24(3), 405–418

Marks, D (1999). *Disability: Controversial debates and psychosocial issues*. London: Routledge

McCabe, MP (1999). 'Sexual knowledge, experience and feelings among people with disability', *Sexuality and Disability*, 17(2), 157–170

McCabe, MP, Cummins, RA, & Reid, SB (1994). 'An empirical study of the sexual abuse of people with intellectual disability', *Sexuality and Disability*, 12(4), 297–306

McCarthy, M (1993). 'Sexual experiences of women with learning difficulties in long-stay hospitals', *Sexuality and Disability*, 11(4), 277–286

Mgwili, VN, & Watermeyer, B (2006). 'Physically disabled women and discrimination in reproductive health care: Psychoanalytic reflections'. In Watermeyer, B, Swartz, L, Lorenzo, T, Schneider, M, & Priestley, M (eds.), *Disability and social change. A South African agenda*, pp. 261–272. Cape Town: HSRC Press

Milligan, MS, & Neufeldt, AH (2001). 'The myth of asexuality: A survey of social and empirical evidence', *Sexuality and Disability*, 19(2), 91–109

Mulindwa, IN (2002). 'Study on reproductive health and HIV/AIDS among persons with disabilities in Kampala, Katakwi and Rakai districts (knowledge, attitudes and practices)', Disabled Women's Network and Resource Organization, http://v1.dpi.org/lang-en/resources/details.php?page=355 [accessed 14th August 2007]

Munthali, A, Mvula, P, & Ali, S (2004). *Effective HIV/AIDS and reproductive health information to people with disabilities: A final report*. Centre for Social Research: University of Malawi, www.dpi.org/en/resources/documents/FinalReportforFedomaStudyOctober2004.doc [accessed 25th June 2005]

Njoki, E, Frantz, J, & Mpofu, R (2007). 'Health-promotion needs of youth with a spinal cord injury in South Africa', *Disability and Rehabilitation*, 29(6), 465–472

Nosek, MA, Howland, C, Rintala, DH, Young, ME, & Chanpong, GF (2001). 'National study of women with physical disabilities: Final report', *Sexuality and Disability*, 19(1), 5–39

Parritt, S, & O'Callaghan, J (2000). 'Splitting the difference: An exploratory study of therapists' work with sexuality, relationships and disability', *Sexual and Relationship Therapy*, 15(2), 151–169

Peinkofer, JR (1994). 'HIV education for the deaf, a vulnerable minority', *Public Health Reports*, 109(3), 390–396

Philander, JH (2007). 'The development and evaluation of a pilot school-based programme for prevention of HIV/AIDS among visually impaired and blind South African adolescents', Unpublished doctoral dissertation, Stellenbosch University, Stellenbosch, South Africa

Philander, JH, & Swartz, L (2006). 'Needs, barriers, and concerns regarding HIV prevention among South Africans with visual impairments: A key informant study', *Journal of Visual Impairment and Blindness*, 100, 111–115

Pillay, AL, & Sargent, C (2000). 'Psycho-legal issues affecting rape survivors with mental retardation', *South African Journal of Psychology*, 30(2), 9–13

Potgieter, C, & Khan, G (2005). 'Sexual self-esteem and body image of South African spinal cord injured adolescents', *Sexuality and Disability*, 23(1), 1–20

Pueschel, SM, & Scola, PS (1988). 'Parents' perception of social and sexual functions in adolescents with Down's syndrome', *Journal of Mental Deficiency Research*, 32, 215–220

Rohleder, P (2007). 'HIV and the "other"', *Psychodynamic Practice*, 13(4), 401–412

Rohleder, P (2008). 'HIV/AIDS and Disability: An exploration of organizations' responses to HIV/AIDS as it affects people with disabilities', Unpublished doctoral dissertation, University of Stellenbosch, South Africa

Rohleder, P, & Swartz, L (2009). 'Providing sex education to persons with learning disabilities in the era of HIV/AIDS: Tensions between discourses of human rights and restriction', *Journal of Health Psychology*, 14(4), 601–610

Rohleder, P, Braathen, SH, Swartz, L, & Eide, AH (2009). 'HIV/AIDS and disability in southern Africa: A review of relevant literature', *Disability & Rehabilitation*, 31(1), 51–59

Saloojee, G, Phohole, M, Saloojee, H, & Ijsselmuiden, C (2007). 'Unmet health, welfare and educational needs of disabled children in an impoverished South African peri-urban township', *Child: Care, Health & Development*, 33(3), 230–235

Schneider, M, Claassens, M, Kimmie, Z, Morgan, R, Naiker, S, Roberts, A, & McLaren, P (1999). *"We also count": The extent of moderate and severe reported disability and the nature of the disability experience in South Africa*. CASE Disability survey prepared for the Department of Health, Pretoria, www.doh.gov.za/facts/1997/case.pdf [accessed 9th April 2005]

Shakespeare, T (2000). 'Disabled sexuality: Towards rights and recognition', *Sexuality and Disability*, 18(3), 159–166

Shisana O, Rehle T, Simbayi LC, Zuma K, Jooste S, Pillay-van-Wyk V, Mbelle N, Van Zyl J, Parker W, Zungu NP, Pezi S & the SABSSM III Implementation Team (2009). *South African national HIV prevalence, incidence, behaviour and communication survey 2008:A turning tide among teenagers?* Cape Town: HSRC Press

Sinason, V (1992). *Mental handicap and the human condition: New approaches from the Tavistock*. London: Free Association Books

Smith, E, Murray, SF, Yousafzai, AK, & Kasonkas, L (2004). 'Barriers to accessing safe motherhood and reproductive health services: The situation of women with disabilities in Lusaka, Zambia', *Disability and Rehabilitation*, 26(2), 121–127

Sobsey, D, & Doe, T (1991). 'Patterns of sexual abuse and assault', *Sexuality and Disability*, 9(3), 243–259

Sobsey, D, Randall, W, & Parrila, RK (1997). 'Gender differences in abused children with and without disabilities', *Child Abuse & Neglect*, 21(8), 707–720

Sontag, S (1991). *Illness as metaphor and AIDS and its metaphors*. London: Penguin

Statistics South Africa (2005). *Census 2001: Prevalence of disability in South Africa*. Pretoria: Statistics South Africa, www.statssa.gov.za/Publications/Report-03–02–44/Report-03–02–44.pdf [accessed 9th April 2005]

Sullivan, PM, & Knutson, JF (2000). 'Maltreatment and disabilities: A population-based epidemiological study', *Child Abuse & Neglect*, 24(10), 1257–1273

Taegtmeyer, M, Hightower, A, Opiyo, W, Mwachiro, L, Henderson, K, Angala, P, Ngare, C, & Marum, E. (2009). A peer-led HIV counselling and testing programme for the deaf in Kenya. *Disability and Rehabilitation*, 31(6), 508–514

Touko, A (2008). *About a neglected group in the fight against HIV/AIDS: Sexual behaviour and HIV prevalence among the young deaf population in Cameroon*. Paper presented at the XVII International AIDS Conference, Mexico City, August 2008. Available from: http://www.aids2008.org/Pag/ppt/WEAD0205.ppt [accessed 10th June 2009]

UNAIDS (2007). *AIDS epidemic update: December 2007*, Geneva: Joint United Nations Programme on HIV/AIDS and World Health Organization. Available from: http://www.unaids.org

Visser, MJ, Schoeman, JB, & Perold, JJ (2004). 'Evaluation of HIV/AIDS prevention in South African schools', *Journal of Health Psychology*, 9(2), 263–280

Watermeyer, B (2006). 'Disability and psychoanalysis', in Watermeyer, B, Swartz, L, Lorenzo, T, Schneider, M, & Priestley, M (eds.), *Disability and social change: A South African agenda*, pp. 31–44. Cape Town: HSRC Press

Wazakili, M, Mpofu, R, & Devlieger, P (2006). 'Experiences and perceptions of sexuality and HIV/AIDS among young people with physical disabilities in a South African township: A Case study', *Sexuality and Disability*, 24, 77–88

White, MJ, Rintala, DH, Hart, KA, Young, ME, & Fuhrer, MJ (1992). 'Sexual activities, concerns and interests of men with spinal cord injury', *American Journal of Physical Medicine & Rehabilitation*, 71(4), 225–231

White, MJ, Rintala, DH, Hart, KA, & Fuhrer, MJ (1993). 'Sexual activities, concerns and interests of men with spinal cord injury', *American Journal of Physical Medicine & Rehabilitation*, 72(6), 372–378

World Bank (2004). *Disability and HIV/AIDS at a glance*, http://web.worldbank.org/WBSITE/EXTERNAL/TOPICS/EXTSOCIALPROTECTION/EXTDISABILITY/0,,contentMDK:20208464~pagePK:148956~piPK:216618~theSitePK:282699,00.html [accessed 3rd October 2007]

Yousafzai, A, & Edwards, K (2004). *Double burden: A situation analysis of HIV/AIDS and young people with disabilities in Rwanda and Uganda*, London: Save the Children, www.savethechildren.org.uk/temp/scuk/cache/cmsattach/1600_DoubleBurden.pdf [accessed 12th March 2005]

Yousafzai, AK, Dlamini, PJ, Groce, N, & Wirz, S (2004). 'Knowledge, personal risk and experiences of HIV/AIDS among people with disabilities in Swaziland', *International Journal of Rehabilitation Research*, 27(3), 247–251

Yousafzai, AK, Edwards, K, D'Allesandro, C, & Lindström, L (2005). 'HIV/AIDS information and services: The situation experienced by adolescents with disabilities in Rwanda and Uganda', *Disability and Rehabilitation*, 27(22), 1357–1363

Chapter 10
Assistive Technology in Low-Income Countries

Arne H. Eide and Tone Øderud

10.1 Introduction

World Health Organization (WHO) has estimated that 10% of the global population has a disability, with social educational and/or economical consequences. Although such estimates have a weak basis (Metts, 2000; Eide and Loeb, 2006a) it might be about 600 million people around the world with special needs in terms of health care, education, rehabilitation, appropriate assistive devices and social support. Furthermore it is indicated that 80% of people with disabilities live in low-income countries and also in very poor life conditions with limited access to health care services, rehabilitation and assistive devices. Case studies in developing countries show that higher disability rates are associated with higher rates of illiteracy, poor nutritional status, lower immunization coverage, lower birth weight, higher rates of unemployment and underemployment, and lower occupational mobility (Elwan, 1999). Disability can cause poverty by preventing the full participation of persons with disabilities in the economic and social life of their communities, especially if the appropriate supports and accommodations are not available. This chapter draws on results from recent studies on living conditions among people with disabilities in southern Africa (Eide et al. 2003a, b; Loeb and Eide, 2004; Eide and Loeb, 2006b) and aims at describing the situation for disabled people in low-income contexts with regards to assistive technology.

Assistive devices and technologies such as mobility aids, hearing aids, visual aids, wheelchairs, prostheses, and adapted computer software and hardware increase the possibilities for individuals with disabilities to participate in their societies and live independently.

The UN Resolution "The Standard Rules for Equalization of Opportunities for People with Disabilities" (UN, 1994) is an important document with strong impact on the future of people with disabilities. Standard Rule 4 on Support Services states: "States should ensure the development and supply of support services, including assistive devices for persons with disabilities, to assist them to increase their level

A.H. Eide (✉)
SINTEF Health Research, Oslo, Norway
e-mail: ArneHenning.Eide@sintef.no

M. MacLachlan and L. Swartz (eds.), *Disability & International Development: Towards Inclusive Global Health*,
DOI 10.1007/978-0-387-93840-0_10, © Springer Science+Business Media, LLC 2009

of independence in their daily living and to exercise their rights". The resolution also states "States should ensure the provision of assistive devices and equipment according to the needs of persons with disabilities, as important measures to achieve the equalization of opportunities" and "States should support the development, production, distribution and servicing of assistive devices and equipment and the dissemination of knowledge about them."

The 58th World Health Assembly adopted the resolution "Disability, including prevention, management and rehabilitation" in 2005 (WHO, 2005). The resolution states that 80% of people with disabilities live in low-income countries and that poverty limits access to basic health services, including rehabilitation services. On assistive technology the resolution urges member states to "facilitate access to appropriate technology and to promote its development and other means that encourage the inclusion of persons with disabilities in society" and to "ensure provision of adequate and effective medical care to people with special needs and to facilitate their access to such care including prostheses, wheelchairs, driving aids and other devices."

The recent UN Convention on the Rights of Persons with Disabilities (UN, 2006) calls for member states to provide individuals with disabilities mobility aids, devices and assistive technologies, including new technologies, as well as other forms of assistance, support services and facilities. In spite of important high-level policy support (UN, 1994, 2006; WHO, 2005), the majority of people with disabilities living in low-income countries, however, have little or no access to assistive devices that could contribute to improving their life situation and help many to a more independent life (Øderud and Grann, 1999). Supply of assistive devices is very far from meeting the needs, and service delivery systems are either non-existent or limited.

WHO reports that rehabilitative services in the developing world reach only 1–2% of the disabled population (Frye, 1993). Production is low and often of limited quality. There is a scarcity of personnel trained to manage the provision of such devices and technologies, especially at provincial and district levels. In many settings where access might be possible, costs are prohibitive. The priorities of health care in low-income countries are largely preventive or promotive, and rehabilitation is not given priority. May-Teerink (1999) underlines the lack of knowledge and research on assistive technology and rehabilitation in low-income countries. In her study carried out in Uganda, May-Teerink found that the use of assistive devices were indicative of greater mobility, which led to better opportunities for formal education or employment. She further reported that gender-related issues may limit women's access to rehabilitative equipment due to limited financial resources of women living in low-income countries.

It has been estimated that there are around 37 million people in the world who are blind, and that an additional 135 million have a severe visual impairment (http://www.cbmicanada.org). It has further been estimated that 90% of the worlds' blind children have no opportunity to attend school, and that 80% of blind adults cannot work, because they lack training facilities and assistive devices. WHO has further estimated that there are around 250 million people worldwide with disabling hearing loss that could benefit from hearing aids (AUDINEWS July 2002). The large majority of these live in low-income countries without any type of hearing aids.

The United Nations Statistical Office estimates there are 20 million people in the world who need a wheelchair but don't have one. Recently the global Consensus Conference on Wheelchairs organized by WHO, the International Society for Prosthetics and Orthotics (ISPO) and USAID (2003) have indicated that 1% of the world's population, or about 60–65 million people, are in need of a wheelchair. According to estimates by Hotchkiss and Knezevitch (1990), 1 million wheelchairs per year are needed if the supply of wheelchairs is going to meet the demand by the year 2020. This is most likely a gross underestimation, as it does not take the expected 5-year life span of a wheelchair into account. Distribution of wheelchairs to developing countries over the past several decades has, however, cumulatively provided less than half a million units (Pearlman et al. 2006), and there is currently a staggering and growing demand.

There is limited data and knowledge on assistive technology in low-income countries. This goes for demand, supply, quality and effect of assistive technology on the welfare of disabled individuals. Critics have for instance argued that wheelchairs supplied in low-income countries in many instances are sub-standard (Pearlman, 2006). Armstrong et al. (2007) state that two of the most common methods for distribution of wheelchairs are either mass produced in high- or middle-income countries or used wheelchairs delivered with minimal service provision. Furthermore, for wheelchairs that are damaged, replacement parts are typically not available. Most donated products are originally designed for indoor use and do not perform well for active users in rugged environments (Mukherjee and Samanta, 2005). Locally adapted and small-scale production found in low-income countries has amounted to around 50,000 units during the last two decades (Pearlman et al. 2006).

Supply of assistive devices is clearly more than a question of quantity and distribution. Equally important is the quality of what is offered. Unfortunately, much of the AT in use in these countries are either technically outdated and not adapted to local circumstances or imported sophisticated technology beyond common people's reach. There are furthermore many examples indicating that supply of AT without considering the need for a service delivery system that includes individual assessment, adaptation, training in use, follow up, maintenance, proper distribution, qualified personnel, etc., is the reality in many countries (Øderud, 2000).

Assessment of user needs and prescription of appropriate devices are key issues in the process of ensuring that people with disabilities are receiving equipment that is correctly fitted and meets the individual needs that could positively influence their quality of life. A poor fit can mean the development of complications like pressure sores and infections, which may even be life-threatening (Armstrong et al. 2007). The width, height and length of a wheelchair should be adapted to fit the individual size of the person and especially for children. If the wheelchair is not fitted correctly the child is at a risk of developing postural problems (scoliosis, kyfose, etc.) and possibly digestive problems. Individual adapted postural support including a cushion is needed to prevent the increase of disability, prevent possible pressure sores and development of additional problems.

In many low-income and middle-income countries, only 5–15% of people who require assistive devices and technologies have access to them. Production is low and often of limited quality. There is a scarcity of personnel trained to manage the provision of such devices and technologies, especially at provincial and district levels. In many settings where access might be possible, costs are prohibitive (WHO).

Since the development, production and distribution of assistive devices and technologies are not an integral part of the health care system in many countries, their provision falls to nongovernmental organizations and other groups. Because there is no central coordination for these efforts, in many instances assistive devices and technologies are produced without adequately taking into account the needs of people with disabilities, their living conditions or environments. In cases were external funding is in place, related programs often collapse when the funding is no longer available (WHO).

The following citation from Zimbabwe indicates the importance of availability of appropriate assistive technology and a service delivery system. Poor fit and/or lack of relevant assistive technology may imply a question of life and death in poor countries.

"We were 19 people being rehabilitated in 2001 and discharged in 2003. I am now the only person alive. The rest have died because of pressure sores. If someone can't afford a wheelchair and is using a wheelbarrow and doesn't have a cushion, what do you expect?" (Ms. Gladys Charowa, Chair of Disabled Women's group DWSO, Zimbabwe) (Personal communication, T. Øderud).

10.2 New Knowledge About Assistive Devices in Developing Countries

In Malawi, Namibia, Zimbabwe and Zambia, studies on living conditions among people with disabilities have recently been carried out (Eide et al., 2003a, 2003b; Loeb and Eide 2004; Eide and Loeb, 2006b) by SINTEF Health Research in collaboration with national universities, central statistical offices and national affiliates of the Southern Africa Federation of the Disabled (SAFOD). The studies were all National, representative household surveys with two-stage sampling; activity-based screening was carried out in a sample of small geographical areas (enumeration areas) drawn from the national sampling frames. Households with a disabled member were later revisited for data collection. One section in the research instrument was about disability, one on general living conditions in the households, and one on activity and participation. Individuals with disabilities responded to the disability related questions, otherwise the head of the household was interviewed. In some households the main respondent also reported for the individual with a disability if this person were unable to respond for some reason. Research instrument was based on previous surveys in the region and adapted to each context through a comprehensive process involving all relevant stakeholders in each country. Although the different national studies are comparable, research instruments thus vary somewhat between the countries. All studies were carried out in close collaboration with the national federation of disabled people affiliated with Southern Africa Federation of the Disabled (SAFOD), Central Statistical Office in each country, and the National Universities. The Norwegian Federation of Organizations for Disabled People (FFO) has initiated, funded and supported all four studies. For further details on methodology (see Eide et al. 2003a, 2003b; Loeb and Eide, 2004, Eide and Loeb, 2006b).

Table 10.1 provides information about the sample in each country. The following analyses concern the sub-population of individuals with disabilities. The number of respondents in the tables below corresponds to the number of individuals with disabilities for each country given in Table 10.1 with small variations due to missing information, unless other information is given in the tables.

Some variables may differ between the countries with regards to formulations and number of answer categories. Whenever this is the case, footnotes in the tables provide explanation, and some results are referred to in the text if this is found most practical.

In all four countries assistive devices for personal mobility is by far the most frequent, followed by devices for sensory impairments (eye glasses, hearing aids, Braille). This reflects the proportion of the different impairment categories (see Table 10.2). The majority of those who reported that they had an assistive device stated that it was in good working condition (Malawi: 53.6%, Namibia 69.2%, Zimbabwe: 74.7%, Zambia: 77.2%).

Table 10.1 Sample

	Namibia		Zimbabwe		Malawi		Zambia	
Disability	With	W/out	With	W/out	With	W/out	With	W/out
No. of households	2,286	1,356	1,943	1,958	1,521	1,537	2,885	2,886
Total no. of individuals in HH	16,459	6,855	11,460	10,252	8,038	7,326	15,210	12,979
Individuals with disabilities	2,537		2,071		1,623		2,898	

Table 10.2 Source of assistive device (percentage of individuals with a device[a])

Source	Namibia	Zimbabwe	Zambia	Malawi
Private	29.1	31.2	42.8	34.4
Government Health Service	59.1	27.4	14.8	17.9
Other Government Service	0.7	3.2	3.2	1.4
NGO	2.3	8.3	8.8	9.3
Other	8.2	28.8	24.7	36.8

[a]Individuals with an assistive device. N = 304 (Malawi), 446 (Namibia), 372 (Zambia), 506 (Zimbabwe)

Different sources of the assistive devices were given.

In three countries, sources outside Government dominated, while in Namibia Government health service provided close to 60% of the devices. Private sources are here largely donations from the commercial sector. The domination of Government as a source in Namibia is also reflected in the reported information on maintenance of the assistive device (Table 10.3). In Namibia more than one third (36.3%) report that their device is maintained by Government, while this figure is between 3 and 6% for the other three countries. The combination of "self-repair" or "maintained by other family member" exceeds the figures for Government for all countries, but this is not as pronounced in Namibia as compared with the other three countries. The proportion of assistive devices that are not maintained at all is particularly high in Malawi (36%) and low in Namibia (12%).

Table 10.3 further reveals that a large proportion of assistive device users, in Malawi it is even a majority, do not get any information or guidance with regards to use. Between 22 and 42% state that the device (i.e. the main device) is not in good working condition. Combining these quality indicators may indicate that the situation is most difficult in Malawi and least in Namibia.

Respondents were asked to describe their impairment, and this was later used to categorize into some main impairment groups. Table 10.4 shows that the largest group of impairments fall into the "physical category", followed by sensory impairments, mental impairments and impairments related to communication.

The figures in Table 10.4 also indicate differentiation in needs with regards to different types of assistive devices. In the data material from Zambia for instance, the most frequent devices in use were mobility devices (wheelchairs, crutches, etc.) (78% of those with an assistive device). This was followed by sensory devices (eye glasses, hearing aids, Braille, etc.) (38% of those with a device), and communication devices (sign language, interpreter, portable writer, computer, etc.) (14% of those with a device). Other types of devices, i.e. for personal care and

Table 10.3 Quality aspects of service delivery with regards to assistive devices

Quality indicator	Namibia	Zimbabwe	Malawi	Zambia
Device maintained by owner or family	43	66	38	58
Device not maintained	12	15	36	11
No information or help given on use of device	28	23	59	37
Device not in good working condition	31	22	42	25

Table 10.4 Types of impairment (%)

Types of impairment (%)	Namibia	Zimbabwe	Malawi	Zambia
Physical	40	46	43	42
Sensory; Visual/hearing	28	32	39	44
Psychological	16	11	12	11
Communication	6	–[a]	3	3
Others	10	11	3	–[a]

[a]Answer category not included in the questionnaire

protection, for handling products and goods, and household items, were reported in use by very few individuals.

Table 10.5 first of all shows that impairments in this context are inflicted upon individuals early in life, contrary to what is the case in richer parts of the world. While demographic distribution in the populations explains some of this difference, it also reflects the vulnerability of children in poor contexts as well as problems related to health care services. This information further indicates the importance of a child perspective on service delivery in this particular context.

Table 10.6 indicates that the largest "service gaps" are found with regards to assistive devices and vocational training. Largely, the assistive device/service gap is around 50%, the vocational training gap around 30%, and the health service gap between 0 and 20%. As this is self-reported, it can be assumed that the real gap is larger as many individuals are not aware of, for instance, what kind of assistive devices could have helped them.

Zimbabwe stands out in this comparison as both the assistive device/service gap and the vocational training gap is considerably smaller than for the other three countries. The study in Zimbabwe was carried out before, or rather in the early stages of, the economic downfall of the country, and the result may reflect particularly developed services for individuals with disabilities in the country. With regards to health services, Zimbabwe and Zambia appears to have no gap, while Namibia and Malawi has reported around 20%. It is also indicated that the need for traditional healers is met and that this type of service is also given in excess of the stated need, indicating that this culturally embedded service to some extent replaces other types of services.

Table 10.5 Age of onset of impairment (%)

Age of onset	Namibia	Zimbabwe	Malawi	Zambia
From birth	31	20	23	30
1–10	21	24	36	21.4[a]
11–20	12	9	11	43.1[b]
21–60	32	32	23	
61+	4	15	7	

[a]Acquired disability between birth and age of 10
[b]Acquired disability as children or young adults (less than or equal to 20 years)

Table 10.6 Types of services that are needed and received (%)*

	Namibia	Zimbabwe	Malawi	Zambia
Services	Need/Received	Need/Received	Need/Received	Need/Received
Health services	91/73	94/92	83/61	77/80
Assistive device/service	67/17	57/37	65/18	57/18
Vocational training	47/5	41/23	45/6	35/8
Traditional healer	33/47	49/90	58/60	32/63

Need: Percent of total number of disabled.
Received: Percent of those claiming they needed the services actually receiving the services.

The proportion of individuals with disabilities having an assistive device varies from 14.9% in Zambia to 25.8% in Zimbabwe. A clear gender difference is demonstrated in Malawi and Zambia in that females have less access to assistive devices as compared with men. Also in Zimbabwe, more men have an assistive device, but the gender difference is not pronounced. In Namibia this question was phrased differently and it was asked for experience rather than ownership, and hence Namibia is not reflected in the table. Also in Namibia a clear gender difference was demonstrated, confirming the findings presented in Table 10.7; male individuals with disabilities report more experience with assistive devices than females.

A clear urban/rural difference is demonstrated, in that individuals with disabilities living in an urban setting report to a larger degree than rural dwellers state that they have an assistive device (Table 10.8).

There are marked differences with regards to type of impairment, as could be expected. Individuals with a physical disability report significantly higher access than other impairment groups, sensory comes as second, followed by age/other and lastly psychological. Controlling for gender revealed that there is a pronounced difference when it comes to physical and sensory impairments in that the proportion with an assistive device is significantly higher among men. For age/other and psychological impairments gender differences are smaller and not statistically significant due to low numbers (Table 10.9).

Table 10.7 Assistive device by gender

	Do you have any assistive device? (% Yes)		
Gender	Malawi	Zambia	Zimbabwe
Male	25.3	15.7	26.6
Female	14.1	11.9	25.0
Total	19.8	14.9	25.8

Table 10.8 Assistive device by urban/rural (%)

Yes, have an assistive device	Urban	Rural
Zimbabwe	35.1	22.2
Namibia	24.7	16.0
Zambia	17.2	11.9
Malawi	20.4	19.7

Table 10.9 Assistive device by impairment type

	Do you have any assistive device? (% Yes)			
Impairment	Malawi	Zambia	Zimbabwe	Namibia
Sensory	14.2	12.7	21.1	14.2
Physical	30.3	19.1	37.6	31.5
Psychological	3.2	2.2	2.7	1.2
Age/other	10.7	–	17.0	2.2
Total	19.6	14.2	25.8	18.4

In Table 10.10, the population of disabled is split in age groups of largely equal size. The proportion of disabled having an assistive device increases with age. Comparing the oldest age category with the youngest shows seven times higher proportion of individuals having an assistive device among the 61+ than the ones who are between 0 and 10 years of age. For all age categories women report lower figures than men. For the three oldest age categories, the gender difference is particularly high in that men report twice or more as high figures as boys. The gender differences in the younger categories are non-significant although among the 0–10 age group girls report 3.1% as compared to 6.8% among boys. The lack of significance is due to the low number having a device in this age group.

Table 10.11 demonstrates that individuals who report that they attend or have attended school are more likely to have an assistive device as compared to those who have never attended.

For the Namibian and Zimbabwean samples different answer categories were applied with regards to employment. No significant differences in use of assistive devices were found in these two samples when comparing those who were currently working with those who had been previously or never employed. For Malawi and Zambia (Table 10.12), it is demonstrated that those without any working experience

Table 10.10 Assistive device by age groups

	Do you have any assistive device? (% Yes)			
Age group (years)	Malawi	Zambia	Namibia	Zimbabwe
0–10	4.9	10.0	5.5	11.2
11–20	9.7	10.2	11.0	14.9
21–40	19.5	29.7	25.0	15.3
41–60	23.8	31.4	35.7	27.9
61+	35.4	15.1	22.9	41.7
Total	18.7	12.1	17.8	25.5

Table 10.11 Assistive device by school attendance

Have you ever attended school?	Do you have any assistive device? (% Yes)			
	Malawi	Zambia	Namibia	Zimbabwe
Never attended	17.8	11.3	12.9	15.2
Attending/finished/left	21.9	16.6	21.6	18.6

Table 10.12 Assistive device by employment

	Do you have any assistive device (% Yes)	
Are you currently working?	Malawi	Zambia
Yes, currently working	26.1	19.7
No, but have been employed previously	39.6	22.6
No, never been employed	20.1	15.0
I am a housewife	11.3	14.3

more often report that they do not have an assistive device as compared to those with work experience. Between 20 and 30% of the population of individuals with disabilities state that they are currently working, and between 15 and 25% have no working experience whatsoever.

10.3 Discussion

The need for assistive devices among the majority of individuals with disabilities living in low-income countries are far from being met. Furthermore, the quality of much of what is offered is often not up to acceptable standards, and service delivery systems are underdeveloped or non-existent. Good intentions, charity and small-scale model programs characterize this arena in many poor countries. Individuals with disabilities are thus denied assistance that clearly could have increased their independence, level of activity and social participation, and thus their living conditions.

Research on assistive technology in low-income countries is scarce. We do have a broad picture of the situation, but lack more precise knowledge that could be of importance in policymaking, resource allocation and measures to improve the situation for individuals with disabilities in low-income countries. The four studies on living conditions among people with disabilities in Zimbabwe, Namibia, Malawi and Zambia provide unique representative information about disability in the Southern African Region, including information about use of assistive devices, quality aspects and service delivery.

The studies have indicated pronounced problems in service delivery when it comes to the quality of the devices (working conditions), instructions for use and maintenance which is to a large extent left to the owner of the device and his/her family or simply not maintained at all. Clearly this situation has negative consequences for the users of devices as well as their families, with increased risk for complications and secondary conditions due to wrong use or wrongly fitted devices (Armstrong et al. 2007). The role of Government vs. private sources on the supply side varies between the countries, and there are indications in the results that the relatively strong Government involvement in Namibia puts this country in a somewhat better position than the other countries in the study. There is, however, not sufficient information to conclude that the model in Namibia necessarily is optimal, as it is also the case that the "assistive device/service gap" in fact is comparatively largest in Namibia and actual use of devices is lower than Zimbabwe and equals the figures from Malawi. The relatively positive results from Namibia may simply reflect a comparatively better economic situation and that there is more money in place to import devices. The results are rather indications of a service delivery system in the region that is fragmented and that does not deliver the services needed to the population in question.

The four data materials have shown a large "needs gap" with regards to assistive devices, and that females and rural dwellers have less access to this technology. May-Teerink's observation with regards to gender is thus confirmed. Furthermore, as the demographic profile of most low-income countries is characterized by a large proportion (often around 50%) of children and adolescents, the results indicate a pronounced need for taking a children's perspective in future service delivery systems.

With regards to school attendance and employment, the results bring support to May-Teerink's (1999) findings from Uganda and other literature on this issue (Armstrong et al. 2007). While the analyses here show that there is a positive association between having an assistive device and school attendance and having a job or work experience, this is, however, not sufficient to conclude that there is a simple cause and effect relationship. Other mechanisms may also be present, but the indication is clear and in line with previous findings and assumptions.

It is vital to promote the possibilities for people with disabilities to take part in education, employment and social activities in society using AT as a tool in order to improve their quality of life. The use of assistive devices is influenced by general knowledge, local supply, technical competence, adaptation to individual, follow up and environmental conditions, as well as local services. There is a chain of links that has to be fulfilled so that the assistive devices can be of best use in different contexts.

Although in no way sufficient, there are currently many ongoing, often small-scale, programs for production, import and distribution of assistive devices in low-income countries. There is a need for studying the many different models in order to extract the most promising experiences. In this way ongoing and new programs can learn from each other. It is further necessary to strengthen research-based knowledge about the role of assistive technology in reducing the link between disability and poverty in order to develop and improve current practice further. Assistive devices should contribute to improve the opportunities for individuals with disabilities to be active integrated members in their local community and in the society in general.

References

Armstrong, W, Reisinger, KD, & Smith, WK (2007). 'Evaluation of CIR-Whirlwind Wheelchair and service provision in Afghanistan', *Disability and Rehabilitation*, 29 (11–12), 935–948

Eide, AH, & Loeb, ME (2006a). 'Reflections on disability data and statistics in developing countries', in Albert, B *In or Out of The Mainstream? Lessons from Research on Disability and Development Cooperation*, University of Leeds, The Disability Press

Eide, AH, & Loeb, ME (2006b). 'Living Conditions Among People with Disabilities in Zambia. A National Representative Survey', SINTEF Report No. A262, Oslo: SINTEF Health Research

Eide, AH, Nhiwatiwa, S, Muderedzi, J, and Loeb, ME (2003a). 'Living Conditions Among People with Activity Limitations in Zimbabwe. A representative regional survey', SINTEF report no. STF78A034512, Oslo: SINTEF Unimed

Eide, AH, van Rooy, G, & Loeb, ME (2003b). 'Living Conditions Among People with Disabilities in Namibia. A National, Representative Study', SINTEF Report no. STF 78 A034503, Oslo, SINTEF Unimed

Elwan, A (1999). 'Poverty and Disability; a Survey of Literature', Social Protection Discussion Paper (np) 9932, Washington, DC: World Bank

Frye, B (1993). Review of the World Health Organization's Report on Disability Prevention and Rehabilitation, New York: Longman Scientific & Technical and Wiley

Hotchkiss, R, & Knezevitch, J (1990). 'Third World Wheelchair Manufacture. Will it ever meet the needs?', in RESNA 13th Annual Conference 1990.Washington, DC: RESNA, pp. 309–310

Loeb, M, & Eide, AH (eds.) (2004). 'Living Conditions Among People with Activity Limitations in Malawi', SINTEF Report no. STF78 A044511. Oslo: SINTEF Health Research

May-Teerink, T (1999). 'A survey of rehabilitative services and people coping with physical disabilities in Uganda, East Africa', *Disability and Rehabilitation*, 22, 311–316

Metts, R (2000) Disability Issues, trends and implications for the World Bank. Washington DC: World Bank

Mukherjee, G, & Samanta, A (2005). 'Wheelchair charity: A useless benevolence in community-based rehabilitation', *Disability and Rehabilitation*, 27, 591–596

Pearlman J, Cooper, R, Krizack, M, Lindsley, A, et al. (2006). 'Towards the development of an effective technology transfer of wheelchairs to developing countries', *Disability and Rehabilitation: Assistive Technology*, 1 (1–2), 103–110

UN (1994). 'The Standard Rules for the Equalization of Opportunities for People with Disabilities', New York: United Nations

UN (2006). 'United Nations Convention on the Rights of Persons with Disabilities', New York: United Nations

USAID (2003). US Agency for International Development. Annual Program Statement, Washington, DC: USAID

WHO (2005). 'Disability, Including Prevention, Management and Rehabilitation', Resolution Adopted at the 58th World Health Assembly. Geneva: World Health Organization

Øderud, T (2000). 'Assistive Technology for People with Disabilities in Namibia and Zimbabwe', SINTEF Report STF78 A900525, Oslo, SINTEF

Øderud T, and Grann, O (1999). 'Providing Assistive Devices and Rehabilitation Services in Developing Countries', The 5th European conference for the Advancement of Assistive Technology, Düsseldorf, November 1999

Chapter 11
Childhood Disability in Burkina Faso and Sierra Leone: An Exploratory Analysis

Cliona O'Sullivan and Malcolm MacLachlan

11.1 Introduction

In 2006, close to 9.7 million children died before their fifth birthday worldwide and 4.8 million of these deaths occurred in sub-Saharan Africa. The main causes of global child mortality are: neonatal disorders (33%), diarrhoea (22%), pneumonia (21%), malaria (9%), AIDS (3%), measles (1%), other (9%) and unknown causes (1%). Neonatal disorders are those which occur in the first month of life and include: preterm birth, severe infections, asphyxia and congenital abnormalities (Lawn et al., 2005). The highest rates of neonatal mortality are found in sub-Saharan Africa (UNICEF, 2008a; Lawn et al., 2005).

Whilst statistics pertaining to mortality rates for various illnesses are available, little is known about the survivors of these illnesses, although many are left with significant impairments and disability. For example, in Burkina Faso, West Africa, the World Health Organization reported more than 22,000 suspected cases of meningococcal disease including 1,490 deaths between January and April 2007 (WHO, 2007a). However, there is no data available pertaining to residual disabilities experienced by survivors of this recent outbreak of meningitis.

In 2000, world leaders agreed to a set of timebound and measurable goals for tackling poverty, hunger, disease, illiteracy, environmental degradation and discrimination against women by 2015; these goals are now known as the UN Millennium Development Goals, (MDGs). While disability was not specifically targeted in these goals, issues around disability are intrinsically linked to several of them.

For instance, with regard to the first MDG, "Eradicate extreme poverty and hunger," it is acknowledged that there is a strong correlation between disability and poverty (Mont, 2007). With regard to the second MDG, "Achieve universal primary education," there is evidence that people with disability in developing countries are more likely to have lower education levels and higher illiteracy levels than people without disability (UN Enable, 2008). Disability in childhood often means that a child is unable to walk

C. O'Sullivan (✉) and M. MacLachlan
School of Physiotherapy and Performance Science, University College Dublin, Belfield, Dublin,
e-mail: cliona.osullivan@ucd.ie

M. MacLachlan and L. Swartz (eds.), *Disability & International Development: Towards Inclusive Global Health*,
DOI 10.1007/978-0-387-93840-0_11,

to school or parents may feel that it is best to 'invest' in a non-disabled child's education. Moreover, schools often report that their teachers are not trained to teach children with special needs and therefore will not give a child a place in school.

The fourth MDG, "Reduce child mortality," is benefiting from increased international attention and there is evidence that child mortality rates are reducing (UNICEF, 2008b). However it is not yet known whether child disability rates are increasing as a result. It is not known whether the major causes of childhood mortality in low-income countries are also the major causes of childhood disability. It is feasible that while more children are now surviving illnesses such as meningitis and malaria; they may be left with residual disabilities as a result; thereby concurrently increasing childhood disability rates.

Accurate information regarding childhood disability is necessary to plan intervention programmes, provide resources for services, develop and monitor policies at a national level, and to compare disability rates and experiences internationally. Currently, there is a dearth of information on a range of childhood disability issues including the prevalence of disability; severity of disability, causes of disability, impact of disability on development, function and social integration; need for services; access to services and cultural views of disability in developing countries. Without such information, the lives of disabled children in low-income countries are unlikely to improve and the key goal of poverty reduction in low-income countries is unlikely to be achieved.

11.2 Measuring Disability

Measuring disability has proven problematic mainly due to the use of differing definitions and parameters. The World Health Organization's (WHO) International Classification of Functioning Disability and Health (ICF) describes the outcome of disability at three different levels (WHO, 2001). Firstly, as an impairment of a body function or structure; secondly; in terms of limitations of activities; and, finally, in terms of participation restrictions. This framework acknowledges the complexity of defining disability and has great potential for the collection of meaningful disability data.

Collecting disability data on children is even more complex as children naturally change from being fully functionally dependent from early infancy to being fully independent in late adolescence. The first two decades of life are characterized by rapid growth and significant changes in the physical, social and psychological development of children and youth (WHO, 2007b). The International Classification of Functioning, Disability and Health for Children and Youth (ICF-CY) is derived from the ICF and is designed to record the characteristics of the developing child and the influence of its surrounding environment. The ICF-CY was published by the WHO in 2007 and uses a common language and terminology for recording problems involving functions and structures of the body, activity limitations and participation restrictions, manifested in infancy, childhood and adolescence and relevant environmental factors (WHO, 2007b).

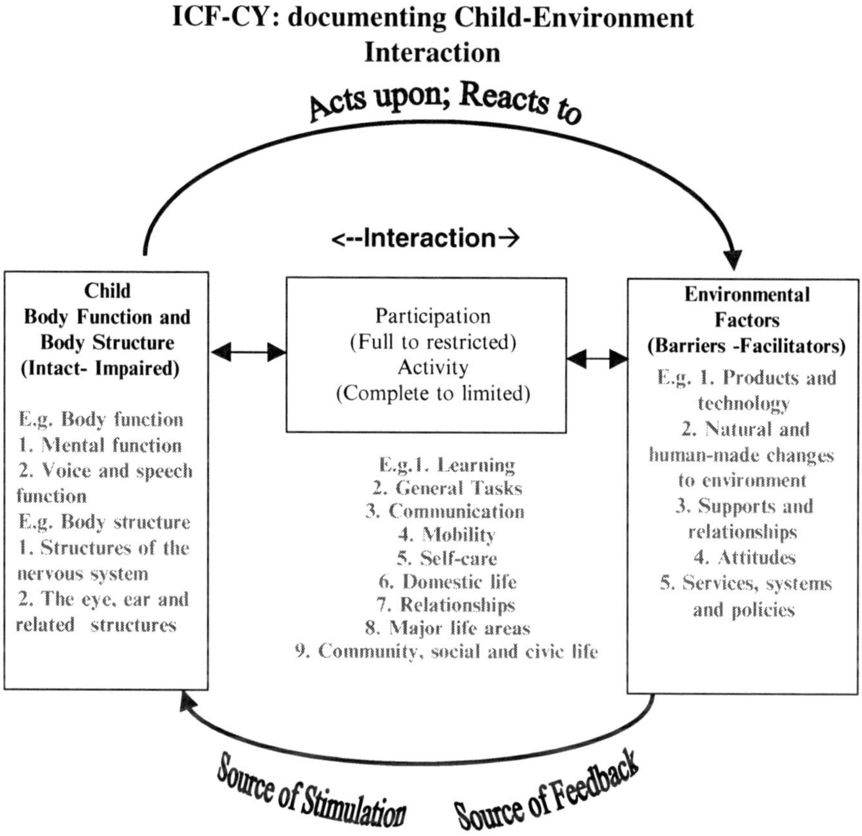

Fig. 11.1 ICF-CY Framework

The ICF-CY model (see Fig. 11.1) stresses three broad issues: body structures and function, participation, and the environment, and it explores how each of these issues is interlinked.

11.2.1 Body Structures and Function

During childhood and adolescence, there are variations in the timing of emergence of body functions and the acquisition of skills associated with individual differences in growth and development. Delays in the emergence of capacities may not be permanent but in some cases can reflect developmental delay or may indeed be a permanent manifestation of impairment at the level of body structure or function. Examples of body structures within the ICF-CY framework include structures of the nervous system and structures related to movement (Fig. 11.1). Examples of body functions include mental functions, Neuromusculoskeletal, and movement-related functions (Fig. 11.1). Generic qualifiers are used to indicate the extent or magnitude of an impairment of body structure or function (WHO, 2007b).

The qualifiers are rated according to the following scale:

0 No impairment
1 Mild impairment
2 Moderate impairment
3 Severe impairment
4 Complete impairment
8 Not specified
9 Not applicable

11.2.2 Activities and Participation

Activity is defined as "the execution of a task or action by an individual," while participation is defined as a person's "involvement in a life situation" (WHO, 2007b). Participation from the point of view of a child differs dramatically from that of an adult, and indeed also from that of an older child or adolescent. For example, in early childhood, a child's participation is dependent on family, service providers and its immediate environment. Examples of participation within the ICF-CY framework include communication, mobility, community, and social and civic life (Fig. 11.1). Two qualifiers are used to rate this component: a performance qualifier and a capacity qualifier. The performance qualifier describes what an individual can do in his/her environment and the capacity qualifier describes an individual's ability to execute a task or action. The qualifiers are rated in accordance with the following scale (WHO, 2007b):

0 No difficulty
1 Mild difficulty
2 Moderate difficulty
3 Severe difficulty
4 Complete difficulty
8 Not specified
9 Not applicable

11.2.3 Environmental Factors

Environmental factors are defined as "the physical, social and attitudinal environment in which people live and conduct their lives" (WHO, 2007b). A child's environment changes dramatically from infancy to adolescence and is related to their increasing functional capacity and independence. For example, a baby is significantly dependent on people in his/her immediate environment. Older children are closely connected to home and school life, while the environment of an adolescent includes broader aspects of society such as work or sport. Examples of environmental factors within the ICF-CY framework include products and technologies and attitudes (Fig. 11.1). The following is the negative and positive scale for the extent to which an environmental factor acts as a barrier or a facilitator (WHO, 2007b):

0 No barrier
1 Mild barrier
2 Moderate barrier
3 Severe barrier
4 Complete barrier
  +0 No facilitator
  +1 Mild facilitator
  +2 Moderate facilitator
  +3 Severe facilitator
  +4 Complete facilitator
8 Barrier (Not specified)
  +8 Facilitator (Not specified)
9 Not applicable

It must be noted that for all of these scales to be used in a uniform manner, assessment procedures have to be developed through research (WHO, 2007b).

This chapter describes an exploratory study of people's perceptions of childhood disability in Burkina Faso and Sierra Leone. Although these two countries are closely related geographically, they also have quite different profiles in relation to childhood disability, presenting the possibility of instructive comparison for understanding disability in the wider region. Sierra Leone has gone through a long period of civil war (1991–2001) and a severe humanitarian crisis. The war has created high levels of disability due to poverty and resultant ill health and also due to traumatic injuries such as amputations as a result of landmines and machete assaults. While Burkina Faso has been relatively politically stable for the past two decades, it suffers from chronic food shortages as a result of drought, desertification and falling export prices. The country also faces major challenges in health due to the spread of HIV/AIDS and outbreaks of meningitis, cholera and yellow fever. Services for children with disability in Burkina Faso are negligible; in 2006, there were 32 physiotherapists working in Burkina Faso, with most concentrated in the urban area of Ouagadougou (Handicap International Burkina Faso, Personal Communication, 2008). Table 11.1, which presents some descriptive statistics for these two countries, clearly illustrates their distinctive and contrasting profiles. Table 11.1 also contrasts these statistics with those of

Table 11.1 Health statistics of countries of interest

	Ireland	Sierra Leone	Burkina Faso
Human Development Index Ranking (of 177 countries)	5	177	176
Life expectancy at birth	78.4	41.8	51.4
Under 5 Mortality Rate (per 1,000 live births)	6	282	191
Infant Mortality Rate (per 1,000 live births)	5	165	96
Maternal Mortality Rates Adjusted (per 1,000 live births)	1	2,100	700
Physicians (per 100,000 people)	279	3	5

(*Source*: UNDP Report 2007/2008)

Ireland, as an example of a comparatively much wealthier country and the country where the authors of this chapter reside.

To eliminate poverty, the prevalence of disability must be reduced, through both interventions that prevent disability and the implementation of programmes that address issues around childhood disability like access to health care, education and acceptance and integration/participation into family and community life. While the problem of disability in this region is acknowledged by most government bodies and non-governmental organizations, the extent of the problem and its repercussions are unknown. The access to slim resources for health care is competitive and priority is often given to interventions that influence a reduction in mortality rates. For this reason, disability is often not on the agenda, and, if it is addressed, the resources are patchy, both in continuity and geographical distribution. Research that accurately reflects the issue of childhood disability is imperative if effective strategies to prevent and manage childhood disability in sub-Saharan Africa are going to be implemented. The objectives of the exploratory research to be reported here were to gain an insight into childhood disability in Burkina Faso and Sierra Leone, identify what research questions are important to examine from the point of view of a range of different stakeholders, and to determine the optimum methods of conducting such research. The proposed study objectives were explored with the relevant stakeholders and modified or expanded upon to incorporate their interests.

11.3 Methodology

Initial contacts were made via colleagues working in or who had previously worked in the sub-Saharan region: Irish NGOs including Trocaire, Concern, VSO, and Goal, and international NGOs working on disability or health issues, including Handicap International, Leonard Cheshire Foundation, International Service Ireland, Mercy Ships, and the World Health Organization. Once in-country, the following cohort were contacted: international and national NGOs working on disability and health issues, schools for children with disabilities, health and rehabilitation programmes, community programmes, universities, third level institutes, research institutes and ministries of health. The objectives of the project were explained to them and a variety of personnel were invited to participate in an interview. The interview was semi-structured and the interview template is outlined in Appendix.

Persons interviewed included parents/guardians of children with disabilities, children with disabilities, teachers, doctors, nurses, physiotherapists, occupational therapists, community leaders, development workers, programme directors, researchers and staff of health ministries. Answers to questions were given in French and English and were transcribed in English. Where local language was used, answers were translated by an interpreter into English. All interviews were conducted and transcribed by the first author, except interviews in local language. It was decided at an early stage that interviews would not be taped, as due to the nature of the project, ethical approval had not been sought prior to the visit.

Responses to questions during the interviews were transcribed by the first author. Questions were then categorized, using thematic content analysis, under headings or topics, (e.g. Causes of childhood disability). The various responses given to each question category were then themed for similar topics, (e.g. medical causes). The contents of each topic are then described in the text, (e.g. cerebral palsy).

11.4 Results and Analysis

In all, 36 interviews using purposive snowball sampling to ensure a broad range of stakeholders were included in the sample. The interviews were conducted over a 4-week period. Figure 11.2 outlines the number and the participants of interviews undertaken. Numbers are pooled for both countries to prevent identification of participants.

Seven broad topics emerged from the analysis of interviews: Disability policy; Meaning of disability; Prevalence of disability; Causes of childhood

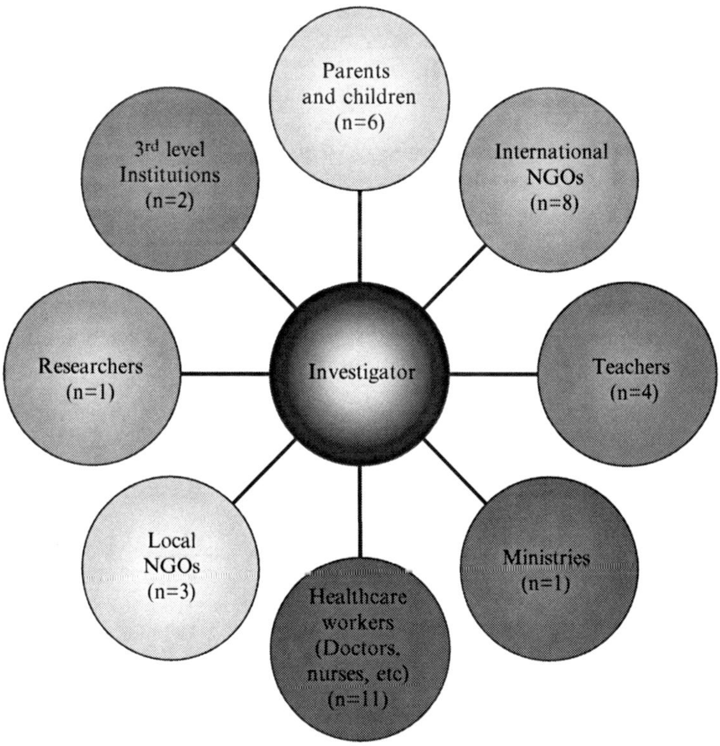

Fig. 11.2 Number and Participants

disability; Impact of disability on the child, family, mother, community, nationally; What would most improve the lives of children with disabilities? and, finally, Challenges facing the disability movement.

11.5 Disability Policy

In Burkina Faso, while disability issues come under the realm of the Ministry of Health, there is no dedicated government post for disability issues. Issues around disability are driven by an umbrella organization of NGOs working on disability. In Sierra Leone, government responsibility for disability issues is divided between the Ministries of Health and Welfare. Similar to Burkina Faso, disability issues are highlighted by an umbrella organization of NGOs working with disability issues called SLUDI (Sierra Leone Union for Disability Issues). Respondents in Sierra Leone reported that disability issues were not a priority as efforts to improve mortality rates took precedence and therefore there was a lack of commitment to disability issues generally. Neither country has a government policy on disability.

11.6 Meaning of Disability

We use the ICF-CY conceptual framework to describe child disability through two case studies, one drawn from each country. This is one of the first published accounts of the use of the ICF-CY in a low-income country setting. These case studies are presented so as to give an impression of the meaning that people's disabilities had, both at the personal and community level. Tables 11.2 and 11.3 expand on the basic framework and illustrate how the classification system can be implemented to capture components of individual cases of childhood disability in Burkina Faso and Sierra Leone.

Table 11.2 ICF-CY classification system related to components of "J's" story

	Body function and structure	Participation and activity	Environmental factors
Level 1 classification	Mental functions	General tasks and demands	Attitudes
Level 2 classification	Emotional functions (b152)[a]	Managing one's own behaviour (d250)[a]	Individual attitudes of immediate family members (e410)[a]
Detailed classification	Regulation of emotion (b1521)[a]	Acting predictably (d2503)[a]	
Qualifier	3 – Severe impairment	3 – Severe difficulty	2 – Moderate barrier

[a]ICF-CY detailed classification codes (WHO, 2007b)

Table 11.3 ICF-CY classification system related to components of 'P's' story

	Body function and structure	Participation and activity	Environmental factors
Level 1 classification	Neuromusculoskeletal and movement related function	Mobility	Products and technology
Level 2 classification	Muscle function (b730–b749)[a]	Changing and maintaining body position (d410–d429)[a]	Assets (e165)[a]
Detailed classification	Muscle tone function (b735)[a]	Sitting (d4103)[a]	Financial assets (e1650)[a]
Qualifier	3 – Severe impairment	4 – Complete difficulty	3 – Severe barrier

[a]ICF-CY detailed classification codes (WHO, 2007b)

11.7 Case Scenario 1

"J" is 11 years old and is cared for by her maternal grandmother. "J" has severe learning difficulties and behavioural problems. She is unable to speak and doesn't understand questions or commands. Her grandmother is unsure of the cause but thinks that it may be since birth or since having meningitis as a baby. "J" has no physical disabilities – she can eat, dress and toilet independently but needs assistance to toilet and dress appropriately. However her grandmother worries about her behaviour and personal safety. "J" was rejected by parents; her parents separated soon after she was born and when her mother re-married, her new husband didn't accept her. She then went to live with her father who didn't care for her properly – Her grandmother used to see her running wild around the market. She worried about her safety and decided to look after her 10 months ago. In her community "J" is not well treated. Her neighbours mock her and other children laugh at her and call her "mad girl." "J"s experience is conceptualised using the ICF-CY framework in Fig. 11.3.

11.7.1 Case Scenario 2

"P" is 1 year and 5 months old. When he was 1 month old, his parents noticed that his head was beginning to swell and he was diagnosed with hydrocephalus. A philanthropist paid for him to undergo surgery in another country. Further surgery is required in 2–3 years but his parents do not have the finances to fund this. Currently his communication is age appropriate. He has no head control, and poor muscle tone, but he can move his arms and put food in his mouth if his head is supported. He attends regular physiotherapy. He is accepted well into his family. His mother and father now both work part-time so that they can share his care. He is not well accepted in his community – he is perceived as a 'snake'. His family have become isolated in their own community. His father worries about this isolation and they keep "P" cov-

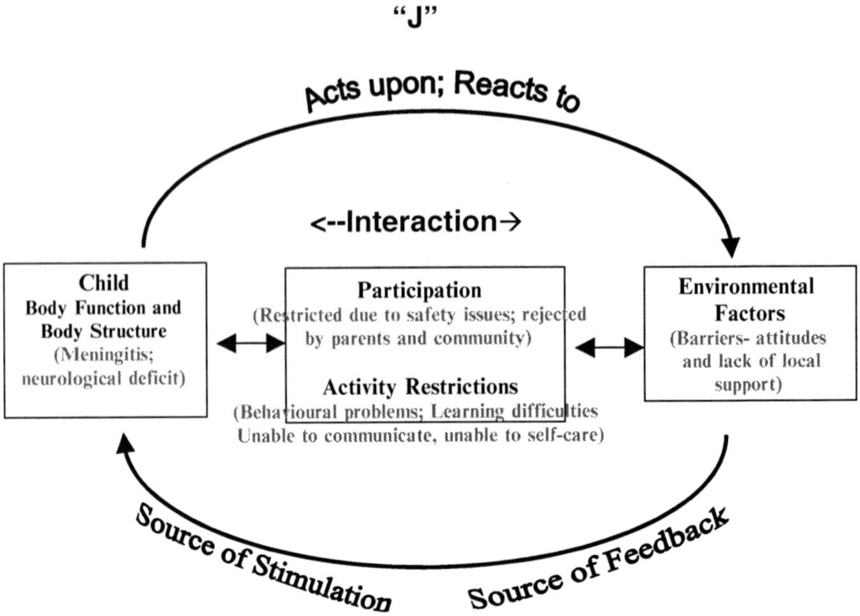

Fig. 11.3 Describing "J's" Experience using the ICF-CY

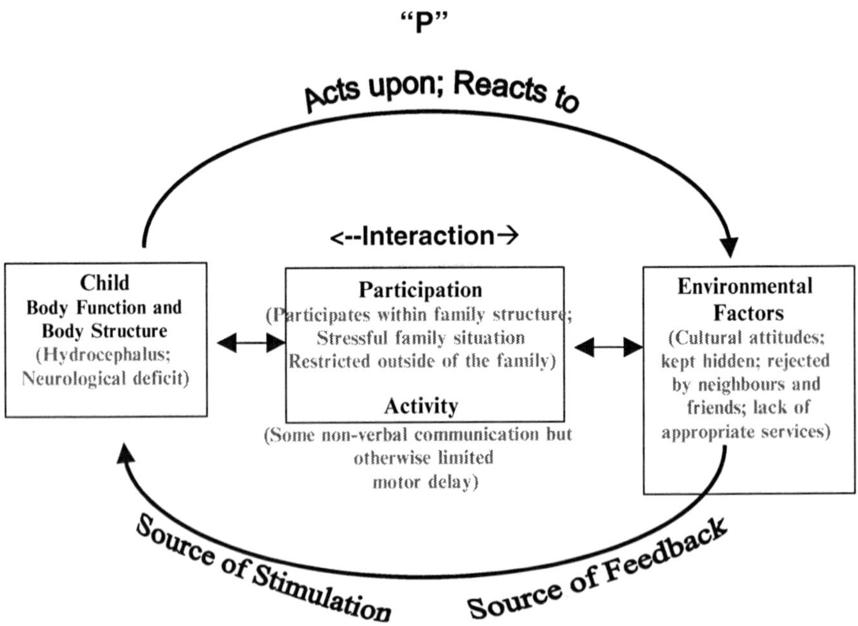

Fig. 11.4 Describing "P's" experience using the ICF-CY

ered when he is in public. His father worries that he will get too heavy to carry and that there are no services for him in their country. He hopes that they will get support from their friends and that "P" will get better in the future. "P"s experience is conceptualised using the ICF-CY framework in Fig. 11.4.

11.8 Prevalence of Disability

Respondents in both countries said that the respective prevalence of disability is unknown. In Sierra Leone, a question on disability was included in the most recent census – however the results were considered to be unreliable. The prevalence of disability in Sierra Leone is estimated to be between 7 and 10%.

11.9 Causes of Childhood Disability

The reported causes of childhood disability fell under four broad themes: medical, social, traditional/cultural beliefs and environmental causes. Medical causes include: cerebral palsy (as a result of antenatal and postnatal complications, difficult labours, meningitis or malaria), neonatal complications, meningitis, malaria, congenital deformities/club foot, accidents, amputations, fractures, malnutrition, polio, "high fever," epilepsy, injections (polio virus), osteomylitis, measles, unknown-or sometimes "difficult to diagnose" problems, and blindness. Causes of blindness included river blindness, traditional medical practices, malnutrition, lack of Vitamin A, corneal ulcers, glaucoma, and war-associated physical trauma.

Social causes were mostly related to poverty, and included malnutrition, lack of vaccines, lack of mosquitoe nets, lack of knowledge, delay in seeking medical help, reduced access to medical services, transport issues and war. The Sierra Leoneon war resulted in more than 5,000 upper limb amputees and in Sierra Leonne upper limb amputation is regarded as a symbol of the conflict.

Most respondents reported that for some people, the causes of disability were closely linked to traditional beliefs and cultural values. Strong traditional belief systems associated with disability were evident in both countries. A disabled child was often regarded as punishment for something that parents or ancestors had done. Disability was often associated with witchcraft, as a result of a "spell" imposed on a child, their family or ancestors. One interviewee with polio since childhood reported: "I was in my twenties and a university graduate when I realized that my disability was due to a medical cause and not because of something that my ancestors had done."

Attributions to environmental causes included the climate, for example increases in the incidence of meningitis during the Harmattan season in Burkina Faso. Other environmental causes included lack of sanitation, accessibility to medical services and poor transport due to difficult terrain.

11.10 Impact of Disability

Most respondents reported that children with disabilities were often isolated, neglected and marginalized at times both within and outside of their family. Traditional beliefs often dictated that disabled children were not considered human and were thought of as spirits or snakes. Disabled children were feared and seen as a sign of bad luck or an omen, resulting in them being hidden within their households. One interviewee reported: "When I was 6 or 7, one morning I went to buy bread at the market – however the man refused to serve me as I was his first customer and it would be bad luck for the day."

As a result, there was a huge stigma associated with disabled children and their families. Access to education or basic stimulation was therefore denied, meaning that their full potential could not be realized. Children with disabilities were often subject to abuse and in both countries it was reported that they were sometimes abandoned by one or both parents. In some instances, children with physical disabilities were used as beggars and provided income for their families. In one situation a teenage girl with severe physical impairments was fully supported by an NGO to attend school – however her mother refused this help, as she was the main breadwinner for the family.

The impact of a disabled child on the family was also negative. Traditional beliefs dictate that people believe that having a disabled child is punishment for something that a family member or their ancestors have done in the past. Families are marginalized and "mocked." Having a disabled child creates many tensions within the family. There are fears over what people think, and/or blame is apportioned. It also places an extra financial strain on families. A parent may have to stay at home from work to look after the child. Medical or rehabilitation services that may be available are costly. One respondent reported that "a disabled child is not a good investment."

Some interviewees highlighted how mothers were often marginalized by their spouse and the community, which placed huge stress on the mother. One interviewee reported: "I was put in residential care at the age of four and didn't meet my mother again until I was nearly 30 – my father had divorced her because she had given him a disabled child." Having a disabled child often meant that mothers had little time for other children. Mothers were often ill equipped to deal with a disabled child and it often affected the productivity and income generation of the mother.

The impact of childhood disability on the community mostly related to traditional belief systems. It resulted in gossip and fear within the community and strong community bonds could be broken as families were rejected. It was perceived that at a national level, childhood disability put a strain on public resources, imposed poverty on families and ultimately limited development.

11.11 What Would Most Improve the Lives of Children with Disabilities?

The responses to this question fell under three broad themes as follows: social inclusion, education, and rehabilitation. The most common answer to the above question was the idea of creating a "disable aware society." It was reported that there was a need to raise awareness and knowledge in the general population that "children with disability have potential to be useful in society." It was acknowledged that negative attitudes and beliefs had to be addressed. Methods that could be employed to achieve this included: education through the media and through sport, employing more people in the area of integration, and the use of role models (e.g. involving people with disabilities who have had successful careers, etc., in the awareness campaign). Other areas included improving infrastructure, transport and general accessibility for people with disabilities. Some respondents also called for commitment from the relevant ministries including the development of policies and legislation that would ultimately protect children with disabilities.

It was widely acknowledged that children with disabilities have reduced access to adequate education in both countries. In both Burkina Faso and Sierra Leone, many NGOs are advocating inclusive education, whereby children with disabilities can attend mainstream schools and special needs schools are coordinated or amalgamated with mainstream schools. Some of the challenges to this include the lack of specialist teacher training and lack of or unreliable government funding.

A high proportion of births in both countries are attended by traditional birth attendants (TBAs). It was reported by many respondents that there is a need for more training and resources for community midwives, TBAs and traditional medicine practitioners, particularly in the area of early recognition of signs of foetal or maternal distress. The need for more comprehensive community-based rehabilitation (CBR) and primary care coverage was also highlighted. Lack of human resources and retention of well-trained local health professionals in both countries was also a challenge – it was reported that in Sierra Leone, out of a total of 30 medical graduates in 1 year, only six remained in Sierra Leone 1 year later.

Resources for all health services should be adequate so that services are provided free of charge. There is also a need for resources for adequate equipment, maintenance and infrastructure. While a few respondents advocated residential care for children with disabilities, most were in favour of supporting children and their families so that they could be cared for at home and therefore didn't become institutionalized; "Organizations should not take children out of the outside world as it is harder to get back in later in life."

11.12 Challenges Facing the Disability Movement

The challenges facing those in the disability movement fell under five broad themes: government commitment, cultural attitudes and beliefs, financial issues, education and mental health. Respondents in both countries reported that disability is not a priority and as a result, government funding for disability services is insufficient and unreliable. There was a need for national policy, legislation and monitoring. There was a strong feeling that the negative social and cultural beliefs associated with disability permeated all levels of society and needed to be addressed.

The lack of adequate funding or unreliable funding for disability resulted in poorer quality of services, poor training levels and staff retention problems.

There was also a lack of awareness of existing services. Corruption was also reported to be a problem. Insufficient funding means that there are poor training levels for staff working with people with disability, particularly a lack of specialist training (e.g. specialist teacher training or training for technical support). This adds to staff retention problems. Lack of access to education for children with disabilities is also currently a major challenge.

One of the biggest challenges facing the disability movement, particularly in post-war Sierra Leone, is mental health issues. During the war, traumatic incidents such as machete assaults, rape and the high level of drug-use and alcohol abuse by rebels means that a high proportion of Sierra Leoneons are suffering from psychological illnesses such as stress, depression and addiction. Current research being carried out in-country has already noted high levels of depression in Sierra Leone. A particularly vulnerable sub-group are the former child soldiers of Children Associated with Fighting Forces (CAFF). In Sierra Leone, it is estimated that there were between 1,700 and 3,000 child soldiers during the war, some of whom joined forces as young as 5 years (Medeiros, 2007). There is evidence that many of the worst atrocities committed during the war were committed by children, often under the influence of drugs and alcohol (Medeiros, 2007). These children are now teenagers or young adults and many have been marginalized and not accepted back into their communities, as they are feared. Coupled with this is the fact that many suffer from depression and drug and alcohol addictions and there is anecdotal evidence of a high suicide rate within this cohort. The lack of services for mental health in Sierra Leone is startling: There is currently one psychiatrist in Sierra Leone and one addiction centre in Freetown.

11.13 Research Needs

In addition to getting a better understanding of the circumstances of persons with disabilities in Sierra Leone and Burkina Faso, we also sought to identify at least some elements of a possible research agenda. In doing so it is clearly important to include the point of view of all stakeholders (children, parents, people working with childhood disability, NGOs, ministries, universities). As a result of the interviews, numerous topics and ideas for pertinent research were evident. It was widely agreed that the outcome of research should promote efficient and effective progress in the introduction of programs that reduce the burden of childhood disability. Interviewees felt that current research was often of poor methodological quality and that relevant findings didn't always filter down to those working on disability issues at grass roots level. It was also acknowledged that research undertaken should be communicated to the relevant Ministries so that findings can be acted upon systematically, ensuring that information was also provided at a national level.

Table 11.4 summarizes the research questions identified and the tick marks outline whether these research questions arose from interviews in-country or from gaps in the literature identified by the authors.

Table 11.4 Summary of research topics

Topic	Source: Interviews in West Africa	Source: Literature
Prevalence of childhood disability	√	√
Type		
Regional variation		
Causes		
Cultural attitudes and beliefs towards children with disabilities	√	√
Optimum methods of raising awareness of issues relating to childhood disability	√	
Existing services and programs working on childhood disability issues	√	√
Effectiveness		
Quality		
Service mapping		
Prevention strategies		√
Legislation and policy	√	√
Needs assessment	√	
Parent-related research	√	
Resources spent on disabled child		
Perceptions		
Obstacles		
Child development	√	
Europe V West Africa		

In addition to rich qualitative studies, randomized control trials and longitudinal studies are needed, along with a long-term commitment to this chronically underserved area from funding agencies and universities. Research should incorporate collaboration between universities, international and national NGOs and Ministries of health, as well as other Ministries that provide services that can promote the inclusion and participation of persons with disability in society. Such research also needs to take into account not only the relevance of local cultural practices but also the power relationships between disabled and non-disabled people, and between different institutions within and between different countries (MacLachlan et al., 2010). There are also significant barriers to research that need to be overcome and these include financial constraints, the fact that funding for disability has to be sought in a very competitive market, a lack of suitably trained personnel in-country, language differences, poor infrastructure, as well as access to children with disabilities and their families.

In conclusion, there is no doubt but that the life of a child with a disability in both Burkina Faso and Sierra Leone is a difficult one. Childhood disability can immerse vulnerable families in poverty. Cultural beliefs dictate that children may be neglected, isolated and subject to abuse. The lack of appropriate health and rehabilitation services and opportunity for education, coupled with a lack of funding and commitment from government ministries and donors, serve to confound negative perceptions associated with disability and to make the attainment of basic human rights for persons with disability frustratingly difficult.

Acknowledgements We acknowledge the Health Research Board, Ireland, and Irish Aid for funding this project.

Appendix: Interview Template

Introduction

My name is Cliona O'Sullivan and I work as a lecturer in the School of Physiotherapy and Performance Science at University College Dublin. I have worked as a clinical physiotherapist for 9 years and for that reason, I am experienced in rehabilitation of disability. I am very interested in issues around disability in developing countries since working in Ouagadougou, Burkina Faso, where I worked in a local NGO for children with disabilities.

As we know, in Sub-Saharan Africa, one in every five children dies before their 5th birthday. The main causes of global child mortality are: neonatal disorders, meningitis, malaria, diarrhoea, pneumonia, AIDS, measles and other, sometimes unknown, causes. While we have valid statistics on the causes of child mortality, little is known about the survivors of such illnesses, although many are left with gross neurological difficulties, among other things.

Because there is so little that we know about such children, I am interested in investigating/studying/researching these issues a little further here in Burkina Faso/ Sierra Leone. I am interested in people's views about the most pressing area that needs research and most effective way to carry out research in this area. I am hopeful that by carrying out good research, we will gain answers to these questions. By knowing this information, it is then possible to implement interventions that will prevent disabilities, reduce disability and improve functional abilities and social participation.

The purpose of my meeting with you is to gain an insight into disability in Burkina Faso/Sierra Leone through your eyes and to gain a better understanding of the causes of disability and the problems faced by children with disabilities and their families in Burkina Faso/Sierra Leone. I am also interested in your opinions on the best way to engage children with disabilities and their parents to participate in research about disability.

The objectives of my visit to Burkina Faso and Sierra Leone are to:

1. Identify the need for research in this area, specifically what research questions are important to examine from the point of view of all stakeholders (children, parents, people working with childhood disability, NGOs, ministries, universities)
2. Identify the best way to conduct such research in the context of Burkina Faso and Sierra Leone (methodologies/difficulties/obstacles)?
3. Identify the best way to form collaborations with NGOs and local universities

Questions

Families

Do you have a child with a disability? Gender/Age?
What was the cause of the child's disability? What happened/Describe events.
How would you describe the child's disability? What can the child do?
What are they unable to do and what do they need assistance with?
Does the child interact with the family/siblings? Play?
Does your child go to school? Do you think your child will be able to go to school? If not, what are the reasons?
Do you have help with the child? Family/community/health services/local or traditional healers?
Do you think that the disability will get better?
How do you think that the child's quality of life will improve?
What are your aspirations and hopes for the child?
In your opinion, how has the disability of your child affected your life/the life of the rest of your family?
In your opinion what is the area/s that need research? What are the questions that need to be answered?
In your opinion, how would you carry out this research?
What are the solutions?
What is disability?
How are people with disability seen by other people in your community?
What would most improve the lives of people with disabilities?

Children/Adolescents:

What age are you?
How would you describe your disability?
What caused your disability? Can you remember how it happened?
What are your abilities? What can you do? What are your skills?
What do you have difficulty doing? What do you need assistance with? What kind of assistance do you need?
Do/did you go to school? If not, why not?
In your opinion, do you participate in the normal activities that a boy/girl of your age would do?
What would you like to be able to participate in? What are the barriers to this at the moment?
Do you work? What do you do?
What are your aspirations and hopes for the future?
In your opinion what is the area/s that need research? What are the questions that need to be answered?

What is disability?
How are people with disability seen by other people in your community?
What would most improve the lives of people with disabilities?
In your opinion, how would you carry out this research?
What are the solutions?

NGO/Ministries/University:

Do you work in the area of disability? Describe your work in this area?
What are the aims or the philosophy of your work in this area?
Are there statistics on the prevalence of childhood/adult disability? What are your opinions on the causes of childhood/adult disability/impact of childhood/adult disability/concerns for the future/obstacles or influencing factors to full participation?
Has childhood disability been measured in Burkina Faso/Sierra Leone? Is there a question on disability on the census?
In your opinion what is the area/s that need research? What are the questions that need to be answered?
In your opinion, how would you carry out this research? Would you be interested in collaborating/facilitating research in this area?
What are the solutions?
Are there reports/publications in this area?
Similar work carried out by other associations?
What is disability?
How are people with disability seen by other people in your community?
What would most improve the lives of people with disabilities?

References

Lawn, JE, Cousens, S, & Zupan, J (2005). '4 million neonatal deaths: When? Where? Why?', *The Lancet*, 365:891–900

MacLachlan, M, Carr, SC, & McAuliffe, E (2010). *The Aid Triangle: Human Dynamics of Dominance, Justice and Identity*, London: Zed

Medeiros, E (2007). 'Integrating Mental Health into Post-conflict Rehabilitation. The case of Sierra Leonean and Liberian "Child Soldiers"', *Journal of Health Psychology*, 12(3):498–504

Mont, D (2007). 'Measuring Disability Prevalence', SP Discussion Paper, The World Bank

UN Enable: 'Promoting the Rights of Persons with Disabilities'. http://www.un.org/disabilities/ [accessed 19th August 2008]

UNICEF (2008a). 'The State of the World's Children', 2008 Report

UNICEF (2008b). http://www.unicef.org/childsurvival/index_40850.html [accessed 19th August 2008]

United Nations Millennium Development Goals. http://.www.un.org/millenniumgoals/ [accessed 19th August 2008]

WHO (2001). 'International Classification of Functioning, Disability and Health (ICF)', Geneva: WHO

WHO (2007a). 'Epidemic and pandemic alert and response: Meningococcal disease in Burkina Faso – update'. http://www.who.int/csr/don/2007_04_17/en/index.html [accessed 19th August 2008]
WHO (2007b). 'International Classification of Functioning, Disability and Health for Children and Youth (ICF-CY)', Geneva: WHO

Acknowledgement We are very grateful to the staff from International Services (Ireland) and other local, national, international and governmental organisations who kindly facilitated the research described in this chapter.

Chapter 12
Education, Disability, and International Development

Petra Engelbrecht, Ansie Kitching, and Willy Nel

12.1 Introduction

One of the biggest challenges facing education systems throughout the world is that of inclusion in education. In general, inclusion is about a philosophy of acceptance where all people in society are valued and treated with respect (Carrington and Robinson, 2004) and in education there is specific emphasis on the development of inclusive learning communities in which diversity is acknowledged and welcomed. In wealthier countries inclusion in education efforts tend to focus on the merger between well-resourced segregated forms of special schooling for learners with disabilities with equally well-resourced mainstream education facilities. In economically poorer countries, however, where a separate education system for people with disabilities has never been fully developed and where mainstream education lacks resources, efforts tend to focus on all learners who are unable to access education. Compounding the challenge to building inclusive education communities globally is the prevailing understanding of why some learners experience difficulties with learning. According to Howell (2006), this understanding is deeply rooted in a historical assumption that learners of all ages can be identified and classified through notions of what is normal and abnormal.

Against this background, this chapter will discuss the global development of inclusion in schooling as well as inclusion in higher education for persons with disabilities in more detail. In conclusion, the integration of research, policy and practice will be evaluated.

P. Engelbrecht (✉)
Educational Sciences, North-West University, Potchefstroom campus,
Potchefstroom, South Africa

M. MacLachlan and L. Swartz (eds.), *Disability & International Development: Towards Inclusive Global Health*,
DOI 10.1007/978-0-387-93840-0_12, © Springer Science+Business Media, LLC 2009

12.2 Inclusion in Schooling and Disability

12.2.1 Background

The development of education for people with disabilities has involved specific stages during which education systems have explored a variety of ways to respond to children with disabilities. In most countries, there has been a tendency to identify and categorize school children through notions of "normality" and a strong belief that the learning needs of children with disabilities should be met with additional specialized support or intervention. A result of this distinctive categorization was the development of a dominant mainstream school system for "normal" learners and a secondary educational system for learners with "special needs" (Howell, 2006). The first 70 years of the twentieth century were characterized by the "medical model" (or deficit discourse), which conceptualized those with disabilities as "abnormal" and in need of the attention of specialists in "special" schools. Placement in special educational settings therefore excluded groups of children from the mainstream of education and of society in the genuine belief that this was in their best interests (Green and Engelbrecht, 2006).

12.2.2 Movement to Inclusive Education

Since the 1970s the appropriateness of separate systems of education has been challenged, both from a human rights and an effectiveness point of view. Opponents of the medical model argued that this way of looking at disability has contributed to the ongoing discrimination against and marginalization of people in a number of ways. For example, by focusing on the impairment and the "objective" degree to which a person cannot undertake some activities in the "normal" way, attention is drawn away from issues of discrimination and the rights of people with disabilities. People with disabilities and the organizations that they have formed also questioned the notion of disability as an individual tragic occurrence that classifies a person as incapacitated in some way and dependent on the good will of others (Howell, 2005). Segregated special education was increasingly condemned as part of an oppressive social system through which people with disabilities were excluded from participation in society (Barton, 1998). For several years, "mainstreaming" or even "integration" were recommended strategies for addressing this concern. Both involved placing specific selected learners with disabilities in mainstream schools under certain conditions, but neither approaches assumed that all learners have an unquestioned right to belong in a mainstream school and classroom or that schools should adapt to the needs of their pupils (Green and Engelbrecht, 2006).

Increasingly it was argued that perspectives that assume that the sources of difficulties in learning are *within* the learner ignore environmental influences (e.g. home and school influences) on learning and do not explain the quality of learning and educational difficulties that can arise from sources other than impairment (Ainscow and César, 2006). If environmental influences are taken into consideration, a definition of disability must describe the relationship between a person with an impairment and the society or environment of which they are part, the so-called social model of disability. A social model of disability derives from social and political understandings of disability, where the focus is on the nature and organization of society and its response to people with impairments rather than on the nature/extent of the individual's impairment (Howell, 2005).

The international development of inclusive education for people with disabilities is therefore essentially based on a social model of disability and the rights of children with disabilities to be included in mainstream schools. The rights discourse lends itself easily to international declarations of which the Salamanca Statement on Special Needs Education (UNESCO, 1994) has exerted a powerful influence on education policies across the world (Artiles and Dyson, 2005). The Salamanca Statement (UNESCO, 1994), for example, argues that mainstream schools with an inclusive orientation should be the most effective way of combating negative attitudes and can contribute to the development of an inclusive society and achieving education for all. Subsequently there have been considerable efforts globally to move educational policy and practice in a more inclusive direction. It is also more widely recognized that reorganizing mainstream schools through school improvement strategies is an effective way of ensuring that all children, and not just those with disabilities, can learn effectively (Ainscow and César, 2006).

The development of inclusive practices in schools is contextually determined by the social learning processes that influence people's actions as well as the thinking that informs these actions in specific contexts (Ainscow et al., 2006; Green and Engelbrecht, 2006). However the following key elements in the implementation of inclusive education that tend to feature strongly in all contexts have emerged internationally:

- Inclusion in education is a never-ending search to find strategies that effectively address diversity in schools.
- Globally, inclusion in schools is concerned with the identification and removal of barriers to participation in educational settings.
- Inclusion is not only about the presence of children with disabilities in mainstream schools but also about the quality of their learning experience (Green and Engelbrecht, 2006).

Even a cursory review of literature on the development of inclusive schools leaves one in no doubt that despite the high status the concept of inclusion in education has gained and the successful inclusion of children with disabilities in some schools, challenges regarding implementation remain complex. Issues of quality, efficacy and morale of teachers in implementing inclusive education policies are key, and differing notions of equity may increase complexity. Entrenched attitudes and discriminatory practices towards people with disabilities play a major role in the development of inclusive school communities in various countries (Howell, 2005, 2006; Carrington and Robinson, 2004; Green and Engelbrecht, 2006).

Applying the social model of understanding disability implies that the relationship that exists between a person and the society in which he or she lives is dependent on how that society is structured and functions. If the society is critical of differences, it is likely to be more difficult to remove the barriers that restrict access for children with disabilities to inclusive schooling.

12.2.3 Inclusion at Tertiary Level and Disability

12.2.3.1 Background

The inclusion in higher education of students with disabilities has become a matter of concern in recent years. As discussed in the previous section, the deficit discourse that stigmatized, disempowered and marginalized people with disabilities is being replaced by a discourse that focuses on the rights of people with disabilities to take up their rightful place in society. These discourses are useful when examining the participation of students in higher education.

For students with disabilities, the first barrier to higher education can be the schooling system they were exposed to and the advice they received regarding future career paths. That is, even if they do complete their schooling they would not have completed the necessary subjects at the appropriate level for entry into a higher education institution. These problems are most often informed by attitudes within schools that reinforce the notion that people with disabilities do not have a future in higher education. Other barriers arise from the way in which universities are structured and function, the role that higher education plays within a specific society as well as the attitudes that inform selection criteria (Howell, 2005; Parker, 1998; Ryan and Struhs, 2004). Furthermore, those responsible for the entry and participation of people with disabilities in higher education frequently lack sufficient knowledge to carry out their responsibilities under disability discrimination legislation (Ryan and Struhs, 2004).

In some countries, especially the wealthier countries, initiatives to promote greater inclusion have had some success in improving access to higher education and raising awareness across the sector of the need to ensure full participation by learners with disabilities once they enter the university (Parker, 1998). Legislation and government education policies, for example in the United Kingdom, United States of America and Australia, have facilitated the inclusion of learners with disabilities into higher education but negative attitudes still play a role. Evidence of what was termed "a shortfall in the attitude budget" was found in an inquiry in Australia into the effectiveness of programmes aimed at students with disabilities across the spectrum (Senate Employment, Workplace Relations and Education References Committee, 2002). Results indicate that students in higher education are frustrated by the fact that they have to invest time and energy in order to negotiate their requirements with staff and lecturers with an additional inhibiting factor, the requirement that prospective students at Australian higher education institutions have to self-identify their disability status. In less wealthy countries, for example South Africa, the failure of university management to either formulate or implement policy has been exacerbated not only by negative stereotyping but also by the lack of funding to implement effective learning support strategies in higher education (Howell, 2005; Matshedisho, 2007).

12.2.4 Higher Education, Disability and the Professions

In addition to the general barriers students with disabilities experience in entering higher education, those who choose a professional career, for example in engineering, law and medicine, experience additional barriers. Lack of clarity regarding decision-making about admission criteria as well as the position of practical placements has, for example, been problematic. Where professional or registration bodies stipulate that certain competencies need to be met before practicing rights are granted (e.g. nursing), universities are placed in the difficult situation where the needs of their students with disabilities, who may require adjustments or accommodations to facilitate the demonstration of such competencies are not met (Ryan and Struhs, 2004). Regarding admission criteria, Roberts (2004) for example found in a study on four medical schools in the United Kingdom that there was no standardization regarding admission criteria for students with disabilities. This means that an applicant with the same disability may get accepted at one medical school while rejected at another. The result has been that people with disabilities are globally underrepresented in the professions, with lower academic achievement and employment success (Foreman et al., 2001).

Without question, successful job entry, job advancement and attainment of leadership roles in the workplace are dependent on the quality of education and training individuals have received. The importance of university-wide policies and practices that ensure that students with disabilities derive maximum benefit from their educational opportunities cannot be overstressed (Foreman et al., 2001).

12.2.5 Postgraduate Training and Disability

Concurrent with the growing criticism of the medical model, a growing awareness of the rights of people with disabilities and an increasing need for in-depth knowledge on support for people with disabilities, the discipline of disability studies on postgraduate level has emerged as an independent academic field within higher education (Lorenzo et al., 2006).

The development of postgraduate training programmes in disability studies has not been limited to specific academic fields. Internationally, programmes exist in the fields of education, counselling psychology, social work as well as nursing and dental training. The programmes seem to have become more generic in nature over the years.

Sweeney and Dalton (2007) identified similarities in contemporary international perspectives that indicate a clear shift of focus from a medical-based approach to a more holistic multi-disciplinary approach in disability studies. They recommend that compartmentalization in terms of disciplines, ideas and practice should be challenged and changed if disability studies is to go forward and offer an alternative, effective perspective. In view of the above arguments it seems imperative that postgraduate training in working with people with disabilities moves towards inter-professional training since it provides the students with opportunities to learn some specific information about interacting with the other professions and gain knowledge about the roles, knowledge and contributions that can be made by professions other than their own (Cook, 2005).

In the development of postgraduate programmes it is also important to emphasize issues that are important to people with disability, rather than address the needs of academics and scholars of disability. To ensure the relevance of themes addressed in postgraduate studies on disability it is imperative therefore to have a collaborative and multi-agency approach (Parkinson, 2006), through acknowledging the input of people with disabilities and sustaining healthy links with academics, campaigners and disability organizations. Three important focus points for learning and teaching of postgraduate students include an understanding of disability, an awareness of the experience of people with disabilities and a contribution to social change (Parkinson, 2006).

Barton and Olivier (2000), warn that "Fashionable issues like postmodernism, representation and embodiment may well turn on disability studies scholars but their immediate relevance to the struggles of people with disabilities to lead a decent life are hard to justify". The same authors suggest that courses in disability studies should critically engage with the writings, poetry and songs of disabled scholars, writers and activists from within the disability movement. This will ensure that they are in touch with important ideas, insights, understandings and questions that concern the disabled community. They also suggest the involvement of people with disabilities in the designing and teaching of such courses, but at the same time warn against tokenism. Parkinson (2006) furthermore emphasizes the importance of a client-centred approach rather than a service-driven approach to the training of postgraduate students. Recent literature (Parkinson ,2006) refers to the emerging affirmative model that embraces a positive view of disabled identities that are social rather than tragic in type, based on the belief that there are benefits of being disabled and impaired in terms of both lifestyle and life experiences. This approach appreciates that not all people with disabilities look upon themselves in the same way, and therapeutic practice needs to reflect the range and variety of perspectives of self and society when constructing a context in which to explore their own attitudes to disability and impairment.

The development of postgraduate programmes on the African continent brings the issue of the strong Eurocentric basis of current theories and literature to the fore and addresses the necessity to focus on Afrocentric approaches in development of postgraduate programmes in order to accurately reflect local and regional experiences Priestly (2005). A programme introduced at the University of Cape Town, South Africa, in March 2003 is an example of a collaborative approach to such a programme. This programme developed through dialogue between the academic community at the University, the Centre for Disability Studies at the University of Leeds and disability rights movements in South Africa. The aim of the programme is to foster a research community that will mobilize and inform disability transformation in society (Lorenzo et al., 2006). The postgraduate students enrolled in the first year of the programme included students from the fields of occupational therapy, speech therapy, nursing and human resources and art. The contents of the course are multidisciplinary in nature, involving academics from sociology, psychology, health and rehabilitation.

12.3 Conclusion

Education is recognized as crucial to the aspirations of people with disabilities to enjoy full and equal opportunities (O'Connor and Robinson, 1999). The global focus on the rights and equity of people with disabilities in education has resulted in a number of stated intentions and written policies in various countries. Throughout this chapter it was indicated that despite the magnitude of written and stated policies regarding the inclusion of people with disabilities in education on all levels, ample evidence exists which indicates the lack of successful outcomes of current policies and the implementation of research results on implementation issues (Dyer, 1999; Chafouleas and Riley-Tillman, 2005; Vlachou, 2004; Welgemoed, 1998).

One of the most critical issues in implementing inclusive education policies is the abstract and idealistic articulation of rights and equal opportunities in policy documents, which through their abstraction have been disconnected from the composition of the education contexts in which policies must be implemented. Through their abstraction, policies fail to take the implications of dominant discourses for implementation into consideration and are constrained in particular by the fact that no strategies for bringing about change are included (Vlachou, 2004). The dominant and persistent societal focus on an individual deficit approach that is detrimental and counterproductive to the successful implementation of the inclusion of people with disabilities in education systems continues to dominate education. By doing so, it totally overlooks disabling barriers of an institutional, attitudinal and ideological nature and directly affects the implementation of inclusive educational policies (Vlachou, 2004).

It is clear that enforcing implementation through policy change at a macro level cannot change human behaviour, values and attitudes (Welgemoed, 1998). Enhancing the recognition and acceptance of the basic rights of all learners with disabilities to be accommodated in inclusive education communities on all levels involves an acknowledgement of the complexity of the dynamic interactions between societal as well as contextual factors and continuous efforts to integrate policy and research results in the daily work of school and university-based practitioners. Bridging the gap between the idealism expressed in policy documents and the realities of education systems is a challenge that needs to be addressed on an ongoing basis.

References

Ainscow, M, Booth, T, & Dyson, A (2006). *Improving schools, developing inclusion*, London: Routledge

Ainscow, M, & César, M (2006). 'Inclusive education ten years after Salamanca: setting the agenda', *European Journal of Psychology of Education*, 11(3): 231–238

Artiles, A, & Dyson, A (2005). 'Inclusive education in the globalization age: the promise of comparative cultural-historical analysis', In Mitchell, D (ed), *Contextualizing inclusive education, evaluating old and new international perspectives*, London: Routledge, pp. 37–63

Barton, L (1998). *The politics of special educational needs*, London: Falmer

Barton, L, & Olivier, M (2000). 'The emerging field of disability studies: a view from Britain', Paper presented at Disability Studies: A Global Perspective Washington DC, October 2000

Carrington, S, & Robinson, R (2004). 'A case study of inclusive school development: a journey of learning', *International Journal of Inclusive Education*, 8(2): 141–153

Chafouleas, SM, & Riley-Tillman, TC (2005). 'Accepting the gap: an introduction to the special issue on bridging research and practice', *Psychology in Schools*, 42(5): 455–458

Cook, DA (2005). 'Models of interprofessional studies in Canada', *Journal of interprofessional care*, 19(1): 107–115

Dyer, C (1999). 'Research the implementation of educational policy: a backward mapping approach', *Comparative Education*, 35(1): 45–61

Foreman, P, Dempsey, I, Robinson, G, & Manning, E (2001). 'Characteristics, academic and post-university outcomes of students with a disability at the University of Newcastle', *Higher Education Research & Development*, 20(3): 313–325

Green, L, & Engelbrecht, P (2006). 'An introduction to inclusive education', In Engelbrecht, P, & Green, L (eds), *Responding to the challenges of inclusive education in Southern Africa*, Pretoria: Van Schaik Publishers, pp. 2–9

Howell, C (2005). *Higher education monitor: South African higher education responses to students with disabilities: equity of access and opportunity?*, Pretoria: Council on Higher Education

Howell, C (2006). 'Changing public and professional discourse', In Engelbrecht, P, & Green, L (eds), *Responding to the challenges of inclusive education in Southern Africa*, Pretoria: Van Schaik Publishers, pp. 89–100

Lorenzo, T, Katoni, M, & Priestley, M (2006). 'Developing a disability studies programme: engaging activism and academia', In Watermeyer, B, Swartz, L, Lorenzo, T, Schneider, M, & Priestley, M (eds), *Disability and social change*, Cape Town: HSRC Press, pp. 179–191

Matshedisho, KR (2007). 'The challenge of real rights for disabled students in South Africa', South *African Journal of Higher Education*, 2(4): 706–716

O'Connor, U, & Robinson, A (1999). 'Accession or exclusion? University and the disabled student: a case study of policy and practice', *Higher Education Quarterly*, 53(1): 88–105

Parker, V (1998). 'UK initiatives to promote inclusion in higher education for students with disabilities', *European Journal of Special Needs Education*, 13(2): 189–199

Parkinson, G (2006). 'Counselors' attitudes towards disability equality training (DET)', *British Journal of Guidance & Counseling*, 34(1): 93–105

Priestly, M (2005). 'Developing disability studies programmes: the international context', In Watermeyer, B, Swartz, L, Lorenzo, T, Schneider, M, & Priestley, M (eds), *Disability and social change*, Cape Town: HSRC Press

Roberts, T (2004). Medicine, dentistry and veterinary medicine: disabled students. Disabled students-Disabled doctors and time for change? Mini-project topic, http://www.ltsn-01.ac.uk/resources/features/docs/roberts.pdf [accessed 11th February 2008]

Ryan, J, & Struhs, J (2004). 'University education for all? Barriers to full inclusion of students with disabilities in Australian universities', *International Journal of Inclusive Education*, 8(1): 73–90

Senate Employment, Workplace Relation and Education References Committee (2002). Education of students with disabilities. http://www.aph.gov.au/senate/committee/eet_ctte/completed_

inquiries/2002–04/ed_students_withdisabilities/report/report.pdf [accessed 12th February 2008]

Sweeney, J, & Dalton, C (2007). 'Intellectual disability nurses' interest in undertaking postgraduate education', *Learning Disability Practice*, (10) 2: 30–37

UNESCO (1994). Final report: world conference on special needs education: access and quality, Paris: UNESCO

Vlachou, A (2004). 'Education and inclusive policy-making: implications for research and practice', *International Journal of Inclusive Education*, 8(1): 3–21

Welgemoed, A (1998). 'Democratizing schools in South Africa', In Harber, C (ed), *Voices for democracy: a North-South dialogue on education for sustainable democracy*, Nottingham: Education Now Publishing Co-operative, pp. 37–47

Chapter 13
Listening to the Voices of Disability: Experiences of Caring for Children with Cerebral Palsy in a Rural South African Setting

Joanne Barratt and Claire Penn

> *For some of these people it is very difficult. They do not have help and they do not have money and there is nobody to help them care for the child but what must they do? This is the child that God has given them.*[1]

13.1 Introduction

For the majority of persons living with disability in South Africa, the experience is inexorably linked with huge challenges imposed by poverty and access, together with the burden imposed by other diseases and by profoundly restricted choices. Nowhere did this lesson become clearer than in our research conducted in Tonga, a rural village in the Nkomazi municipality of the Mpumalanga province of South Africa, which has recently been defined as a "pocket of poverty" (Nkomazi Spatial Development Framework (2003)).

After a year's community service as a speech and hearing therapist in this community, the first author was granted access to this community in 2006 to gather material for a research project using ethnographic methods. These methods enabled a profoundly powerful snapshot of the link between disability and daily life; the interface between historical, social and demographic factors; and the relationship between the individual and the community, which are described elsewhere in this volume.

J. Barratt (✉)
Speech Therapy Department, University of the Witwatersrand, Johannesburg, South Africa

[1] Comment made by the research mediator after collecting data for this study.

M. MacLachlan and L. Swartz (eds.), *Disability & International Development: Towards Inclusive Global Health*,
DOI 10.1007/978-0-387-93840-0_13,

In this chapter we will foreground the narratives of the participants of this research in an attempt to demonstrate the relationship between these variables and to inform intervention and training models. While the focus of our study was on the condition of cerebral palsy, it became clear that the voices of this study seemed to echo those of many other individuals and communities living with the challenge of disability and highlights the relationship between disability and contextual aspects such as poverty and social exclusion.

13.2 Service Provision in a "Uniquely South African" Setting

13.2.1 Childhood Disability in South Africa

In South Africa, between 5.2 and 6.4% of children under the age of 9 years are estimated to be affected by motor, sensory, or intellectual disabilities (Christianson et al., 2002; Couper, 2002). One of the most common childhood disabilities, particularly in rural areas, is cerebral palsy, which is estimated to affect as many as 8% of live births (Christianson et al., 2002). Significantly, 32% of the causes of cerebral palsy in rural areas are postnatal and include brain injury resulting from, among other factors, meningitis, malaria and gastroenteritis and subsequent dehydration (Potterton, 1996).

Socio-economic variables which contribute to disease exposure and healthcare access, place children at risk for disability in South Africa, and poverty plays a pivotal role in predisposing neonates to conditions which may result in cerebral palsy. Mothers, particularly in rural areas, often do not have access to prenatal care, have limited health literacy, are exposed to the spread of infectious diseases, such as HIV/AIDS and tuberculosis, and do not take in sufficient nutrition (Levin, 2005; Nutbeam, 2000). Additionally, there may be limited access to running water and high levels of stress related to poverty (Bhorat et al., 2006; Hutcherson, 1991). Thus children in poor families are more at risk for acquiring chronic health problems and disabilities, and caring for these children imposes substantial costs on their families.

13.2.1.1 Setting

The small rural village of Tonga falls within the Nkomazi municipality in the Mpumalanga province of South Africa and is situated approximately 30 km northwest of the Mananga border post into Swaziland and approximately 40 km west of the Mozambiquan border. The Nkomazi municipality forms the eastern section of the Lowveld region and is located approximately 350 km east of Gauteng, consisting of a wedge of land between the Kruger National Park in the

North, Mozambique in the East, Swaziland in the South, and the Mbombela and Umjindi Municipalities in the west. The closest towns are Malelane, which lies 45 km northwest of Tonga, and Komatipoort, which lies 60 km northeast of Tonga. The Nkomazi municipality is made up of two areas with vastly different characteristics in terms of economic and social development. Tonga falls into the Kangwane region in the south, and has approximately 350,000 people living in approximately 45 informal settlements. The majority of inhabitants are black SiSwati speaking residents (Nkomazi Integrated Development Plan, 2006–2007).

According to the Nkomazi Spatial Development Framework (2003) the last national election reflected that almost 90% of the adult population's political persuasion is to the African National Congress (ANC). There is very little land ownership as all land belongs to the State. All settlements are growing at a rapid rate and in the absence of proper planning the settlements are expanding in an uncontrolled manner. Urban sprawl is rife and places stress on existing infrastructure and has the effect of sustaining the current state of underdevelopment (Nkomazi Spatial Development Framework, 2003).

Economically, Tonga has always served a dormitory function, meaning that residents commute from the area to their place of work. There is very little investment or economic development in the area and the inhabitants have to travel long distances for consumer goods. Businesses are mostly represented by small general dealers and liquor stores. Informal industrial businesses such as car repair shops, exhaust repairs, tyre sale and fitment, and welding shops are found in all settlements (Nkomazi Spatial Development Framework, 2003).

Social and community facilities are limited. Recreation facilities are provided in the form of two libraries, a formal sport facility that is in a state of disrepair, and numerous informal soccer fields. No public parks exist. Almost all cemeteries are informal. Bus shelters are widely unavailable or are of an insufficient standard. Very little provision is made for the disabled, at both public and council buildings. There are grave concerns about the conditions that pensioners and disabled persons have to endure on pension payout days, as there is a lack of water, sanitation, and shelter. Most of the infrastructure needs upgrading and there is a general lack of equipment and furniture (Nkomazi Spatial Development Framework, 2003). Emergency services and the judicial system are insufficient and no correctional facility exists in the region (Nkomazi Integrated Development Plan, 2006–2007). The area has a high prevalence of HIV/AIDS, although since 2004 antiretroviral medications have been available at some hospitals and clinics.

Environmental degradation is taking place at an alarming rate and is attributed to a number of factors, including the under-provision of municipal services, the extent of urban sprawl and unsustainable subsistence farming methods (Nkomazi Spatial Development Framework, 2003).

Table 13.1 below provides a summary of the community profile for the Nkomazi municipality as determined by the Nkomazi Integrated Development Plan (2006–2007):

Poverty levels among people with disabilities have been documented by the Mpumalanga Province Community Based Rehabilitation (CBR) Disability Support

Table 13.1 Community profile for Tonga

Employment	40% of the economically active population are unemployed
Income level	73% of households bring in less than R2,000 per month
Dependency ratio	1:8
Household density	6 persons per household
Population distribution	50% of population under 17 years old
Population growth rate	20–30% per annum
Water provision	41% of households have water supplied in their houses
	14% of households have access to an outside tap
Sanitation	55% of households make use of a chemical sanitation system
	20% of households make use of pit latrines
	7% of households make use of chemical toilets
	5% of households have access to flush toilets
	13% of households have no sanitation at all
Electricity	60% of households have access to electricity
Roads	40% tarred, with internal roads almost inaccessible
Health	2 × 24-h hospitals functioning at a primary healthcare level
	1 × 24-h clinic
	27 × day clinics
	6 × home-based care initiatives
Education	32% of the population have no formal education
	113 primary schools
	40 secondary schools
	3 combined schools
	45 adult education centres
	Teacher:pupil ratio of 1:54
Literacy levels	24% of the population are illiterate
Community/social facilities	2 libraries
	Informal soccer fields
	Informal cemeteries only

Project (Nkomazi Spatial Development Framework, 2003). This research was conducted in the Lowveld district of the Mpumalanga province between August 1999 and July 2000 among 907 predominantly rural African households with disabled family members and revealed the following:

- 38% of families have no regular monthly cash income
- 49% of families rely on R530 or less income per month
- 11% of families have a regular monthly income of between R531 and R1,199
- 2% of families have a regular monthly income of between R1,200 and R1,999
- None of the 907 families had a monthly income exceeding R3,000
- 82% of disabled school-age children do not attend school

These statistics illustrate the strong relationship between disability and socio-economic status (Anderson and Phohole, 2003), and strongly justified the goals and framework of the current study.

13.2.2 Access to Setting

During a year's compulsory community service at Tonga hospital, the first author provided an in- and out-patient therapy service at the hospital, outreach services at 15 clinics in the surrounding area, and home visits to patients who were unable to access the clinics or hospital. This year enabled a first-hand experience of many of the frustrations that local people have, including poor provision of municipal services, poor conditions of the roads and limited access between the hospital and many of the homes in the community, as well as the frustration of travelling long distances in order to acquire basic products. Considerable time was spent with the community elders, in order to gain access to the community and visiting the homes of local leaders in order to obtain an understanding of the needs of the community and to deliver a basic rehabilitation service. This experience provided a degree of understanding of the way of life within the community, the beliefs and cultural practices, as well as the support structures and roles of various members of the community.

Access to both community structures and patients was achieved through collaboration with a Community-Based Rehabilitation Worker (CBRW) who is a local SiSwati-speaking woman, confined to a wheelchair. The CBRW understands the nature and experience of living with a disability in a rural area, and in this way was able to provide insight into the community, their culture and belief systems. These factors motivated us to return in order to explore in more depth the contextual aspects related to disability, so as to better inform healthcare policies, service delivery and the training of students. We chose to interview and observe caregivers of children with cerebral palsy. The CBRW was employed and trained to assist with this in terms of accessing caregivers and carrying out narrative interviews in SiSwati in the homes of the caregivers.[2] The interviews were audio-recorded and later translated and transcribed. We then derived and extracted themes which were linked to detailed ethnographic notes and to the results of interviews with the CBRW after each consultation.

Appendix A provides a paraphrased ethnography and interview to demonstrate the type of questions asked and the data collection process.

13.2.3 Caregiver Informants

The informants in this study were 27 caregivers of children with cerebral palsy. Caregivers who at the time were currently accessing services at the hospital and clinics, as well as those who were not accessing such services were included. Caregivers included 12 mothers, three fathers, seven grandmothers, one grandfather,

[2] In line with the basic fundamentals of qualitative research and participant observation, we employed a range of methods including ethnographic field notes, interviews and personal reflections in order to triangulate results.

one aunt, one step-mother, one male cousin, and one male neighbour. The age of children with cerebral palsy ranged from 8 months to 14 years.

13.2.4 Disability Narratives

The informants' narratives revealed an intricate web of variables, which emerged as relevant and framed the experience of caring for a child with a disability in the context of poverty. The link between poverty and disability emerged clearly and illustrated how poverty renders persons vulnerable to disability and how disability impoverishes individuals' chances of breaking the poverty cycle. Most apparent was the way in which individuals are not only disabled by a physical impairment but remain disabled by their living conditions (Table 13.2).

Of the many possible ways of coalescing the data that emerged, the following seemed to have particular relevance for the purpose of this chapter. We conceptualize these themes schematically in Fig. 13.1.The core themes that emerged are discussed as follows:

- *Macro-variables* are those aspects emerging in the data that relate to broader issues such as government policies, the disease profile of the country and how these factors play out at a local level and how they affect accessibility to services.

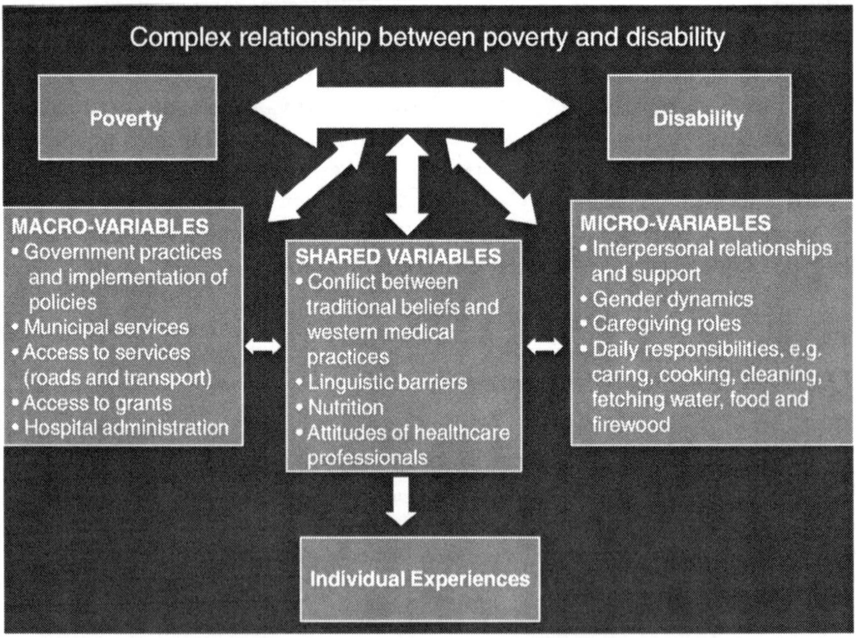

Fig. 13.1 Relationship between poverty, disability, and macro-, micro-, and shared variables. Some illustrative voices…

Table 13.2 Summary of living conditions of informants

	Distance of home from road	Electricity	Water	No. of people in house	Sanitation	Grant recipient	Other financial support	Support structure	Father involved
1	500 m	Yes	Rainwater reservoir	23	Long-drop 15 m from house	No	Father pays maintenance and grandfather's pension	Family and community	Maintenance only
2	2 km	No	No – walks 3 km	4	On neighbour's property	No	Mother's boyfriend (R300 per month)	None	No
3	4 km	No	Water point on property	3	None	Disability grant	Father pays maintenance	Boyfriend	Maintenance only
4	1.5 km	Yes	Running water in house	7	Long-drop 5 m from house	Child support grant	Mother's cousin	Both parents, family and neighbours	Yes
5	1 km	Yes	Running water in house	16	Long-drop 5 m from house	Disability grant	Father employed and grandfather's pension	Parents, family and neighbours	Yes
6	1 km	Yes	Running water in house	16	Long-drop 5 m from house	Disability grant	Grandfather's pension	Parents, family and neighbours	Yes
7	On tar road	Yes	Rainwater reservoir	8	Long-drop 5 m from house	No	Grandmother's pension	Grandmother and family	No
8	5 km	No	No	14	Long-drop 100 m from house	Child support grant	Grandmother's pension	Grandmother	No
9	10 km	Yes	Water point on property	11	Long-drop behind house	Disability grant	Father is employed	Family and community	Yes
10	45 km	No	Water point on property	5	Long-drop behind house	No	Grandmother's pension	Grandmother	No
11	50 km	Yes	No	8	Long-drop 100 m from house	No	Live off land	Father and step-mother	Yes
12	45 km	No	No	5	None	No	Father is employed	Male cousin and neighbour	Yes
13	15 km	Yes	Water point on property	17	Long-drop	Disability grant	Uncle	Aunt	Yes
14	8 km	Yes	Water point on property	13	Long-drop	Disability grant	Father is employed	Extended family and neighbour	Yes
15	8 km	Yes	Water point on property	3	Long-drop	Disability grant	Father is employed	Mother's family and neighbour	Yes

- *Micro-variables* which relate to personal, family, and community experiences, cultural practices, and roles within the family, and how these factors influence individual experiences of disability.
- *Shared variables* relate to variables which link to both macro- and micro-variables. They include the interface between traditional and western models of treatment-seeking behaviours as well as religion.

This division though somewhat overlapping and artificial seemed to capture the themes and our observations. Figure 13.1 above provides a graphic representation of the relationship between poverty and disability, and the effect that this relationship has on the individual as a consequence of the macro-, micro-, and shared variables.

13.3 Macro-variables

13.3.1 Information on and Access to Government Resources

Part of the attempt made by the South African government to ensure accessible healthcare services has been the implementation of the "free healthcare policies". Currently, free healthcare is accessible to children under the age of 6 years, pensioners, disabled persons and pregnant women. Additionally, a wide variety of grants are available, including child support grants, care-in-aid grants and disability grants. While every child with cerebral palsy in this study should have been eligible for a State financial assistance as a result of their disability, only seven children were receiving any and there was much confusion regarding the process of accessing grants. These voices illustrate this:

> I tried to apply for a disability grant but I haven't got my reply yet. They told me at the hospital that the child won't get a disability grant until she is 7 years old, so I went to the pension office and they gave me a child support grant form that I filled and sent back. I thought that the child dependent form is the same as the child disability grant.

> I don't have the right information on how to apply for a disability grant.

In addition to accessing grants, difficulty was reported in accessing social services in order to register the child so as to make them eligible for financial assistance. One grandmother reported:

> The child does not have a birth certificate so he does not get the government grant.

Some caregivers reported difficulty in accessing so-called "free" assistive devices, available through the government healthcare system. One mother whose child was in need of orthotic shoes reported the following:

> My child needs the special shoes. They told us to write our names on the list in 2004 as the shoes were not available at the time. So we have been waiting for three years with no reply from anyone.

Consistent with findings from other studies conducted in South Africa (Meyer and Moagi, 2000) it was found that six out of 15 children were supported by a grandparent's pension. In some instances it was found that the grandparents actually felt that it was their responsibility to use their pension money to care for their children and grandchildren. One grandmother reported,

> When he got sick I knew it was my duty to take him to all the medical professionals for help using my pension funds.

The powerful role of kinship is explained by Maverick (1966) who reports that within the Swazi culture, the grandparents are instrumental in teaching, and bring up the young. In addition, he reports that should a child fall ill he or she is often sent to live with the maternal grandparent until health returns. While this was not explicitly reported in any of the narratives, there was evidence that this practice still exists today.

13.3.2 HIV/AIDS

While the focus of the present study was on cerebral palsy, the influence of other health variables, specifically the HIV/AIDS pandemic in this community was pervasively detectable. Having the largest number of persons living with HIV/AIDS in the world residing in South Africa (Rehle and Shisana, 2003), this epidemic has profoundly affected rural areas due to, amongst other factors, lack of access to appropriate information, illiteracy, and in many cases, restricted life choices. With a few exceptions, the disease was seldom directly acknowledged in the interviews, reflecting the stigma and silence that surrounds it. However there were frequent allusions to family deaths, absent and ill family members and artefacts evident in the homes (such as medication, and t-shirts and tablecloths with HIV/AIDS logos), which fore-grounded the local presence and impact of the disease. Ironically, this disease provides family members with access to disability grants, which were acknowledged to be helpful in addressing the needs of disabled children.

13.3.3 Infrastructure and Access

The interviews confirmed that transport remains a major barrier to healthcare services for people living in rural areas (Anderson and Phohole, 2003). Common complaints among the caregivers included travelling long distances from sites barely accessible by motor vehicles, combined with expensive, unreliable transport, making regular follow-up visits difficult to achieve. One grandmother whose grandchild was not receiving any form of financial assistance reported,

> When he needs to go to the hospital it is difficult because I have to find someone with a car and loan money from people to pay them to take us to the hospital because there are no taxis from here.

Another mother who lived 45 km off the tar road in an area where there is no public transport and whose only source of income was R180 child support grant reported “I loan money from people, usually R50 to take him to the hospital or clinic”.

13.3.4 Inability to Work

Five of the mothers of the children with cerebral palsy felt that they were unable to go out in search of work as their children required constant care and they felt they were unable to leave their child with anyone else while they went out to work. Reports of this included:

> I always have to take him everywhere I go because no one is able to help look after him – they complain that he cannot even say when he wants to go to the toilet and that he is just an inconvenience.

> When I am away for any reason I get back and find (the child) refusing to eat because I am not there. She will only eat if I am there.

> Neighbours take (the child) if I am here at home otherwise I don’t want them to take her because (the child) needs constant care.

Such comments reflect the fact that the mothers may not trust others to take care of them as they would a non-disabled child. Whereas generally after weaning, a child in this community is frequently left in the care of older children (Kuper, 1963), at each of the 15 homes we visited, the child with cerebral palsy was always in the care of a mother or grandmother.

13.3.5 Hospital Administration

Hospital administration, particularly problematic filing systems, were reported by all of the informants and proved to be a major barrier affecting accessibility of healthcare services. As a result, informants reported that they are hesitant to make follow-up appointments at the hospital. Comments such as the one below were common:

> I often stay there for two to three hours waiting for the child’s file with the nurses sending me everywhere.

13.4 Micro-variables

13.4.1 Support Within the Family and Community

The majority of informants reported that lack of support both from within the family and the community were barriers to accessing quality healthcare. This related both to the physical assistance in caring for a child with a disability, as well as emotional support. In many instances, the emergence of a disability in the family came as a shock and was regarded with much suspicion, particularly in relation to traditional and cultural beliefs. One caregiver reported fleeing from Mozambique in the middle of the night to escape the father of the child, after being given an ultimatum to choose between the child and himself. The mother reported:

> He chased me away. He said he didn't want the baby because it was so tiny. He said I must choose. I can stay or I must kill the baby.

Another caregiver reported having lost all support from persons in the community whom she had previously regarded as friends. She said:

> I have no friends. Now they just laugh at me saying my child is disabled.

Another instance where a significant lack of support was reported was in this narrative obtained from a mother in response to asking how the neighbours respond to the child with cerebral palsy:

> If it was according to them I would have taken (the child) and given him away or thrown him in the dustbin. They don't think he will ever be a normal person at all. Even his father's family doesn't like (the child).

13.4.2 Reactions to Disability: Acceptance, Guilt, Disappointment and Depression

During the interviews a range of reactions to disability were noted. Of the 27 participants interviewed 22 reported that they had accepted their child's condition, while five reported that they had not come to terms with having a disabled child. A combination of positive and negative responses was obtained in response to acceptance, illustrated by the voices below:

> It took me a while to understand. I just prayed and said he is my blessing from God. It was very painful though.

> (The child's) father did not have any problem with him being disabled.

> The neighbours like him like any other child.

> (The child's) father's mother doesn't want (the child). She is ashamed of her.

> I have not seen any of the neighbours who like (the child).

> I don't think (the child's) mother has accepted that he is disabled because she doesn't show care or love for (the child) at all. She doesn't want (the child) to touch her and when he cries she just leaves him there without caring.

> He has no relationship with his granny and I don't know why she dislikes (the child). I think she needs counselling to help her and then stop disliking the child.

Sixteen participants reported a sense of sadness related to bearing, bringing up and caring for a child with a disability. Some of the comments included:

> I was very disappointed since it was my first-born. I expected that since she was my first-born she would be everything I ever wanted from a child.

> It is difficult to see other children walk and yours cannot.
>
> It is very painful because I did not ask for a disabled child.

Guilt was an emotion that was frequently alluded to; however, only two informants overtly discussed bearing the burden of guilt for giving birth to a child with a disability. When asked what she thinks assists the child in his development, one caregiver reported:

> There is nothing I can do. I just keep telling him that I am sorry.

Some evidence of despair and desperation especially at the time of diagnosis, as well as the experience of depression was evident in the following narratives:

> At first I felt terrible. I lost weight and I used to spend time alone thinking about (the child's) disability, but after two years I accepted the situation as it is and I regained weight.
>
> We can't even resolve things like adults. She is always upset without reason. She doesn't even communicate what is wrong. She just becomes angry and upset without reason.
>
> It took me a whole year to accept. During that time I was just crying all the time.
>
> It took me nine years to accept her disability. From time to time I still become upset.
>
> I left (the child) with his father because I didn't know what to do with him because he was very sick and no one was able to help him so I came to his father for help. I always thought about him.
>
> When (the child's) granny is here she usually says bad things about the child. She even said she wishes this situation would be over. I don't know what she meant about the situation being over or maybe she wishes (the child) to die. I don't know.

13.4.3 Family Roles and Gender Dynamics

In this study, 12 of the children were cared for primarily by their mothers, two were cared for by a grandmother, and one by a father. The complexities of the rural context in regard to gender roles were reflected in some of the narratives. Like in many other rural contexts, men frequently become migrant workers, and relocate to the cities in search of work, while the roles of women include growing and harvesting crops and caring for children and the sick (Cancian and Oliker, 1998). In the community we researched we noticed a marked absence of men yet of the 15 families who participated in the study, nine of the fathers lived with the family and were actively involved in the child's upbringing, two paid maintenance regularly, and four did not have any contact with the child.

In situations where the father was not involved, this put obvious strain on the caregiver who was taking care of the child both from an emotional and a financial point of view. Some of the comments made by the female primary caregivers in instances where the father was not involved included:

> We do not have any relationship since he denied the child after he was born. It is easy for him to say that he does not love the baby because he is disabled.

> One day we had a fight and the father told me that he knows (the child) is not his son because they have never had a disabled person in their family.

Of the 15 children with cerebral palsy, seven had been abandoned by one or more family member(s). Of these seven children, five had been abandoned by their father and the father's family (indicating the role and power of the paternal family), two had been disowned by their mother, one of whom was now cared for by her grandmother, and the other child was now in the care of his father. Comments that arose from this discussion included:

> We broke up after the birth of (the child) because of bad influence from his mother.

> While I was living with his family (the child) got sick. I then decided to leave and come back home because the father's mother was saying that (the child) is not her son's boy.

Another common theme that emerged in relation to gender was the issue of kinship, and it appeared that in many instances the paternal grandmother had enormous power over her son's relationships and would make the decisions regarding her son's involvement with the child. This is explained by Kuper (1963) whose perspectives on kinship, although produced over 40 years ago, suggest that the legal authority of the father is in contrast to the more indulgent relationship with the mother, for whom Swazi men express affection and appreciation, as well as respect. This description is evident in the quotation below where a mother reveals that the father's family are denying that the child is part of their family, due to the presence of the disability:

> The father's mother says the child is not her son's boy. They have never had a disabled person in their family. They do not want the child in their house.

13.5 Shared Variables

13.5.1 Traditional Beliefs and Western Medical Practices and Religion

A wide range of responses to cultural beliefs and practices in relation to the causation and treatment of cerebral palsy were elicited. All except for two families had consulted with traditional healers regarding their child's condition and a variety of responses to traditional treatment were elicited. The narratives revealed that grandmothers and grandfathers were consulted first before any action was taken in terms of managing the child's disability. It appeared that for the most part it was the grandparents who recommended going to the traditional healers, while the parents of the child held conflicting beliefs about which approach to follow. In many instances, traditional healers and western healthcare practitioners were consulted concurrently. This conflict and family responsibility for the child's wellbeing is described in the narrative below:

> My mother said we must take him to the traditional healer. They said it is witchcraft and evil spirits. They said they can cure it and gave us herbs to chase the evil spirits away, but

> we haven't seen any improvements in the child's condition so now I have decided to stick to the hospital ways. It is much simpler.

Another explanation for disability obtained through the narratives was that of *umuthi*. Translated into English, *umuthi* can mean either "medicine" or "poison", and refers to substances fabricated with an expert hand, designed to achieve either healing or illness (Ashworth, 2005). Dangerous substances deployed as *muthi* can enter the body through the mouth in the form of food or drink, through the lungs, through the skin, or through sexual contact, so anyone who puts their body in contact with another person or substance needs to be careful (Hammond-Tooke, 1970). This narrative obtained from a father describes this concept of *umuthi*, while the final sentences expose conflict and confusion between the traditional and western explanatory models:

> I heard the elders saying that if a child is disabled it is because of cross-dressing of males and females in the house or older people wearing younger people's clothes. So they say all this cross-dressing causes confusion in the family and can lead to disability. Now I have confirmed it is not this, but something that I don't understand.

Further conflict is evident in the quotations below, both obtained from mothers:

> I think that there was a problem while I was giving birth to him. Traditionally we call it umuthi.

> I don't know. At the hospital they told me she was affected and that is what I believe now.

However, this "confusion" must be interpreted with caution since both the researchers and research mediator were affiliated with the hospital. Scheper-Hughes (1990) warns that patients may respond to the doctor's explanation of disability or illness by shifting his or her explanatory model towards that of the doctor in order to make a working alliance possible.

Consistent with the view that disability and spirituality are intertwined (Pfeiffer, 2003; Mweshi and Mpofu, 2001), seven participants spoke about disability in terms of religion and stated that they had accepted the children with cerebral palsy as a religious blessing. Exploring the experience of cerebral palsy included:

> I don't know. I just think (the child) is my gift from God and God is tempting me to see if I can rise above this challenge.

> We believe God knows what he is doing.

A main concern of one grandmother was who would care for the child should she be unable to do so. She reported, "It is something I think about everyday. I always pray that God will bring a solution to this problem because there is no one I trust to take good care of (the child) the way I do".

> There is only one woman from the church who comes near her. She comes and prays for her recovery.

> I took him to (name withheld) Church and that's where he became better through our prayers. He started crawling and walking again before I took him to physiotherapy training at the hospital.

> I cried and I prayed to God to help me and to help (the child) to be strong so that he will be able to walk again.

13.5.2 Attitudes of Healthcare Professionals

Just under half of the total number of participants reported that the negative attitudes of healthcare professionals affect their willingness to access services at the hospital or clinics. While reports of poor attitudes of staff members towards patients are grave and carry enormous implications for the success of service delivery and for the commitment of caregivers to the management techniques recommended by the healthcare professional, cognizance must be taken that for any healthcare provider working with a population with whom they do not share a common language is extremely difficult, and that working in the presence of such a language barrier is likely to give rise to miscommunications. This is particularly true in the South African context where hospitals do not employ interpreters and therapists frequently need to make use of other parents or hospital cleaners as translators, and in this way much meaningful conversation is lost. In addition to language barriers, working cross-culturally can be a major barrier to effective therapy. The western bio-medical model on which so much of the therapy is based is a foreign concept to the majority of patients (Potterton, 1996), and for this reason cognizance needs to be taken of cultural issues and the patient's worldview must be taken into account (Penn, 2000). This is highlighted in the comment below:

> I want to know why the physiotherapists don't listen to what we need.

Additionally, an instance where it became evident that the caregiver's expectations had not been met at the hospital is apparent in the following quotation obtained from a father:

> I have gained nothing. They just show me exercises but don't give me medications to help the child.

This highlights a misconception relating to the extent of the neurological impairment of cerebral palsy and the nature of the management thereof. One can understand the assumption that a condition such as cerebral palsy, which is managed at the hospital, should be treated with medication. This emphasizes the need for healthcare professionals to develop their communication skills, as well as to develop resources detailing predisposing factors and aetiologies of disability, and the treatment and management thereof.

Another alarming concern was that of the communication skills of the nurses, particularly since in most cases the nurses shared a common language with the patients. The majority of informants made claims similar to the one below obtained from a mother:

> What I have found to be a problem is the nurses' listening skills. When I try to explain about the child's condition they try to disagree with me, thinking I am lying or something.

This complaint highlights both the possible lack of counselling skills, but also a power dynamic between the caregivers and the nurses, which may well be linked to cultural beliefs surrounding disability. This is explained by Crawford (1994) who demonstrates how the societal beliefs of a community affect how the members of that community construct beliefs about who becomes ill and who remains healthy and how this serves to marginalize an already marginalized community. In turn, Crawford (1994) demonstrates how the language of health has come to signify those who are responsible from those who are irresponsible, those who are respectful from those who are disreputable, those who are safe from those who are not, and ultimately those who have the right to rule from those who need supervision, guidance or reincarnation. In this way the sick and disabled are not only made responsible for their illness, but they are also made different. This gives rise to a social distancing from the "unhealthy" – a further stereotyping of an already stigmatized group.

13.5.3 Support Narratives

A large number of participants reported that the primary reason for returning to the hospital even though accessibility was difficult was because of the emotional and peer support received at the hospital. A comment from a mother revealed this:

> It is very difficult dealing with the changes I have had to go through to accommodate my baby. Most of the time I just let it pass but I deal better with it when I go to the clinic and find other women with children with the same problems. It feels good to know that I am not alone.

References to peer support are important for us as healthcare service providers to acknowledge as they have implications for refining our role in service provision within the community. It is important to consider that with significant neurological impairment, compounded by living conditions which do not allow the patient easy or regular access to healthcare facilities, and inexperienced therapists who do not have advanced training in working with such conditions, it may not be possible to achieve full or even partial recovery. However, it is achievable to set up information centres and support groups and in this way empower members of the community to stand up for their rights and the rights of their children. Narratives relating to support obtained through healthcare provision included the following:

> It took me three years to accept. All this time I have been looking for alternatives to help (the child) to get better. However, in all my hospital visits I have seen many people there that are disabled like (the child) and that made me to accept and put things into perspective.

> Also to see other disabled children at the hospital helped very much because I was able to see and compare (the child's) condition, and what I have realized is that (the child) is less disabled than any other children I have seen at the hospital.

13.6 Conclusions

Over 250 years ago, Olwen Hufton (as cited by Ngwisha, 2003, p. 8), wrote "The approach to the study of poverty must be predominantly qualitative not quantitative. There is no such thing as a graph of human suffering". As the above examples demonstrate, contextual factors have a powerful influence on the experience of caring for a child with a disability in a rural area. Our findings have profoundly challenged traditional methods of intervention and the goals and outcomes of rehabilitation. The narratives of the participants provide a rich tapestry for understanding disability. Rising to the surface are glimpses of how persons make sense of their circumstances and the role of hope, acceptance, gender, family structure, and religion in this regard. The stories highlighted a universal experience of caring for a child with a disability and also culture-specific features of this experience. Listening to these stories was both remarkably inspiring and humbling. As Tonga is clearly one of the most under-serviced and poverty stricken areas of South Africa, we had expected much discussion surrounding this topic and complaints regarding the accessibility of services, the provision of water and electricity, the conditions of the roads and long distances walked each day in order to collect water, firewood and food. To our considerable surprise none of the participants complained in any way! There were reports of difficulties encountered but these were merely mentioned as part of life, not as a complaint.

Similarly, as speech-language therapists we had expected an emerging theme to be one which highlighted the frustrations of having a family member with a communication disability resulting from cerebral palsy. This type of response emerged from only one of our 27 informants, again reinforcing the powerful need for reframing our scope of practice and the role of our profession in a rural context.

The powerful experience of asking and listening highlighted the need for a deeper understanding of the important variables mediating the experience of disability and the influence of both extrinsic and intrinsic factors on individuals, their communities and cultures. We have tried as far as possible to let the narratives speak for themselves, rather than interpret them. The narratives helped to clarify even the unspoken themes of fear and stigma in the community and provide meaning, context and perspective for the caregivers. In addition, they were used to define how, why and in what way the child and the families have been affected by the disability.

Writing anthropological accounts such as this one necessarily involves a power relationship. Our account is not only a dialogue with the participants but also with a body of scholarly theory about disability and its impact. As feminists and professionals, our perceptions undoubtedly and inevitably influenced our interpretations and themes which have informed our analysis. Our account, even though effectively facilitated by our research mediator, makes no claims to be speaking directly for the people of Tonga. However, through the methods used we hope to have borne witness to their lives and we have tried to understand as far as we could *what* things look like from their perspective. In asking *why* they look like this, we are cautious of falling into an oversimplified model but hope that the framework may be useful for advising policy-makers and hopefully in bringing about positive change to this marginalized community.

The stories of our informants revealed many things about the provision of services within the disability sector of South Africa. Since April 1994, some strides have been made in the area of service provision to previously disadvantaged communities. However, as this study has shown, in many areas, these changes have had little impact on the lives of those who are truly marginalized. The narratives depict a disempowered and fragmented community, with discrepancies in the provision of basic services and healthcare practices. They also, however, represent the strength and power and capability of a marginalized community in standing together and supporting each other. The need to be heard is a basic right of any individual and is the first step towards achieving a caring nation, with recognized democratic values and a social justice system that is based on equality, non-racism, non-sexism and human dignity.

The worldview of the caregiver is pivotal in a medical context for assessment and treatment and highlights the imperatives of issues such as food security and access. Social advocacy must begin by listening to those who truly know and understand the effects of disability and the barriers to service provision. Persons with disabilities and service consumers should be the main judges of service provision within a context of informed social transformation. The transformation of healthcare service provision in the presence of enabling national strategies can similarly only take place within the framework of empowerment of individuals and communities with the realization that disability is a social construct which needs to be mediated within a human rights and development framework, rather than viewed solely as a health and welfare problem. Such an approach cannot be implemented without the use of sensitive methods and effective communication amongst disabled people, their families, professionals, and researchers and with the knowledge of community resources. The essence of this is reflected on by Father Smangaliso Mkhatshwa (as cited in Goldstein et al., 1998) who states that "The struggle for health and the struggle for social justice in South Africa are the same".

Acknowledgements We pay tribute to the informants in this study whose qualities of resilience and endurance in the context of profound marginalization will hopefully influence future policy and practice for all those living with disability in South Africa.

The authors are grateful to Dr L Vivian, Dept of Anthropology, University of Cape Town for valuable comments on an earlier version of this manuscript.

Appendix

Participant M – Paraphrased Ethnography and Interview

Distance of home from tar road:	*8km*
Electricity	Yes, electricity meter
Water:	Yes, tap on property
Number of people living in house:	13
Sanitation:	Long-drop
Disability grant recipient:	Yes

Other financial support:	Father
Belief in cause of disability:	Umuthi
Child's difficulties:	Holding things and eating solid food
Perception of child's needs:	Unknown, something to support her in sitting
Support structure:	Extended family and neighbours

The interview took place in village XXX. We arrived at participant M's home only to find that another participant, X, was the next-door neighbour. These two participants live approximately 8 km off the main road, and their homes are barely accessible by car. We phoned for directions, and the mother came to meet us at a nearby primary school.

Upon arrival we were clearly expected! Plastic chairs had been set out in a circle and the mother, grandmother, aunt and two men were sitting there. The child was in her buggy that had been issued by the hospital. A little boy who was about 5 years old was chasing chickens, while a toddler of about 18 months was wandering around playing with a ping-pong ball.

Soon after we arrived the men got up and left, leaving the property and walking down the street. They did not bid farewell or say where they were going. After explaining the purpose of our visit L (CBRW) took the mother aside to the edge of the property so that she could conduct the interview. The grandmother took responsibility for the child with cerebral palsy and sat with her on a grass mat under the trees talking softly. From time to time she also spoke to and scolded the other children.

I sat under a tree, observing what was going on and taking down field notes. Two of the men that had walked down the road came back. The one man lay down on the grass and lit a cigarette, while the other man came and sat next to me. He introduced himself to me in English and told me that he had completed matric last year and was unable to find a job. We sat and chatted for a while. The aunt had gone back to cleaning the house and a young man came out of the house, filled a bucket with water and took it to the wash area at the back of the plot. The house had a water point on the property and an electricity meter in the house.

The main house was modern and made out of brick and African jive music was drifting through the open windows. There was also a second smaller house on the property and a mud shack at the side of the house. The yard consisted of grass, swept ground and trees.

I noticed the close proximity of the neighbours and the fact that one could easily see what was going on in the neighbours' gardens. I observed women doing washing, hanging washing up to dry, tending vegetable gardens and filling buckets of water. Once again the absence of male contributions to the daily chores was noticed.

One of my thoughts as I sat there was "I wonder how open these women will be able to be" given that there were three men sitting around trying to listen in on the interview. At one point the aunt stopped cleaning and sat a metre or two from where the interview was being conducted and seemed to be listening to what was being said in the interview.

The toddler wandered over to where the interview was being conducted and started disrupting the proceedings. The man who had been sitting next to me went over and picked the toddler up and brought her back to where we were sitting to play.

At one point the grandmother got tired of holding the child with cerebral palsy. The aunt went inside and fetched a walking ring, which she put the child into. In this way the child was able to navigate her way around the yard and sit with fairly good trunk control.

At around lunchtime the mother went inside and brought out a plate of soft porridge and gravy. The grandmother held the child with cerebral palsy on her knee and fed her by rubbing the porridge into her mouth then waiting for a few minutes for it to slide down her throat.

Later on in the afternoon I went and sat down on the patio near to where the research mediator was conducting the interview. The mother stood up immediately and brought me a chair.

Just after the children started arriving home from school the grandmother called for one of the young boys. She spoke to him in SiSwati and then placed some money into his hand. He ran off down the road. About half an hour later I saw the same child running back down the road in the direction of the house, carrying a 1-l bottle of Fanta Grape. He handed it to the grandmother who came over and handed it to me. L (research mediator) translated for her that she was giving this to me as a token of thanks to the white doctor who had come to visit them in their home and to thank me for all I had done to help the child.

The sense of support came through strongly in the interview. The mother reported "As soon as I knew I was pregnant my family-in-law took me into their home. I then gave birth at their home. (The child) was born one month early, so she had a breathing problem. I then took her to the hospital and had to stay for 1 week because at that time she was not even crying. She only cried after two weeks".

In general it seemed that all of the family and the neighbours were fond of the child. However, the mother said she was not sure if she would be able to leave the child with any of the neighbours.

When asked about the cause of disability, the grandmother said she believed it was *umuthi*. She reported, "Anyway, I heard elders saying that if a child is disabled it's because of cross-dressing of males and females within the house or young people dressing in older people's clothes. So they say all this cross-dressing causes confusion within the family and can lead to disability". The father took the child to traditional healers who said that the disability was the result of evil spirits and gave her herbs and liquids to drink but no improvement was noted. The mother reported "The father took her traditional healers and none of them were able to help her so he decided that we should leave (the child) as she is because he is sick and tired of all the run around". The grandfather agreed that they should stop taking the child to traditional healers.

The mother reported that the first time she visited the hospital was because she thought there was a problem with the child's tongue. The doctor found nothing wrong but referred her to the rehabilitation department. The mother said that she had noticed improvement at the hospital "...because before (the child) couldn't move her body and she couldn't roll herself but now she can". Once again the mother's main complaint was that it takes a long time to get a file at the hospital.

Both mother and grandmother reported that they found it difficult to accept the child's disability. The grandmother added, "We believe God knows what he is doing".

The mother reported that she needs something to help support the child's body in sitting. She reported that she is currently using a tire to seat the child in. She has received a buggy from the hospital but there is no space in the house to keep the buggy so it has become damaged as a result of exposure to the elements.

Once again the issue of HIV and the prevention of contractible diseases was discussed. The mother reported, "I trust that I won't contract anything that will affect (the child's) well-being. But I don't know about (the child's) father because he is not with me all the time – he is working far from here. Anyway, I trust he is not doing anything that could affect (the child)". When L asked if the mother thought that the father would agree to using condoms she replied "I don't know if he will use it, and if I ask him and he doesn't want to use it I don't know what I will do".

References

Anderson, G, & Phohole, M (2003). 'Situational Analysis of Children Living in the Molanantsi Area of the Northern Province: Childhood Disability Research Unit: University of Pretoria', (Unpublished document)

Ashworth, A (2005). 'Muthi, medicine and witchcraft: Regulating African science in post-apartheid South Africa', *Social Dynamics*. 31(2):211–242

Bhorat, H, Poswell, L, & Naidoo, P (2006). Dimensions of poverty in post-apartheid South Africa: 1996–2001. Available online at: http://www.commerce.uct.ac.za/poverty_status_report [Accessed 23 February 2007]

Cancian, F, & Oliker, J (1998). *Caring and Gender*. Alla Mira Press: Walnut Creek, CA

Christianson, A, Zwane, M, Manga, P, Rosen, E, Venter, A, Downs, D, & Kromber, J (2002). 'Children with intellectual disability in rural South Africa: Prevalence and associated disability', *Journal of Intellectual Disability Research*. 46(2):179–186

Couper, J (2002). 'Prevalence of childhood disability in rural KwaZulu Natal', *South African Medical Journal*. 92:549–552

Crawford, R (1994). 'The boundaries of the self and the unhealthy other: Reflections of health, culture and AIDS', *Journal of Social Science and Medicine*. 38(10):1347–1365

Goldstein, S, Ntuli, A, & Coulson, N (1998). *Promoting health in South Africa*. Heineman Higher and Further Education: Johannesburg

Hammond-Tooke, D (1970). 'Urbanization and the meaning of misfortune', *Africa*. 40(1):25–38

Hutcherson, P (1991). 'Community based rehabilitation in the Diocese of Eldoret, Kenya' (Anglican Church of Kenya), http://www.kenyamission.org/kehidrehab.htm [Accessed 18th November 2005]

Kuper, H (1963). *The Swazi: A South African Kingdom*, Holt, Rinehart, and Winston: New York, NY

Levin, K (2005). 'I am what I am because of who we all are: International perspectives on rehabilitation: South Africa', *Paediatric Rehabilitation*. 9(3):285–292

Maverick, B (1966). *The Swazi: An Ethnographic Account of the Natives of the Swaziland Protectorate*. Frank Cass/Cambridge University Press:London/Cambridge

Meyer, C, & Moagi, S (2000). 'Determining priority needs of mothers with disabled children in Winterveldt', *South African Journal of Occupational Therapy*. 30(2):7–11

Mweshi, M, & Mpofu, R (2001). 'The perceptions of parents and caregivers on the causes of disabilities in children with cerebral palsy: A qualitative investigation', *South African Journal of Physiotherapy*. 57(2):28–31

Ngwisha, J (2003). 'The concept of poverty: It's analysis and application to Swaziland', in Kanduza, A, & DuPont-Mkhonza, S (eds), *Poverty in Swaziland: Historical and Contemporary Forms*. (pp.8–34) OSSREA Swaziland Chapter

Nkomazi Spatial Development Framework (2003). http://www.ledc.co.za/docs/Nkomazi local municipality/spatial development framework [Accessed 14th April 2005]

Nkomazi Integrated Development Plan (2006–2007). Available from: http://www.nkomazimun.co.za/idp.html [Accessed 6th August 2008]

Nutbeam, D (2000). 'Health literacy as a public health goal: A challenge for contemporary health education and communication strategies into the 21st century', *Health Promotion International*. 15:259–267

Penn, C (2000). 'Cultural narratives: Bridging the gap educating speech-language pathologists to work in multicultural populations', *The South African Journal of Communication Disorders*. 47:71–78

Pfeiffer, J (2003). 'International NGO's and primary healthcare in Mozambique: The need for a new collaborative model', *Journal of Social Science and Medicine*. 56:725–738

Potterton, J (1996). 'Cerebral palsy in Giyani'. *South African Journal of Physiotherapy*. 52(3):66–68

Rehle, T, & Shisana, O (2003). 'Epidemiological and demographic HIV/AIDS projections: South Africa', *South African Journal of AIDS Research*. 2(1):1–8

Scheper-Hughes, N (1990). 'Three propositions for a critically applied medical anthropology', *Social Science and Medicine*. 30(2):189–197

Index

Lightning Source UK Ltd.
Milton Keynes UK
19 September 2010

160020UK00005B/53/P